SOLITARY CONFINEMENT

SOLITARY CONFINEMENT

Social Death and Its Afterlives

LISA GUENTHER

University of Minnesota Press
Minneapolis
London

A different version of chapter 2 was published as "Subjects without a World? An Husserlian Analysis of Solitary Confinement," *Human Studies* 34, no. 3 (June 2011): 257–76; reproduced with kind permission from Springer Science + Business Media B.V. A different version of chapter 6 was published as "Beyond Dehumanization: A Post-Humanist Critique of Intensive Confinement," *Journal for Critical Animal Studies* 10, no. 2 (2012): 46–68.

Published by the University of Minnesota Press
111 Third Avenue South, Suite 290
Minneapolis, MN 55401-2520
http://www.upress.umn.edu

LIBRARY OF CONGRESS CATALOGING-IN-PUBLICATION DATA
Guenther, Lisa, 1971–
Solitary confinement : social death and its afterlives / Lisa Guenther.
Includes bibliographical references and index.
ISBN 978-0-8166-7958-4 (hc)
ISBN 978-0-8166-7959-1 (pb)
1. Solitary confinement—United States—History. 2. Solitary confinement—History. I. Title.
HV9471.G84 2013
365'.644—dc23   2013014540

Printed in the United States of America on acid-free paper

The University of Minnesota is an equal-opportunity educator and employer.

20 19 18 17 16   10 9 8 7 6 5 4 3

For REACH Coalition, in solidarity

CONTENTS

ACKNOWLEDGMENTS

This book would not have been written if not for Angela Davis. In my first year teaching at Vanderbilt University, I audited a graduate course on slavery with Dr. Davis, who was a visiting professor in the philosophy department at the time. This course, along with her written work on slavery, prisons, and torture, changed the course of my research and my life. I thank her.

I am also grateful to many friends, colleagues, and students for engaging in what must seem like endless conversations, projects, conference papers, blog posts, and even Facebook updates about prisons. My most steadfast interlocutors are the past and present members of REACH Coalition, who meet on Wednesday nights in Unit 2 of Riverbend Maximum Security Institution to discuss philosophy and to build community: Abu Ali Abdur'Rahman, Geoffrey Adelsberg, Devin Banks, Kevin Burns, Ron Cauthern, Natalie Cisneros, Gary Cone, David Duncan, Joshua Hall, Kenneth Henderson, Carmela Hill-Burke, Olen Hutchison, Akil Jahi, Don Johnson, Katie Kelly, Donald Middlebrooks, Harold Wayne Nichols, Richard Odom, Pervis Payne, Andrea Pitts, Derrick Quintero, Donika Ross, Sandy Skene, Rebecca Tuvel, Sarah Tyson, and Scott Zeman. Many thanks to Donald Middlebrooks for his painting *Midnight,* which appears on the cover of this book. Thank you to Janet Wolf and Jeannie Alexander for making this group possible and for providing guidance when I needed it most. It has been an honor and an inspiration to correspond with Russell Maroon Shoats, who has been held in solitary confinement for thirty years at State Correctional Institution Greene and other prisons.

At Vanderbilt, Kelly Oliver, David Wood, Jose Medina, Idit Dobbs-Weinstein, Rob Talisse, Colin Dayan, and Ellen Armor have been incredibly supportive and insightful colleagues. Thank you to the Vanderbilt philosophy department, the Black Cultural Center, the Robert Penn Warren Center, and the Curb Center for Art, Enterprise, and Public Policy for collaborating with me on various projects and public events related to prisons and the death penalty. Keramet Reiter, Drew Leder, Gayle Salamon, Kelly Oliver, David Wood, Larry May, Colin Dayan, Alejandro Arango, Garrett Bredeson, Chris Wells, Maxime Doyon, and Caleb Smith offered invaluable feedback on chapter drafts. Melinda Hall performed life-saving work formatting the book for publication, and Lara Giordano prepared the index. Doug Armato at the University of Minnesota Press was a wonderfully supportive editor.

I have drawn inspiration and intellectual guidance from old friends (Hasana Sharp, Will Roberts, Chloe Taylor, Bettina Bergo, Ann Murphy, and Abbie Levin) as well as newer friends—Alexis Shotwell, Ami Harbin, Florentien Verhage, Talia Welsh, Claire Katz, Steve DeCaroli, John Protevi, Adrian Switzer, Naomi Beeman, Jérôme Brillaud, Kirk Smith, Ira Helderman, and an ever-burgeoning community of scholars and activists who are committed to resisting isolation in all its forms, behind and beyond the prison walls. Finally, thank you to Rohan Quinby for his love and support, fresh bread, and dog walks.

INTRODUCTION

A Critical Phenomenology of Solitary Confinement

Capture, imprisonment, is the closest to being dead that one
is likely to experience in this life.
—George Jackson, Soledad Brother

THERE ARE MANY WAYS to destroy a person, but one of the simplest and most devastating is through prolonged solitary confinement.
Deprived of meaningful human interaction, otherwise healthy prisoners become unhinged. They see things that do not exist, and they fail
to see things that do. Their sense of their own bodies—even the fundamental capacity to feel pain and to distinguish their own pain from
that of others—erodes to the point where they are no longer sure if they
are being harmed or are harming themselves. Not only psychological
or social identity but the most basic sense of identity is threatened by
prolonged solitary confinement. As Jack Henry Abbott wrote in his
memoir *In the Belly of the Beast: Letters from Prison,* "Solitary confinement can alter the ontological makeup of a stone" (1991, 45).

We have known this for almost as long as solitary confinement
has been practiced. In the 1830s, just years after the establishment of
Eastern State Penitentiary in 1829, reports were already beginning to
emerge of a sharp increase in mental disorders among prisoners, including hallucinations, "dementia," and "monomania" (Grassian 1983, 1450;
P. Smith 2006, 457). While penal codes, theories of criminal justice, and
psychological terminology have all changed over time, the symptoms
of solitary confinement have remained strikingly consistent: anxiety,
fatigue, confusion, paranoia, depression, hallucinations, headaches,
and uncontrollable trembling (P. Smith 2006, 488). Similar symptoms

are reported in the United States, Canada, Denmark, Germany, and South Africa—wherever the psychological effects of solitary confinement have been studied.[1] Not only are these symptoms historically and geographically consistent, but they are also experienced by an overwhelming proportion of those who have undergone solitary confinement.[2] But despite numerous lawsuits and overwhelming evidence of its harm, solitary confinement continues to form a basic component of federal and state prison systems in the United States, especially in supermax penitentiaries, where all prisoners are kept in twenty-three-hour-a-day lockdown with almost no human contact.

Many prisoners describe their experience in solitary confinement as a form of living death. Harry Hawser, a poet and inmate at Eastern State Penitentiary in the 1840s, called his cell "a living tomb" (quoted in C. Smith 2009, 5).[3] Angela Tucker, an African American woman held at California's Valley State Prison for Women in the 1980s, said, "It's like living in a black hole" (quoted in Shaylor 1998, 386).[4] Jeremy Pinson, a prisoner at the U.S. Penitentiary Administrative Maximum Facility (ADX) in Florence, Colorado, said, "You feel as if the world has ended but you somehow survived" (quoted in Greene 2012). What does it mean to recognize, as the effect of a standard method of incarceration, the possibility of a suffering that blurs the distinction between life and death? What must subjectivity be like in order for these effects to be possible? Who are we, such that we can become unhinged from ourselves by being separated from others?

In the context of this inquiry, "becoming unhinged" is not just a colloquial expression; rather, it is a precise phenomenological description of what happens when the articulated joints of our embodied, interrelational subjectivity are broken apart. Solitary confinement deprives prisoners of the bodily presence of others, forcing them to rely on the isolated resources of their own subjectivity, with the (perhaps surprising) effect of eroding or undermining that subjectivity. The very possibility of being broken in this way suggests that we are not simply atomistic individuals but rather hinged subjects who can become unhinged when the concrete experience of other embodied subjects is denied for too long. Even if the people in one's life are not particularly sympathetic or supportive, it becomes difficult to bear the weight of existence in isolation from others. In this sense, solitary confinement makes even solitude impossible; isolated from social life, even one's sense of individuated personhood threatens to dissolve. As a woman who experienced pretrial solitary confinement in Denmark explained, "The person subjected to solitary confinement risks losing her self and disappearing into a non-existence" (quoted and translated in P. Smith 2006, 497).

How could I lose myself by being confined to myself? For this to be possible, there must be more to selfhood than individuality. Prisoners in a supermax unit may have everything that individual human beings need in order to survive; they may even have access to "extras" such as television or closed-circuit television (CCTV) video conferencing with visitors. And yet there is something about the absence of regular bodily contact with others, the absence of even the *possibility* of touching or being touched, that threatens to unhinge the subject. My thesis is this: solitary confinement works by turning prisoners' constitutive relationality against themselves, turning their own capacities to feel, perceive, and relate to others in a meaningful world into instruments of their own undoing. This self-betrayal is only possible for beings who are complicated, whose subjectivity is not merely a point but a hinge, a self-relation that cannot be sustained in absolute solitude but only in relation to others.

Critical Phenomenology

My aim in this book is to develop a critical phenomenology of hinged (inter)subjectivity by tracking the effects of solitary confinement in the U.S. penitentiary system from the mid-nineteenth century to the present. By critical phenomenology I mean a method that is rooted in first-person accounts of experience but also critical of classical phenomenology's claim that the first-person singular is absolutely prior to intersubjectivity and to the complex textures of social life. The critical edge of this approach emerges through an engagement with the work of Frantz Fanon, Maurice Merleau-Ponty, and Emmanuel Levinas— each of whom could be considered postphenomenologists, given the degree to which they challenge the basic concepts and methods of phenomenology—as well as with other discourses such as history, sociology, anthropology, and critical race theory.

These discourses are not just relevant to what Edmund Husserl would call the "lifeworld," understood as a level of social meaning that is ultimately founded on the transcendental condition of absolutely singular and nonworldly first-person consciousness. Rather, these discourses show, in different and sometimes divergent ways, how embodied subjects have been racialized through (for example) the colonization of the Americas, the trans-Atlantic slave trade, the practice of plantation slavery and its partial abolition, followed by the hyperincarceration of black men and women in what is now the United States. This history, and the stories interwoven in this history, affect the formation of subjects in such deeply constitutive ways that the contemporary phenomenologist is compelled to rethink basic concepts and methods in order to do justice to the social life—and social death—of consciousness. This demand for critique is particularly intense where the breakdown of meaningful experience is concerned, as in prolonged isolation. While phenomenology provides a rich conceptual language for describing the ontological, epistemological, and even ethical effects of solitary confinement, classical phenomenology alone is not enough to explain why some subjects are more likely targets of this violence than others, nor to launch a sufficiently radical political critique of solitary confinement.

Critical phenomenology raises thorny methodological questions, not all of which will be resolved in this book. It is not clear, for example, where critical phenomenology ends and postphenomenology begins. Nor is it clear which particular social and cultural analyses do justice to the testimony of prisoners, nor even whose testimony should be taken as exemplary of *the* experience of solitary confinement. Some prisoners have written memoirs; others have been interviewed by psychologists, anthropologists, lawyers, and other researchers, each having distinct agendas. Countless others have left no record of their experiences—if we can even call what happens in isolation "experience." Access to the written word, as well as access to interview opportunities or any other form of interaction, is shaped by race, class, gender, and geographic location. Most of my sources in this book are men, and many are white men whose relative privilege still makes a difference, even in spaces of civil and social death. My way of interpreting the testimony of these prisoners is shaped by my own social and intellectual formation as a white feminist, a phenomenologist, a volunteer prison educator, and a Canadian (not necessarily in that order, and no doubt in ways that have escaped my own awareness). Time and again while writing this book, I have run into conflicting desires and investments: Is it wrong to spend so much time thinking about solitary confinement, when arguably the more urgent problem is the mass incarceration of nonviolent drug offenders and the criminalization of poverty and addiction? Why write about living death when the majority of U.S. states still have the death penalty? How critical can "critical phenomenology" become, given its constitutive commitment to the first-person singular as an absolute starting point, prior to the "levels" of race, class, sex, and other dimensions of social subjectivity? How has my own intellectual and social formation shaped my tendency to reflect on certain testimonies at length and to exclude others or consign them to footnotes?

Confronting these questions, and without claiming to have solved them, I have sought to develop a method of critical phenomenology that both continues the phenomenological tradition of taking first-person experience as the starting point for philosophical reflection and also resists the tendency of phenomenologists to privilege transcendental *subjectivity* over transcendental *intersubjectivity*. In the spirit of Merleau-Ponty, I have engaged in what I hope will be a fruitful, non-reductive dialogue between phenomenological analysis and concrete social scientific research in fields such as psychology and anthropology. The work of Levinas and Fanon has been indispensable for my attempt to address the ethical and political dimensions of the lived experience of solitary confinement, and of social and civil death more generally. For me, what is most valuable about the phenomenological tradition is the insight that there is no individual without relations, no subject without complications, and no life without resistance. Persons who are structured as intentional consciousness but are deprived of a diverse, open-ended perceptual experience of the world, or who are structured as transcendental intersubjectivity but are deprived of concrete relations to others, have the very structure of their Being-in-the-world turned against them and used to exploit their fundamental relationality. This is the worst form of torture and the principle upon which all more determinate forms of torture are based.

Three Waves of Solitary Confinement in the United States

The book has two trajectories. The first is phenomenological; it moves from Husserl's account of transcendental subjectivity and intersubjectivity, through Fanon's account of racialized embodiment and Merleau-Ponty's account of intercorporeality, to Levinas's account of solitude, ethical temporality, and the investment of freedom as responsibility and social justice. The second trajectory is historical and political; it moves through three waves of solitary confinement in the United States (Shalev 2009, 23–25). The first wave was led by moral and religious reformers in the 1850s; it gave rise to the penitentiary system as a site of redemption through prolonged solitude. The aim of this first wave was to transform the criminal into an upright citizen or, in Benjamin Rush's words, a "republican machine." The second wave took place in the 1960s and '70s and was led by behavioral scientists who applied the principles of behavior modification developed in the wake of the Korean War to domestic prisoners in the United States. Their aim was not to redeem but to rehabilitate criminals, to treat and recondition their antisocial behavior, and to turn them into productive members of society. The third wave of solitary confinement began in the 1980s and was led by prison administrators who sought less to redeem or rehabilitate criminal subjects than to isolate and control prison populations in ways that best suited the needs of wardens, prison staff, legislators, planners, and other stakeholders in the political economy of crime and incarceration. The aim of this current policy is not to enable prisoners to adapt to a new, noncriminal life beyond prison but, rather, to adapt to the rules and structures of the prison itself. We are living in the era of the control prison, where the immobilization of inmates has become an end in itself rather than a way of breaking through to the inwardness of criminals' souls or even the outwardness of their abnormal behavior. Prisoners have become risks to be managed, resistances to be eliminated, and organisms to be fed, maintained, and even prevented from taking their own lives.

These three waves of solitary confinement in the United States cannot be understood apart from the broader context of mass incarceration and the hyperincarceration of people of color. Today, the United States has less than 5 percent of the world's population but more than 25 percent of the world's prisoners (Liptak 2008b). We have both the highest rate of incarceration in the world and the largest number of prisoners in the world.[5] In 2007, there were 7,225,800 adults in prison, jail, or on probation or parole; that is more than 3 percent of the total adult population. Another 86,927 children were held in juvenile detention that year, some in solitary confinement.[6] A hugely disproportionate number of these prisoners are people of color. A young black man between the ages of twenty and thirty-four has a 1 in 9 chance of being incarcerated (Public Safety Performance Project 2008). While it is difficult to say exactly how many prisoners are being held in solitary confinement, most researchers agree on a figure between 25,000 and 80,000 (Solitary Watch 2012a). A disproportionate number of these isolated prisoners are people of color (Arrigo and Bullock 2008, 633).[7]

We cannot account for this hyperincarceration and hyperisolation of young men of color without tracking the material and symbolic legacies of slavery in the U.S. prison system. As Angela Davis and others have pointed out, the Thirteenth Amendment only partly abolished slavery in the United States, making an exception for convicted criminals: "Neither slavery nor involuntary servitude, *except as a punishment for crime whereof the party shall have been duly convicted,* shall exist within the United States, or any place subject to their jurisdiction" (emphasis added). Even today, prisoners in Georgia and Texas are not entitled to compensation for their labor, and every able-bodied prisoner is required to work (Mayeux 2010). Joy James argues that, by leaving open a loophole for the enslavement of convicted criminals, the Thirteenth Amendment did not abolish slavery; rather, it

> resurrected social death as a permanent legal category in U.S. life, yet no longer registered death within the traditional racial markings. Breaking with a two hundred-year-old tradition, the government ostensibly permitted the enslavement of nonblacks. Now not the ontological status of "nigger" but the ontological status of "criminal" renders one a slave. (2005, xxviii–xxix)

As long as this loophole remains open, the work of abolition will be incomplete, and the social death of slavery will continue to haunt us.

Basic Concepts: Civil Death and Social Death

Michel Foucault's brilliant account of the production and surveillance of the prisoner-subject in *Discipline and Punish* and in his later accounts of biopower and governmentality are indispensable for understanding the disciplinary logic of the penitentiary system and the neoliberal logic of the control prison. But they do not quite capture the feeling of living death described in many prisoners' accounts of their *experience* in solitary confinement. The isolated prisoner may be a docile body, an industrious worker, and a member of a targeted population, but none of these concepts speaks directly to the problem of feeling like a ghost in one's own life or losing one's ability to see straight after ten years in solitary confinement. Giorgio Agamben's account of *homo sacer,* or bare life, comes closer to articulating the sense of living death in prisoners' testimonies, but I find his account of resistance so insufficient and his invocation of the *Muselmann* so problematic that I have not relied on his concepts or methods for my own analysis.[8] Rather, I have found rich and relatively unexplored resources in Colin Dayan's account of the civil death of slaves, prisoners, and detainees in the War on Terror and Orlando Patterson's account of the social death of slavery.

Civil Death

Civil death is a legal fiction; it refers to someone who has been (legally) positioned as dead in law. Their body may be alive and their mind sharp, but they have been deprived of the legal status of a person with civil rights such as the rights to own or bequeath property, to vote, to bring a legal case to court, and so on.

English common law allowed for the application of civil death for four cases: entrance into a religious order such as a monastery; abjuration, or permanent flight from punishment; banishment or exile; and the more radical form, attainder, or "corruption of blood" ("Civil Death Statutes" 1937, 969), resulting from a conviction on charges of felony or treason. Attainder deprived convicts not only of their property, income, and civil status but also of the right to pass down these goods as an inheritance. In effect, one's blood was corrupted, or deemed legally incapable of bequeathing an estate to future generations. The meaning of physical death was thus altered by attainder; death became final, individual, and permanent, bearing no fruitful seeds for a (civil) connection to life beyond death. Attainder renders the civil dead both dead in life and dead beyond life; convicts are declared both prematurely and posthumously dead, even if, from a different perspective, they are arguably too alive to be dead in the first case and too dead to die again in the second case.

While attainder is forbidden by the U.S. Constitution, various forms of civil death persisted in many states well into the twentieth century, and they arguably persist today in the form of felon disenfranchisement.[9] The author of a 1937 *Harvard Law Review* article called civil death a "medieval fiction in a modern world":

> With living men regarded as dead, dead men returning to life, and the same man considered alive for one purpose but dead for another, the realm of

legal fiction acquires a touch of the supernatural under the paradoxical doctrine of civil death. ("Civil Death Statutes" 1937, 968)

In her most recent book, *The Law Is a White Dog,* Colin Dayan elaborates the consequences of this "paradoxical doctrine" for slaves, prisoners, and detainees:

> In the fiction of civil death, broadly understood, the state reinvents what happens after literal death. In a secular world, the enthusiastic embrace of something vague like the *soul's salvation* allowed reformers to point to an abstraction, thus masking the concrete object of punishment: the *mind's unraveling.* (2011, 70)

Dayan tracks the remarkable traces of civil death and attainder in antebellum southern case law, including Judge Joseph Henry Lumpkin's claim in *Bryan v. Walton* (1853)[10] that "social and civil degradation, resulting from the taint of blood, adheres to the descendants of Ham in this country, like the poisoned tunic of Nessus" (quoted in Dayan 2011, 155), and Judge Roger B. Taney's ruling in *Dred Scott v. Sandford* (1857)[11] that "no black had been or could be a citizen of the United States" (cited in Dayan 2011, 134; Dayan's phrasing). After the (partial) abolition of slavery, the burden of civil death shifted from the slave to the convicted criminal. For example, in *Ruffin v. Commonwealth* (1871),[12] Judge J. Christian ruled that the bill of rights did not apply to convicts:

> The bill of rights is a declaration of general principles to govern a society of freemen, and not of convicted felons and men civilly dead. Such men have some rights it is true, such as the law in its benignity accords to them, but not rights of freemen. They are the slaves of the State undergoing punishment for heinous crimes against the laws of the land. (Quoted in Dayan 2011, 61)

And in *Avery v. Everett* (1888),[13] Judge Robert Earl offered this dissenting opinion:

> As the convict could no longer discharge any of his obligations to society, he was to possess no civil rights whatever. As he could not discharge any of the duties of husband or father, the family ties were severed. As he could have no use for property and no power to manage or possess the same, that was to pass away from him. He became civilly dead in the law, and the law ceased to know or to take any notice of him. He no longer possessed any rights growing out of organized society or depending upon or given by law. As to all such rights he was in law dead and buried. (Quoted in Dayan 2011, 56)

Just as persons are made in law, they can be unmade in law. But as Dayan's analysis suggests, the *meaning* of personhood is not fully captured by legal constructions and destructions. In this book, I trace the social–phenomenological constitution of personhood and its unraveling up to the point where "personhood" becomes too narrow a term to account for the constitutive relationality of living beings. I look to Husserl, Fanon, Merleau-Ponty, and Levinas for ways of accounting for this relationality without assuming that individual persons precede their relations with others and can persist without them. In resistance to legal constructions and destructions of personhood, I propose a range of terms—"intercorporeality," "interanimality," "hinged (inter)subjectivity," "the creature"—to describe the texture of this constitutive relationality in a way that does justice to the testimony of prisoners exposed to civil death but also engaged in creating their own this-worldly afterlives of resistance.

Social Death

Social death is the effect of a (social) practice in which a person or group of people is excluded, dominated, or humiliated to the point of becoming dead to the rest of society. Although such people are physically alive, their lives no longer bear a social meaning; they no longer count as lives that *matter.* The social dead may speak, act, compose symphonies, or find a cure for cancer, but their words and deeds remain of no account.

Orlando Patterson defines the social death of slavery as "*the permanent, violent domination of natally alienated and generally dishonored persons*" (Patterson 1982, 13). Positioned at the edge of social life, neither included nor expelled, the slave is "in a permanent condition of liminality and must forever mourn his own social death" (60). Patterson calls the slave's relation to the master a "peculiar mode of reincarnation on the margin of his master's society" (66). Socially dead but maintained as a living being in order to render services to the master, slaves are inclusively excluded in the master's world as "non-born" or "born outside birth" (Meillassoux 1991, 40, 107, 121).[14] As such, they can be represented as "social nonperson[s]" (Patterson 1982, 5), or "*pro nullo* [for nothing]" (40).

It takes a whole network of interconnected obligations, both in the present and extending into the past and future, to create and sustain social personhood, and it takes a whole network of exclusions, interruptions, and violations, not only against individuals but against the social and temporal horizons of their lives, to destroy that personhood. Patterson writes:

> Not only was the slave denied all claims on, and obligations to, his parents and living blood relations but, by extension, all such claims and obligations on his more remote ancestors and on his descendants. He was truly a genealogical isolate. Formally isolated in his social relations with those who lived, he also was culturally isolated from the social heritage of his ancestors. He had a past, to be sure. But a past is not a heritage. Everything has a history, including sticks and stones. Slaves differed from other human beings in that they were not allowed freely to integrate the experience of their ancestors into their lives, to inform their understanding of social reality with the inherited meanings of their natural forbears, or to anchor the living present in any conscious community of memory. (1982, 5)

To be socially dead is to be deprived of the network of social relations, particularly kinship relations, that would otherwise support, protect, and give meaning to one's precarious life as an individual. It is to be violently and permanently separated from one's kin, blocked from forming a meaningful relationship, not only to others in the present but also to the heritage of the past and the legacy of the future beyond one's own finite, individuated being. Of course, slaves *did* manage to form strong ties with one another, both vertically (between the generations) and horizontally (along the lines of language group, geographic proximity, friendship, and so forth).[15] But these relationships were formed and sustained precisely in resistance, and even in opposition, to the structures that deliberately and systematically sought to foreclose them. The families of slaves could be broken apart at any moment: parents separated from children, siblings dispersed, lovers separated with no way of finding one another again. Even relationships that were respected by the slave master were different from ordinary kinship relations in that their legal and social legitimacy was contingent upon the consent of a single person, which could be withdrawn at any moment without warning or justification.

Patterson argues that the hallmark of slavery is this replacement of a whole social network with a single "fictive" kinship relationship to the master (66). Even if the master does not explicitly abuse his power, the exclusivity of this relationship is itself a form of abuse.[16] Slavery reduces the range of possible responses to the child's question, Where do I come from? with a single answer: You owe your life to the master.

To the extent that you have any relation to a legitimate social world, it is through him. The point of this replacement is to delete and suppress any countergenealogies that might challenge the legitimacy of the transaction by which one was bought and sold. Not only does this threaten to block or interrupt one's relation to concrete others—to *this* mother, *this* lover, *these* children, *this* friend—but it also affects one's relation to *possible* others and to the fecundity of time. Our embodied relations to others in a shared but contestable world create and sustain the sense that the present moment is open to new beginnings and is not merely the culmination of the past. These relationships hold open the promise of an escape route from present domination and exclusion, a sense that things could be otherwise, that the future is not always already determined by the master's intervention. This book is an extended argument for the insight, which I learned from Levinas and continue to relearn through my conversations with prisoners, that an intercorporeal, ethical, and political relation to time and to others is the condition for the possibility of a meaningful life.

Consider the ethical implications of reducing all of slaves' (legitimate) social relations to a single, nonreciprocal relation to a master. This reduction not only circumscribes slaves' personal freedom and exposes them to radical domination by the master, since they are no longer protected by a network of kin who would intervene on their behalf, but it also bans slaves from interceding on behalf of others. Patterson cites Callicles's definition of the slave in Plato's *Gorgias* as one who is "unable to help himself, or any other about whom he cares" (cited in 1982, 8). This ban on helping others is confirmed by an American ex-slave, Mr. Reed, interviewed by Ophelia Settle Egypt of Fisk University around 1930:

> The most barbarous thing I saw with these eyes—I lay on my bed and study about it now—I had a sister, my older sister, she was fooling with a clock and broke it, and my old master taken her and tied a rope around her neck—just enough to keep it from choking her—and tied her up in the back yard and whipped her I don't know how long. There stood mother, there stood father, and there stood all the children and none could come to her rescue. (Quoted in Patterson 1982, 8)

There are countless examples like this from the history of antebellum slavery, all of which testify to the importance of the power not only to help oneself but also to help and defend others. This is the power of social life: not (just) the autonomy of a sovereign subject, but the mu-

tual support of a concrete but open-ended network of protective relationships.[17] Not everyone with access to kin is guaranteed this kind of
support; families can be abusive or overprotective. But the structure of
natal alienation attacks the very *possibility* of mutual support among
kin. The social death of slavery blocks and even criminalizes slaves'
capacity to respond to the others who matter most to them. As such,
it seeks to undermine the social, ethical, and political subjectivity of
slaves right at the very site of its emergence.

What makes social death different from milder forms of exclusion
is its intensity, its pervasiveness, and its permanence. The social dead
are not just excluded from this society; they are excluded—in principle,
though not necessarily in fact—from belonging to any society whatsoever. This is not to imply that a society that produces the social death of
others always notices what it is doing. The social dead may be subject
to explicit disregard and disrespect, but also to casual indifference;
they may appear as abject others whose constant threat of pollution
helps reinforce the boundaries of the social world, or they may not appear at all. This invisibility does not diminish the intensity of social
death; rather, it may intensify it.

Social death excludes not only individuals but also their descendants. Patterson calls this "natal alienation"; it involves the systematic
separation of individuals from their kin, including from past and future generations. Only the stain of social death remains transmissible.
In this sense, social death is less a matter of being denied the natural
rights and freedoms of an individual than of being *isolated in one's
individuality,* confined to one's separate existence and blocked from
a meaningful sense of belonging to a community that is greater than
oneself. Without a living relation to past and future generations, who
am I? Do I still have a stake in historical time? If the meaning of my
life is confined to my biological existence, then it amounts to almost
nothing; one swift blow to the head, and it could all be over.

And yet, we must remember that social death is a distinctly *social*
phenomenon, just as civil death is a distinctly legal exclusion from legal
status as a full citizen. It is produced and sustained by a range of social
practices and institutions, including the law; police surveillance; arrest and confinement; the court system; economic exchange; norms of
gender, race, and sexuality; and so forth. In this sense, the social dead
are not merely nonpersons but rather, in Dayan's words, "depersonalized persons" (2011, 32). They are persons whose social significance

has been crossed out, as if they were *no longer with us*. But precisely as crossed-out persons, the social dead bear a resemblance to persons, and this resemblance can be exploited if necessary, for example, to hold socially dead slaves accountable for criminal violations of the law, even while they remain dead in law as anything but criminals. This opportunistic ambiguity with respect to the personhood of slaves can also be exploited by the slaves themselves, for example by deliberately transgressing the law in order to assert legal personhood. But this is not the only, or even the primary, source of resistance against social death; the bond between criminal and slave is too tight in this country to support Hannah Arendt's claim that the criminal is better off than the stateless person, whose status has been reduced to the merely human.[18] Today, as much as 50 years ago or 250 years ago, a death penalty hangs over the social dead and the civil dead, like Poe's swinging pendulum.

As we will see, both slaves and prisoners have engaged in creative ways of resisting social death and mutually supporting social life. The testimony of slaves and prisoners bears witness not to the utter anni-hilation of the person, not to an absolute indifference of life and death, but to a *life against death* that is more than bare survival, a relational-ity that is exploited but not annihilated. This book is dedicated both to those who have managed to find and sustain an afterlife of resistance and to those who have not.

A Ghost of the Civil Dead

I conclude these introductory remarks with the testimony of a prisoner who both survived and succumbed to civil death in prison: Jack Henry Abbott. In his memoir, *In the Belly of the Beast,* Abbott describes him-self as a "state-raised convict" (1991, 3). The son of a Chinese American prostitute and an Irish sailor, he grew up in a series of foster homes, juvenile detention centers, industrial schools, and prisons. Throughout his life, he refused to "adjust" to these institutions or to accept the blame for the way they shaped his habits and desires (10, 14–18).[19] Abbott's worst crime before entering prison at the age of eighteen was passing a bad check; for this, he received an indeterminate sentence of up to five years. While in prison, Abbott killed another inmate in a fight; he was given another indeterminate sentence of three to twenty years. In the late 1970s, Abbott began exchanging letters with Norman Mailer, who was researching violence in prisons for his book *The Executioner's Song* (1980). Mailer was moved by Abbott's brilliant capacity to analyze and articulate his experience in prison; he supported Abbott's successful bid for parole in 1981 and introduced Abbott to the New York literary scene. Six weeks after his release from prison, Abbott stabbed and killed a man in a dispute over access to a restroom; he was sentenced to fifteen years to life for manslaughter. In 2002, after his parole application was denied, Abbott committed suicide in his prison cell. Less than a year of his life since the age of twelve had been spent out of prison or some other form of detention.

Abbott's name is often invoked by those who wish to expose and undermine the starry-eyed liberal fantasy that convicted killers can be rehabilitated. But what does Jack Henry Abbott have to say for himself?

> He who is state-raised—reared by the state from an early age after he is taken from what the state calls a "broken home"—learns over and over and all the days of his life that people in society can do anything to him and not be punished by the law. . . . In *any* state in America someone who is state-raised can be shot down and killed like a dog by anyone, who has no "criminal record," with full impunity. (10–11)

> In the American judiciary, anyone who is sent to prison suffers *civil death*. . . . There is no legal *relationship* between prisoners, and *any social* relationship among prisoners [that is] not monitored directly—a "forced" social relationship—by the pigs is in violation of the rules. It is insubordination. (114)

> When they talk of ghosts of the dead who wander in the night with things still undone, they approximate my subjective experience of this life. (4)

In his lifetime of incarceration, Abbott spent between fourteen and fifteen years in solitary confinement. Some of this time was spent in blackout cells that isolated him in complete darkness for weeks at a time (26–27). Some of it was spent in a strip cell with no running water and no bed, only a toilet hole in the middle of the concrete floor (27–29). I will discuss Abbott's account of the perceptual, cognitive, emotional, and even ontological derangement that he experienced in isolation later, in chapters 2, 6, 7, and 8. For now, I want to address Abbott's broader claim that "anyone who is sent to prison suffers civil death" and that the "subjective experience" of this civil death is like the half-life of a ghost.

Abbott argues that an open social relationship between prisoners is undermined in advance by the prison system, not only because prisoners are deprived of their individual freedom but also—more importantly—because the web of their legitimate social relations has been reduced to a single "forced" relationship to the "pigs." The same institutional structure that enjoins Abbott to accept personal responsibility for his own lifetime of incarceration also blocks his attempt to assume responsibility for other prisoners: "No prisoner can claim an obligation to other prisoners without declaring war" (114). According to Abbott, prisoners cannot obligate or be obligated to each other, except in the specific ways that are sanctioned by prison wardens and correctional officers. This constriction of legal and social relationships to a single legitimate relationship structurally undermines the possibility of meaningful relationships between prisoners, to the point of civil and social death.

To illustrate this point, Abbott recounts his own attempt to initiate a legal inquiry into the apparent suicide of a fellow inmate named Blackie, who was found dead in his cell under suspicious circumstances. No autopsy was performed, and the same guards who allegedly discovered Blackie's corpse also wrote the official report on his death. Blackie had no living kin, no one with a recognized legal claim on his life and death. In order to establish his own right to demand an autopsy, Abbott argued that Blackie owed him money and that he therefore had a legal and financial interest in determining the circumstances of Blackie's death. This is a brilliant appropriation of the language and assumptions of a legal system that supports capitalism against the interests of the chronically poor state-raised convict. If financial interest consistently trumps ethical responsibility and justice, then why not use the claim of financial interest as a vehicle for one's ethical and political demands? But the court blocked Abbott's counterstrategy; it ruled that "no prisoner can have obligations of any kind to other prisoners" (115). Without some sort of legally recognized and socially supported relationship and without the legal and social obligations that make this relationship concrete, the circumstances of Blackie's death cannot be questioned in anything but a personal, private, and ultimately ineffective way.

Abbott is condemned, in a sense, to be free; he is removed from the thicket of legal and social obligations that bind one person to another in civil society. But this freedom from obligation casts both Abbott and Blackie into a limbo of meaningless death and meaningless life.

Blackie's death is rendered permanent and individual: a closed case, no longer open to question or critique. In turn, Abbott's life becomes a living death: the wanderings of a ghost whose words, actions, and relations are no longer effective or meaningful to others. Abbott asks, "How am I going to get [Blackie] out of his grave? How am I going to get justice for him? As long as I am nothing but a ghost of the civil dead, I can do nothing" (115).

Without obligations, social relations can become meaningless; and without social relations, individual lives can become unhinged. This is Abbott's analysis of his own experience in prison, but it is also the basic point of Levinas's ethics. In order to reflect on the full significance of this point for the U.S. prison system, we need to develop the ethical implications of Abbott's memoir, to expand the political dimensions of Levinas's thought, and to situate both within the concrete social context of mass incarceration and the hyperincarceration of racialized subjects. But the basic insight is clear: the civil and social dead are excluded from full participation in life, like ghosts who can still speak and act but whose speech and actions no longer make an impact on the world. They can neither intervene on behalf of another nor receive the help of others who come to their aid. All of their social relations run through the mediation of an official power invested with the right to grant or withhold their civil and social legitimacy.

What is it like to be exposed to this sort of death-in-life as a prisoner in the U.S. penitentiary system? Who is more likely to face social and civil death, and why? How has the situation of living death shifted from the early penitentiary system where inmates were targets of redemption, to Cold War penitentiaries where they were targets of rehabilitation, to contemporary supermax prisons where they are targets of management and control? What forms of resistance have emerged for the creation and mutual support of (social and civil) life after (social and civil) death?

Social Death and Its Afterlives

This book is organized into three parts: the early penitentiary system, the modern penitentiary, and the postmodern penitentiary or supermax.

Part I takes a critical look at the early penitentiary system and its implicit understanding of personhood, offering an alternative phenomenological account of what it means to be a person. Chapter 1 examines eighteenth- and nineteenth-century arguments in support of solitary confinement and against it. It focuses in particular on advocates such as Benjamin Rush, who believed that the health of both the individual and the body politic depended on the proper functioning of "republican machines" characterized by self-discipline, emotional restraint, and industrious habits of work, study, and prayer. I argue that the humanitarian impulses of nineteenth-century penal reform worked against prisoners' well-being precisely to the extent that their advocates endorsed a vision of human beings as separate, autonomous individuals who thrived best when they could support themselves without depending on others.

Chapter 2 develops an alternative phenomenological account of personhood and its destruction. What must a person be like in order to experience his or her life as a "living death" as a result of prolonged solitary confinement? If we were really autonomous individuals, then there would be no reason to expect a wholesale derangement of personhood in solitary confinement. Through a reading of Husserl's classical phenomenology of consciousness, embodiment, and intersubjectivity, I argue that the sense of concrete personhood relies essentially upon embodied relations to other embodied consciousnesses in a shared world. The world is not just the "environment" of an organism that responds to stimulation; rather, it is the ultimate horizon of meaningful experience. The sense of the world is coconstituted with others, even if its ultimate condition of possibility is first-person consciousness. Husserl offers a convincing critique of the sort of mechanistic naturalism upon which Rush based his defense of solitary confinement, and yet Husserl's own insistence on the absolute priority of first-person consciousness produces a certain ambivalence toward the role of others in coconstituting the world. How far down does transcendental intersubjectivity go, and to what extent can we account for the social dimensions of personhood by starting with the singularity of first-person consciousness? I argue that classical phenomenology must become critical by engaging with social and political analyses of particular, historically situated social relations.

In chapter 3, I develop such a critical analysis of social death from plantation slavery to postabolition plantation prisons and beyond. While white male offenders were being targeted for redemption through the "humane" punishment of solitary confinement in the penitentiary system, black men and women continued to be held as slaves and punished with physical violence, sexual assault, forced separation from loved ones, and death. Even after the partial abolition of slavery, African Americans were subject to judicial and extrajudicial execution, disproportionate punishment for an expanding range of offenses outlined by the black codes and the later Jim Crow laws, and unpaid work in a convict lease system that was, by some accounts, "worse than slavery" (Oshinsky 1996). This chapter explores the racialization of crime and the criminalization of race in the wake of the Thirteenth Amendment, drawing on the work of Frederick Douglass, W. E. B. Du Bois, and Frantz Fanon. Fanon's work in particular helps address the lived experience of criminalized racial embodiment and helps develop a preliminary outline of critical phenomenology.

Part II looks at the modern penitentiary, beginning with Cold War behaviorism and its influence on twentieth-century penal policy. In chapter 4, I trace the connections among Cold War research on sensory deprivation, the development of behaviorist training programs and coercive interrogation techniques for use on noncitizens, and the application of these and other techniques to U.S. domestic prisoners in the mid-to-late twentieth century, in particular to Black Muslims, Latino/a activists, Puerto Rican *independentistas,* and other politically active prisoners. By tracing the application of behaviorist research in military contexts (the SERE [Survival, Evasion, Resistance, and Escape] program and the KUBARK manual) and domestic prison contexts (START [Special Treatment and Rehabilitation Training], Asklepieion, and other behavior modification programs), I offer a critical analysis of the intersections among psychiatry, prisons, and global politics in the mid-to-late twentieth century.

In chapter 5, I build on the work of Merleau-Ponty to develop a critical phenomenology of behavior, not as a set of causal mechanisms but, rather, as patterned structures of interaction between self-organizing living beings in the context of a shared world. Merleau-Ponty's approach also resists classical phenomenology's focus on pure transcendental consciousness; his account of intercorporeality and interanimality offers a rich conceptual language for articulating the ontological structure of the constitutive relationality that is exploited by solitary confinement and sensory deprivation.

Chapter 6 develops this critical phenomenology of behavior in relation to two specific sites of intensive confinement: the factory farm and the supermax prison. I argue that the discourse of human rights, while important for strategic reasons, ultimately rebounds against both prisoners and nonhuman animals who are harmed by intensive confinement not merely as rational human beings but also—perhaps even more fundamentally—as sensible, affective, corporeal, and intercorporeal living beings. I follow the political implications of my argument by critically analyzing the discourse of "dehumanization" and "human dignity" in *Madrid v. Gomez,* a 1995 Eighth Amendment case concerning the treatment of prisoners at California's Pelican Bay State Prison, a supermax penitentiary.[20]

Part III turns to contemporary supermax prisons, which both reflect and accomplish a shift in U.S. penal policy from the goal of redemption and rehabilitation to the task of perpetual control. Chapter 7 explores the experience of space in supermax confinement by drawing on Merleau-Ponty's account of spatial depth in *Phenomenology of Perception.* Chapter 8 reflects on the temporality of supermax experience by drawing on Levinas's account of ontological solitude, in which the existent's relation to impersonal being, or the *il y a,* feels like an unbearable weight that threatens one's sense of identity precisely by riveting one too closely to the burden of having to be (oneself). Finally, chapter 9 develops a critique of the rhetoric of "accountability" in supermax prisons by drawing on Levinas's account of responsibility as the investment of one's own arbitrary and potentially meaningless freedom as ethical responsibility for the other and political solidarity (or fraternity) with a community of others. An important part of my critique is a discussion of Levinas's own account of rhetoric as "anti-language," where language is understood as an ethical orientation toward the other who commands one to respond. For Levinas, the task of philosophy is to perform an ethical reduction of rhetoric; in other words, to trace anti-language back to the ethical responsibility that it both presupposes and denies. In each of these chapters, I engage with prisoners' own reflections on the meaning—and the meaninglessness—of their experience.

I
THE EARLY U.S. PENITENTIARY SYSTEM

1 AN EXPERIMENT IN LIVING DEATH

SOLITARY CONFINEMENT first emerged as a standard technique of punishment with the establishment of the penitentiary system in the early nineteenth century in the United States. The penitentiary was devised as a humanitarian response to the penal customs of public humiliation, torture, and execution inherited from English colonial rule. In the latter system, punishment was largely based on retribution—an eye for an eye, a life for a life—and its purpose was not to reform the individual criminal but to demonstrate the glory of the sovereign to the entire community, both for its own sake and as a deterrent to further crimes (Foucault 1979, 3–69). Punishments tended to be brutal and violent, focused on producing a public spectacle of pain in the body of the criminal, but not all crimes were punished, and not all destructive or "antisocial" behavior was classified as a crime. For the most part, imprisonment was used in this premodern period not as punishment but as a way of holding those who were still awaiting trial.

The Great Law of Pennsylvania, enacted in 1682, made a first step to transforming the blunt instrument of public corporal and capital punishment into a subtler, more expansive web of private punishments for increasingly private offenses, such as cursing and bestiality (Dumm 1987, 78–79). Under the influence of Quaker reformers, the Great Law restricted the application of the death penalty to murder alone and shifted the emphasis of punishment from retribution to correction and even redemption of the prisoner. Imprisonment, particularly solitary imprisonment, was the central mechanism of this new approach. No longer would prisoners be subject to the whips, cudgels, and gallows of corporal and capital punishment; rather, they would be confined to their own cells, forced to confront their own consciences in solitude, and made to reflect on the wickedness of their own souls. At the same time, they would acquire the habits of good citizens and industrious workers; left to their own devices for years on end, with no contact with family or friends and no news of the outside world, prisoners would learn how to rely on their own moral and physical strength. Like Robinson Crusoe, they would emerge from the ordeal of solitude stronger, more capable, and more industrious, and therefore more useful to society as a whole.

But the Great Law did not accomplish this transformation of the penal system; it merely initiated it. The practice of public punishment was carried over in the newly independent United States through laws such as the "wheelbarrow law" in the 1786 Pennsylvania code. The wheelbarrow law called for "hard labor, publicly and disgracefully imposed . . . in streets of cities and towns, and upon the highways of the open country" (quoted in Masur 1991, 78). Prisoners worked in chain gangs with "shaved heads and coarse uniforms lettered to indicate the crime committed" (Masur 1991, 78; see also Dumm 1987, 97–98).[1] The purpose of the law was, in essence, to give the prisoners a taste of social death by putting the degrading consequences of their life of crime on display, both exposing prisoners to public view and excluding them from membership in the public. In this sense, reforms of 1786 did not so much *replace* the death penalty as transpose it into a form of living death based on public humiliation combined with heavy physical labor. The expectation was that criminals would be encouraged to repent of their crimes by suffering both the psychic pain of social exclusion and the (socially useful) physical pain of hard work. They would be forced to contribute to society, precisely as a consequence of having betrayed the social contract. But this neat solution to criminality produced its own messy consequences. The presence of wheelbarrow gangs turned out to have a deleterious effect on the public; passersby enthusiastically contributed to the humiliation of the prisoners with insults and random violence, to the point where advocates of penal reform feared that the wheelbarrow law was encouraging more crime rather than deterring it. Moreover, many upstanding citizens were horrified at the sight of white men being forced to work like black slaves.[2] I will address the relation between slavery and the early penitentiary in chapter 2. For now, let us focus on the views of an influential penal reformer, Benjamin Rush. Why did Rush advocate solitary confinement as an alternative to public punishment, and what view of personhood did his advocacy presuppose?

Benjamin Rush and the Privatization of Punishment

In March 1787, just six months after the wheelbarrow law was passed, Benjamin Rush wrote "An Enquiry into the Effects of Public Punishments on Criminals, and on Society." Rush was a prominent physician, psychiatrist, essayist, educator, abolitionist, and signatory to the Declaration of Independence. Like other penal reformists of the time, Rush advocated private punishment, particularly solitary confinement, as a technique for producing repentance and reform in criminals and for fostering appropriate moral sympathies in the public. The problem with public punishment, according to Rush, was that it excited in prisoners a feeling of their own power and infamy, and in the public witnesses of punishment a feeling of "abortive sympathy" or even admiration for criminals, destroying in both "the sense of shame, which is one of the strongest outposts of virtue" (in Rush 1806, 141, 138). If punishment was to serve as an effective deterrent to crime, it must work with rather than against this natural sense of shame, stimulating a horror of crime without abasing criminals to the point where they could no longer be reintegrated into society. Rush recalled with admiration a scene that he witnessed as a student of the Reverend Samuel Finley:

> I once saw him spend half an hour in exposing the folly and wickedness of an offense with his rod in his hand. The culprit stood all this while trembling and weeping before him. After he had ended his admonitions, he lifted his rod as high as he could, and then permitted it to fall gently upon his hand. The boy was surprised at this conduct. "There go about your business (said the doctor). I mean *shame* and not *pain* in the present instance." (Quoted in Thorp 1946, 51–52)

The beauty of shame was that it inflicted a psychic wound that was invisible and yet visceral, affecting transgressors right at the level of their personhood. While physical pain tends to produce resistance in offenders by providing them with a concrete object of aversion, shame undermines resistance from within, deploying their own sense of dignity against their desire to transgress. Even in more serious cases than a schoolboy's misconduct, shame promises to transform criminals into respectful, productive, and morally upright members of society. In this sense, Rush's humanist campaign for penal reform shares with the early advocates of the wheelbarrow law a common confidence in the transformative power of shame; he merely relocates this shame to the private interior of a penitentiary cell.[3]

In his "Enquiry into the Effects of Public Punishments," Rush justifies private punishment from a philosophical and physiological perspective by offering "an analogy from animal economy" (142). Rather than relying upon abstract reason to reform criminals and educate the public, he puts bodily sensibility at the center of his biopolitical account of punishment. For Rush, the sensibility of the body is expressed both actively and passively; active sensibility produces a feeling in the subject along with an active response, and passive sensibility produces a spontaneous affect without corresponding action. While active sensibility is increased through the repetition of impressions, such that, for example, a doctor gets better and better at treating patients in response to their expressions of pain and distress, passive sensibility is decreased through repetition, such that the doctor's spontaneous feelings of sympathy diminish through the constant exposure to the pain of others. The danger of public punishment, according to Rush, is that it both impairs onlookers' development of active sympathy by forbidding them to relieve prisoners' distress, and also damages the public's capacity for passive sympathy by exposing them to the pain of others so frequently that they become indifferent to the suffering of others and unable to sympathize (appropriately) with widows and orphans, as well as (inappropriately) with prisoners (142–43). Even criminals are ill-served by public punishments, because their sensibilities are either inured to the benefits of punishment—having become so insensible to pain and humiliation that they are no longer susceptible to the moral dimension of such feelings—or their worst passions are intensified by the infamy of public punishment, thus escalating the depravity of their criminal life rather than causing them to repent and be redeemed.

For Rush, the issue of public punishment was of supreme importance in the new American republic, where one could no longer rely upon a common sovereign or universally shared traditions to bind the people together. Sympathy and sensibility would have to do the work of forming citizens or, in Rush's own words, converting them into "republican machines" governed by reliable mechanisms of self-discipline, emotional restraint, and industrious habits of work, study, and prayer (Rush 1806, 14). This production of republican machines was necessary in order for citizens "to perform their parts properly, in the great machine of the government of the state" (14–15). Rush's formula for producing republican machines was based on New Testament religion and supported by love of country, a moderate dedication to private life and family, a desire to amass wealth in harmony with the interests of the state, and (among other things) a simple diet consisting of hearty broths and little or no alcohol. Above all, the republican machine should avoid overstimulation of the nervous fibers, as produced, for example, by the excitement of public punishment. "Moderate sleep, silence, occasional solitude and cleanliness, should be inculcated upon [the people], and the utmost advantage should be taken of a proper direction of those great principles in human conduct,—sensibility, habit, imitations, and association" (Rush 1806, 13). Once these republican machines were properly wound up, they were bound to produce "happiness and perfection" in the republican state, which was itself a machine of machines.

Rush's views on sensibility and sympathy reflect a flourishing of interest in the emotional, physiological, and social dimensions of politics in the postrevolutionary United States (see Knott 2009). Sensibility was seen as the capacity that forms individuals into social creatures; it was the glue of society—which, of course, presupposes that individuals already exist prior to being stuck together. Rush moves very freely between physiological, emotional, mechanistic, social, and political claims in his analysis of sympathy and sensibility. For Rush, the body is a living machine composed of sensible matter, or nerve fibers. When stimulated in the proper way, these fibers produce impressions of sympathy that are socially and politically necessary for the functioning of a healthy state; however, when overstimulated or improperly stimulated, they produce physical, emotional, and social ills such as disease, madness, criminality, and even racial difference.

Rush believed that black skin and African American morphology was caused by a kind of leprosy. In a 1797 presentation to the American Philosophical Society entitled "Observations Intended to Favour a Supposition That the Black Color (as It Is Called) of the Negroes Is Derived from the LEPROSY," Rush argues that while blacks were not inferior to whites, poor diet, greater "heat," "savage manners," and "bilious fevers" conspired to darken their skin, flatten their noses, widen their lips, and cause their hair to become kinky. He cites cases of white women becoming black as a result of cohabitation with African Americans, as if blackness were an infectious disease. The cure for this disease was physical labor supplemented by bleeding, purging, and abstinence (Rush 1799, 296). Rush proposed to solve the problem of slavery by removing African Americans from circulation among whites and relocating them to a blacks-only farming "colony" to be established in Bedford County, Pennsylvania. This proposed colony would offer freed slaves a quiet place to be educated and cured of their blackness, while providing whites with the necessary time to shed their own habits of degrading, abusing, and oppressing blacks (D'Elia 1969, 421).

In his 1799 "Lectures on Animal Life," Rush explains physiological phenomena in terms that are continuous with his analysis of punishment and public sensibility. For Rush, "life is the effect of certain stimuli acting upon the sensibility and excitability which are extended, in different degrees, over every external and internal part of the body" (Rush 1847b, 136).[4] The imagination and the passions "pour a constant stream upon the wheels of life," stimulating the organism in both healthy and potentially unhealthy ways (144). In the prelapsarian paradise of Eden, all stimulations were positive and life affirming, but in our fallen world, negative emotions such as anger, fear, and jealousy act upon the body in a way that is comparable to the stimulus of a dislocated bone; they antagonize the muscles of the body and disrupt its equilibrium rather than facilitating productive movement (145). Diseases of the body and the mind, as well as social disorders such as criminality, are caused by "excessive, or preternatural excitement in the whole, or a part of the human body, accompanied generally with irregular motions, and induced by natural, or artificial stimuli" (177). Therefore, "the cure for all diseases depends simply upon the abstraction of stimuli from the whole, or from a part of the body, when the motions excited by them, are in excess" (177). However, a physician's care must be taken in the administering of silent and solitary cures, since the total "abstraction of all the stimuli which support life" results in death, just as the sound of a violin ceases altogether when the bow is "abstracted" from its strings (175).

For Rush, the model institution for curing diseases of any kind was the asylum; it offered a place where the disordered body could be removed from an overstimulating environment and given a chance to "reset" itself in the relative absence of stimuli. He designed a special chair called the tranquilizer that was designed to calm and restrain mental patients. The tranquilizing chair is a precursor to the restraint chairs used in today's prisons; a patient's arms, legs, chest, and belly would be strapped to the chair, and his or her head fit inside a wooden box lined with linen that prevented the head from moving up or down, left or right. A small window was cut out of the front of the box so that the patient could look forward, presumably to receive food and to see the doctor. A slot in the chair and a chamber pot obviated the necessity for potentially disruptive trips to the bathroom (Opton 1974, 611).

Given Rush's account of sensibility, it is no surprise that he should recommend the same treatment—solitude and silence—for a wide range of different mental, physical, and social disorders. In "The Influence of Physical Causes upon the Moral Faculty," he proposes solitary confinement as a cure for "bodies that are predisposed to vice" (1947a, 198).[5] The same treatment was effective in curing nervous disorders, reforming criminal behavior, and correcting the misdemeanors of children over the age of three or four.[6] Rush took this principle so seriously that he applied it to the treatment of his own children, both as infants and as adults; when his son, John, showed signs of depression after killing a friend in a duel, Rush admitted him to solitary confinement in his own institution, the Pennsylvania Hospital. John died there after twenty-seven years of confinement (Opton 1974, 613).

Rush approached the problems of political life in exactly the same way that he approached physiological life. He reasoned that if society was dysfunctional, it must be sick; and if it is sick, it must be healed by following the same sound principles that hold in the body-machine. For Rush, the mind, the body, the asylum, and the republic were all interlocking mechanisms or machines governed by similar principles of cause and effect, machines that relied upon each another for their own successful performance. What the fledgling republic needed in order to balance and regulate stimulations in the social body was an asylum for criminals, a place where the overly exciting stimuli of their dissolute lives could be diminished or removed, and their body-machines reset or reconditioned with the habits of healthy citizens. In a letter to John Adams, reflecting on their shared experience of the American Revolution, Rush proposed, "Were we to live our lives over again and engage in the same benevolent enterprise, our means should not be reasoning but bleeding, purging, low diet, and the tranquillizing chair" (quoted in Takaki 2000, 35). Rush believed that criminality, like insanity, was a disease; both were caused by "an original defective organization of those parts of the body, which are occupied by the moral faculties of the mind" (quoted in Dumm 1987, 92–93).[7] And he was not the only one of his contemporaries to hold this view. As one author wrote in 1790: "Let every criminal, then, be considered as a person labouring under an infectious disorder. Mental disease is, indeed, the cause of all crimes" (quoted in Masur 1991, 77). For Rush, the cure for political problems—perhaps the cure for politics itself—was medicine, and the best medicine for criminals, as for the insane, was solitude and silence.

Rush was by no means alone in his enthusiasm for the healing powers of solitary confinement. One reformist argued in April 1790 that "solitude and darkness are known to have a powerful influence on the mind. When the avenue of external sense is shut, and every accession of ideas from without precluded—the soul becomes an object to herself, her agitations subside: and her faculties tend to the natural equipoise" (quoted in Masur 1991, 81). Reverend James B. Finley, chaplain of the Ohio Penitentiary argued that the prisoner might even have a certain advantage over the "free" or nonincarcerated citizen:

> "Could we all be put on prison fare, for the space of two or three genera-
> tions, the world would ultimately be the better for it. Indeed, should society
> change places with the prisoners, so far as habits are concerned, taking to
> itself the regularity and temperance and sobriety of a good prison," then
> the grandiose goals of peace, right and Christianity would be furthered.
> "As it is," concluded Finley, "taking this world and the next together . . . the
> prisoner has the advantage." (Aynes 1975, 444, quoting J. Finley 1851, 41–42)

While Rush's own arguments for private punishment were largely biomedical, other advocates of penal reform in the late eighteenth and early nineteenth centuries, especially Quaker and other Protestant reformists in Pennsylvania, made religious arguments for the same practices. One author in the *Maryland Gazette* of October 31, 1788, argued, "Conscience cannot long sleep in *solitude*. The worst of men, when left for a while to themselves, are made prisoners by their own reflections. These reflections are the messengers of Heaven to bring them to repentance, and a sense of their duty" (quoted in Masur 1991, 83). This sentiment is reflected—albeit in secular language—in the words of Eastern State Penitentiary's first board of directors, who defined the purpose of solitary confinement as "to turn the thoughts of the convict inward upon himself, and to teach him how to think" (quoted in C. Smith 2009, 100).

But in the early reformist movement a tension had already emerged between the desire to heal or redeem and the desire to punish. Enoch Edwards—a close friend of Rush, a fellow physician, and the president of the Philadelphia Court of Quarter-Sessions—supported solitary confinement as a replacement for capital punishment, not on the grounds that it was more humane but because the anxiety of prolonged solitude was, in his words, a "greater evil than certain death" (quoted in Masur 1991, 83). Francis Calley Gray thought that solitary confinement would "leave a deeper remembrance of horror on the mind of the culprit. . . . Solitude, complete and entire solitude, should be left to do its effectual work" (Gray 1848, 37). And Rush himself praised the power of solitude to intensify the suffering of criminals, even as he prescribed the same treatment to his patients and children in order to cure them or alleviate their suffering:

> A wheelbarrow, whipping post, nay a gibbet, are all light punishments compared with letting a man's conscience loose upon him in solitude. . . . A bad man should be left for some time without anything to employ his hands in his confinement. Every thought should recoil wholly upon himself. (Quoted in Takaki 2000, 26)

As we will see in chapter 4, this ambiguity between treatment and punishment continues to haunt the U.S. penal system, even as the humanitarian agenda has long since faded away.

Imagining the Penitentiary

Rush's solution to the problem of public punishment raised by the wheelbarrow law and, more generally, by the inheritance of British penal customs was the construction of a penitentiary or "house of repentance." The proposed design for this asylum for criminals was based on the principles of active and passive sensibility expounded in Rush's medical work:

1. Let a large house of a construction agreeable to its design be erected in a remote part of the state. Let the avenue to this house be rendered difficult and gloomy by mountains or morasses. Let its doors be of iron; and let the grating occasioned by opening and shutting them, be increased by an echo from a neighbouring mountain that shall extend and continue a sound that shall deeply pierce the soul. Let a guard constantly attend at a gate that shall lead to this place of punishment to prevent strangers from entering it. Let all the officers of the house be strictly forbidden

ever to discover any signs of mirth, or even levity, in the presence of the criminals. To increase the horror of this abode of discipline and misery, let it be called by some name that shall import its design.[8]

2. Let the various kinds of punishment, that are to be inflicted on crimes, be defined and fixed by law. But let no notice be taken, in the law, of the punishment that awaits any particular crime. By these means, we shall prevent the mind from accustoming itself to the view of these punishments, so as to destroy their terror by habit. The indifference and levity with which some men suffer the punishment of hanging is often occasioned by an insensibility that is contracted by the frequent anticipation of it, or by the appearance of the gallows suggesting the remembrance of scenes of criminal festivity, in which it was the subject of humour or ridicule. Besides, punishments should always be varied in degree, according to the temper of criminals, or the progress of their reformation.

3. Let the duration of punishments for all crimes be limited, but let this limitation be unknown. I conceive this secret to be of the utmost importance in reforming criminals, and preventing crimes. The imagination, when agitated with uncertainty, will seldom fail of connecting the longest duration of punishment with the smallest crime. (Rush 1787, 148)

Each of these axioms is designed to intensify the association of criminal behavior with a secret and indefinite yet irremissible and horrifying punishment. Rather than overstimulating the organism with direct impressions of physical pain (be it the pain of others or one's own), Rush proposes to heighten the anxiety of both the prisoner and the public about the site, nature, and duration of punishment. The focus of this punishment is not so much the body of the criminal as the mind, especially the imagination, of both the criminal and the public; not knowing what the law has in store for one is a more effective deterrent, on this account, than knowing the law and perceiving its power directly.

And yet, the body of the criminal is not absent from Rush's vision of biopolitical reform. As always, Rush connects the political to the physiological: "The punishments should consist of BODILY PAIN, LABOUR, WATCHFULNESS, SOLITUDE, and SILENCE. They should all be joined with CLEANLINESS and a SIMPLE DIET. To ascertain the nature, degrees, and duration of the bodily pain will require some knowledge of the principles of sensation and of the sympathies which occur in the nervous system" (Rush 1806, 154). He adds, "I have no more doubt of every crime having its cure in moral and physical influence than I have of the efficacy of the Peruvian bark in curing the intermitting fever. The only difficulty is, to find out the proper remedy or remedies for particular vices" (155). The prison warden, like the government whose punishing arm he represents, ought to be both politician and doctor, curing social ills by drawing on the model and methods of medical science:

> The great art of surgery has been said to consist in saving, not in destroy-ing or amputating, the diseased parts of the human body. Let governments learn to imitate, in this respect, the skill and humanity of the healing art. Nature knows no waste in any of her operations. . . . The soul of man alone, with all its moral and intellectual powers, is, when misled by passion, aban-doned by the ignorance or cruelty of man to unprofitable corruption or ex-tirpation. (Rush 1806, 161–62)

In effect, the "house of repentance" or penitentiary that Rush proposes is a machine for isolating, breaking down, and resetting the habits of diseased or criminal subjects, and for (re)producing healthy citizen-subjects; it is a machine for (re)producing the republican machines that were necessary for the healthy functioning of the great machine, the republic itself. This, at least, is the theory. Now what of the practice?

The Machinery of Living Death

The first penitentiary was the Walnut Street Jail, established in Philadelphia in 1790. Eastern State Penitentiary followed in 1829; it became the prototype of the Pennsylvania system, which subjected prisoners to solitary confinement by day and by night. The commis-sioners of Eastern State required that "the exterior of a solitary prison should exhibit as much as possible great strength and convey to the mind a cheerless blank indicative of the misery that awaits the un-happy being who enters within its walls" (quoted in Yanni 2007, 49). This "cheerless blank" was extended to the prison's interiors, and even to its inhabitants. In the design by architect John Haviland, each cell was a bare stone box with the dimensions of twelve feet by eight feet by ten feet, with a twenty-foot-long, unroofed, enclosed exercise yard.[9] The yard was accessible—again, in solitude—for one hour a day, half an hour in the morning and half an hour in the evening. A small round skylight known variously as a "deadeye" or the "eye of God" provided ventilation and enough light to read. The interior door was solid, with only a one-way peephole for the guards and a small food hatch that converted into a table for the prisoner. Otherwise, the cell was furnished with a bed, a workstation, a toilet and a Bible. Silence was to be maintained at all times in the cells, and in order to not disrupt this silence, guards wore woolen socks over their shoes as they walked in the hallways. Until 1904, prisoners had to wear a mask or hood whenever they were removed from their cells (Yanni 2007, 49).[10]

Upon entry at Eastern State, prisoners' hair would be shaved and their clothes fumigated or burnt. Their first two weeks would be spent in total isolation, with no reading materials, no opportunity to work, no permission to sleep during the day, and almost no contact with guards or inspectors. Thomas Dumm compares this phase of confinement to what is now called sensory deprivation; prisoners were cut off not only from social life but from all forms of meaningful activity and engagement with the world (Dumm 1987, 108). After this initial period of disorientation, they would be given a Bible and put to work in the solitude of their cells. Most of the accounts from prisoners of Eastern State refer to this work as a lifeline without which they would not have survived confinement; it was the only source of distraction, the only way to fill their time day after day, week after week, year after year (109). Prisoners would work, eat, and sleep in their cells, knowing that there were others all around them in exactly the same situation but permanently separated from them by thick stone walls. Once a year, they might receive a visitor; at the most once a year, they might receive a letter. All contact with the outside, including news, would be severely limited so that, after their time was served, they could emerge as new persons, unconnected to their old community or way of life. This was the gift of the penitentiary: the privilege of becoming a tabula rasa, a blank slate from which to begin again as a newly made republican machine, an individual without a past and with nothing but a clear, bright, productive future ahead.[11]

While the Pennsylvania system was getting underway at Eastern State, an alternative penitentiary system was already being developed at New York's Auburn Prison, beginning in 1819. In the Auburn system, prisoners were confined in their cells by night but ate and worked in common during the day in strictly enforced silence. While Auburn began, like Eastern State, with a policy of total solitary confinement, within six months it was forced to adjust its policy: five of the original eighty prisoners had died, and at least half of those remaining suffered from serious physical and emotional problems (Dumm 1987, 116). In response to the crisis provoked by full solitary confinement, the inspectors at Auburn were forced to moderate their initial plans, introducing a common work space along with a code of silence, strict regimes of surveillance, and corporal punishment for those who broke the code. In the words of Dumm, the Pennsylvania system was designed to teach prisoners "one fundamental lesson, that they were alone in the world," and the Auburn system was designed to teach a second lesson: "that loneliness was to be a shared condition" (111–12; see also C. Smith 2009, 109).

In both systems, the penitentiary was designed to reflect its name as a place of penitence, a place to reflect on one's sins, to repent and to be redeemed (Dumm 1987, 85). In his recent book, *The Prison and the American Imagination* (2009), Caleb Smith argues that the penitentiary was imagined by its founders not just as a place for quiet reflection but also as a place of death and resurrection; through the civil and social death of the criminal, a newly born citizen and productive worker would emerge. As Benjamin Rush put it:

> I am so perfectly satisfied of the truth of this opinion that methinks I already hear the inhabitants of our villages and townships counting the years that shall complete the reformation of one of their citizens. I behold them running to meet him on the day of his deliverance.—His friends and family bathe his cheeks with tears of joy; and the universal shout of the neighbourhood is, "This our brother was lost and is found—was dead, and is alive." (1806, 157)

But for Smith, and for nineteenth-century critics of the penitentiary system such as Hans Christian Andersen, Charles Dickens, and Alexis de Tocqueville, the penitentiary did not function as a site of spiritual reflection, moral improvement, religious conversion, and happy reunions; rather, it was a machine for producing civil and social death without a chance for redemption. Prisoners emerged from this machine with eyes like blanks, a deranged nervous system, and a diminished capacity for coherent thought or conversation. From this perspective, the penitentiary was not a place of death and resurrection but, in the words of Harry Hawser, a poet and inmate at Eastern State Penitentiary in the 1840s, "a living tomb," a site of living death (quoted in Smith 2009, 5).

In their 1833 report on the U.S. penitentiary system, Gustave de Beaumont and Alexis de Tocqueville observed that while in theory solitary confinement was intended to ennoble prisoners by forcing them to reflect on the state of their souls, in practice, "absolute solitude, if nothing interrupts it, is beyond the strength of man; it destroys the criminal without intermission and without pity; it does not reform, it kills" (quoted in C. Smith 2009, 82). A prisoner becomes "dead to the world, and after a loss of several years, he re-appears in society, to which, it is true, he brings good resolutions, but also perhaps, passions, the more impetuous, from their being long repressed" (quoted in Dumm 1987, 122). Hans Christian Andersen uses similar language to describe what he saw at a Swedish penitentiary modeled on the Pennsylvania system in 1851:

> [A] silence deep as the grave rests over it. It is as though no one lived there or it was an abandoned house in time of plague. . . . Galleries run along the various storeys and, at the hub, the chaplain has his pulpit; where he holds his Sunday sermons for an invisible congregation. Door upon door of the cells is half-opened to the gallery. The prisoners hear the chaplain, but they cannot see him, nor he them. It is all a well-built machine, a nightmare for the spirit. (Andersen 1852, 55–56)

To be imprisoned in such a machine was to be buried alive, removed from the world to an enclosure with no vantage points from which to gain a perspective on one's spatial situation. In this sense, the architectural design of the cell reflected and produced the social and political situation of the prisoner; it was a machine for dying, or what Caleb Smith calls a "concrete sign of civil death" (2009, 83). Elam Lynds, warden at Sing Sing from 1825 to 1830, spoke frankly about this harsh reality in his address to a group of incoming prisoners in 1826: "While confined here, . . . you are to be literally buried from the world" (quoted in C. Smith 2009, 39). Buried from the world and confined to this living tomb, prisoners were reduced to their single individualities, their "cellular souls" (92). The walls of this cell were meant to function as a surrogate or support for the "straightened" body: both a tomb for the death of the criminal subject and a case or cocoon for the rebirth of the righteous citizen-subject (96).[12] But in practice, this ideal process stalled somewhere between life and death, rendering the distinction almost indiscernible.

According to Caleb Smith, the penitentiary's founders imagined the inmate as "a redeemable soul but also an offending body; a citizen-in-training but also an exile from civil society; a resurrected life but also an animate corpse" (2009, 39). But as Rush's biomechanistic account of the human animal suggests, the division between body and soul may not have been so clear; the body itself, with its complex network of nervous fibers, sensible impressions, and healthy or unhealthy habits, might have been just as important a target of "treatment" in the penitentiary as the soul was a target of religious redemption. Arguably, these two ways of imagining the death and rebirth of the criminal subject—religiously and medically—map onto the distinct characters of the two penitentiary systems. The aim of the Pennsylvania system was to redeem the soul of the offender; the Auburn system had more modest and practical goals: to reform behavior and to reduce repeat offenses (Dumm 1987, 116–20). In the words of Lynds, who was head warden at Auburn in the early 1820s and the architect of the Auburn system:

> I do not put great faith in the sanctity of those who leave the prison; I do not believe that the counsels of the chaplain, or the meditations of the prisoner, make a good Christian of him. But my opinion is, that a great number of old convicts do not convict new crimes, and that they even become useful citizens, having learned in prison a useful art, and contracted habits of constant labor. This is the only reform which I ever expected to produce, and I believe that it is the only one that society has a right to expect. (Quoted in Dumm 1987, 117)

According to Dumm, Auburn "produced timid and hardworking animals, in the form of people who worked out of habit," and Eastern State sought not only to train prisoners but to save their souls as well (136). It is not clear which form of punishment is less cruel.

A Proto-Phenomenology of Living Death: Charles Dickens on the Pennsylvania System

What was it like to be confined as a prisoner in the early penitentiary systems? There are few direct reports of prisoners' experiences from this period, but Charles Dickens paints a vivid picture of living death in the early penitentiary in *American Notes,* a series of reflections based on his 1842 tour of the United States, during which he visited the Tombs prison in New York (officially known as the Halls of Justice), Eastern State Penitentiary, and a House of Correction and House of Reformation for Juvenile Offenders in Boston.

While Dickens admired what he saw of the Auburn system, he

denounced the Pennsylvania system in the strongest possible terms as a punishment "which no man has a right to inflict upon his fellow creature":

> I hold this slow and daily tampering with the mysteries of the brain to be immeasurably worse than any torture of the body; and because its ghastly signs and tokens are not so palpable to the eye and sense of touch as scars upon the flesh; because its wounds are not upon the surface, and it extorts few cries that human ears can hear; therefore the more I denounce it, as a secret punishment which slumbering humanity is not roused up to stay. (Dickens 1957, 99; see also 109)

What is it about solitary confinement that Dickens finds so absolutely objectionable? It is not the silence or the constant surveillance to which prisoners are subjected, nor is he squeamish about punishment as such.[13] Dickens expresses much enthusiasm for the Auburn system, or "the silent system" as it was also called, because its ingenious organization of space allowed for the maximum surveillance of prisoners, both in the factories where they worked silently side by side and in the cells where they ate and slept in solitude. According to Dickens, "The whole of this arrangement struck me as being admirable; and I hope that the next new prison we erect in England may be built on this plan" (53).

Dickens is not Foucault; he is not concerned with how the mechanisms of separation and surveillance individualize and normalize body-subjects in order to make them docile, productive workers. But he is concerned about the effects of the prisoners' near-total deprivation of the bodily presence of other people in the Pennsylvania system. This deprivation alone marks for him the difference between a system that is just, humane, and admirable and one that is so "strict, rigid and hopeless," so "cruel and wrong," that one can scarcely imagine the lengths and depths of the violence to which it afflicts the prisoner (99). Dickens argues that while both penitentiary systems seem to be motivated by a humanist desire to facilitate reform and repentance, advocates of the Pennsylvania system "do not know what it is that they are doing" (99). Not only do they mete out an "unknown punishment" in the sense that they dare to tamper with the mysteries of the brain, but they also use secrecy and prisoners' lack of knowledge of their place in the system as weapons against them (100). As we saw in Rush's axioms for penal reform, secrecy was a strategic component of the penitentiary system: not knowing where they were within the architecture of the prison—whether they were abandoned in a remote corner of the prison or surrounded by fellow prisoners in their cells—intensified prisoners' sense of disorientation to the point of sensory deprivation and social death.[14]

Whereas from Rush's perspective this disorientation was therapeutic and even redemptive, for Dickens it constituted a fundamental violence against the person as a social being who is intrinsically related to and supported by others. For Dickens, the violence of solitary confinement hits prisoners at a level that is so basic that we can scarcely locate it, measure it, or even describe the damage done. This violence leaves no bruises, and yet it effects a general demolition of the person, both "body" and "soul." Dickens notes the trembling of the prisoners, their nervous tics such as picking at their fingers, their difficulty in meeting his eye or sustaining conversation, their cringing posture and nervousness to the point of bursting into tears. He asks his guide if the prisoners "trembled very much" upon their release:

> "Well, it's not so much a trembling," was the answer—"though they do quiver—as a complete derangement of the nervous system. They can't sign their names to the book; sometimes can't even hold the pen; look about 'em without appearing to know why, or where they are; and sometimes get up and sit down again, twenty times in a minute. This is when they're in the office, where they are taken with the hood on, as they were brought in. When they get outside the gate, they stop, and look first one way and then the other: not knowing which to take. Sometimes they stagger as if they were drunk, and sometimes are forced to lean against the fence, they're so bad:—but they clear off in course of time." (105–6)

Dickens notes that even prior to their release, the sensory awareness of prisoners, their very capacity to see and hear clearly and to make sense of their perceptions, was radically diminished by solitary confinement. Their faces took on "something of that strained attention which we see on the faces of the blind and deaf, mingled with a kind of horror, as though they had all been secretly terrified. . . . That it makes the senses dull, and by degrees impairs the bodily faculties, I am quite sure" (108–9).

Dickens believes that we cannot even begin to imagine the ferocious intensity with which solitary confinement afflicts prisoners, because the level at which this affliction takes place is so fundamental to the very *personhood* of prisoners that it is impossible to locate the damage. Is it a physical affliction? But prisoners have adequate food and drink and a bit of daily exercise and are free from physical violence. Is it a mental affliction? But solitary confinement was meant to stimulate prisoners' capacity to think and reflect, to "abstract" them from overstimulation so that they could find new reserves of moral and intellectual strength. And yet, in practice, this withdrawal from concrete social relations did not impose upon prisoners the habits of reflective, penitent souls; rather, it brought about a general demolition of their personhood: not an affliction of this or that *part* of their person but a generalized incapacitation of their Being-in-the-world. Of one prisoner, Dickens remarks that he has become "a helpless, crushed, and broken man" who has "lost all care for everything" (104). It is not just that he misses his friends and family, or even his criminal cohorts for that matter; it is that his capacity to care about things, to comport himself toward something that matters to him, to have a meaningful relation to himself or to the world, has been evacuated from his life.

How could a person die from being deprived of the company of others, as many did in the first years or even months of the penitentiary experiment? And for those who survived, how and why was their life transformed into a form of living death? What does it mean to become a ghost in one's own life, unable to communicate with others, and even unable to determine the line between imagination and reality? These transformations are only possible if the person in solitary confinement is not simply an atomistic individual, separable from others and from the world, and constructed of different interlocking but separable parts. If the person is a machine, as Rush had theorized—even if it were a highly excitable, sensible, and sympathetic machine—then there would be no reason to expect that its separation from others would provoke such a wholesale collapse of its integrity as a person and its capacity for meaning or care. It is only because we depend on the world, and on the others who coconstitute both the meaning of the world and our own sense of personhood, that solitary confinement and the sensory deprivation that inevitably accompanies it have the power to damage us at the very level of our being.

I will have more to say about this phenomenological sense of personhood in chapter 2. For now, I wish to draw on Dickens's proto-phenomenological description of what it is like to be kept in solitary confinement. While he does not express himself in the phenomenological vocabulary that I develop in chapter 2, Dickens clearly understands that personhood cannot be sustained on its own and that an experience of shared space—of the bodily presence of others—is minimally necessary to sustain a sense of personhood. In the end, he overestimates the benefits and benevolence of the Auburn system, but he nevertheless presents a powerful critique of solitary confinement. And even in his problematic endorsement of the Auburn system, he at least confirms the importance of sharing some form of collective space in common with other embodied persons, even if one is condemned to total silence.[15]

Reflecting on his visit to Eastern State Penitentiary, Dickens tries to imagine what it must be like to be thrown into solitary confinement:

> Over the head and face of every prisoner who comes into this melancholy house, a black hood is drawn; and in this dark shroud, an emblem of the curtain dropped between him and the living world, he is led to the cell from which he never again comes forth, until his whole term of imprisonment has expired. He never hears of wife and children; home or friends; the life and death of any single creature. He sees the prison-officers, but with that exception he never looks upon a human countenance, or hears a human voice. He is a man buried alive; to be dug out in the slow round of years; and in the meantime dead to everything but torturing anxieties and horrible despair. (100–101)

At first, the prisoner is stunned and disoriented; his first impulse is throw himself on the bed in despair. Then, he becomes desperate for work, or for anything that will distract him from his solitude. But this work can only absorb him for so long. The silence begins to drive him mad. Who are the other prisoners? Where are they? Are they near or far? In desperation, he conjures up shadowy figures, imagining first one man and then another, lurking in the corners of his cell, their faces hidden from view. He becomes obsessed with these mysterious figures of his own imagination, to the point where they expand to fill the whole cell, invading his sleep, leaving him no room to be and (ironic as this might seem) no meaningful experience of solitude. At this point, everything in the prisoner's cell becomes animate; the smooth white walls become dreadful and horrifying; even the ceiling seems to be looking down on him. There is nowhere to hide from this impersonal gaze, and yet no one to encounter, no one to whom one may appear.

Everything that ought to bring comfort now takes on the appearance of a threatening other: "The blessed light of day itself peeps in, an ugly phantom face, through the unchangeable crevice which is his prison window" (107). The figments of his imagination take on a life of their own, turning against him and threatening to overpower him. "Now, [his cell] is every night the lurking-place of a ghost: a shadow:— a silent something, horrible to see, but whether bird, or beast, or muffled human shape, he cannot tell" (107). A generalized anxiety comes to replace his sense of separate, autonomous personhood; it undermines the subject for whom there once existed a meaningful world. But soon, even this anxiety becomes impossible to sustain. Hypersensitivity gives way to insensible dullness; the animated world collapses into dead, inert blankness: meaningless existence, emptied of even the ambiguous presence of the phantom other. The hallucinations return now and then, unexpectedly, but now the prisoner's life has become the site of an emptiness, a placeholder for the absence of a subject. "He is easily moved to tears; is gentle, submissive, and broken-spirited" (108). If the imprisonment persists for long enough, he may never recover from this state where the possibility of a meaningful world has been reduced to the tomblike space of the cell, and where the occupant's existence has been stuck to itself to the point of self-annihilation.

The prisoners that Dickens meets and describes have each developed strategies for survival. The receiver of stolen goods, midway through his six-year sentence, has made himself a paper hat and a Dutch clock out of scavenged materials; both he and the German convicted of larceny have painted their cells with little bits of colored yarn; another man has been permitted to raise rabbits. But none of these strategies could adequately compensate for the bodily presence of others—even if that presence was merely the silent presence of a coworker. Even the rabbit keeper looks "as wan and unearthly as if he had been summoned from the grave," and when he darts back into his cell in pursuit of a rabbit, Dickens finds it "very hard to say in what respect the man was the nobler animal of the two" (103).[16]

In the end, the mode of punishment that attempted to humanize the U.S. penal system, to redeem the souls of criminals, and to convert them into "republican machines," threatens to destroy the very matrix of personhood. What must a person be like, in order for this destruction to be possible?

2 PERSON, WORLD, AND OTHER

A Husserlian Critique of Solitary Confinement

DICKENS PAINTS A VIVID PICTURE of living death at Eastern State Penitentiary in the early nineteenth century. Taking this description as my starting point, I now develop a phenomenological analysis of what personhood must be like in order to be affected in this way by prolonged solitary confinement. What are the conditions for the possibility of such a radical physical, emotional, cognitive, and social deterioration of the prisoner in isolation? How must concrete personhood be structured in order to be diminished so radically by the prolonged deprivation of the bodily presence of other people? To explore these questions, I turn to Husserl's phenomenological account of subjectivity, intersubjectivity, and the world. In this preliminary discussion of phenomenology and social confinement, my focus is on the following questions: What is consciousness? How is it distinct from concrete personhood, while still forming the ultimate condition for its possibility—and what are the further conditions for personhood, beyond the transcendental level of consciousness? What is a world, and how integral is the world to personhood? How does the experience of other people beyond myself support my own experience of the world as the most general context for meaningful experience, even if (or perhaps because) these others contest my own account of what this or that particular object or situation means? And finally, what role does embodiment play in my experience of other people, and by extension of the world, and even of myself as a concrete person in the world?

If the person were really a living machine, republican or otherwise, governed by causal mechanisms in which each stimulus from the environment provoked a predictable response in the organism, then there would be no reason to expect a wholesale deterioration of personhood in solitary confinement. Likewise, if the mind were a tabula rasa, as Rush believed, then solitary confinement might be therapeutic; to clear the mind of all worldly attachments would be to wipe the slate clean in preparation for a new beginning. Solitary confinement would be as Rush intended it when he locked his own son up in his asylum for the rest of his life: a gift, a source of spiritual and physical healing, the chance to begin a new and better life. But precisely because consciousness is more than just a blank slate upon which external objects impress themselves—because the world is essentially correlated to consciousness, while at the same time remaining irreducible to it—one cannot deprive individuals of their world without doing grievous damage to their beings as consciousness. This chapter proposes a phenomenological alternative to Rush's account of sensibility in order to initiate a broader philosophical critique of the violence of solitary confinement.

For the phenomenologist, experience is not the inscription of impressions on the blank slate of the mind but, rather, the intentional relation of consciousness to a world that is neither "out there" in a separate realm beyond consciousness nor "in here" in the form of an innate idea. For the phenomenologist, consciousness is not a thing—it has no extension, no location in the brain or in nervous fibers. It is a relation of intentional acts *(noesis)* to intentional objects *(noemata)*, the widest context for which is the world. One could no more separate these two sides of intentionality than one could separate two sides of a sheet of paper; they are essentially correlated, such that consciousness is always consciousness *of* something—whether or not the particular object of consciousness actually exists. The task of phenomenology is to trace these correlations, uncovering the structure of each noema and describing the ways in which different noemata are given in a shared context, or the same noema is given differently in perception, imagination, memory, and so forth. While perception is "original consciousness" for Husserl in the sense that it provides our most fundamental way of getting to know the world, he is nevertheless careful not to reduce all modes of awareness to the specific structure of perceptual awareness.

My argument in this chapter is twofold; it involves both an appropriation and a critique of Husserl's approach to phenomenology. On the one hand, Husserl offers a convincing critique of the sort of mechanistic naturalism upon which Rush based his defense of solitary confinement, and he develops a much richer account of personhood as essentially oriented toward a world shared with other subjects. For Husserl, persons do not exist as such without a world to which they belong; they are not solitary individuals but rather selves among others, where those others are both encountered within the world and coconstitutive of that world's objective reality. In this sense, Husserl's phenomenology helps explain why the very techniques intended to heal or even save criminal subjects ended up diminishing them to the point of social, and sometimes physical, death. But on the other hand, Husserl's own insistence on first-person consciousness, not just as a necessary methodological starting point for phenomenological reflection but also as an irreducible ontological structure—as the transcendental being upon which the meaning of the world ultimately and absolutely depends—puts him in an uncomfortably close proximity to the early humanist advocates of solitary confinement. I am not trying to suggest that Husserl himself would have endorsed solitary confinement if pressed to take a position; I am suggesting, rather, that his account of personhood is not sufficiently intersubjective to provide the grounds for my own critique of solitary confinement as a mechanism of social death. And yet, the precise way in which Husserl's account falls short is instructive in my further development of a phenomenological critique of solitary confinement as social death.

From the Transcendental Ego to the Full Monad: An Introduction to Phenomenology

The challenge of phenomenology is to reveal, through a careful description of intentional consciousness, the transcendental conditions for the possibility of any experience whatsoever, as well as for particular varieties of experience. Husserl proposes the phenomenological reduction as a method for demonstrating both that there is an irreducible *distinction* between consciousness and world—such that consciousness is not just "a little tag-end of the world" (1991, 24), a substantive thing that can be studied like an object—and also that there is an essential *correlation* between consciousness and world, such that it would be incoherent to speak of the mind as if it were separable from that of which it is mindful. To perform the reduction, one must suspend one's belief that the world exists in a realm apart from consciousness, as an unproblematically objective reality to which one's mind somehow connects. One must bracket what Husserl calls "the natural attitude," the assumption that characterizes both everyday life and also prephenomenological natural and social sciences. The natural attitude is an unreflective experience of the world as if one's own consciousness did not constitute the very possibility of experience. To bracket the natural attitude is to shift one's attention from the objects of experience to the *way* in which these objects are given to consciousness and the way that consciousness orients itself toward these objects.

For example, when I perceive a cup in the natural attitude, I fail to notice that the cup is given to me in a series of profiles, one side at a time, always from a particular perspective and in relation to a background or external horizon. I never perceive the whole cup all at once, and yet if I were asked what I am looking at, I would say "a cup" rather than "a partial view of one side of what appears to be a cup." The experience of objects as such involves more than just the impression of a stimulus on the mind of the perceiver, because the "stimulus" that we receive at any given time never matches what we actually *intuit* as a cup, rather than as a side or profile. From a phenomenological perspective, then, the experience of a cup is not the straightforward apprehension of an empirical reality; rather, it involves a blend of presence and absence, something given but also something just-given (retention) and not-yet-given (protention). But we only notice that this is the case by taking a step back from our natural absorption in the world to see how perceptual objects are given to us, and how we constitute their meaning through active and passive synthesis.

For Husserl, the phenomenological reduction reveals consciousness as the most fundamental condition for the possibility of experience. This is not to say that the world is just a dream, and consciousness the dreamer; rather, it means that any conceivable *sense* of the world, or of any object within the world, is founded in the transcendental ego rather than in a set of empirical or naturalistic facts.[1] Even ideas such as *reality, nature,* or *fact* depend not upon something real, natural, or factual for their meaning but, rather, upon consciousness as a correlation of noesis and noema, the meaning and the meant, the subjective flow of impressions and the objects that are given in this flow. Every possible meaning, even the meaning of absurd, nonsensical, or nonexistent things, is a sense that is constituted in consciousness and ultimately founded on the flowing stream of impressions that form the most basic level of ego-life. In constituting the sense of the world, the ego does not simply decide what will count as real; it relies on *evidence,* which for Husserl is an experiencing or "mental seeing" of something as it is given to consciousness, in just the way that it is given (1991, 12).

Husserl accepts Descartes's argument in the *Meditations* that the ego receives apodictic, or indubitable, evidence of its own existence; however deceived I may be about the world, or even about myself, it is simply unthinkable that the subjective processes of thinking, doubting, wanting, remembering, and so forth do not exist (Husserl 1991, 17). In addition to this apodictic evidence of itself, the ego has access to potentially endless manifolds of evidence about the world, but this evidence, insofar as it is founded in and dependent upon the ego's subjective processes, can never attain the status of absolute apodicticity. To say this is not to condemn the ego to a permanent skepticism about the nature and existence of the world but, rather, to promote a critical vigilance based on evidence with various degrees of adequacy, the ultimate acceptance basis of which is the transcendental ego itself. Drawing on this evidence, the ego constitutes the sense of a "fixed and abiding being" as something to which it can return again and again to investigate further, confirming or correcting its initial impressions. This evidence of the world may be indefinitely enriched and refined, but it can never be "completed as an adequate evidence" (62). This implies that the sense of the world remains forever open to modification, refinement, and correction by new discoveries and new perspectives.

Husserl distinguishes between different levels or strata of consciousness, each of which is nested within other, more fundamental levels. At the foundation of all possible experience is the transcendental ego, the pure stream of consciousness that unfolds in the first person in a singular, unsharable way for any given consciousness. Husserl calls the transcendental ego "the acceptance-basis of all Objective acceptances and bases" (1991, 26); it is that without which there would be no experience of anything whatsoever, and therefore no world. The transcendental ego is not some kind of transpersonal being of which each individual ego would be a token or particular manifestation; it is just the transcendental dimension of any ego whatsoever, human or nonhuman, taken in its most basic sense as the sheer capacity for awareness. No one can access my singular stream of consciousness, nor can I access the singular flowing stream of any other consciousness. To say this is not to condemn the ego to solipsism, as if the singularity of the transcendental ego prevented it from getting to know other egos or coming to share a certain way of looking at the world; it simply means that it cannot experience the world *as* that other ego.

In addition to this transcendental ego, and founded upon it, each ego has its own personal history of flowing impressions, which includes everything from mundane experience, such as glancing from left to right across a room, staring down at one's shoes, wondering what's for dinner, and so forth, to the experience of momentous world events, personal traumas, and other formative experiences that dramatically shape one's personal habits, style, and character. The transcendental ego is singular and unsharable, or "absolutely simple" and "absolutely clear" (1991, 111), and therefore does not have specific attributes or characteristics beyond the sheer capacity for experience; but the personal ego that is founded upon it does have its own distinctive shape, history, and habits, its own idiosyncratic way of relating to the world. I am both a transcendental ego and a person; but these levels should not be confused or collapsed; while the transcendental ego is the pure power of constituting, with nothing behind it or underneath it as a cause, persons "are constituted not only in relation to a pure Ego and a stream of consciousness with its manifolds of appearances but also in relation to an intersubjective consciousness, that is, in relation to an open manifold of their streams of consciousness which, by reciprocal empathy, are unified into a nexus which constitutes intersubjective objectivities" (118). As I will explain in more detail below, the personal ego is essentially constituted in relation to a world and to other egos. The most fundamental condition for its possibility is the transcendental ego, but this alone is not sufficient for a concrete sense of personhood. For that, experience of other embodied egos in a shared world is needed, where each has a singular, unsharable perspective on a shared world.

The highest level of ego-life is what Husserl calls "monad," or "*the ego taken in full concreteness*" (1991, 67–68). Although the word "monad" suggests a self-enclosed bubble complete unto itself, for Husserl it refers to the whole nested structure of transcendental ego, personal ego, and world. The full monad has personal habits and a sedimented history that makes him or her both available to others and inextricably involved with them. For this reason, the monad is not a self-sufficient individual but rather a whole nexus of concrete relations, and is therefore

dependent on others, and not merely on individual persons but on communities of persons, social institutions, morals, the law, the church, etc. The apprehension of a man as a real personality is determined throughout by such dependencies. A man is what he is as *a being who maintains himself* in his commerce with the things of his thingly, and with the persons of his personal, surrounding world, and who, in doing so, *maintains his individuality throughout.* (Husserl 2002, 148)

When I refer to concrete personhood in this chapter, it is the full monad that I have in mind: the whole complex of interrelations within and among a multileveled self, a concrete world, and the other concrete egos who coconstitute this world. It is precisely this sense of personhood that is threatened with derangement or even destruction in solitary confinement. But before I can address this collapse of personhood phenomenologically, I need to say a bit more about how personhood is constituted in the first place.

Husserl acknowledges the essential role that the body plays in constituting the sense of an objective reality in which I exist as a concrete person among others. In *Ideas Pertaining to a Pure Phenomenology and to a Phenomenological Philosophy: Second Book. Studies in the Phenomenology of Constitution,* he offers a phenomenological analysis of touch as the most fundamental sense involved in constituting an awareness of my body as my own. My right hand touches my left hand, and in this simple everyday experience, a whole nexus of bodily interrelations unfolds. Let us address each strand of this nexus separately, with the understanding that they are all interwoven as a whole in experience. As my right hand touches my left, I feel in my right hand the kinesthetic sensation of moving something simultaneously, without any intermediary objects; this is an experience of the phenomenal body in the mode of "I can," as a seamless extension of consciousness, or as a moving, living corpus that is completely suffused with consciousness. Reflecting on this simple experience reveals that the body is not like a marionette controlled by a puppeteer-mind; it is experienced in kinesthetic unity with consciousness, and only when I have a radically disruptive experience of "I cannot" does the body appear to me as an object to be prodded, coerced, manipulated, or moved by a separate or disjointed consciousness.[2]

At the same time that I experience my body as a kinesthetic unity by touching my left hand with my right, I also experience tangible sensations on my right hand; my body is not just an animate being infused with consciousness but also a sensible being that perceives the world by exploring it. The avocado is rough, the teapot is hot, the table is smooth, and my left hand is warm with smooth and rough sides. But I only perceive the latter as *my* hand, rather than as a nonbodily object, by experiencing a total ensemble of coordinating touch-sensations on my left and right hands. At the same time that I experience my left hand as warm, I have sensations of pressure on my left hand; likewise, if I shift my attention slightly, my left hand becomes the "active" side touching my "passive" right hand. When it comes to touch-sensations of my own body, no side is absolutely active or passive; it is precisely the reciprocity of touch—and the interweaving of activity and passivity to the point of indiscernibility—that constitutes my body as *mine*. Husserl is emphatic on this point:

> *A subject whose only sense was the sense of vision could not at all have an appearing Body.* . . . The Body as such can be constituted originarily only in tactuality and in everything that is localized with the sensations of touch: for example, warmth, coldness, pain, etc. (2002, 158)[3]

Without the sense of touch and the capacity to *feel* oneself touching oneself, one would not be able to relate to one's body as one's own; rather it would be perceived as a material thing somehow attached to itself, like a prosthetic limb that has not yet been incorporated. To the extent that prosthetic limbs are incorporated into this kinesthetic-sensible nexus of reciprocity, they too become part of one's body. In this sense, the phenomenal body (*Leib,* or the body as experienced from a first-person perspective) is not exactly the same as the objective body (*Körper,* or the body as viewed from a third-person perspective), although they do overlap; while the objective body may be more or less stable over time, barring grievous accidents or disease, the phenomenal body is highly flexible, acquiring certain habits and patterns such that, for the most part, we do not even think about how to run, jump, type on a keyboard, or drive a car (151–69; see also Merleau-Ponty 2002, 159–70).

Already it is clear that the phenomenological view of the body is very different from Rush's view of the body as a machine. While both acknowledge the sensibility of the body, Rush views the body not as a flexible nexus of interrelations with itself and the world but, rather, as a mechanism that reacts with certain determinate outputs in response to inputs or external stimulus and whose behavior can therefore be manipulated through changes in the environment. Husserl would not deny that, for example, a brain injury can affect one's cognitive capacities, but this alone says nothing about the lived experience of embodiment or *Leib* (2002, 151–69, 172–75, 294–310). For Husserl, the body is not just a mechanism caught in the web of cause–effect relationships; rather, it is the "turning point" or hinge between the physical and the psychical, the objective and the phenomenal, the causal and the conditional. This "'turning point,' which lies in the Body, the point of transformation from causal or conditional process, is hidden from me" (168–69; see also 70). I will have more to say about the body's conditionality later, when I address the constitution of the sense of an objective world. For now, let this stand as a preliminary discussion of how the sense of my body as mine is constituted through reciprocal relations of touch. If the phenomenological account of embodiment has merit, then imagine the effect that prolonged sensory deprivation, especially the deprivation of touch, could have on one's sense of embodied consciousness.[4]

For Husserl, the body is a hinge not only between causal and conditional processes but also between self and other, or between the artificial construction of an abstract, solipsistic subject (posited for the sake of methodological simplicity) and the intersubjectivity of an objective world, which the full human person shares with others. Since transcendental consciousness is singular and unsharable, such that I can never experience the world as another person, my access to others is constituted primarily through the body.[5] The body of the other is not just an outward sign pointing to the inner psyche of the other but, rather, the locus of the other *as* alter ego, as the "there" that is essentially correlated to my "here." My own body is "the zero point of all these orientations"; it is "the ultimate central here: that is, a here which has no other here outside of itself, in relation to which it would be a 'there'" (2002, 166; see also 88). Wherever I go, whatever I do, I am always oriented toward the world from the starting point of my body; I am always here at the point where the world unfolds for me, in a singular unsharable way. But as long as I can move my body, I can always explore what the world is like from different places within the world; I can move around a sculpture, noticing how it changes with every step. In this experience, I have already become aware of the possibility that another ego could be looking at the same object from a different position and could be seeing more or less what I saw just a moment ago.

This structure of a multiplicity of different perspectives on the same object has important implications, both for the constitution of the sense of an *alter ego* and for the sense of a shared, objective world. But it also raises a question of primordiality, a chicken-and-egg question that, in my view, haunts Husserl's phenomenology. On the one hand, I encounter others within the world, just as I encounter cups, tables, and other objects, but on the other hand, the alter ego is not just an object within the world but another subject with his or her own perspective on the world. Just as an alter ego is "there" from the perspective of my "here," so too am I "there" from the perspective of that ego's "here." Precisely because the world does not merely appear to me but also coappears to others from their own singular perspectives, I am able to experience the world as something more than just a subjective projection or hallucination, as an objective world that exceeds my own personal experience of it. The experience of other subjects oriented toward a common world is crucial for the constitution of objective reality. But if this is the case, which comes first: My solitary constitution of the sense "other ego" or the mutual coconstitution of a world in which I encounter both myself and the other as concrete persons? Is transcendental subjectivity the most primordial condition for the possibility of a world, or is transcendental intersubjectivity even more primordial to the extent that we are never actually solitary in the first place but instead always already exist in relation to others whose perspective on the world was developed long before we could even "learn to see"?[6]

Husserl proposes to solve this problem by appealing once again to levels. At the most basic level, the world is the horizon of horizons, the widest possible context for the "meant" of my "meaning." At the level of the personal ego, the world acquires a certain determinate but openended character for me; it is the world of my concrete experience, a world with particular historical, cultural, and natural dimensions. But at the highest and most concrete level, the world is not just my own; it is the intersubjective world of a community of monads, each of whom has a singular *and* particular perspective on "*one identical world*" (1991, 107). This is the fully concrete objective world, or what we could call the "real world." While the first two senses of "world" can be plausibly understood to be constituted by a solitary or solipsistic ego (a plausibility that I wish to contest in the following section), the sense of a *real* world can only be coconstituted with others. As Husserl puts it, the intermonadic community "is an essentially *unique connectedness*, an actual community and precisely the one that makes transcendentally possible the being of the world, a world of men and things" (129). This intermonadic community is not just added onto the absolute primacy of a solitary ego:

> On the contrary (and this carries over to the sociality of brute animals), in the sense of *a community of men* and in that of *man*—who, even as solitary, has the sense: member of a community—there is implicit a *mutual being for one another,* which entails an *Objectivating equalization* of my existence with that of all others—consequently: I or anyone else, as a man among other men. (129)

There is an "*Objectivating equalization*" of my existence with that of others because "*the Other's animate bodily organism*" is "the intrinsically first Object, just as *the other man is constitutionally the first <Objective> man*" (124). Even though the transcendental ego is the ultimate condition for the possibility of any experience whatsoever, the sense of my own concrete personhood is not "first" from my perspective but is, rather, transferred over to me analogically through my experience of the *first* objective person in my world: the other.

Husserl makes a similar point in *Ideas II* in relation to the constitution of the sense "I as man," or I as concrete person. While the sense of the phenomenal body is constituted through relations of self-touching, the sense of an embodied person, with a real existence in the world, is first constituted by me as the personhood of an other and is only then transferred to myself:

> It is only with empathy and the constant orientation of empirical reflection onto the psychic life which is appresented along with the other's Body and which is continually taken Objectively, together with the Body, that the closed unity, man, is constituted, and I transfer this unity subsequently to myself. (2002, 175)

The first concrete *person* (or "man") is not myself but the other; I transfer this sense of personhood to myself through empathy with an other who is encountered within an objective world that was itself made possible by the appearance of an alter ego within my solipsistic sphere. In this sense, self–other relations are not simply or straightforwardly built outward, starting from a core self, toward a shared, objective world that includes myself and others; rather, these relations are constituted both outward (from myself toward others) and inward (from the other to myself). There is an "Objectivating equalization" of myself with all the others, which suggests that while the other is my alter ego, I am also the alter ego of these others.

But in spite of this radical thesis of the other as the "first man," Husserl maintains that transcendental intersubjectivity is ultimately nested within and made possible by transcendental subjectivity:

> We need hardly say that, as existing for me, [the community of monads, or transcendental intersubjectivity] is constituted purely within me, the meditating ego, purely by virtue of sources belonging to my intentionality; nevertheless it is constituted thus *as* a community constituted also in every other monad (who, in turn, is constituted with the modification: "other") as the same community—only with a different subjective mode of appearance—and as necessarily bearing within itself the same Objective world. (1991, 130)[7]

On the one hand, the very possibility of a world presupposes a transcendental ego; stones and chairs do not have worlds (although nonhuman animals do have worlds for Husserl; he does not take the later Heideggerian position that they are merely "poor in world" [Heidegger 1995, 186–200]). But on the other hand, the ego alone cannot constitute the full sense of the world as objectively real or as more than just the correlate of its own subjective processes. The ego may be able to constitute a personal world or "Nature" full of harmonious relations, consistent patterns, and more or less reliable evidence, but it cannot constitute the higher level of an "Objective world" without a community of others with whom it partakes in a transcendental intersubjectivity. And yet, in spite of the many nested layers of ego-being and world-being, and in spite of the essential intertwining of the concrete ego with the egos of others, the core of all possible experience remains for Husserl the singular, subjective transcendental ego. The lifeworld is essentially a world shared with others, but it nevertheless "derives its necessity from the transcendental ego *and then* from the transcendental intersubjectivity which discloses itself *in that ego*" (136; emphasis added). This is precisely the point that I would like to contest by reading certain moments in Husserl's work in relation to concrete accounts of the experience of solitary confinement.

The testimony of survivors of solitary confinement suggests that if one is deprived for long enough of the experience of other concrete persons in a shared or common space, it is possible for one's own sense of personhood to diminish or even collapse, while the transcendental ego, or the pure capacity for experience, remains, now unhinged from a shared world in which its perpetual flow of impressions could receive the bodily validation of others. Without the concrete experience of other embodied egos oriented toward common objects in a shared world, my own experience of the boundaries of those perceptual objects begins to waver.[8] It becomes difficult to tell what is real and what is only my imagination playing tricks on me, and this difficulty increases with the length of solitary confinement. I may begin to hallucinate, spontaneously generating an experience of imaginary others in the absence of concrete bodily relations. Or I may have less dramatic but no less unnerving perceptual distortions, like the supermax prisoners for whom the wire mesh on their door begins to vibrate or the surface of the wall seems to bulge (Grassian 1983, Shalev 2009, 186–206).[9] To the extent that we regard the prisoner as an individual who is separable from the world and from others, even if we acknowledge that this individual is a "social animal" whose "environment" has some sort of effect on physical and mental health, we fail to grasp the depths of the harm inflicted by solitary confinement.[10] It's not just that prisoners grow depressed or psychotic, although this could very well happen; it's that the intersubjective basis for their concrete personhood, and for their experience of the world as real and objective, as irreducible to their own personal impressions, is structurally undermined by the prolonged deprivation of a concrete, everyday experience of other people. Some prisoners are able to resist the collapse of worldhood and personhood for longer; some keep their sense of personhood alive by becoming absorbed in world-supportive activities such as work, physical exercise, puzzles, games, and elaborate fantasies; and some prisoners even feel strengthened by a certain degree of solitude in prison because for the first time in their lives, they are removed from an intersubjective community that has consistently undermined their attempts to make sense of the world.[11] But as we will see, the evidence overwhelmingly suggests that prolonged solitary confinement undermines prisoners' capacity to make and sustain meaning. It not only dulls the senses and impairs the cognitive faculties (as if these were two different parts of the body-mind-machine) but also attacks the structure of intentional consciousness by impoverishing the world to which consciousness is essentially and irrevocably correlated. In this sense, the practice of solitary confinement does not merely punish prisoners by limiting their freedom and blocking their access to family and friends; it exploits the most fundamental capacities of their embodied existence, turning the constitutive relationality of their consciousness against themselves, using their most impressive power—the power of coconstituting a meaningful world—as a weapon against them.

Phenomenology at the Limit

To get a sense of the limits of Husserlian phenomenology for understanding the experience—and the unraveling of experience—in prolonged solitary confinement, consider Jack Henry Abbott's account of his confinement alone in a blackout cell with absolutely no light for twenty-three days. Abbott describes his ordeal as a dissolution of the very capacity for coherent experience, a mashing together of his senses in which his vision, hearing, touch, and even breath trampled over one another. His eyes "*hungered* for light, for color, the way someone's dry mouth might *hunger* for saliva" (1991, 27). His sense of hearing diminished, as if "darkness muffle[d] sound" (26). It became difficult to breathe, as if darkness swallowed air along with light (25). This crisscrossing of the senses in prolonged solitary darkness suggests that even in normal perception, our senses collaborate to a greater extent than we may think; the deprivation of sight brings pain and diminishment to other senses, as well as a more general deterioration of bodily integrity. But it was not just Abbott's subjective experience of embodiment that was affected by prolonged darkness; the normal experience of light and darkness and the conditional relations that pertain to opening and closing one's eyes became disordered and even reversed. Abbott reports, "The only light I saw was when I closed my eyes. Then there was before me a vivid burst of brilliance, of color, like fireworks. When I opened my eyes it would vanish" (26). His eyes "became so sensitive if I touched them, they exploded in light, in showers of white sparks shooting as if from a fountain" (27). Deprived of the light they need to function normally, his eyes began to respond to the stimulus of touch, and the otherwise unnoticed pressure of eyelids on the surface of his eye produced intense, unavoidable flashes of light. Abstracted from the illuminated world, his eye was forced to become a tactile organ, producing its own impressions of the light for which it hungered.[12] After twenty-three days of darkness, Abbott came unhinged, no longer able to identify with his own body and voice: "I heard someone screaming far way and it was me. I fell against the wall, and as if it were a catapult, was hurled across the cell to the opposite wall. Back and forth I reeled, from the door to the walls, screaming. Insane" (27).

Husserl's phenomenological account of experience and of concrete personhood in a shared world helps us begin to understand what is at stake in the insanity produced by solitary confinement and sensory deprivation. But it only goes part of the way, for two distinct reasons, only one of which I have explored in this chapter.

First, Husserl's insistence on the absolute primacy of the singular transcendental ego underestimates the sense in which even our own capacity to localize our sensations, to feel our body as our own, to have coherent perceptions of an objective world, to tell the difference between reality and hallucination, and even to exist as concrete persons, presupposes embodied social relations with others. For example, in *Ideas II,* Husserl asks us to imagine that it has become "permanently night":

> Light is now no more—could such a consciousness arise for me, as a solipsistic subject, if I became blind, for instance by being struck on the eyes? Or is this the consciousness that is more likely to be motivated: there is day and night as before, but I do not see it any longer? It depends on the apperceptions of the respective Objective and subjective perceptual circumstances as such. In any case one fact remains: I still have eyes, which touching tells me, but I do not see with them any more. (2002, 75)

At what point for the person in solitary confinement—or even worse, for the person held in social and sensory isolation—does it become impossible to distinguish between a subjective and an objective sense of permanent night? At what point does even the fact that "I still have eyes" lose its obviousness? Without a more robust account of transcendental intersubjectivity, or what Merleau-Ponty calls "intercorporeality," it remains difficult, perhaps impossible, to account for Abbott's experience in phenomenological terms.

Second, even in its expanded and enriched form, phenomenology is limited in how much it can tell us about the specific subject positions of concrete persons, the power relations among them, and the history of punishment in which they are embedded. How does race in particular affect the likelihood of being exposed to the violence of solitary confinement in prison? How is race perceived, and how is its meaning constituted and reconfigured over time, in specific social worlds and in the lived experience of intercorporeal subjects? To address these questions, I return to the scene of the early penitentiary system in order to track its relation to slavery and to the racialized bodies that have circulated from one system to the other. I will follow this up with a phenomenological analysis of racism and physical violence as forms of social death, drawing on the work of Frantz Fanon and Elaine Scarry.

3 THE RACIALIZATION OF CRIMINALITY AND THE CRIMINALIZATION OF RACE

From the Plantation to the Prison Farm

> My recall is nearly perfect, time has faded nothing. I recall
> the very first kidnap. I've lived through the passage, died
> on the passage, lain in the unmarked, shallow graves of
> the millions who fertilized the Amerikan soil with their
> corpses; cotton and corn growing out of my chest, "unto the
> third and fourth generation," the tenth, the hundredth. My
> mind ranges back and forth through the uncounted genera-
> tions, and I feel all that they ever felt, but double. I can't
> help it; there are too many things to remind me of the 23½
> hours that I'm in this cell. Not ten minutes pass without a
> reminder. In between, I'm left to speculate on what form the
> reminder will take.
>
> —George Jackson, *Soledad Brother*

> Because, that's what prison looked like. It looked like
> slavery. It felt like slavery. It was black people and people of
> color in chains.
>
> —Assata Shakur, "Assata Shakur Speaks from Exile"

THE BLACK EXPERIENCE OF INCARCERATION during the
first wave of the U.S. penitentiary system was not, by and large, an
experience of (failed) redemption through solitary confinement in the
penitentiary system but, rather, one of forced labor, bodily pain, public humiliation, and isolation to the point of social death. Slaves were
punished for not working, for not working hard enough or fast enough,
for disobeying orders, for stealing, for fighting, for "sassing," for trying
to see loved ones at neighboring plantations, for attempting to escape,
or just for being in the path of a master or overseer who was drunk

and felt like wreaking havoc or who just felt like punishing.[1] After the Emancipation Proclamation of 1863, many black Americans found they were still not treated as citizens and full human persons; rather, they were stigmatized as criminals and exposed to a whole new set of justifications for the ongoing deprivation of their freedom. Blacks who had been forced to pick cotton as slaves found themselves picking cotton as convicts—sometimes on the same plantations as before. Their labor power was often counted the same way it had been under slavery, in measures of "full hands," "half-hands," and "dead hands."[2] They were not paid for their work, and when they failed to work fast enough or were caught breaking rules, they were punished—as convicts, and as slaves—with whips whose nicknames bore the stain of racist and sexist oppression, such as "Black Annie" or "Black Betty" (B. Jackson 1999, 60–61). Some of the prison farms, such as Parchman and Angola (still operating today as Mississippi State Penitentiary and Louisiana State Penitentiary, respectively) were actually built on former slave plantations; they replicated not only the look and feel of slavery but also the same geographic territory, the same fields of cotton or sugarcane. As raúlrsalinas, a prisoner at the U.S. Penitentiary, Marion, observed, "Prison is a backyard form of colonialism" (quoted in Gómez 2006, 58).

Even the northern penitentiaries—whose development in the 1830s coincided with an expansion and intensification of plantation slavery in the South—managed to incarcerate black men and women at much higher rates than their white counterparts. In 1830, blacks formed 2.8 percent of the population of Pennsylvania but 46 percent of the inmate population at the Walnut Street Jail; whites, by contrast, formed 97.2 percent of the state population but only 54 percent of the inmate population (Patrick-Stamp 1995, 109).[3] Some black prisoners literally bore the scars of slavery on their bodies (117). Their most common occupations prior to incarceration were physical labor for men and domestic service for women; their crimes were overwhelmingly crimes of poverty and desperation (116, 121).

The very first inmate received into Eastern State Penitentiary was black. His intake record from 1829 reads:

> Charles Williams, Prisoner Number One. Burglar. Light Black Skin. Five feet seven inches tall. Foot: eleven inches. Scar on nose. Scar on Thigh. Broad Mouth. Black eyes. Farmer by trade. Can read. Theft included one

twenty-dollar watch, one three-dollar gold seal, one, a gold key. Sentenced
to two years confinement with labor.[4]

While (white) citizens of Philadelphia grew uncomfortable seeing
crews of (largely white) "wheelbarrow men" in their midst, such treatment remained the norm for black slaves in the South. Indeed, this
visual proximity of the white criminal to the black slave arguably
played a significant role in the northern rejection of public punishments (C. Smith 2009, 9). Even after the abolition of slavery in 1865,
and in spite of the rhetoric of humane punishment through solitary
confinement, brutal forms of corporal and capital punishment were inflicted on African Americans as a result of the black codes of the 1860s,
the convict lease system (1865–1928), the vast prison farms that sprang
up across the South, and the extralegal but socially supported violence
of lynching and other forms of racial terror. Whereas in the North,
the social death of the prisoner was produced through the touchless
torture of prolonged solitary confinement in a penitentiary cell, in the
South, social death followed a different logic, much closer to the logic of
today's supermax prisons: a logic of containment, control, and exploitation. It begins with the material conditions of slavery, is transposed
into the prison system, and continues all the way to the squeaky-clean,
fluorescent-lit control of today's supermax units. Throughout, this logic
of punishment is intensely racialized, but the patterns of racialization
have shifted over time to include what Joy James calls "the enslavement of nonblacks" and the relocation of the slave's "ontological status"
from "nigger" to "criminal" (2005, xxix). As Ruth Gilmore observes in
her analysis of California's prison system from the 1980s to the present, "You have to be white to be prosecuted under white law, but you
do not have to be Black to be prosecuted under Black law" (2007, 227).
Gilmore defines racism, following Foucault, as "the state-sanctioned
or extralegal production and exploitation of group-differentiated vulnerability to premature death" (28, 247; see also Foucault 2003 and
McWhorter 2009).

In this chapter, I track this vulnerability to premature physical and
social death from plantation slavery to plantation prisons and beyond,
to the forced idleness of supermax control units. I begin with an analysis of punishment during slavery, followed by a political-historical
account of the shifting site of racialized punishment from slavery to

prisons, concluding with a critical phenomenology of punishment and resistance inspired by the work of Frantz Fanon.

The Punishment of Slaves: Containment, Control, and Exploitation

While the northern penitentiary systems failed to deliver on their promise of redemption and resurrection, this promise was not even extended to black slaves—nor even to black penitentiary inmates. Slaves were generally punished not by the state legal system but by their masters. This applied to white women as well, especially to poor and working-class women.[5] The ideal target of penitentiary punishment was someone who was free enough to experience the deprivation of freedom as a meaningful punishment—namely, a white man with a redeemable Christian soul. In order for the penitentiary to make sense—in order for the deprivation of freedom to function as a *punishment,* but also as a stimulus for improvement—offenders had to be free to begin with. This could not be said for slaves, for women, or for the very poor. Even manumitted or emancipated blacks could not be considered free in the sense presupposed by the ideals of the penitentiary system; to the extent that they were released into poverty and into the minefield of the black codes, freed slaves became eligible for incarceration but not for the redemptive punishment of prolonged solitude. As Angela Davis puts it, "Black men and women . . . could not even fall from grace, a state they were deemed incapable of attaining in the first place" (2002, 66).

A former slave, Squire Irvin, confirms this point:

> I ain't never seen no jail till after peace was declared. In slavery times, jails was all built for the white folks. There warn't never nobody of my color put in none of them. No time for them to stay in jail. They had to work. When they done wrong, they was whipped and let go. (In Mellon 1988, 247; see 235–50 for more oral histories of punishment during slavery)

The punishment of black slaves in the South targeted not the soul or conscience of offenders but their body. Thomas Cobb justifies this in his 1858 *Inquiry into the Law of Negro Slavery*:

> The condition of the slave renders it impossible to inflict upon him the ordinary punishments, by pecuniary fine, by imprisonment, or by banishment. He can be reached only though his body. (Quoted in C. Smith 2009, 104)

Black offenders were excluded in advance from the redemptive aspect of the penitentiary project, in part because a slave was seen, in Thomas Jefferson's words, as an "animal . . . who does not reflect" (quoted in C. Smith 2009, 104). Without reflection, what redemption could be found in the solitary-confinement cell? A slave in prison would be little more than an animal in a cage, and a less productive worker as a result.

In contrast to the "humane" torture of forced solitude in a penitentiary cell, black slaves in the South were subject to brutal physical and psychological domination. Some of these punishments involved exposing slaves' bodies to physical torment and humiliation, literally flaying them alive. A former slave, Robert Burns, describes his master's favorite method of punishment:

> My moster would put slaves in a calaboose at night to be whipped de next morning. He always limited de lashes to five hundred. After whipping dem, he would rub pepper and salt on deir backs, where whipped, and lay dem before de fire until blistered, and den take a cat, and hold de cat, and make him claw de blisters, to burst dem. (In Mellon 1988, 241)

Other forms of punishment involved riveting slaves to their own bodies, as with the "bell rack" used on a plantation in Alabama:

> This apparatus, a reminder of racial terrorism, consists of an iron collar that was closed by a bolt, attached to an upright bar or post. A belt went around the slave's waist and through an iron loop. When in use, a bell hung from a hook at the top, above the slave's head. This hook kept the slave confined to the highways and open places, for it would catch in the limbs of the trees and cause the bell to ring if the slave tried to run away through the woods. The slave could move around, but had no chance to make a getaway. (Gorman 1997, 442)

Mrs. Thomas Johns, a former slave, reports a particularly outrageous form of this self-binding punishment:

> My husband said there was a family named Gullendin which was might hard on their niggers. He said ole Missis Gullendin, she'd take a needle and stick it through one of their nigger women's lower lip and pin it to the bosom of her dress, and that woman would go roun' all day with her haid drew down thataway, and slobberin'. Ole Missis Gullendin done her that-away lots of times. There was knots on her lip where the needle had been stuck in it. Me, I don't b'lieve I coulda stood that no time, without goin' crazy. (Quoted in Mellon 1988, 240)

Another former slave, Callie Elder, recalls slaves being bound not only to their own bodies but to the corpse of another slave:

> If one slave kilt another, Marse Billy made de overseer tie dat dead nigger to de one what kilt him, and de killer had to drag de corpse round till he died, too. De murderers never lived long a-draggin' dem dead ones round. Dat jus' piorely skeered 'em to death. (Quoted in Mellon 1988, 248)

Whereas some forms of punishment fastened slaves to others or to themselves, other forms of punishment forcibly separated slaves from their loved ones and sought to undermine relations of care among slaves. Recall the testimony of the former slave quoted by Patterson, whose family was prevented from coming to the rescue of his sister (Patterson 1982, 8). Or Frederick Douglass's moving account of being unable to help his Aunt Hester as she was beaten by their master (Douglass 1987, 343–44). Or Sethe in Toni Morrison's *Beloved,* who would sooner kill her children than expose them to a lifetime of slavery and torture (Morrison 1998; see also Gordon 2008). In *Black Reconstruction,* Du Bois cites advertisements offering rewards for the return of runaway slaves in southern newspapers. Note how these ads indirectly acknowledge the pain of being separated from loved ones and the determination with which slaves sought to reconnect with their kin:

> Fifty Dollars reward.—Ran away from the subscriber, a Negro girl, named Maria. She is of a copper color, between 13 and 14 years of age—bareheaded and barefooted. She is small for her age—very sprightly and very likely. She stated she was *going to see her mother* at Maysville. Sanford Tomson. (Quoted in Du Bois 1935, 12; emphasis added by Du Bois)

> Fifty Dollar reward.—Ran away from the subscriber, his Negro man, Pauladore, commonly called Paul. I understand Gen. R. Y. Hayne *has purchased his wife and children* from H. L. Pinckney, Esq., and has had them on his plantations at Goosecreek, where, no doubt, the fellow is frequently *lurking.* T. Davis. (Du Bois 1935, 12; emphasis added by Du Bois)

It is impossible to imagine what such torture feels like. But if we let such descriptions stand on their own—or if we avoid such descriptions because of the intense affect they may generate in readers, whether traumatic or prurient—then we risk allowing the violence of slavery to impose silence on both the tortured and the unwilling beneficiaries of torture, to suppress critical analysis and protest, and to substitute fear or disgust. What the above forms of torture have in common is that they were specifically developed to contain, control, and exploit black slaves.

While the northern penitentiary systems undertook to *separate* punishment from domination and to improve the offender rather than to destroy him, the punishment of slaves sought to *accomplish* domination and to secure white supremacy. It produced not a "cellular soul" (C. Smith 2009, 92) but a contained and controlled body, pinned to itself and to the master's will, immobilized just to the point of remaining available for exploitation. Even slaves' powers and pleasures were used against them, to undermine and betray their own capacity for life beyond social death. Frederick Douglass describes a typical response to theft on a plantation:

> For instance, a slave loves molasses: he steals some. His master, in many cases, goes off to town, and buys a large quantity; he returns, takes the whip, and commands the slave to eat the molasses, until the poor fellow is made sick at the very mention of it. (Douglass 1987, 397; see also his account of the drunken festivals and boxing matches encouraged by slave owners, 397)

To be forced to gorge on something that would otherwise bring one pleasure, to the point of becoming ill and disgusted both with the object of pleasure and with oneself, is a particularly insidious form of torture. Rather than punishing offending slaves straightforwardly, and so engaging them in a battle of wills, an overdose of pleasure induced by a master seeks to undermine their resistance from within. The whip, and the overseer who wields it, can be hated. But who is to blame for the slave's molasses binge?

In her now-classic account of torture, Elaine Scarry describes the logic of this type of punishment as a forced self-betrayal. "Each source of strength and delight, each means of moving out into the world or moving the world in to oneself, becomes a means of turning the body back in on itself, forcing the body to feed on the body" (1985, 48). The torturer "uses the prisoner's aliveness to crush the things that he lives for" (38). The torturer not only inflicts pain from the outside but also exploits the prisoner's own capacities for feeling, enjoyment, perception, and thought, turning these capacities against the prisoner in order to make him an instrument of his own undoing. And yet many slaves, in spite of these tortures, managed to create and sustain a sense of meaningful resistance in solidarity with others. Douglass testifies to this resistance in his moving tribute to his fellow slaves at Mr. Freeland's estate:

> They were noble souls; they not only possessed loving hearts, but brave ones. We were linked and inter-linked with each other. I loved them with a love stronger than any thing I have experienced since. . . . I believe we would have died for each other. We never undertook to do any thing, of any importance, without a mutual consultation. We never moved separately. We were one; and as much so by our tempers and dispositions, as by the mutual hardships to which we were necessarily subjected by our condition as slaves. (1987, 402–3)

Douglass's words bear witness to the possibility of coming back to life from the social death of slavery—even *in the midst* of this social death sentence. But the history of abolition is also the history of the growth of the prison industrial complex. What can we learn from what Douglass calls "the prison-house of slavery" (402) about the logic of punishment in today's prison system, which has long since awoken from its dreams of rehabilitation and redemption? And what can we learn from his resistance about the possibilities for solidarity in the abolition movements that continue to this day?

Included as Criminals, Excluded as Citizens

The legacy of civil and social death from slavery raises a series of questions: Whom are we allowed not to care about today? Whose lives matter so little that they may become indistinguishable from death? Who is marked as "disposable" (Balibar 2002, 24), "ungrievable" (Butler 2006, 35–36), "wasted lives" (Bauman 2004), "extraneous persons" (Dayan 2011, xi), or "the regime's durable nonhumans" (Rodríguez 2006, 79)? And how is the "we" of social and civil life shaped by its own excretions?

Colin Dayan has argued that both the slave and the convict—and later the "terrorist"—are constructed in law as a form of "negative personhood" (2001, 23). Although physically alive and nominally persons, they are stripped of rights and recognition to the point of being dead in law:

> Using the legal fiction of "civil death" as anchor, I return to what has been deemed a remnant of obsolete jurisprudence: the state of a person who, though possessing *natural life,* has lost all *civil rights.* Unnatural or artifi-

cial death as punishment for crime entailed a logic of alienation that could extend perpetually along constructed lines of racial kinship. I argue that its legal paradoxes, its gothic turns between tangible and intangible, life and death, became necessary to the racialized idiom of slavery in the American social order. The alternating moves between the idea of civil death and the meaning of servitude operated both forward and backward along a temporal continuum to exclude, subordinate, and annihilate. (6)

Dayan proposes "a continuum between being declared dead in law, being made a slave, and being judged a criminal" (6). To put this in the language of Agamben's biopolitics: slaves, and convicts as a remnant of slavery, are inclusively excluded in the law as legal persons whose status as full and proper citizens has been withdrawn or withheld in suspension, as persons who do not have social access or legal claim to the rights that would normally accrue to a person (Agamben 1998, 8).

In the antebellum South, slaves were "alive" with respect to their responsibilities but "dead" with respect to their rights. To the extent that they obeyed their masters, they had no will of their own, no rights as citizens, and no social recognition as persons with dignity. But to the extent that they disobeyed or transgressed, they were interpolated as criminals with unruly wills to be punished and tamed. Dayan analyzes the case *Creswell's Executor v. Walker* (1861) to show how, in southern case law, "slaves were only granted a mind or legal personality when committing a crime." Judge R. W. Walker ruled that the slave "has no legal mind, no will which the law can recognize" with respect to civil acts, but is nevertheless "treated as a person, as having a legal mind, a will, capable of originating acts for which he may be subjected to punishment as a criminal" (quoted in Dayan 2005, 79n74).

Even after the abolition of slavery, the association of convict status with slave status persisted. In the introduction to this book, I quoted Judge Christian's decision in *Ruffin v. Commonwealth,* which explicitly describes convicted felons as "slaves of the State" and as "men civilly dead" (quoted in Dayan 2011, 61). By contrast, Dayan notes, "White persons . . . do not need the law in order to exist or be recognized" (2001, 34n16). They are socially alive and enjoy social recognition at least insofar as they are white, even if they are deprived of this recognition to some extent because of their gender, class, sexuality, and so forth. The legal reinscription of brute punishment and forced labor for blacks, even beyond the abolition of slavery, was made possible by the terms of abolition themselves: the Thirteenth Amendment continued to allow such practices in the United States for those convicted of crimes.

The exceptional status of convicted criminals positions them, in Dylan Rodríguez's words, as "both the state's abstracted legal property/obligation and intimate bodily possession" (2006, 42). Joy James argues that this transposition of slavery into incarceration helps constitute the meaning of whiteness as well as blackness:

> The white civic body was strengthened by feeding off those designated as socially dead. The encoding of slavery or criminality onto blackness reflected a counterpart construction: the inscription of "whiteness" and nonincarceration as freedom and civility, hence as property or existential wealth. (2005, xxv; see also Harris 1993)

The hyperincarceration of African Americans in the wake of the Thirteenth Amendment—a pattern that continues to this day—racializes the status of criminal as black, even while it draws in other racialized groups such as Latinos/as, Pacific Islanders, Native Americans, and even denigrated whites, such as poor "white trash." This *political ontology* of social death is both connected to slavery and different from it. Dylan Rodríguez calls the current U.S. prison system "a direct derivative of racial chattel slavery as a practice of genocidal nation building and as a formative inscription of property relations in the general sense" (2006, 12). In what follows, I seek to chart the series of investments, transpositions, interventions, and reinventions that accomplished this derivation of the current prison system from the civil and social death of slavery.

From the Plantation to the Prison Farm

In *Black Reconstruction,* W. E. B. Du Bois explains the process by which the promise of abolition turned "back toward slavery" as a result of social, economic, political, and legal reactions to the sudden appearance of almost four million free blacks on the American scene (1935, 670–710). For Du Bois, the freed slave is still (or already) "a caged human being," not only in literal terms but also in psychological and cultural terms as a result of the oppressive policies and unofficial violence that arose after abolition (701). The black codes enacted in every former slave state after abolition allowed police to arrest blacks for a wide range of "crimes" such as vagrancy, unemployment, breaking a labor contract, making a public speech, selling certain goods or services, and possessing a firearm (see 166–80). Du Bois summarizes:

> The Negro's access to the land was hindered and limited; his right to work was curtailed; his right of self-defense was taken away, when his right to bear arms was stopped; and his employment was virtually reduced to contract labor with penal servitude as a punishment for leaving his job. And in all cases, the judges of the Negro's guilt or innocence, rights and obligations were men who believed firmly, for the most part, that he had [quoting the Dred Scott decision] "no rights which a white man was bound to respect." (1935, 167)

As Bruce Franklin puts it, southern blacks were punished both for "moving around" and for "staying still" (quoted in Gilmore 2007, 12). This criminalization of black mobility foreshadowed contemporary control prisons, whose goal is not to redeem or even to reform prisoners but, rather, to immobilize and incapacitate them.

As a result of the black codes, rates of incarceration for African Americans skyrocketed during Reconstruction. Once arrested and convicted, prisoners were leased as unpaid laborers to private companies for as little as a dollar a month to clear swamps, build railroads and roads, work in coal mines, and, of course, to work on plantations.[6] Convict lease systems sprang up in every former slave state; they operated between 1868 (with Georgia as the first state to institute such a system) and 1928 (with Alabama as the last state to outlaw it). During its period of operation, incarceration rates in those states skyrocketed, with a 10-fold increase in the prison population in Georgia from 1868 to 1908, more than a 10-fold increase in North Carolina from 1870 to 1890, an 8.5-fold increase in Florida from 1881 to 1904, a 4-fold increase in Mississippi from 1871 to 1879, and a 6.5-fold increase in Alabama from 1869 to 1919 (Shelden 2005). A vastly disproportionate number of these convicts were black.[7] Mortality rates were outrageously high, with many prisoners dying before they could serve out their full sentence.[8]

David Oshinsky calls the convict lease system "worse than slavery" because it granted white property owners access to a ceaselessly renewed source of labor while removing the incentive to provide even a minimal degree of care for the workers. As one southern employer explained in 1883:

> Before the war we owned the negroes. If a man had a good nigger, he could afford to take care of him; if he was sick get a doctor. He might even put gold plugs in his teeth. But these convicts: we don't own 'em. One dies, get another. (Quoted in Oshinsky 1996, 55)

Working and living conditions were abominable for convict slaves. For example, in the 1880s in Mississippi, convicts laid railroad track while wading through the Canay Swamps:

> In water ranging to their knees, and in almost nude state they spaded rooty ground, their bare feet chained together. They were compelled to attend to the calls of nature as they stood, their thirst compelling them to drink water in which they deposit their excrement. (Report in the *Raymond Gazette*, March 8, 1885, quoted in Adamson 1983, 566)

The convict lease system was specifically designed for black prisoners: "While black felons in Mississippi worked on plantations and railroads, not a single white left the penitentiary" (Vernon L. Wharton, in 1965, quoted in Adamson 1983, 565). But it was not the only mechanism of social death in the postabolition South. Prisons such as Parchman and Angola were developed as southern counterparts to the northern penitentiary systems; they were built on former slave plantations and were run in strikingly similar ways.

Whereas in the North, the work of (ideally white) inmates was meant to be first redemptive and then punishing, in the South, the work of (predominantly black) inmates was meant to be first punishing and then redemptive. Part of the soul's redemption involved the inculcation of good work habits, an indispensable mechanism for the production of both republican machines and docile slaves. But even when blacks and whites received the same punishment, the meaning of that punishment was distributed differently. African Americans were seen as destined to do the work that whites did not want to do; a life of hard physical labor was fit punishment for the simple fact of having darker skin or darker-skinned parents. By contrast, the hard physical labor to which white prisoners were sometimes condemned was not generally seen as a natural, fitting punishment; rather, it was meant to show white prisoners that they could be deprived of the privileges of whiteness if they did not use these privileges properly.

In the northern penitentiary system, prison work often functioned as a kind of substitute for social relations, a tenuous scaffolding for meaningful experience in the absence of other embodied beings to support a capacity for meaning through embodied interaction and the mutual perception of objects in a shared space. This forced reliance on work as a substitute for social relations was not incidental to the original conception of the penitentiary; prisoners (implicitly white) were supposed to be redeemed in equal measure by their extrication from a socially destructive life of crime and by their inculcation with socially useful habits of work. This is, indeed, what Dickens found attractive about the Auburn system. As problematic as this endorsement may be, the fact that meaningful work can play a positive supporting role in prolonged isolation does not begin to grapple with the debilitating effects of slave labor, both before and after abolition. Comparatively few accounts remain of what it is like to work from sunup to sundown, but Frederick Douglass gives a sense of the soul-crushing weight of embodied existence when people are forced to work at the outermost limits of their capacities without respite or recovery:

> I was broken in body, soul and spirit. My natural elasticity was crushed, my intellect languished, the disposition to read departed, the cheerful spark that lingered about my eye died; the dark night of slavery closed in upon me; and behold a man was transformed into a brute! (1987, 387)[9]

To work until one is *dead tired,* unable to think clearly or to feel the expansiveness of one's own creaturely existence: this, too, is a form of social death. It is *social,* and not "merely" physical, because the body is both the site of lived experience as first-person consciousness and also the site of intersubjective relations with others as the embodied "there" to one's own embodied "here." Physical punishment and exhaustion puts intense pressure on the capacity to relate to other people and to the self. Dylan Rodríguez writes about this in relation to the current prison system:

> Bodily punishment does indeed impart intelligence that physically inscribes something akin to a common sense of abjection, in which subjects are reminded that they will spend the remainder of their lives in a perpetual intimacy with regulated bodily violence. Such captives, both current and former, embody a regulated proximity (often, a physical vulnerability) to an occupying state that can instantly mobilize to reach, catch, and punish, while bearing a gravity of movement—engraved by the state's operational policing and imprisonment protocols—that invokes a state of perpetual martial law, if not warfare. It is within this biopolitics of the punitive that a profoundly personalized proximity and familiarity with death and suffering—what the imprisoned U.S. activist Viet Mike Ngo eloquently names

as an "intimacy with despair"—becomes a central political and (anti)social logic of the prison regime. (2006, 22)

We get a sense of this "biopolitics of the punitive" *avant la lettre* in the words of a black inmate interviewed by folklorist Bruce Jackson at a Texas prison farm in the summer of 1964:

A heap see and a few know.
A heap start and a damn few go.
It's just like that. It goes down the road like this here, that's just the way it start out. You see and don't see, *yeah* and don't *yeah*. 'Cause if you want to live a long time and stay healthy that's what you do, 'cause another dead man can't help you. (Quoted in B. Jackson 1999, 3)

"Another dead man can't help you," and you can't help another when you are utterly broken in body, soul, and spirit. Prison work songs, like the slave songs whose tradition they both continued and transformed, functioned to some extent as a way of remaking the world in the midst of its destruction. In the song "Go Down Old Hannah," a plantation prisoner imagines waking up his work partner, who has fallen asleep on the job due to exhaustion and overwork:

Wake up, oh dead man,
Help me carry my row. (Quoted in B. Jackson 1999, 116)

"Help me carry my row": help me bear the burden of this work, this sentence, this life. Another dead man can't help us, but as long as we can maintain that minimal resistance by which living beings stay alive, even when they have been stretched beyond the limits of what can be tolerated—then we can help each other to carry that row.

Convict work songs did not only make it possible for workers to coordinate with each other and to regulate the pace of work; they also helped them support and rebuild the world of social life, even on the terrain of social death, and even while using the instruments of their own punishment.[10] This possibility of finding, creating, and amplifying resistance, even in the midst of social and civil death, even at the verge of physical death, and even by using the resources of death as a semiotic field, has a rich and underexplored history in the past hundred years of prison writings, particularly by prisoners of color.[11] Their voices speak for themselves.

From George Jackson:

Born to a premature death . . . that's me, the colonial victim. . . . I've lived with repression every moment of my life, a repression so formidable that any movement on my part can only bring relief, the respite of a small victory or the release of death. In every sense of the term, in every sense that's real, I'm a slave to, and of, property. (1990, 7; quoted in Rodríguez 2006, 86)

Down here we hear relaxed, matter-of-fact conversations centering around how best to kill all the nation's niggers and in what order. It's not the fact that they consider killing me that upsets. They've been "killing all the niggers" for nearly half a millennium now, but I am still alive. I might be the most resilient dead man in the universe. The upsetting thing is that they never take into consideration the fact that I am going to resist. (1970, 174)

As you know, I'm in a unique political position. I have a very nearly closed future, and since I have always been inclined to get disturbed over organized injustice or terrorist practice against the innocents—wherever—I can now say just about what I want (I've always done just about that), without fear of self-exposure. I can only be executed once. (1990, 181, quoted in Rodríguez 2006, 121)

From Viet Mike Ngo:

My role is to dig or be dug out. Some may say this kind of change is unproductive. I say these "some" don't live in grave yards. Or if they do, they forgot the smell of wholeness; they forgot because the stink has commensurated with the marrow of their souls, and now this smell seems natural; and they forgot that to purge this stink, we need graves and diggers.

So while some preach reform inside classrooms and churches, I'll sharpen my shovel. For revolutions need grave diggers. Revolutions need role players to fill them. You fill the desks and pews. I'll fill the graves. We all have roles to play. (Quoted in Rodríguez 2006, 221–22)

From Hugo "Yogi" Pinell:

If we ever get real close and you happen to leave this world before me, which I hope doesn't happen, you're still going to live. I'm going to carry you with me. I'm going to need your energy to keep me going anyway. If I happen to go, I hope that you can feel my energy because I'm going to be there. I'm going to wake you up at night and say, Hey, have you forgotten about me or what? I'm there. Don't let me go. Don't let me die. It's not that easy. Dying is too easy. Living is what's happening. (Quoted in Rodríguez 2006, 221)

These prisoners are resisting social death by embracing a certain relation to death and to the possibility of meaningful relationships to oneself, to others, and to the world both within and beyond the constraints of social death. They have found ways of cultivating death as a way of life—without ever accepting their living death sentence, but also without being able to protect themselves from the officially and unofficially sanctioned violence of the state. After all, Jackson was shot and killed by prison guards at the age of thirty; Ngo has been in prison since the age of seventeen and continues to be denied parole; Pinell has been in prison since 1965 and has been isolated in a supermax unit since 1990. These men are by no means invincible, but they are the teachers we need in order to complete the work of abolition, from slavery to the prison industrial complex, solitary confinement, and the death penalty.

Fanon's Critical Phenomenology of Social Death

Fanon's work is not explicitly about slavery, prisons, or even social death, and yet he may be the most brilliant theorist of all three. In what follows, I present a reading of *Black Skin, White Masks* as a critical phenomenology of social death as a feeling of isolation and containment in a racialized body that one can neither inhabit nor escape. While *The Wretched of the Earth* (1963) is often read in opposition to *Black Skin, White Masks* (1967) as a political manifesto and call to arms rather than a philosophical text, I will read the two works as continuous rather than opposed. They explore two sides of colonial domination: its lived experience for the colonized subject, and its social and political meaning as containment, control, and exploitation—as well as resistance, solidarity, and the creation of a new possibilities for collective life.

For Fanon, not only blacks but also whites are imprisoned by the logic of colonization:

> The white man is sealed in his whiteness. The black man in his blackness. (1967, 9)

Both races are "sealed" in their particularities, which for all their parallelism still bear asymmetrical meanings:

> The disaster of the man of color lies in the fact that he was enslaved. The disaster and the inhumanity of the white man lie in the fact that somewhere he has killed man. (231)

Fanon isolates these claims in separate paragraphs, as if they were not even able to share the same textual location, let alone the same social location. And yet these positions are mutually defining; the colonizer cannot exist without the (coerced nonbeing) of the colonized, and when a colonial regime is violently overthrown, both the colonizer and the colonized will be destroyed as such.[12] This destruction is the "No!" that makes possible the "Yes!" of a new, postcolonial humanity.

The black man who discovers the social meaning of his blackness for the colonizer finds himself suddenly "imprisoned on his island," even when he occupies a respectable place in the metropol (1967, 21).[13] Racial stigma functions as a portable prison or tomb, exposing the racialized subject to psycho-affective disorders as well as to the alienation of social exclusion.[14] These social and political dynamics of imprisonment are experienced by the racialized subject as a feeling of simultaneous exposure and isolation, to the point of explosion or implosion:

> Sealed into that crushing objecthood, I turned beseechingly to others. Their attention was a liberation, running over my body suddenly abraded into nonbeing, endowing me once more with an agility that I had thought lost, and by taking me out of the world, restoring me to it. But just as I reached the other side, I stumbled, and the movements, the attitudes, the glances of the other fixed me there, in the sense in which a chemical solution is fixed by a dye. I was indignant; I demanded an explanation. Nothing happened. I burst apart. Now the fragments have been put together again by another self. (109)

The gaze of the other both opens the possibility of a liberating escape from the crushing objecthood of racialized embodiment and also slams the door in the face of the racialized other, "riveting" him to a fixed identity.[15] The colonized subject bursts apart in response to the unbearable constraints into which it has been forced, and it gathers these fragments together as another self—a black-man-constructed-by-white-colonization, a black man with a white mask.

Fanon argues that "every ontology is made unattainable in a colonized and civilized society" (1967, 109). The black man has no being in the colonial world beyond his opposition to the white man, who reduces him to a negative foil for his own identity while exploiting his labor and resources and disavowing their contributions to his own wealth.[16] The black man cannot simply *be* himself under these conditions; his existence is interrupted by an inescapable relation to an other who devalues and degrades him, who shatters his being and remakes him (or forces him to remake himself) in the white man's image, with a mask that he can neither assume nor remove. As Fanon puts it, "The black man has no ontological resistance in the eyes of the white man" (110). His being does not *matter* to the white man; he might as well be dead, if his material and symbolic labor were not so profitable.[17] For the black man, this is not a "feeling of inferiority" but rather "a feeling of nonexistence" (139).

This negation and dislocation is experienced by the black man at the level of the bodily schema (1967, 110). In the work of Jean-Paul Sartre and Merleau-Ponty, the bodily schema is a pattern of habitual gestures or ways of moving, acting, and being that help organize one's intentional relations to the world on a prereflective level. My bodily schema generates a reserve of implicit meanings so that I don't need to pay explicit attention to everything all the time. My bodily schema carries me along, subtending and supporting my explicit awareness of the world. But the unlivable structure of racialized embodiment shatters the ease of comportment for colonized subjects; they are given only a racial-epidermal schema that leaves them no place to be, and yet no avenue of escape. The racial-epidermal schema is also a pattern, but a pathological one: a pattern that does not support but, rather, thwarts and disrupts any attempts to make sense of the world. It is constituted not by a web of interconnecting visual, tactile, kinesthetic, and other perceptions experienced in the first person, but "by the other, the white man, who had woven me out of a thousand details, anecdotes, stories" (Fanon 1967, 111). The racial-epidermal schema imprisons blacks in a pattern of traumatic repetition rather than an open, dynamic gestalt.

Fanon describes this shattering of experience in a language of imprisonment, slavery, and self-mutilation:

> On that day, completely dislocated, unable to be abroad with the other, the white man, who unmercifully imprisoned me, I took myself far from my own presence, far indeed, and made myself an object. What else could it be for me but an amputation, an excision, a hemorrhage that spattered my whole body with black blood? (1967, 112–13)

> I am overdetermined from without. I am the slave not of the "idea" that others have of me but of my own appearance. (116)[18]

The material location of this feeling of isolation and exclusion is the plantation, the slum, the ghetto, the favela, the shantytown, the reservation—in short, the sector of the colonized. In *The Wretched of the Earth*, Fanon describes this sector as a prisonlike site of containment, control, and exploitation. It is "a disreputable place inhabited by disreputable people"; moreover:

> You are born anywhere, anyhow. You die anywhere, from anything. It's a world with no space, people are piled on top of the other, the shacks

squeezed tightly together.[19] The colonized's sector is a famished sector, hungry for bread, meat, shoes, coal, and light. The colonized's sector is a sector that crouches and cowers, a sector on its knees, a sector that is prostrate. It's a sector of niggers, a sector of towelheads. (1963, 5)

The racialized other is contained within this sector by the police and the military, both of which use brute force in addition to disciplinary surveillance to control the native population (3–4). The distinction between violent repression and productive rehabilitation—a distinction on which the early penitentiary systems relied—becomes indiscernible in this context. As Fanon explains, "Colonialism is not a machine capable of thinking, a body endowed with reason. It is naked violence and only gives in when confronted with greater violence" (23). The resistance of the colonized, whether violent or not, is always already criminalized by the colonial regime.

The Algerian under French colonial occupation is a "born criminal," a "senseless killer" who is set off by the slightest offenses; he breaks into homes and kills or assaults the owners before stealing their things, often preying on their fellow Algerians in a "closed circle" of violence (Fanon 1963, 221–29). The colonizer interprets this behavior as evidence that "the Algerian has no cortex," that there is something wrong with his "brain structure," that he is "mentally retarded" and has "no inner life," that "the normal African is a lobotomized European" (224–27). The regime must "discipline, tame, subdue, and now pacify" the Algerian, both for his own good and for its own self-defense (228). And yet, it is the colonized rather than the colonizer who must struggle for mere survival: "For the colonized, living does not mean embodying a set of values, does not mean integrating oneself into the coherent, constructive development of a world. To live simply means not to die. To exist means staying alive" (232).

Fanon identifies two distinct problems with the racialization of crime, both of which continue to haunt the U.S. prison system: (1) Colonization engenders violence and criminality among the colonized, most often directed against members of their own community, and (2) colonization marks the colonized as "born criminals," always already guilty, and never quite open to rehabilitation (1963, 16).

It is worth noting that current "commonsense" penal policy, as articulated by people like Supreme Court Justice Antonin Scalia, replicates the structure of this colonial foreclosure of rehabilitation. In

Miller v. Alabama (2012), which raised the issue of life imprisonment without parole for juvenile offenders, Scalia said:

> Well, I thought that modern penology has abandoned that rehabilitation thing, and they—they no longer call prisons reformatories or whatever, and punishment is the—is the criterion now. Deserved punishment for crime.[20]

This view—that convicted criminals are in prison for a reason, that they are incorrigible, and that there is no point wasting time and money trying to rehabilitate them (even if they are only fourteen years old!)— follows the same basic logic as the French colonial view of Algerians, as Fanon describes it. What we find in the United States today is the generalization of this colonial logic beyond the slave or the "nigger" (as Joy James puts it) to the disinherited more generally: the poor, the state-raised, the learning disabled, the disaffected and disposable remnants of global capitalism and the "postcolonial" management of surplus populations.[21] Individual prisoners are saddled with the blame for their own disinheritance, for their own natal alienation and social death. Fanon argues that according to this logic, the self-destructive cycle of violence among the colonized is not "the consequence of how his nervous system is organized or specific character traits, but the direct result of the colonial situation" (1963, 233).

Fanon shows how the hyperindividuation of criminal responsibility works in tandem with the depersonalization of colonized subjects and communities:

> For colonialism has not simply depersonalized the colonized. The very structure of society has been depersonalized on a collective level. A colonized people is thus reduced to a collection of individuals who owe their very existence to the presence of the colonizer. (1963, 219–20)

Fanon argues that "when we see the notion of the Algerian or North African as born criminal dislodged . . . then yes, we can say the revolution is making progress" (228).

The Wretched of the Earth is often read as an endorsement and justification of anticolonial violence, in part because of Sartre's preface to the book, in which he warns Europeans that "it is through this mad rage, this bile and venom, their constant desire to kill us, and the permanent contraction of powerful muscles, afraid to relax, that they [the colonized] become men" (Sartre 1963, lii). But Fanon's own views on the role of violence in revolutionary action are much more complex than this. While violent force may be a necessary, or at least an inevitable, response to the brute force of colonialism, it is by no means sufficient for the creation of a new humanity and a new humanism. What is needed, in addition to strategic acts of violence, is a transformation of the collective consciousness or "brain" of the people. This is a cultural and artistic project as well as a material one. Fanon writes:

> The meeting of the local cell or the committee meeting is a liturgical act. It is a privileged opportunity for the individual to listen and speak. At every meeting the brain multiplies the association of ideas and the eye discovers a wider human panorama. (1963, 136)

> Let us reexamine the question of cerebral reality, the brain mass of humanity in its entirety whose affinities must be increased, whose connections must be diversified and whose communications must be humanized again. (237–38)

> No, it is not a question of back to nature. It is the very basic question of not dragging man in directions which mutilate him, of not imposing on his brain tempos that rapidly obliterate and unhinge it. The notion of catching up must not be used as a pretext to brutalize man, to tear him from himself and his inner consciousness, to break him, to kill him. (238)

I interpret these references to the "brain" *(cerveau)* of the community as a nonreductive materialist account of collective subjectivity. This concept fleshes out the social and political dimensions of what Husserl calls "transcendental intersubjectivity"; it offers a suggestive starting point for a critical phenomenological account of embodied *social life,* in resistance to the disinheritance of natal alienation and social death. Fanon's own inspiration for thinking about the "brain" of the community is, in part, Ahmed Sékou Touré's 1959 address to the Second Congress of African Writers:

> In the realm of thought, man can claim to be the brain of the world; but in reality, where every action affects spiritual and physical being, the world is still the brain of mankind for it is here that are concentrated the totalization of powers and elements of thought, the dynamic forces of development and improvement, and it is here too that energies are merged and the sum total of man's intellectual values is finally inscribed. (Quoted in Fanon 1963, 140)

The revolutionary creators of a new sense of humanity must change the world by changing peoples' minds. But they must also change minds by changing the world. Fanon writes:

> If the building of a bridge does not enrich the consciousness of those work-
> ing on it, then don't build the bridge, and let the citizens continue to swim
> across the river or use a ferry. The bridge must not be pitchforked or foisted
> upon the social landscape by a *deus ex machina,* but, on the contrary, must
> be a product of the citizens' brains and muscles. And there is no doubt ar-
> chitects and engineers, foreigners for the most part, will probably be needed,
> but the local party leaders must see to it that the techniques seep into the
> desert of the citizen's brain so that the bridge in its entirety and in every de-
> tail can be integrated, redesigned, and reappropriated. The citizen must ap-
> propriate the bridge. Then, and only then, is everything possible. (1963, 141)

This renewal of possibility through the material and meaningful transformation of consciousness and the world is exactly what we need to
accomplish the work of abolition.

I catch a glimpse of this renewal in the work of Mothers ROC, or
Mothers Recovering Our Children, an activist group that formed in
resistance to the hyperincarceration of young black men from urban
communities (Gilmore 2007, 181–240). A coalition of mothers, sisters,
aunts, friends, and concerned community members came together to
reclaim their children from the natal alienation and social death of
incarceration. Mothers ROC was *rooted* in the care of specific mothers
and specific children, but it did not limit itself to biological mothers,
or even to those who identify as mothers: "One need not be a woman
or a parent to participate in an action-based critique of vulnerability grounded in, but not bounded by, local conditions" (196). Rather,
Mothers ROC formed a "community of purpose" based on "a simple
inversion: we are not poor because our loved ones are in prison; rather,
our loved ones are in prison because we are poor" (237).[22] This work
embodies what Fanon calls "collective self-criticism with a touch of
humor because everyone is relaxed, and because in the end we all want
the same thing" (1963, 12). It engenders a new sense of humanism that
is rooted in the particular struggles of decolonizing peoples, but it expands the scope of solidarity to include anyone who wants to join in
the struggle, and ultimately to anyone at all.[23]

This is how I interpret Fanon's insistence on the development of
a national culture as a necessary condition for the creation of a new
humanity; ultimately, it amounts to the overcoming of natal alienation
through the collective thought and action of particular people in a particular place and time, but not isolated or "sealed" in its particularity:

The living expression of the nation is the collective consciousness in motion of the entire people. It is the enlightened and coherent praxis of the men and women. The collective forging of a destiny implies undertaking responsibility on a truly historical scale. Otherwise there is anarchy, repression, the emergence of tribalized parties and federalism, etc. If the national government wants to be national it must govern by the people and for the people, for the disinherited and by the disinherited. (Fanon 1963, 144)

This ethical, political, epistemic, and ontological transformation of the disinherited, and of the very terms of inheritance, is a collective process of coming back to life from social death and social murder. This is what abolition looks like: not the relocation of slavery from the plantation to the prison but the creation of new ways of thinking, seeing, feeling, speaking, and experiencing a world that is shared in common with all other human (and, as I will argue later, nonhuman) beings. The rehabilitation or redemption of criminals is not sufficient for this and may even exacerbate the problem of decontextualized, hyperindividualized responsibility. What we need is rather collective resistance and revolution at the scene of "crime" itself.

II
THE MODERN PENITENTIARY

4 FROM THOUGHT REFORM TO BEHAVIOR MODIFICATION

> Treat the criminal as a patient and the crime as a disease.
> —Alfred H. Love, 1874 Congress of the America
> Correctional Association

> Punishment must be used as precisely and as dispassionately
> as a surgeon's scalpel if it is to be effective.
> —Dr. James V. McConnell, "Criminals Can
> Be Brainwashed—Now"

ALMOST ONE HUNDRED YEARS separate James V. McConnell from Alfred H. Love, and there is a vast ideological chasm between Love's Christian humanism and McConnell's scientific antihumanism. And yet their conclusions are strikingly similar: criminals must not only be punished or reformed but also treated and cured of their criminal behavior. The desire to diagnose and treat criminal offenders as if crime were a disease is as old as the Philadelphia prison reform movement, but from the 1950s to the 1970s it was the hallmark of a second wave of solitary confinement in U.S. prisons, which took behavior modification rather than religious redemption as its primary goal. While this focus on the biopolitical dimensions of criminality marks a departure from the earlier, eighteenth- and nineteenth-century religious arguments for solitary confinement, it remains consistent with the enthusiasm of people like Alfred Love and Benjamin Rush for medical solutions to social and political problems such as slavery, crime, mental illness, and even revolution. And yet, the second wave of solitary confinement accomplished a medicalization of crime and a politicization of medicine beyond what Rush might have expected. In the 1960s and '70s, inmates in prisons across the United States were exposed not only to social isolation but also to forms of "treatment" such as sensory deprivation, sensory overload, intensive group confinement, attack therapy, aversion therapy, and the involuntary administration of drugs such as antipsychotics, tranquillizers, and muscle relaxers. Some of these techniques, such as sensory deprivation and the use of psychotropic drugs, persist in the current prison system.[1] The purpose of such treatment in the second wave of solitary confinement—often explicitly stated as such—was to break down the antisocial personalities of inmates and to rebuild them in harmony with dominant social norms.[2] The "criminal personality" was to be destroyed and replaced with the healthy habits of a "winner at the game of life" (Mitford 1973, 19).

As I will demonstrate in some detail, mid-twentieth-century behavior modification programs in U.S. prisons tacitly, and sometimes overtly, targeted African Americans, Latinos/as, and other racialized groups, especially those who were engaged in organized forms of political resistance, such as the Black Panthers, La Raza Unida, and the American Indian Movement (AIM). Behaviorist penal therapies also provided a conceptual framework for the politicization of crime, as if every illegal act were not just a matter of breaking the law but also a rejection of "society," a display of antisocial behavior that the state was justified in repressing as violently as necessary to guarantee its own survival. At the same time, the social and economic context of offenses such as nonviolent property crimes continued to be depoliticized during this period, with the effect of obscuring the racial and class inequalities that continued to shape U.S. social and carceral landscapes more than a hundred years after the abolition of slavery. The "criminal personality" and "criminal behavior" became alibis for the continued racist oppression of African Americans, Latinos/as, and Native Americans as crime was both hyperpoliticized and depoliticized in the mid-twentieth-century United States.

In this chapter, I trace the development and implementation of behavior modification programs in U.S. prisons in the 1960s and '70s back to their theoretical roots in 1950s research on Communist thought reform, or "brainwashing," research that was funded by the Central Intelligence Agency (CIA) and the U.S. Department of Defense in the wake of the Korean War. Many of the same psychologists and psychiatrists who began their careers in the 1950s with research on thought reform went on to apply their research in the 1960s and '70s to behavioral reform in prisons or to the development of interrogation techniques for the CIA. Some even went on to have successful careers in industrial and organizational psychology, applying the same basic insights to business management and corporate self-help in the 1980s and '90s. What is the connection between the apparently discontinuous contexts of psychiatric research, military intelligence, domestic prison policy, and corporate success? And how do these connections continue to shape U.S. prisons to this day?

Cold War Studies in Thought Reform

The Korean War (1950–53) posed interesting problems for both the scientist and the politician, and especially for those in both groups who sought to apply scientific insights and methods to political life. After the war, U.S. soldiers held in solitary and small-group confinement by Chinese forces returned with reports of specialized techniques for "brainwashing" or "thought reform" through which the personhood of the prisoner could be broken down and rebuilt in the form of a Communist sympathizer or revolutionary fanatic. What else could explain the existence of U.S. prisoners of war (POWs) who expressed sympathy with communism after their imprisonment, some even refusing repatriation to the United States?[3] Beginning in the early 1950s, the CIA and the Department of Defense contracted numerous psychologists and social scientists to study Chinese incarceration and interrogation techniques, both in order to develop countertechniques for U.S. soldiers to deploy in resistance to potential brainwashing (known as the SERE [Survival, Evasion, Resistance, and Escape] program), and also in order to refine their own coercive interrogation techniques (as outlined in the CIA's *KUBARK Counterintelligence Interrogation Manual* [1963]).[4]

In their 1956 special report for the Department of Defense, entitled "Communist Interrogation and Indoctrination of Enemies of the State: Analysis of Methods Used by the Communist State Police," psychologists Lawrence E. Hinkle and Harold G. Wolff, both professors at Cornell University, presented a comprehensive account of techniques used by the KGB (the security agency of the Soviet Union) and by the Chinese, both domestically and (in the latter case) in the Korean War. They found that the KGB relied mainly on a combination of solitary confinement and aggressive interrogation techniques in order to break down individual prisoners, but the Chinese used a combination of solitary confinement, interrogation, and intensive group confinement. The socially starved prisoner would be put into close quarters with other prisoners who had already "converted" to communism and whose constant social pressure urged the lone outsider to confess his reactionary ways and be reborn as a soldier for the revolution. As in the early U.S. penitentiary, physical punishment was used sparingly, if at all. Rather, punishment in a Chinese detention camp was represented as a therapeutic treatment in which the traitor, spy, or criminal would be cured of his "bad thoughts" and supplied with a new, healthy identity (Lifton 1957). The basic technique of this treatment was to use the social, emotional, and physical capacities of the prisoner against himself, to break him down in order to then remake him in another form.

In his own 1957 study of Chinese "thought reform," contracted by the CIA as part of the MKULTRA program (an experimental behavioral engineering program),[5] Robert J. Lifton, then a research assistant at Harvard University, articulated the stages of "adaptation" in terms of death and rebirth, echoing the early rhetoric of the U.S. penitentiary system:

> "Thought reform," for the individual prisoner, is an agonizing drama of death and rebirth. The "reactionary spy" who entered the prison must perish; in his place must arise a "new man," resurrected in the Communist image. Such symbolism is frequently spelled out by the Communist officials, so that the prisoner directly perceives that he must "die and be reborn," and may use these words in describing his experience. (639)[6]

These mid-twentieth-century U.S. accounts of the effects of solitary confinement on prisoners in Communist regimes are similar to the death and resurrection narrative of U.S. eighteenth- and nineteenth-century defenses of solitary confinement, with some striking exceptions. While Benjamin Rush argued for the salutary effects of prolonged solitude, Cold War thought reform researchers emphasized the pain of social deprivation in KGB and Chinese incarceration techniques: "In nearly all cases the prisoner's need for human companionship and his desire to talk to anyone about anything becomes a gnawing appetite, which may be as insistent as the hunger of a starving man" (Hinkle and Wolff 1956, 129). Both Rush and the Cold War researchers recognize the importance of social relations for the individual, but only the latter acknowledge the debilitating effects of isolation on the coherence and stability of the prisoner's identity. According to Hinkle and Wolff, the prisoner in a Communist POW camp is severely affected by even a few weeks in isolation. He stares into space, gives up spontaneous activity, begins to fiddle with things absentmindedly, ceases to care about personal hygiene, and even soils himself without seeming to notice or care. He mushes his food together and "stuff[s] it into his mouth like an animal" (128). Passing through stages of initial anxiety and hyperactivity, then depression and extreme passivity, the prisoner eventually reaches a malleable or suggestible state. At this point, the prisoner is ready for interrogation, and (in the Chinese POW camp) for introduction into the group cell.

Where Rush's vision of the penitentiary leaves off, the intensive confinement of the Chinese group cell begins.[7] Once the isolated prisoner has regressed to a state of extreme passivity, the prisoner's situation is inverted from radical isolation to radical social contact, to the point of overexposure and the total obliteration of privacy. Prisoners in the group cell are initiated into a strict regimen of lectures, the study of Communist texts, and "self-criticism sessions" in which their every act and word is subject to critical interrogation (Hinkle and Wolff 1956, 157). In the most intense stage of this process, called "the struggle," prisoners are mercilessly reviled and humiliated by their cellmates for their failure to embody Communist values. Hinkle and Wolff describe the aim of the group cell as "turning prisoner against prisoner, and requiring the enemies of the regime to beat each other into conformity" (157). The only way out of this intolerable situation is to confess and convert, or in the behaviorist language that became the lingua franca of these Cold War studies, to "adapt."

Albert D. Biderman describes this process in "Communist Attempts to Elicit False Confessions from Air Force Prisoners of War," his 1957 study of Chinese incarceration techniques (funded by the U.S. Air Force Personnel and Training Research Center at Lackland Air Force Base in Texas).[8] According to Biderman, the aim of Chinese incarceration techniques in the Korean context was to convert the prisoner into an "ideal confessor" through the use of isolation, monopolization of perception, sleep deprivation, threats, occasional indulgences, and degradation (1957, 623, 619). This combination of techniques "Deprives Victim of all Social Support of his Ability to Resist; Develops an Intense Concern with Self; Makes Victim Dependent on Interrogator"

(619). Biderman is especially interested in the effectiveness of what we would now call stress positions for turning the prisoner against himself without the use of direct or overt force. Rather than being beaten or whipped, the prisoner is forced to stand for extremely long periods of time, until the weight of his own body becomes an insupportable burden, causing massive swelling in his legs and feet to the point of creating edema, blisters, increased heart rate, and even kidney failure.[9] Biderman notes, "The immediate source of pain is not the interrogator but the victim himself. The contest becomes, in a way, one of the individual against himself," and this serves to "exaggerate the power of the interrogator" (620). Stress positions were reported by prisoners to be "more excruciating" than any other form of physical punishment, and they had the additional advantage of remaining "consistent with formal adherence to mythical principles of legality and humaneness important to the Communists" (621).

While the Cold War researchers do not make this connection, we could interpret this use of stress positions as an intensification of the basic structure of solitary confinement, which exploits prisoners' constitutive capacity for social relations by depriving them of concrete, everyday experiences of embodied others, thereby turning what ought to be a source of power and joy into a source of pain and debilitation. Like solitary confinement, and like many of the punishments inflicted on slaves, stress positions use subjects' own powers and capacities against themselves in order to undermine their integrity as persons— not by applying an external force against which they might be provoked to resist more forcefully but by using their own strength against them and blocking the concrete fulfillment of their capacities in order to undermine those capacities from within. Stress positions, like solitary confinement, do not apply power to prisoners as a repressive external force; rather, they redirect prisoners' own powers against themselves, such that the conditions for the possibility of a meaningful world—now unhinged from a concrete context of open-ended exploration—become signs of impossibility, meaninglessness, and the destruction of the world. At this point, prisoners are ready for reprogramming.[10]

Cold War Studies in Sensory Deprivation

In addition to funding the study of Chinese Communist brainwashing techniques, the CIA and the Department of Defense also contracted re-

searchers at universities such as Harvard and McGill to study the effects
of sensory deprivation on the "suggestibility" of experimental subjects.
These studies fell into roughly two groups: those that focused on the
effects of a radical reduction in sensory *patterning,* as in the research
of Donald O. Hebb and his team at McGill University in Montreal,
Canada, and those that focused on the effects of a radical reduction
of the *intensity* of sensory stimuli, as in the immersion tank experiments of John C. Lilly at the National Institute of Mental Health near
Washington, D.C. Most subjects could not bear to continue with either
kind of experiment for more than twenty-four hours; among the twenty-
two people who participated in research funded by Hebb's Contract
DRB-X38 from the Canadian Defense Research Board (DRB), "four
remarked spontaneously that being in the apparatus was a form of
torture" (quoted in McCoy 2007, 405). Nevertheless, Hebb concluded
that "the contract [was] opening up a field of study that is of both
theoretical and practical significance" (quoted in McCoy 2007, 405).[11]

What was the theoretical and practical significance of this research?
Hebb sought to discover whether "*slight* changes of attitude" could be
produced by intensifying short periods of isolation with sensory depatterning (quoted in McCoy 2007, 405). This depatterning was achieved
by confining subjects to a small room or cubicle where they lay on a cot,
moving as little as possible, with their arms and legs covered in card-
board cuffs and their hands in cotton gloves in order to reduce tactual
stimulation. Subjects wore translucent goggles painted medium grey to
diffuse the light and reduce visual patterning to a homogeneously gray
field of vision; they kept these goggles on during food and toilet breaks
in order to minimize disturbances. The white noise of a fan further
diminished the patterning of sound perception. As part of this sensory
deprivation, subjects were socially isolated, although some "tried to
trick the experimenter into talking with them" (McConnell 1970, 15).
Hebb and his colleagues found that sensory depatterning accelerated
the process of "unfreezing" observed by Lifton and others in their research on Chinese thought reform, but they were surprised to find that,
in addition to this acceleration, sensory deprivation produced florid
hallucinations and intense emotional responses in many subjects. Even
after the subject was removed from the experimental situation, perceptual distortions such as a deep intensification of color or the wavering
of boundaries around objects persisted for some time.

The most detailed descriptions of these effects are found in a 1956 study in which three of Hebb's students confined themselves in a small soundproof cubicle with goggles, cuffs, and gloves for six days, twenty-four hours a day, with brief breaks for meals and to use the toilet. They recorded their impressions immediately upon returning from isolation and for several days afterward:

> OBSERVER A: When I fixate here, that box behind you moves, and when I was fixating there, there was something wrong with this thing, which seemed to be swinging out. . . . There is a serious limit to what is in focus. I'm focusing on the midpoint of that rod, and there's a very small area of the rod which is clear. The rest of it is fluctuating all the time. . . . Have you ever looked at the bottom of a stream after you have dropped a stone in? A shallow stream, and you can look down through the circles going out? The centre is still and clear, but the rest is all ripply. Well, that's exactly the impression that I get. Wherever I fixate is the centre of the circle, and the rest of the stuff is behind these ripples. (Heron, Doane, and Scott 1956, 15)

> OBSERVER B: The whole room is undulating, swirling. . . . You were, going all over the fool place at first. The floor is still doing it. The wall is waving all over the place—a horrifying sight, as a matter of fact. . . . The centre of that curtain over there—it just swirls downward, undulates and waves inside. . . . I find it difficult to keep my eyes open for any length of time, the visual field is in such a state of chaos. . . . Everything will settle down for a moment, then it will start to go all over the place. (Heron, Doane, and Scott 1956, 15)

> OBSERVER A: Things just don't stay put. For instance, I'm fixating down there, and out of the corner of my eye I see that upright; but when I fixate the upright, it jumps back. . . . There's no position constancy, that's what it is. As I move, it moves. When I move back and forth like this, I can't orientate against anything. . . . It's most peculiar, I feel as if I'm in a swing. . . . If I turn quickly or move back, it's not me that moves, it's this thing that moves. (Heron, Doane, and Scott 1956, 16)

After six days of social and sensory isolation, the subjects' experience of the world had been altered dramatically. Objects became instable, their boundaries rippling as if in constant flux. Space itself seemed to be set in motion, swirling or undulating chaotically. Surfaces appeared wet or glistening, people's faces appeared rouged, and straight lines or flat surfaces appeared to bend or bulge (Heron, Doane, and Scott 1956, 16–17).

Switching from the role of experimental subject to the role of scientific observer, the researchers reflected on the significance of their experience:

It is unlikely that the effects observed after isolation can be attributed merely to the forgetting of perceptual habits during the isolation period. They seem to resemble somewhat the effects reported after administration of certain drugs (such as mescal and lysergic acid) and after certain types of brain damage. When we consider as well the disturbances which occurred during isolation (e.g., vivid hallucinatory activity), it appears that exposing the subject to a monotonous sensory environment can cause disorganization of brain function similar to, and in some respects as great as, that produced by drugs or lesions. (Heron, Doane, and Scott 1956, 18; see also Doane et al. 1959)

I will reflect on the phenomenological significance of these results in chapter 5, picking up on the connections between sensory deprivation and what psychiatrist Stuart Grassian has called SHU syndrome (named after the Secure Housing Units of many supermax prisons). For now I wish merely to note the dramatic feeling of instability produced by sensory deprivation, to the point of dissolving the coherence of the subject's experience of objects in space, and to raise some questions that I will take up in detail later: What is the relation between the ongoing experience of a heterogeneous, patterned world and the capacity to perceive spatially extended objects in a clear and stable way? What are the effects of this spatial destabilization on the subject's own sense of self? And how do sensory isolation and social isolation reinforce one another?

While Hebb and his students were experimenting with sensory depatterning at McGill, Lilly was conducting experiments of his own at the National Institute of Mental Health (NIMH). Lilly's initial project was to study the possible effects of solitude and low sensory stimulation on U.S. astronauts; his approach was to lower the absolute intensity of perceptual stimulus, including the perception of gravity, through immersion in water-filled tanks.[12] In a 1956 presentation to the American Psychiatric Association, Lilly formulated his guiding question as follows: "Freed of normal efferent and afferent activities, does the activity of the brain soon become that of coma or sleep, or is there some inherent mechanism which keeps it going, a pacemaker of the 'awake' type of activity?" (1956, 1). Reformulated in more psychoanalytic terms: "Is the healthy ego independent of reality or dependent in some fashion, in some degree, on exchanges with the surroundings to maintain its structure?" (1).

In Lilly's experiments, subjects were completely immersed in slowly flowing water, held at a constant temperature of 34.5°C (94.5°F), wearing nothing but a blacked-out mask with a breathing apparatus that fit completely over the head. Under these conditions, subjects feel neither heat nor cold; they see no light and feel almost no gravitational pressure; the only sound they hear is the rhythm of their own breath. According to Lilly, "It is one of the most even and monotonous environments I have experienced" (1956, 5). Subjects typically go through the following stages during immersion: First, the residues of the day cycle through the mind. Then, after about forty-five minutes, they begin to relax and feel restful. But as the immersion continues, tension begins to build, along with what Lilly calls "'stimulus-action' hunger" (6; see also Biderman and Zimmer 1961, 83). In the absence of other stimuli, subjects begin to stimulate themselves by twitching, moving their legs, stroking their own fingers, and so on. At this point, either the tension increases to the point where subjects ask to leave the tank, or they find themselves drawn into an intense awareness of the most subtle stimuli: the feeling of the mask on the face; the slow, rhythmic movement of the water; the sense of suspension; and so forth. This sensitivity either becomes unbearable, or subjects enter into a further phase of personal reverie and fantasy, often accompanied by hallucinations or "visual imagery" (6–7). Lilly compares the feeling of euphoria attained by those who are able to persist to this stage to the feeling of an "intense love of any living things *[sic]*" (3–4).[13]

Unlike the subjects in Hebb's experiments, Lilly's subjects did not typically report sustained perceptual alterations, "depersonalization," or changes in body schema after the period of immersion. Rather, they reported feeling as if their internal clock had been "reset," as if they had just woken up from a deep sleep and were now out of step with everyday time. Lilly argues that, rather than becoming more passive during immersion, "the brain not only stays active despite lowered levels of input and output, but accumulates surplus energy to extreme degrees" (1956, 7). One of the respondents to Lilly's paper, Zigmond Lebensohn, a psychiatrist at Georgetown University School of Medicine, speculates that

the period of life which this [immersion] most closely resembles is the embryonic stage, and the embryo is not instructed by an experimenter not to flex his muscles. Fetal movement is present very early in embryonic development. It seems that even the embryo requires some moving around to assure itself of its own existence! (Quoted in Lilly 1956, 18)

This comparison of the experimental subject to an embryo reveals a nested series of assumptions about solitude and relationality in the emergence of subjectivity. On the one hand, subjects in immersion return to (a fantasized) quasi-embryonic state; they are floating in dark liquid, stimulated only by the slight, even pressure of this fluid, and by the rhythmic sound of their own breath. They are alone, but enclosed and protected from the outside world; and if they can stand the monotony of sensory deprivation for long enough, they will be rewarded with a blissful surge of "oceanic feeling" (Lilly 1956, 4). But on the other hand, even embryos seem to have some (again, fantasized) anxiety about their own identity, to the point of needing to move around in order to generate some minimal evidence of their own existence. Lilly resists the comparison of the experimental subject with a fetus in the womb, while acknowledging that such fantasies do arise: "Fantasies about the experience (such as the illusion of 'return to the womb,' which is quite common) are dispelled; one realizes that at birth we start breathing air and hence cannot 'return to the womb'" (7). Subjects in the immersion tank may feel like a fetus in the womb, but they know (or, at least, Lilly knows) that this is a physiological impossibility. After all, fully born organisms need air to breathe!

However unconvincing this may be as an account of fantasy and its dissolution, Lilly's observation of a tension between feeling and knowing is significant. On the one hand, subjects feel free, no longer encumbered by the weight of the world and the obligation to respond to stimuli, including the social stimuli produced by other subjects. But on the other hand, they are reminded of their dependence on the breathing apparatus, and hence on air itself, and ultimately on the experimenter who controls the environment and assures their continued safety. Immersion is thus a highly ambivalent situation; while it generates a feeling of free-floating solitude and independence, it nevertheless requires a complex apparatus of technology and technicians to make that feeling of solitude possible.

In a paper that Lilly cowrote with Jay Shurley for a 1960 symposium entitled "Psychophysiological Aspects of Space Flight," the authors speculate at greater length on the solitude of the immersed subject, which is produced and maintained by the discreet presence of an other, the "safety man," as Lilly calls him:

> The maintenance of physical–physiological isolation and solitude in the
> midst of a community implies barriers to intrusion by persons or sources of

physical stimuli; i.e., such isolation implies that eventually one is in solitude (of course solitude per se does not necessarily imply physical isolation). Such consideration requires a building which houses the tank and is constructed in such a way as to bar any continuous traffic through its structure and which permits no invasion by people or animals or other objects which may be sensed by the subject; a lock on the door is required but not sufficient. The safety man is instructed to act as a buffer agent for the subject, both before, during, and after the experiments and to maintain privacy. (1961, 243)

A relation to the safety man is the basic condition for the subject's feeling of solitude and freedom. But what does freedom mean in this context? It may feel like the freedom of a solitary individual who is completely independent, weightless, and disconnected from the world, but this feeling of solitude is produced by a highly artificial, technologically mediated relation to an other who cares for the subject and supports the vulnerable "solitude" with intimate, discreet, but attentive care. This careful cultivation of (a fantasy of) solitary freedom, like the solitude of Robinson Crusoe or of the embryo-astronaut beloved of pro-lifers, depends upon an other whose assistance is vital but whose contributions to one's own feeling of solitude must be erased or reinterpreted as an anonymous "environment" or impersonal background in order to sustain the fantasy of solitude.[14] The "privacy" of the subject was of paramount importance to Lilly and Shurley as a condition for maintaining "maximum ego freedom and voluntariness of the subject" (1961, 243). This privacy extended to maintaining the secrecy of subjects' reported fantasies, visual hallucinations, or other intimate experiences within in the tank.

Lilly acknowledges that the initiation into such a radical and ambivalent sense of freedom is initially a kind of "indoctrination," but he argues that it is an indoctrination into *oneself*, as a necessary condition for breaking with the indoctrination of "society":

It is our conviction that the range of phenomena available to the normal human mind is much greater than "society" will apparently permit or accept . . . ; consequently, the safety man becomes the intercessor between the individual and the community. As such, he grants the subject permission to experience whatever he can experience; i.e., the right to exercise any function, strictly leaving open the content of what is experienced. If you will, the individual is "indoctrinated" in the principle of freedom for his own ego with the internal experiential sphere. (Lilly and Shurley 1961, 245)

Confined to himself in solitude, the experimental subject gains access to "sources of *new information* from within" (246). Hence the promise

of psychological and spiritual development through sensory deprivation—and yet, the raw openness of the immersed subject also makes
him susceptible to what the researchers on Chinese brainwashing techniques would call "refreezing" or reprogramming: "Any other person,
observer, or safety man can be made to appear as if he is a 'source'
to which is attributed the origin of the new information" (246). The
conditions of absolute freedom and absolute exposure—not to physical death but to the death of one's "personality" and the unraveling
of one's individuated personhood—overlap in Lilly's account of the
possibilities opened up by sensory deprivation research. The safety
man is positioned as both a support for the freedom and solitude of
the experimental subject—a beneficent, even maternal presence—and
also a master whose exclusive support renders the experimental subject
vulnerable to manipulation, exploitation, and even natal alienation.
While the slave master frankly and openly occupied the role of a sovereign father whose exclusive support allowed him to alienate slaves
from their kin and to remake them as a peculiar blend of property and
personhood, the sovereignty—and the danger—of the safety man is
occluded by his role as a scientific researcher.[15]

In the end, Lilly's scientific research gave way to esoteric spiritu-
alism and a fascination with other limit experiences, such as those
produced by LSD. In 1969 he left the NIMH amid controversy over
his experiments with LSD and continued his research at the Esalen
Institute, where he became a cult hero. And yet Lilly's research on
sensory deprivation was taken very seriously by the military and
the political institutions that commissioned and funded it. In the
next section, I follow the application of this research in the domestic context of incarceration and the international context of military
intelligence.

Applications of Sensory Deprivation Research

In 1961, two influential texts were published: *The Manipulation of
Human Behavior,* which became an important theoretical foundation
for the CIA's coercive interrogation techniques as outlined in the
KUBARK manual (CIA 1963), and *The Power to Change Behavior,*
which became a theoretical and practical foundation for the behavior modification programs that shaped U.S. domestic prison policy in
the 1960s and '70s. Both publications were heavily indebted to the
literature on "Communist" thought reform and sensory deprivation,

and both yielded specific techniques for the production of social death, both within the United States and beyond.

The *Manipulation of Human Behavior* and the KUBARK manual were edited by Albert D. Biderman, whose 1957 research on Communist thought reform I have referenced above, and Herbert Zimmer, an associate professor of psychology at the University of Georgia. The research in the volume was funded by contracts from the U.S. Air Force and was carried out by the Bureau of Social Science Research, of which Biderman was a senior member. Contributors include Lawrence Hinkle, another pioneer of Communist thought reform whose work I have discussed at some length. The cover of *The Manipulation of Human Behavior* depicts a puppet composed of geometrical shapes and attached to strings manipulated by unseen hands. The introduction, written by Biderman and Zimmer, sets the stage for a discussion that ranges from the use of drugs and hypnosis during interrogation, to strategies for blocking the countermanipulation of interrogators by prisoners, to a review of the literature on sensory deprivation. The editors begin with some broad observations on the importance of sensory deprivation research for effective interrogation in a military context and for addressing more general problems of a political and psychological nature:

> Two of the most basic of life's problems are linked to the individual's power position vis-à-vis his fellow men: the inability to make others fulfill one's wishes; and the reverse, the fear of being controlled by others, with the consequent loss of the autonomy that is believed to be fundamental to the conception of the self. (Biderman and Zimmer 1961, 4)

For Biderman and Zimmer, the central problem facing humanity— or, at least, facing the United States during the Cold War—is the challenge of securing one's own freedom and independence while at the same time retaining power over others. Power implies a relation, and even the absolute power of the master over the slave exposes the master to a certain dependence, a mediation of his solitary freedom by subordinate others, and even—if Hegel was right—the eventual dissolution of the master's power. If freedom entails solitude and liberation from constraint, then it is not clear how we can be free while remaining in relation to others, unless there is a way to manipulate the behavior of others like a puppet master who remains aloof from the puppets.

The Manipulation of Human Behavior brings together psychologists, psychiatrists, and social scientists to address this double problem of power and freedom in the context of U.S. military interests. In effect, their challenge is to explain how the U.S. interrogator, armed with the insights of behavioral science, could exploit prisoners' basic capacity for social relations in order to solve the problem of power and freedom that sociality poses in the first place. In his contribution to the volume, "The Physiological State of the Interrogation Subject As It Affects Brain Function," Hinkle (1961, 29–30) argues that isolation and sleep deprivation are more effective than physical pain, hunger, or threats of violence for "disorganizing" a person and reducing the capacity for resistance to interrogation. An untrained interrogator may assume that a violent, aggressive approach is most effective in forcing prisoners to submit to the interrogator's will, but such an approach only grants prisoners a determinate target against which to consolidate their own oppositional subjectivity. A more effective approach to interrogation would be to use prisoners' own capacities, but also their needs or vulnerabilities, to undermine their sense of independent personhood. Prisoners who are determined to remain independent, who refuse to relate to the interrogator on the interrogator's own terms, should be isolated in their independence, forced to bear their solitary freedom alone and without the support of others. They should be blocked from even the temporary relief provided by sleep from this burden of solitude. Their ability to experience the world with their senses, from their own singular perspective on the world, should become a source of fatigue and overexposure rather than a source of understanding or enjoyment. Then, once prisoners have crumpled under the weight of their own solitude—once the personality has become "disorganized"—they should be given the chance to relate to one, and only one, other person: the interrogator. At this point, they should be ready to cooperate.

To be sure, Hinkle does not articulate his position in phenomenological terms such as these; rather, he bases his argument on a mechanistic, functionalist model of cognition: "The brain, the organ that deals with information, also organizes its responses on the basis of information previously fed into it" (1961, 34). If the seat of personality is the brain, and the brain is an input-output machine, then the interrogator should be able to manipulate the personality of the prisoner by controlling the level and type of environmental input. This mechanistic model leads to the same conclusion as my own phenomenological sketch of the "disorganization" of the interrogated subject; but, like Benjamin

Rush's mechanistic account of personhood, it also works to obscure the violence of disorganization as an attack on the social-ontological roots of the victim's relational personhood. As such, Hinkle's behaviorist explanation of isolation allows both researchers and practitioners to explore the possibilities of solitary confinement and sensory deprivation without regard for the ethical, epistemological, or ontological implications of their work, and even to pursue applications of their research under the rubric of apparently legitimate social and political goals such as national security.

The clearest example of this confident disregard for the implications of one's research is Malcolm L. Meltzer's paper "Countermanipulation through Malingering" (1961). At the time, Meltzer was a staff psychologist at the District of Columbia General Hospital; he also taught psychology at George Washington University. Meltzer addresses the problem of dealing with prisoners who pretend to be mentally ill in order to evade coercive interrogation. He focuses on the importance of emotional manipulation in outwitting malingering prisoners and maintaining control of the situation. If the interrogator is the sole person with whom the prisoner has any chance of forming a relationship—is, in effect, the prisoner's "safety man"—then an intense level of intimacy may form between a prisoner and the interrogator, giving rise to ambivalent feelings of guilt and desire in the prisoner:

> In some lengthy interrogations, the interrogator may, by virtue of his role as the sole supplier of satisfaction and punishment, assume the stature and importance of a parental figure in the prisoner's feeling and thinking. Although there may be intense hatred for the interrogator, it is not unusual for warm feelings also to develop. This ambivalence is the basis for guilt reactions, and if the interrogator nourishes these feelings, the guilt may be strong enough to influence the prisoner's behavior. (1961, 297; quoted in CIA 1963, 83)

In effect, the prisoner becomes an overgrown infant, and the interrogator a substitute (phallic) mother: both a source of punishment and a source of life or comfort, however limited. Scraped raw by any or all of prolonged solitude, sensory deprivation, and sensory overload, the prisoner begins to feel guilty. Meltzer suggests that the cause of these guilty feelings is the prisoner's impression "that he is taking advantage of the interrogator and may feel some guilt for misleading the one person who seems to be interested in him and who is looking after his welfare" (297).

The writers of the KUBARK manual build on this suggestion, quoting liberally from *The Manipulation of Human Behavior* and especially from the texts of both Meltzer and Hinkle. The KUBARK manual was the CIA's secret counterintelligence manual; it outlines the methods and rationale for the "coercive counterintelligence inter-rogation of resistant sources" (CIA 1963, 82). KUBARK was updated in 1983 and renamed the *Human Resource Exploitation Training Manual.* This manual was used for intelligence training courses run by the CIA between 1987 and 1991 at the U.S. Army School of the Americas, which trained interrogators from across Central and South America, including El Salvador, Colombia, and Guatemala.[16] Both documents were declassified in 1997 in response to a 1994 Freedom of Information Act request by the *Baltimore Sun.* Both manuals ad-vise sleep deprivation, stress positions, blindfolding, stripping, search-ing body cavities, identifying and exploiting existing fears, and other techniques "designed not only to exploit the resistant source's internal conflicts and induce him to wrestle with himself but also to bring a superior outside force to bear upon the subject's resistances" (CIA 1963, 82).

Both KUBARK and the *Human Resource Exploitation Training Manual* instruct interrogators on how to induce the prisoner to regress to a feeling of infantile helplessness, disorientation, and shock and on how to establish the interrogator as the source of everything that is good, comforting, and familiar—sunlight, food, water, warmth, and protection—all of which are distributed on the condition that the pris-oner cooperate (CIA 1963, 83; 1983, K-1).[17] The KUBARK manual explicitly favors

> methods of inducing regression of the personality to whatever earlier and weaker level is required for the dissolution of resistance and the inculcation of dependence. . . . As the interrogatee slips back from maturity toward a more infantile state, his learned or structured personality traits fall away in a reversed chronological order, so that the characteristics most recently ac-quired—which are also the characteristics drawn upon by the interrogatee in his own defense—are the first to go. (CIA 1963, 41)[18]

As if undergoing a personal evolution in reverse, the prisoner is re-duced to ever-more-primitive levels of human personality, losing his autonomy along with his capacity to resist. And yet, the most effective instrument in this devolution is the prisoner himself:

> It has been plausibly suggested that, whereas pain inflicted on a person from outside himself may actually focus or intensify his will to resist, his resistance is likelier to be sapped by pain which he seems to inflict upon himself. . . . When the individual is told to stand at attention for long periods, an intervening factor is introduced. The immediate source of pain is not the interrogator but the victim himself. The motivational strength of the individual is likely to exhaust itself in this internal encounter. (CIA 1963, 94)

This feeling of self-inflicted pain is intensified by the use of "stress positions" that use the prisoner's own weight against himself, by sleep deprivation, and by relentless exposure to loud noise or extreme temperatures, all of which exploit the body's basic needs and vulnerabilities. In response to such treatment, the prisoner

> turns his awareness inward, upon himself and then projects the contents of his own unconscious outwards, so that he endows his faceless environment with his own attributes, fears, and forgotten memories. (CIA 1963, 88)

As both KUBARK and its 1983 successor observe, and as Rush already pointed out in his "Enquiry into the Effects of Public Punishments," the intense fear and dread of pain is more effective than physical pain in manipulating the behavior of others: "Sustained long enough, a strong fear of anything vague or unknown induces regression. On the other hand, materialization of the fear is likely to come as a relief. The subject finds that he can hold out and his resistance is strengthened" (CIA 1963, 90–91; 1983, K-2). The interrogator need not appear as a diabolical torturer, threatening prisoners with a dental drill and a wicked grin; rather, the regression of prisoners to a state of helpless infancy is best accomplished by turning their own bodies against themselves, and by depriving them of the satisfaction of pinpointing the source of pain.[19]

In the section on solitary confinement and sensory deprivation, the authors of the KUBARK manual draw directly on the research of Hebb and Lilly, listing the typical effects of solitary confinement as superstition, hallucination, delusion, and "an intense love of any other living thing" (CIA 1963, 88; 1983, K-6).[20] What does it mean to recognize, as the effect of one's own standard operating procedure, the production and exploitation of an intense love for any living thing? To produce *love* as a means of torture? What exactly is the "human resource" being exploited here? In order to understand what is at stake, we need to think more carefully about the intimate drama that seeks to regress the prisoner to infancy and installs the interrogator as a source of both punishment and care.

In her impressive study of torture in Algeria, *Torture and the Twilight of Empire,* Marnia Lazreg describes a different but related exploitation of the scene of infancy and birth, this time imagining the tortured body not as an adult regressing to infancy but as a woman giving birth:

> One of the images used by torturers evokes labor pains preceding the birth of a child, an image at odds with the gender of its users who, in the Algerian War, happen to all be men. Nevertheless, in their minds their actions facilitate the release of information. A prisoner is subjected to extreme pain, just like a pregnant woman must endure labor pains as she gives birth to a child. The body of the prisoner must be worked over, and worked through. The imagery used by the torturer helps him to appropriate the ownership of the information he seeks to get. Because it is he who inflicts pain and suffering, and makes the prisoner "labor," *he* has *produced* the information. The pregnancy metaphor enables the torturer to look upon his actions as producing life. After all he is involved in a life-giving process that marks the familiar justification of torture: It saves lives. The metaphor also denotes a trivialization of the prisoner and the information he is assumed to carry in the recesses of his being. The prisoner is but a vessel through which the torturer works. (2008, 132–33)

In this way of imagining the scenario of torture, the torturer is both like a midwife who "delivers" the secret information from the sweating, screaming, suffering body of the prisoner and also like a husband, the symbolic owner of the delivered information. Given that much torture happens whether or not the prisoner has information to give up, the torturer sometimes literally "produces" the secret to be delivered. When a confession is already written, waiting to be signed, torture is both a process of extracting information from the prisoner's body and of planting it there in the first place. The classical image of the pregnant woman's body as a mere vessel for the homunculus planted in her by the man resonates with this fantasy of torture as a birth scene staged on the prisoner's body, and produced by the torturer himself.[21]

Lazreg's analysis of torture in Algeria suggests that the regression of the prisoner is not a solitary affair but, rather, an intensely relational process that implicates the interrogator as a kind of perverse parent, both a supportive mother and a punishing father, but in any case as the *sole* support for the prisoner's life and comfort.[22] The structure of

this (nonrelational, even antirelational) relationality echoes the structure of natal alienation in slavery, where slaves are put in a position
of social death precisely to the extent that they are forced to rely upon
one sole other—the master who "owns" them—for protection and support. Even though both Lilly and the authors of the KUBARK manual
emphasize the importance of freedom, understood as the capacity of
a solitary individual to be liberated from the constraint or control of
others, in practice, prisoners are implicitly, and sometimes explicitly,
targeted as interrelational, intercorporeal beings, whose "human resources" provide the material for their own undoing and become the
site of their most radical exploitation. If prisoners were just autonomous individuals, if they were not (also) relational beings, then they
would not be susceptible to the techniques in this manual.

The KUBARK manual was developed at the same time that the
second wave of solitary confinement in the U.S. domestic prison system
was getting underway. Like the KUBARK manual, this new approach
to solitary confinement sought to incorporate and apply the insights of
behaviorist experiments in sensory deprivation and thought reform.
What sort of programs and techniques did this research yield in the
context of domestic incarceration?

"The Power to Change Behavior" and U.S. Prison Policy

The 1961 symposium "The Power to Change Behavior" brought together prison wardens and behavioral scientists—including Edgar
Schein, an important researcher on Chinese/Communist thought reform—to consider how prisoners could be "treated" with behavior
modification therapy. The forward to the conference proceedings states
this mission clearly:

> Effective treatment of individuals confined in correctional institutions de-
> pends upon the degree to which their unsocial or anti-social behavior can be
> modified. Behavioral change takes place in response to stimuli. Providing
> the stimuli necessary to produce the desired responses requires a broad
> knowledge by the correctional worker of the behavioral sciences. (U.S.
> Bureau of Prisons 1961)

By controlling the prisoners' environment and calibrating their exposure to stimuli, wardens sought to reform their behavior, and even their
personalities, both for their own sake and for the good of society as a

whole. As Bernard Kramer, then of Tufts University Medical School, argues in his contribution to the symposium: "It has always been true that man's social environment and man's behavior have had interlocking effects upon each other. And if this is so then we may reasonably suppose that man has the power to change behavior by manipulating his social environment" (Kramer 1961, 28).

In *The Power to Change Behavior* (the published papers from the symposium), as in *The Manipulation of Human Behavior,* contributors identify two main problems facing humanity. But in this case, the problems are somewhat different: "1) the development and preservation of himself as an individual; and 2) the preservation of his kind in the continuation of the species" (Leiderman 1961, 5). The challenge of life is to survive, and in order to survive—both as an individual and as a species—one must adapt. Armed with the right sort of information, prison wardens should be able to manipulate this adaptive imperative, forcing the criminal offender to adapt to new, more socially acceptable patterns in the environment of the prison. This concern for survival is shared by David Landy, professor of anthropology at the University of Pittsburgh, in his paper for the symposium, "Man's Adaptive Processes: Cultural Influences on Behavioral Change." Landy represents culture as

> the protective screen or group life-patterns, erected by [modern man's] bewildered and shivering Paleolithic ancestors as they scratched and clawed their way to survival in the face of often catastrophic natural events.... The man who half a million years ago in splendid isolation cast his whittled stick at a giant mammoth has evolved to his descendant who, by light pressure upon a smooth button, can destroy the large part of a mammoth society of his fellow-humans. (Landy 1961, 44–45)

For Landy, the rehabilitative aim of prison is

> to serve as an adaptive mechanism by restoring and renewing the bonds between its inmates and the society that has rejected them. Any goal short of this may retard cultural and industrial development by returning inmates to the status of infant dependency from which man has struggled to free himself over the past million years. (51)

The risk of an insufficiently informed prison policy is a biocultural (and even industrial) devolution in which prisoners regress to a state of primitive, infant dependency, eventually dragging the rest of society with them. In order to evade this risk, wardens must become "agents of behavior change" who, educated in the techniques of behavior modification, take advantage of personal, social, and natural mechanisms of adaptation in order to reconcile offenders to society, and society to offenders. The "subjects of change" in this process of mutual adaptation are the inmates themselves, with administrators and technicians as "executors of change" (51).

Landy, like many of the symposium's contributors, represents prisoners both as patients to be cured and as problems to be solved, such that the line between treatment and punishment becomes blurred. In his contribution to the symposium, "Man Alone: Sensory Deprivation and Behavioral Change," P. Herbert Leiderman, professor of psychiatry and behavioral sciences at Stanford University and coeditor of *Sensory Deprivation: A Symposium Held at Harvard Medical School* (1961), argues that the "hope" of behavioral modification programs in prisons is to "enable individuals to harness some of the forces of their inner life . . . for greater creativity, surely of benefit to the individual himself and his society" (Leiderman 1961, 26; see also 51). But it is not at all clear how this enhanced creativity is supposed to blossom, nor how "the individual himself" is meant to benefit from being subject to a rigorous program of behavior change. Leiderman argues that "isolation as a controlling technique will have its major use for prisoners with problems of impulse control" (24), but in the same breath, he acknowledges that for those whose "inner life is under poor control," isolation can "lead to an increase of anxieties, fears, perhaps to the point of psychosis" (24). Nevertheless, these anxieties can be useful instruments in the manipulation of prisoners' behavior: "Suggestibility seems greatest when individuals are anxious, and under conditions when sensory deprivation is combined with social isolation, rather than either one alone" (22). While Leiderman acknowledges that such intensive isolation can produce "mental aberrations" in prisoners, he maintains that "in most instances these are unsought, in a few instances perhaps desired" (11). He leaves it to the reader to imagine the circumstances under which the production of mental illness in the prisoner may be "desired."

Edgar Schein's contribution to the symposium, "Man against Man: Brainwashing," draws on his 1953 research (published in 1956) on Communist brainwashing techniques to reflect on how these techniques might be used to reform U.S. domestic prisoners. Schein was a professor at the MIT Sloan School of Management (then the School of Industrial Management); after his publication of his 1971 book,

Coercive Interrogation, he went on to have a highly successful career in corporate and organizational psychology. Schein's basic argument in "Man against Man: Brainwashing" is that "in order to produce marked change of behavior and/or attitude, it is necessary to weaken, undermine, or remove the supports to the old patterns of behavior and the old attitudes" (Schein 1961, 55). Most important among these supports are the inmate's affective social relations; the warden must therefore find a way to "break those emotional ties" and to replace them with new, healthy social relations. New behavior and attitudes "will be learned as a basic solution to the problem of how to survive in the inflexible environment" established by a strict calculus of punishments and rewards (55).

Schein urges his audience of prison wardens not to let the similarity of his suggested techniques to those used by Chinese/Communists prevent them from seeing the usefulness of these practices in different contexts, attached to different ends. He encourages them to "think of brainwashing not in terms of politics, ethics and morals, but in terms of the deliberate changing of behavior and attitudes by a group of men who have relatively complete control over the environment in which the captive population lives" (1961, 56). If coercive persuasion is approached in the right way, with the proper goals, it can be good for both the individual prisoner and for society as a whole:

> What is cruel and coercive about this process is the control which the agent of change exerts over the individual in the process of undermining and destroying his social and emotional supports. And yet, do we not feel it to be legitimate to destroy the emotional ties of one criminal to another, or of a criminal to a sick community? Do we not break up gangs and denigrate idolized gang leaders in our attempts to rehabilitate the delinquent? And do we not put criminals with the wrong attitude in the midst of others with the right attitude in the hope that they will learn the right ones through the pressure of the group? . . . I am trying to show that the Chinese methods are not so mysterious, not so different, and not so awful, once we separate out the awfulness of the Communist ideology and look simply at the methods of influence used. (63–64)[23]

Once purified of their Communist objectives, the techniques of Chinese thought reform could become useful for reforming the behavior of socially destructive or unproductive subjects in the U.S. domestic context, especially—as the concluding discussions of the symposium show—to control the Black Muslim prison population.

While Schein himself does not explicitly advise the application of Chinese brainwashing techniques to Black Muslim prisoners—and while he later denied that he ever advocated the use of these techniques at all[24]—the connection between coercive persuasion and racial inequality was not lost on him. In his 1956 paper "The Chinese Indoctrination Program for Prisoners of War: A Study of Attempted Brainwashing," he had already noted that Chinese authorities focused in particular on pressuring "low status" Americans,

> including the younger and less intelligent, the malcontent, and the man whose social reference groups made the attainment of status difficult—that is, the members of various racial, religious, national, or economic minority groups. These men had little realization of the benefits of democracy because they had never experienced them in a meaningful way. They felt that the society was more to blame for their failures than they were. Such men were ready to give a serious consideration to an ideology that offered remedies for their misfortunes. (1956, 167–68; see also 153 on the Chinese treatment of African American POWs)

Schein claims that such men were more susceptible to coercive persuasion to the point of conversion, and some declined repatriation, "perhaps in order to stay with the cause which for the first time allowed them to become important" (168). However, the Chinese technique of separating the "Negroes" from other prisoners may have backfired, since, as he observed,

> many Negroes felt that if they were going to be segregated they might as well be segregated in the United States—that there was nothing new or better about communism in this respect. Moreover, the propaganda given to them was too extreme; even the very low-status Negro knew that his circumstances in the United States were not as bad as the Communists painted them. (168)

Schein's recognition that African Americans may have genuine and legitimate reasons for being dissatisfied by their social status in the United States leads him not to a critique of U.S. race relations but, rather, to a confirmation of the evils of communism; for Schein, even antiblack racism is not as bad for blacks as the lack of freedom under a Communist regime.

Some of the most revealing moments of "The Power to Change Behavior" addressed the challenge of controlling Black Muslim prisoners. In the "Discussion Summary," one unnamed discussant tentatively suggests that racism might have something to do with the "behavior problems" of black prisoners in particular:

> About the question of the Muslims, I think it is important to look at some of the underlying aspects of the picture even outside the prison system and to look at it as much as it is humanly possible through the eyes of the others, and this I know is a really difficult task especially when you have the job of keeping order and keeping the place going and all of the things necessary to run an efficient prison. But through the eyes of many of the Negro prisoners, I would guess that they see a pattern in which over 50% of the prisoners are Negro and they constitute only 10% of the population, and they ask—they may not ask it specifically, and they may not realize what's behind it all— but this Muslim business is latched onto because there's an underlying issue of which they may be aware. I think that to close our eyes to this aspect of the problem is not to see the whole picture. (U.S. Bureau of Prisons 1961, 68)

Responding to this issue, Dr. Lowry (not otherwise identified, but presumably a prison psychiatrist) describes how his own attempt to treat Black Muslim prisoners as a group rather than as individuals backfired because it fed "their paranoid behavior" and resulted in "additional recruits." In the end, he had to admit that

> they have as some of their basic premise some truth, and that is that members of their race have been persecuted in many ways and from this premise you can build up the whole system of logic and behavior which looks very fine, but which can be very destructive. (U.S. Bureau of Prisons 1961, 69)

The closing words of the symposium go to James V. Bennett, director of the Bureau of Prisons from 1937 to 1964:

> We have a tremendous opportunity here to carry on some of the experimenting to which the various panelists have alluded. We can manipulate our environment and culture. . . . What I am trying to say is that we are a group that can do a lot of experimenting and research and we can change our methods, our environments, and perhaps come up with something more specific. What I am hoping is that the audience here will believe that we here in Washington are anxious to have you undertake some of these things. Do things perhaps on your own—undertake a little experiment of what you can do with the Muslims—undertake a little experiment with what you can do with some of the sociopath individuals. . . . You are thoughtful people with lots of opportunity to experiment—there's lots of research to do—do it as individuals, do it as groups, and let us know the results. (U.S. Bureau of Prisons 1961, 72)

Not all of the symposium's participants shared Bennett's enthusiasm for experimenting on inmates, and particularly on Black Muslim inmates, in an effort to "restructure" their behavior. Jessica Mitford reports that the one black psychiatrist present at the meeting, Wendell Lipscomb, stormed out midway, telling Mitford in a later interview, "What you were seeing at that meeting were the grant hunters, hungry for money, willing to eat any shit that's put before them" (quoted in Mitford 1973, 30).

In the end, Schein and his fellow researchers walk a fine line between claiming that Communist mind-control techniques are nothing special or new, that they are not effective in the long term, and that they may even end up turning the prisoner more bitterly against his former captors, on the one hand, and suggesting, on the other hand, that these techniques warrant further investigation and that they may be especially helpful in the U.S. context for reforming the antisocial behavior of prisoners—especially Black Muslim prisoners—by controlling them in the short term and even reintegrating them into U.S. society in the long term.

While many of the papers presented at "The Power to Change Behavior" symposium lack concrete suggestions for how to treat prisoners, Schein offers the following recipe for unmaking and remaking the prisoner's "behavior":

> If one wants to produce behavior inconsistent with the person's standards of conduct, first disorganize the group which supports those standards, then undermine his other emotional supports, then put him into a new and ambiguous situation for which the standards are unclear, and then put pressure on him. (1961, 60)

In order to accomplish this disorganization and reorganization of the prisoners' situation, Schein recommends the segregation of natural leaders, the creation of mutual distrust among prisoners, the disruption of contact between prisoners and their families, including the interruption of mail service and visiting schedules, and the use of compliant prisoners as informants and group leaders (58–61; see also Griffin 1993, 3).

In the late 1960s and early 1970s, Schein had a chance to put these ideas into practice. He teamed up with Martin Groder, a psychiatrist who worked at Marion Penitentiary from 1968 to 1972 and later became program development coordinator for the Federal Bureau of

Prisons.[25] Together, Schein and Groder designed the Special Treatment and Rehabilitation Training (START) program, which was implemented at the Federal Medical Center for Prisoners in Springfield, Missouri, from 1972 to 1974. Groder had already spearheaded a similar program, named Asklepieion (after the Greek god of healing), at Marion Penitentiary from 1968 to 1972. Both programs were patterned on techniques used by Chinese forces against U.S. POWs in the Korean War: a combination of solitary confinement and small-group confinement, together with other elements of behaviorist conditioning, such as punishment–reward systems, aversion therapy, and a component that Groder called "attack therapy," in which inmates criticized one another in nightly discussion groups (Aynes 1975, 459). What did these "little experiment[s]" look like in practice, and what did they hope to accomplish?

The Application of Behavior Modification Research in U.S. Prisons: START and Asklepieion

In the early 1970s, around a hundred federal prisoners who were considered to be "disruptive of institutional authority, or who held radical political views" were transferred from other penal institutions to Marion Penitentiary (Eisenman 2009). According to Ralph Aron, a former warden at Marion, "The purpose of the Marion Control Unit is to control revolutionary attitudes in the prison system and in the society at large" (quoted in Griffin 1993, 6; see also Gómez 2006, 58).[26] Politically active prisoners held at Marion have included Leonard Peltier of the American Indian Movement, Sekou Odinga of the Black Liberation Army, Alan Berkman of the Resistance Conspiracy case, and Oscar López Rivera of the Puerto Rican nationalist group FALN (Eisenman 2009; see also Gómez 2006). In 1973, a "Long Term Control Unit" was established at Marion in response to a strike by inmates after a Chicano inmate was beaten by a guard (Gómez 2006, 60). This Control Unit (CU) became a prototype for the CUs and SHUs of the contemporary supermax prisons. In fact, Marion became the first de facto supermax prison in 1983, when the entire facility was locked down in response to the murder of two guards and every cell was treated as a long-term control unit. The lockdown lasted for twenty-three years.

In his important paper "Resisting Living Death at Marion Federal Penitentiary, 1972," Alan Eladio Gómez pieces together archival evidence of prisoners' resistance movements within Marion Prison and traces the connections between "The Power to Change Behavior" symposium and the programs developed to contain these growing resistance movements. The target of these experimental programs went beyond the Black Muslims identified in the papers presented at "The Power to Change Behavior"; they included organizations such as the Black Panthers, the Black Liberation Army, La Raza Unida, and CORA (Chicanos Organizados Rebeldes de Aztlán, or Organized Chicano Rebels from Aztlán). Gómez argues:

> The very existence of political activists behind prison walls challenged the logic of advanced capitalism in the United States; resistance was unacceptable, the internal colonial other was to be buried alive, permanently isolated from human contact, sentenced to the punishment of living death. (2006, 60)

While the CIA was applying behavior modification techniques to noncitizen enemies of the state, programs like START and Asklepieion began experimenting with their application to domestic prisoners, in a form of domestic counterinsurgency against African Americans, Chicanos/as, Native Americans, Puerto Ricans, and others.[27] What did these programs look like in theory and in practice?

START was an incentive-based "treatment" program in which prisoners were placed in solitary confinement and then became eligible for higher degrees of freedom, comfort, and social contact based on good behavior and the successful performance of certain tasks such as "maintaining good hygiene, keeping [their] cell clean, performing well on [their] job, and not physically or verbally assaulting prison officials" (Rangel 1975, 6). These privileges were removed if they resisted, rebelled, or otherwise failed to comply with the rules. Participants did not volunteer for the program; they were chosen by wardens from among the most "highly aggressive and assaultive inmates" (4). Charles Rangel (writing in 1975, at the beginning of his long career as a U.S. Congressman) defended the program, arguing that it had been a successful rehabilitation program but was unfortunately too expensive to justify its continuation (4n4). He characterized statements made against the program by the Commission for Racial Justice as mere "rhetoric" complicit with certain inmates' false perception of themselves as political prisoners (5n12; see also 6–7).[28]

How did prisoners themselves describe the START program?

They put [inmates] in the hole and they chained them, completely nude. So then the following day they give them a pair of shorts, and then the next day they give them a pencil, but no paper, and each day you progress, and if your behavior is not keeping with what they want it to be, then you start back from nothing. The reward punishment trip is what START was about. (Eddie Sanchez, quoted in Gómez 2006, 63)

The whole so-called program was based on racist tidbits of neo-nazi psychology as advocated by the likes of Dr. Jensen, Swell etc., that black people are mentally unbalanced and this manifests itself in aggressive behavior, unwillingness to accept white values (racist concepts of conduct). (Gerard Wilson, quoted in Rangel 1975, 7n15)

I have been subjected to brutal physical assaults, drug assaults, chaining to a steel bed, my mail has been withheld and destroyed, and since none of the above has made me submit to the racist, nazi-like START program, now they're subjecting me to this psychological intimidation, seeking to undermine my mental stability. (Unnamed inmate, quoted in Rangel 1975, 7–8n17)

The U.S. Bureau of Prisons responded to these and other charges of physical, psychological, and racist abuse by claiming that the START program was designed not to "brainwash" prisoners but, rather, to enable them "to maintain their principles and beliefs, while teaching them to express these beliefs in a manner more acceptable to society than they have in the past" (Rangel 1975, 8). The START program was intended as an incubator for programming at a new, experimental prison in Butner, North Carolina, where Schein was the director of the Center for Correctional Research, but the program was terminated in response to a 1974 lawsuit by the American Civil Liberties Union (ACLU) charging that prisoners' rights were violated by forced participation in the program.[29]

Groder's Asklepieion program was similarly controversial but, like START, it has still managed to find supporters, both then and now. The 1996 Dictionary of American Penology, for example, praises the low recidivism rates among participants in the program and, while expressing some reservations about the coerced nature of the program's "volunteer" participation, nevertheless states:

It would be fair to say that there was nothing inherently wrong with the eclectic treatment approach developed by Groder, but the court system and the Bureau of Prisons came to see the folly in attempting to force inmates to participate in programs designed to change their attitudes and behavior. (V. Williams 1996, 29)

Critics of the Asklepieion program in the 1970s described its objectives in terms that resonate with Lifton's account of Communist brainwashing techniques: "to 'unfreeze' the prisoner's former organization of beliefs about himself (i.e., to degrade his self-concept, to shatter his personal identity), to 'change' his personality, and to 'refreeze' the new beliefs into his new personality" (Opton 1974, 630; see also Aynes 1975, 432). Like the inmate in the nineteenth-century penitentiary, the U.S. soldier in a Chinese POW camp, and even the detainee at a CIA black site, the prisoner was encouraged to "directly [perceive] that he must 'die and be reborn'" (Lifton 1957, 639). But not every inmate was equally suited for rebirth. In a prepared statement to a U.S. House of Representatives subcommittee, Groder claimed that most of the inmates, the "typical non-thinking tough guy thug[s]," had already committed "social suicide" and were especially difficult, even impossible to reform, while other "incarcerated individuals, usually with white-collar, selective service or other kinds of milder social infractions had not committed social suicide" (quoted in Aynes 1975, 455).[30] The latter individuals had committed "reasonable" crimes, rather than crimes against society, and so they still had a realistic chance of starting a new life after prison. This concept of social suicide acknowledges the feeling of social death in a peculiar way by attributing the cause of death to the "thug[s]" themselves: they were not willing to live in harmony with society, and so they chose to commit social suicide. What can be done with such people? By deciding against a life in harmony with others, they leave us no choice but to contain and control them, protecting the rest of society from those who have perversely rejected them.

Eddie Griffin, a former inmate at Marion Penitentiary who did not participate in the program but who observed its effects on other prisoners, has a different story to tell. In a 1993 paper published in the *Journal of Prisoners on Prisons*, Griffin describes the participants in the Asklepieion program as if they, rather than the "thug[s]," had been reduced to a state of living death:

The prisoners call the group "groders" or groder's gorillas, named after the psychologist who implemented Dr. Schein's brainwashing program. The "groders" live in a special cellblock that, by prison standards, is plush. They are allowed luxuries and privileges which regular prisoners can not receive.

However, they are convinced that they "earn" these things because they are trying to do something to "better themselves." Generally, they look on other convicts with contempt. When confronted with evidence that they are a brainwash group, they reject the proof and accuse other prisoners of being envious. (5)

The "groders" will not resist or complain. Nor will they go on a strike to seek redress of prisoners' grievances. They are alienated from their environment, and emotional inter-dependency welds and insulates them into a crippled cohesion (of the weak bearing the weak). (4–5)

They are not permitted to discuss these techniques outside the group, because one of the preconditions for admittance is a bond to secrecy. Yet almost anyone can spot a "groder" because the light has gone out of his eyes. He literally wears the look of humiliation. (5)

Griffin explicitly traces the structure of Groder's Asklepieion program to Schein's paper, "Man against Man: Brainwashing," arguing that all but one of Schein's recommendations had been implemented at Marion and that several new strategies had been added (1993, 3). Even in the general prison population, behavioral modification techniques were used to isolate prisoners from their families and from each other, whittling down their access to supportive social relations as a way of intensifying the prisoners' dependence on prison authorities. For example, visitors of inmates at Marion Penitentiary would be arbitrarily strip-searched, or prisoners' friends and family would be removed from the visiting list; according to Griffin, these tactics were used most frequently with interracial families (4). Griffin explains the double isolation of the prisoner from society, and society from the prisoner:

On the one side, prisoners are told they have been totally rejected by society, and that even those who "pretend" to be interested in them are "only using prisoners for their own selfish benefit." By this a prisoner is supposed to believe that he was never a part of a community or of society in general, that his ties among the people were never legitimate, and that their interest in him is a fraud. On the other side, a brutish, bestial, and "sociopathic" image of prisoners is presented to the public. The horror image further alienates the people from the captive, and it sometimes causes a family to fear their own loved ones. This further isolates the prisoner and makes him more dependent on the prison authorities. (4)

Even the physical structure of the prison intensifies this feeling of dependence by inhibiting the movement of prisoners beyond what is required to maintain security. Every hallway is punctuated by a series of locked doors, between which prisoners have to wait for the next door to open. As a result, the prisoner's "motion, the fluidity of his life, is compressed between time locks. There is a sense of urgency to do what prisoners usually do—nothing" (2). This compression of time and space is

> part of the systematic process of reinforcing the unconditional fact of a prisoner's existence: that he has no control over the regulation and orientation of his own being. . . . In essence, a prisoner is taught to be helpless, dependent on his overseer. (2)

Griffin's choice of the word "overseer" here is significant; it emphasizes the structural parallel between the living death of mid-twentieth-century inmates and the natal alienation and social death of antebellum slaves. According to Orlando Patterson and Claude Meillassoux, the enslavement of captives in war spared their lives but rendered them socially dead by alienating them from their kin—from those who were socially obliged to come to their assistance if anyone tried to abuse or exploit them—and by replacing the complex social network of kinship relations with a single "fictional" parent: the slave master (Patterson 1982; Meillassoux 1991). This absolute dependence upon one person, and one person only, made captives vulnerable to the most radical exploitation of their capacities to work or even to exist; they became depersonalized persons, dead to the rights but not to the responsibilities of membership in a community.

Eddie Griffin calls the Control Unit of Marion Penitentiary "a Death Row for the living" (1993, 7). A prisoner in the CU has had his life spared from execution, but a meaningful sense of social life has been drained from his existence:

> A vague but bleak sensation invades a man's being when he passes through the grill doors into the prison's interior. Each electronically controlled grill seems to alienate him more and more from his freedom—even the hope of freedom. A sense of finality, of being buried alive, is raised to the supra-level of his consciousness. (1)

Griffin argues that this feeling of living death was especially intense for "groders" who had been conditioned to accept the terms of their imprisonment, or even to embrace them. Through a blend of transactional analysis (TA) and behavior modification techniques, "groders" learned to accept the authority of wardens or group leaders as a "parent" (5). Griffin explains:

Essentially, TA propagates the theory that people communicate on three different levels: parent, child, and adult. These become character roles. It is up to the corresponding party to figure out which role the first party is playing, then communicate with the person on the proper counter-part level. What this technique actually does is create an artificial dichotomy between people, each straining to fit into the proper character role. Thus, communication becomes artificial, stilted, and utterly meaningless in its content. Everyone sounds like a pseudo-intellectual. Ultimately, it propagates the idea that the authorities always fit the role of "parent" and the prisoners must submit to the role of a "child." Although some "groders" pretend this practice is a fakeout on "the man," it still is a real social practice. Changing the words to describe it *does not* change the reality. . . . These techniques exploit the basic weaknesses in human (aggregative) nature, especially those weaknesses produced by an alienating society, i.e., the need to be loved, cared about, accepted by other people, and the need to be free. (5)

Griffin articulates the logic of thought reform and behavior modification as it was applied to domestic prisoners: to induce subjects' regression to a state of infantile dependence by undermining their basic needs and desires. It is by exploiting their need to be loved, cared about, and accepted that "groders" are socially isolated from other prisoners with whom they might otherwise join in resistance; it is by exploiting their desire to be free that they are turned into helpless dependents of the prison authorities.

But if this is the case, then freedom is not the property of a single individual will but, rather, a *possibility* for the socially constituted, relational person, whose desire for freedom and for meaningful relationships are mutually supportive rather than mutually exclusive. Precisely because freedom depends on the interdependence of (singular, irreducible) beings, this freedom is precarious; it is rooted not in the power of single individual wills, nor in the capacity of those individuals to make themselves immune to the pressures of "society," but rather in a network of open-ended relationships that can be exploited or protected by social institutions such as prisons, courts of law, police forces, and state governments.

Dylan Rodríguez challenges us to "imagine the U.S. prison not as a discrete institution, but, rather, as an abstracted site—or, if you will, a prototype—of organized punishment and social, civil, and biological death" (2006, 9). While the START program and the Asklepieion program are extreme examples of the application of "mind control" and behavioral modification techniques in U.S. prisons, they are by no means exceptional, nor have the basic principles of punishment and reward disappeared from U.S. prison policy. The system of "levels" of increasing freedom, comfort, and social interaction as a reward for good behavior remains standard in most prisons across the United States, although the rewards and punishments are not always directly correlated to good and bad behavior.[31] I will follow up on the legacy of behaviorism in current supermax prisons in chapter 6. While some of the excesses of the 1960s and '70s have been addressed thanks to class-action suits by prisoners, these legal reforms have left their own ambivalent legacy of diminished but increasingly normalized abuse.

In the 1970s, the radicality of behavior modification was already being downplayed and normalized by some of its proponents as an inevitable consequence of social life. For example, Gaylin and Blatte write in their 1975 review of behavior modification in prisons:

> Behavior modification in its generic form has, of course, existed throughout human history. By biological necessity, man is a social animal. Because of our ingenuity, an individual after attaining adulthood may live separated from his fellows; however as a species we are dependent for survival on each other. That being so, a social structure is not merely a choice, but a necessity of survival. Since it is required that people live with each other there evolves a need for codes of behavior defining that which is permissible, and that which is not. (11)

James McConnell offers a more extreme, and decidedly less humanist, formulation of this idea in his 1970 article "Criminals Can Be Brainwashed—Now":

> No one owns his own personality. Your ego, or individuality, was forced on you by your genetic constitution and by the society into which you were born. You had no say about what kind of personality you acquired, and there's no reason to believe you should have the right to refuse to acquire a new personality if your old one is antisocial. I don't believe the Constitution of the United States gives you the right to commit a crime if you want to; therefore, the Constitution does not guarantee you the right to maintain inviolable the personality forced on you in the first place—if and when the personality manifests strongly in antisocial behavior. (74)

Compare this with the statement of a senior prison administrator interviewed by Sharon Shalev in the twenty-first century:

> I think if we regard behaviour modification as brainwashing, then we pretty much have to accept the fact that we've all been brainwashed through our

process of just growing up, by being told what's acceptable in society and what's not acceptable in society if you want to . . . be a part of society. And when I talk of behaviour modification, I'm talking, generally speaking, of giving people access to the same tools that the rest of us not only had access to, but we took advantage of when we were growing up . . . and a lot of these people did not accept them. They accepted an alternate lifestyle that was either stealing or hurting people and they disregarded some of the social evolutionary processes that the majority of people took. . . . If you decide you don't want to [be violent] then we're going to give you an opportunity to go through an evolution, to go through a learning process to give yourself some skills that will give you alternatives to violence . . . and if you want to call it "brainwashing" that's okay. (Quoted in Shalev 2009, 55)

But if Griffin is right in thinking that it is precisely as a person who desires freedom *and* social relations that the prisoner is exploited in programs such as Asklepieion—if it is true that freedom becomes meaningful *in the context* of a social community rather than in opposition to it—then we need a different account of individuation and relationality to make sense of the violence and harm of behavior modification programs in U.S. prisons. In chapter 5, I look to Merleau-Ponty's critique of behaviorism and his development of a critical phenomenological account of behavior in order to develop an alternative philosophical and political discourse on Cold War behavior modification research and its application in U.S. prisons.

5 LIVING RELATIONALITY

Merleau-Ponty's Critical Phenomenological
Account of Behavior

COLD WAR RESEARCH on thought reform and behavior modification provided a scientific foundation and an intellectual justification for a set of practices ranging from the coercive interrogation of enemies of the state, to coercive "therapy" for domestic prisoners, and even to voluntary forms of therapy and self-improvement based on similar principles. These researchers shared a set of basic assumptions and methods that have not altogether disappeared neither from contemporary behaviorist psychology nor from domestic prisons. In this chapter, I develop an alternative to the behaviorist model by drawing on Merleau-Ponty's phenomenological account of behavior. My aim is threefold: (1) to expose the insufficiency of behaviorist discourse, even for explaining the results of its own research; (2) to show that a critical phenomenological account of behavior provides a better framework for understanding behaviorist research; and (3) to argue that this phenomenological account of behavior has ethical and political implications such that we cannot recognize its epistemological significance without also condemning the violence both of sensory deprivation and solitary confinement and of their application in domestic prisons and global detention centers.

The foundational claim of behaviorism is that, in order to develop a properly scientific account of psychological phenomena, researchers must restrict themselves to the observation of an organism's objective behavior without introducing stories about what might be going on inside its "mind" or "consciousness" (Pavlov 2003, 6). This approach could not be more different from the method of phenomenology. While classical phenomenology suspends the naturalistic assumption that the objective world has an independent existence outside of consciousness in order to study the structures of intentionality that give rise to a meaningful *sense* of the world, classical behaviorism takes the opposite approach: it brackets out subjectivity in order to track the correspondence of stimulus and response in objectively observed behavior. For a behaviorist psychologist, it makes no sense to take the perspective of the experimental subject into account; we have no direct access to the perspective of other organisms, and even our own apparent access to first-person consciousness is unreliable as a source of scientific knowledge. The experimental subject must be approached in objective terms as an organism whose behavior is determined by the interaction of its physical structure (which in turn is determined by its evolutionary history) and its environment. Similar forms of stimulus give rise to similar reactions, forming patterns of behavior that may be conditioned through the repetition of positive and negative reinforcement, or reward and punishment. The human subject, just like the rat or the dog, can be trained to salivate in response to a bell, or (in the fantasy of one behavior modification enthusiast) training can "make a bank robber want to vomit every time he saw a bank" (quoted in Opton 1974, 617).

Behaviorists reject the notion that there is something special about human beings that allows us to resist the pressures of our environment or break with the imperatives of survival and adaptation. As Kurt Bayertz explains:

> Human subjectivity does not exist—and this is the true kernel of Skinner's theory—beyond Nature, but is part of it and resides within it. By making physical nature an object, the human being also makes its subjectivity an object—and thus a part of Nature. The strict difference between subjectivity and Nature, which forms the basis for the concept of human dignity, disappears. (1996, 86; quoted in Venter 2004, 537)

The staunch antihumanism of the behaviorist position leads many of its critics to assert the primacy of free will and the inviolable character of a uniquely human dignity.[1] But both behaviorists and their humanist critics leave important questions unaddressed: What is the *meaning* of behavior? What does it mean to exist as a creature who displays certain patterned forms of activity and response within a concrete situation or environment, but who is also capable of deviating from these patterns in more or less radical ways? How does the possibility of having a *perspective* on one's situation affect that situation?

These are questions that Merleau-Ponty takes up in his early work

The Structure of Behavior (1942), as well as in other texts such as
Phenomenology of Perception (1962) and *Nature: Course Notes from
the Collège de France* (1956–60; first published 1995). In what follows,
I present Merleau-Ponty's critique of classical behaviorism and his development of a critical phenomenological account of behavior as the
site of a meaningful, prereflective comportment toward the world. This
alternative account of behavior raises a new set of questions about the
Cold War research on thought reform and behavior modification: Why
would prolonged social and sensory isolation give rise to "an intense
love of any living thing"? What is the relation between social deprivation and sensory deprivation, and to what degree can we separate their
perceptual and psychological effects? Why does sensory deprivation
give rise to hallucinations and perceptual distortions similar to the
effects of psychotropic drugs or even brain damage? What does this
tell us about the relation between the physical and the psychical more
generally? Without addressing the meaning—or meaninglessness—of
the experimental subject's experience, we cannot even begin to understand the epistemological, ethical, and even ontological significance of
solitary confinement and sensory deprivation.

A Critical Phenomenological Approach to Behavior

In *The Structure of Behavior,* Merleau-Ponty challenges the behaviorist account of experience as a causal relation between stimulus and
response, arguing that this account fails to explain behavior as it actually unfolds because it excludes in advance the perspective of the living
organism. In an effort to achieve clear, objective, repeatable results,
the behaviorist observes an organism from the outside, "decomposing"
its behavior into simple, elementary parts and then linking these parts
together in a linear temporal sequence or a logical relation of causality
(2008, 11, 75; see also Pavlov 2003, 9–10). From this perspective, the
organism appears like a machine whose parts are externally attached
rather than intrinsically interrelated (Merleau-Ponty 2008, 11, 75). The
environment, in turn, appears as both a container for the organism
and an external source of inputs; the environment exerts an impact
on the organism while remaining separate from it, just as a billiard
table remains separate from the game that is played upon it.[2] For every
input or stimulus, there is a more or less predictable range of outputs
or behavior (Pavlov 2003, 7–8). Behaviorists situate the organism and

the environment on the same ontological plane (although they would not put it this way). From this perspective, there is no reason to think that there is something ontologically distinctive about the stimulus of another human being's vocalizations such that we would be justified or compelled to treat them as fundamentally different from, say, the acoustic stimulus of a jackhammer or a birdsong.

By isolating the objective components of behavior and situating each of these components on the same ontological plane, behaviorists are able to analyze, predict, and even condition the behavior of their experimental subjects. But can the behaviorist paradigm explain the *meaning* of its own results? Can it further explain the occasional unpredictability or resistance of some experimental subjects to conditioning? Merleau-Ponty argues that, by reducing the complex interrelations within the organism as a whole, along with its distinctive comportment toward the environment or situation, behaviorists distort the way behavior actually unfolds for most living beings. They may achieve consistent results within the lab and other highly controlled environments such as prisons or detention camps, but they risk conflating the highly artificial situation of the lab with behavior as such, and even within the lab, they miss the significance of their own results.[3]

Consider, for example, a monkey who is put in an experimental situation where she has to press a lever in order to gain access to food that is visible but out of reach. The behaviorist interprets the monkey's behavior in terms of a linear sequence of events, each of which is causally related to the next. The monkey sees the food, which produces the reflex mechanism of salivation; in response to this mechanism, she reaches for the food; she is thwarted by the barrier and tries to remove it; through a process of trial and error, she eventually presses the lever and gains access to the food (a "positive reaction"). Over time, this positive reaction is repeated and reinforced; eventually, the monkey is conditioned to associate the action of pressing the lever with access to food. She may even begin to salivate when she sees a similar lever, whether or not food is present. Each of these components could be broken down further, into even simpler physiological processes; for example, light diffracted from the food stimulates the monkey's optic nerve, this stimulus is transferred to the visual cortex, the information is processed, and so on. Such an analysis could be perfectly correct and exhaustively detailed, and yet it would still miss something: the form or gestalt of behavior as a whole, and the *meaning* that this form generates for the subject of experience. For Merleau-Ponty, this meaning is not merely something that the observer attributes to the monkey (with or without justification); it is not added on to the monkey's behavior from the outside; rather, it emerges from within her response to the situation as a whole, organizing both the structure of her behavior and the meaning of her environing world.

Take, for example, the monkey's perception of the food *as* food and as something that is both desirable and out of reach. This act of perception involves the stimulation of nerves and the processing of visual information; the phenomenologist would not deny these facts. But there is nothing in the physical properties of light or the physiological processes of nerve excitation that conveys the *meaning* of food as food. Following Husserl, Merleau-Ponty argues that "perception is not an event of nature" (2008, 145). It is not just a physical process set into motion by the stimulus of light or pressure; if it were, then photographic paper could be said to "perceive" images in the same sense that monkeys or people do. What is at stake in perception, beyond the physical processes involved, is the grasping of a meaning: the orientation of intentional consciousness toward noemata and toward the ideas or essences that they express.[4] Merleau-Ponty emphasizes the embodied character of consciousness to a greater degree than does Husserl, and he further departs from him in supplementing Husserl's eidetic analysis of meaning with a broader analysis of form or structure inspired by Gestalt psychology.[5]

While behaviorism analyzes behavior by breaking it into discrete parts, Gestalt psychology seeks to grasp the form of behavior as a whole: the patterned web of relationships that constitute behavior-in-a-situation (Merleau-Ponty 2008, 22–28). It is in relation to this total situation that both "the organism" and "the environment" emerge as meaningful, and meaningfully distinct, terms. For Gestalt theory, these relata do not preexist their relations; they are not separate entities that are then joined together externally. Rather, perception and other forms of behavior are "total processes whose properties are not the sum of those which the isolated parts would possess" (47).[6] I do not just perceive red patches or sonorous vibrations; I perceive pomegranates and marching bands, and I perceive them as delicious, annoying, inspiring, and so forth. Different species typically display different levels of form and meaning in their perceptual and expressive behavior (104–24). But even a simple sunfish perceives meaningful differences between food and nonfood in its environing world.[7] For Merleau-Ponty, the profound insight of Gestalt theory, and its relevance for a critical appropriation of Husserl's more idealist approach to phenomenology, is the concept of *structure*: "the joining of an idea and an experience which are indiscernible, the contingent arrangement by which materials begin to have meaning in our presence, intelligibility in the nascent state" (206). This concept of structure allows Merleau-Ponty to develop a phenomenological account of behavior rather than simply opposing phenomenology as a transcendental science to behavioral psychology as an empirical science.

Merleau-Ponty does not reject the behaviorist premise that an organism is affected by its environment, but he does offer a critical rejoinder to mechanistic accounts of this effect in terms of linear causality:

> The organism cannot properly be compared to a keyboard on which the external stimuli would play and in which their proper form would be delineated for the simple reason that the organism contributes to the constitution of that form. . . . All the stimulations which the organism receives have in turn been possible only by its preceding movements which have culminated in exposing the receptor organ to external influences. . . . Thus the form of the excitant is created by the organism itself, by its proper manner of offering itself to actions from the outside. Doubtless, in order to be able to subsist, it must encounter a certain number of physical and chemical agents in its surroundings. But it is the organism itself—according to the proper nature of its receptors, the thresholds of its nerve centers and the movement of the organs—which chooses the stimuli in the physical world to which it will be sensitive. . . . This would be like a keyboard which moves itself in such a way as to offer—and according to variable rhythms—such or such of its keys to the (in itself monotonous) action of an external hammer. (2008, 13)[8]

For Merleau-Ponty, even the most mechanistic aspects of animal life, such as the reaction of nerve receptors to stimuli, are distinguished from the operations of a machine by the *perspective* that an animal has on its own reactions. This animal need not be capable of self-reflection in order to have a perspective of its own; it need not be recognizable as the multileveled consciousness that Husserl describes in such meticulous detail. For Merleau-Ponty, even a medusa or a tick has a perspective, or a minimal degree of interest in its own survival, that distinguishes it from a nonliving machine. As such, the animal is open to (even a minimal degree of) possibility; it "offers" itself to some forms of stimulus more than to others, depending on the structure of its behavior. This self-offering is different from a conscious choice to focus on this rather than that; it happens at the prereflective level of comportment, which is informed by both the structure of its body and the pattern of its own personal history.

In Merleau-Ponty's account, the animal does not merely convert environmental inputs into behavioral outputs; rather, it shapes the meaning of its situation by foregrounding certain features of its environment and consigning others to a more diffuse, general background. In so doing, the animal remains embedded in a particular environment with certain material and structural configurations—it does not "choose" its own world in a *real* sense—but it nevertheless opens up a *virtual* dimension within the material world through its comportment toward form and toward the meaning and possibilities that are supported by this form. This is how organisms—even relatively simple organisms like sunfish or ticks—create a meaningful experience of their environment, to the point of constituting that environment as an *Umwelt*, or "surrounding-world," rather than a mere container for survival.

In his *Nature: Course Notes from the Collège de France (1956–60)*, Merleau-Ponty invokes Jakob von Uexküll's concept of Umwelt as "the difference between the world such as it exists in itself and the world of a living being" (Merleau-Ponty 2003b, 167). An Umwelt is neither purely objective nor purely subjective; it is neither the sum of its material parts nor the projection of a consciousness that remains aloof from its surroundings. As a living being, I am not only stimulated by the environment and contained within it; I am also "witness to my *Umwelt*" (216). Merleau-Ponty writes:

> Between the situation and the movement of the animal, there is a relation of meaning which is what the expression *Umwelt* conveys. The *Umwelt* is the world implied by the movement of the animal, and that regulates the animal's movements by its own structure. (175)

This movement need not be grasped in the reflective awareness of a consciousness in order to be meaningful for the animal who comports itself toward it. Rather, an Umwelt is "the aspect of the world in itself to which the animal addresses itself, which exists for the behavior of the animal, but not necessarily for its consciousness" (167). On this view, consciousness is not opposed to behavior or hidden behind it; rather, it emerges as an elaborated "variant" of behavior. We need not posit consciousness as a separate substance located at a mysterious point within the body or outside of it in order to acknowledge the irreducibility of consciousness to a real material process within a naturalistic causal network. Indeed, for Merleau-Ponty reading von Uexküll alongside Raymond Ruyer, E. S. Russell, and others, there is no consciousness apart from behavior, no actor behind the act; behavior goes all the way down to the level of organs and all the way up to the level of human consciousness (167–99).

This understanding of the environment as an Umwelt helps explain why the organism can be compared neither to a keyboard that is "played" by external stimuli nor to a player piano that comes already programmed with its own songbook. If anything, the animal is like a keyboard that attunes itself more readily to certain melodies and rhythms than to others; but ultimately, even this metaphor is insufficient.[9] Rather than forcing the image of the keyboard beyond its signifying capacity, Merleau-Ponty distills what is most essential about it: the possibility of playing a melody. A melody has a recognizable structure that is nevertheless open to modification and improvisation. It can be played in different keys, on different instruments, with different rhythms and variations. A melody is a *form* in the sense articulated by Gestalt psychology: the whole expresses more than the sum of its parts:

> While the notes taken separately have an equivocal signification, being capable of entering into an infinity of possible ensembles, in the melody each one is demanded by the context and contributes its part in expressing something which is not contained in any one of them and which binds them together internally. (2008, 87)

The first note of a melody already implies a certain range of possibilities for resolving the melody in its final notes, but it does not determine the path toward this resolution (2003b, 174).[10] It is just as true to say that the last note of a melody implies its first note, or that the first implies the last. While a melody has a certain linear progression, its structure cannot be reduced to the successive sequence of particular notes; if this were the case, the melody would lose its openness to transposition. Rather, a melody "unfurls" in harmony with its structure, just as an Umwelt unfurls through the attunement of a living, moving animal to its particular environs (2003a, 144 and 173).[11] Both in *The Structure of Behavior* and in the Nature lectures, Merleau-Ponty cites von Uexküll's comparison between the behavior of an animal and a melody that sings itself.[12] The animal is both the singer and the song;

it has its own singular perspective, and also a more or less complex gestalt that both guides its performance and remains open to continuous modification and transposition.

This shift from a causal model of behavior to a melodic one has significant implications for the way we understand the temporality of behavior. For Merleau-Ponty, the difference between past, present, and future is not linear or cumulative; it cannot be measured in terms of different locations in a causal chain of events. Rather, the future emerges from within the dynamic of the present, which itself implies both a reference to the past and an elaboration of it:

> Behavior is neither a simple architectural effect nor a sheath of functions; it is something that is ahead of functioning, which carries a reference to the future, which is beyond the immediate possibles and cannot immediately realize all that it already sketches out. (2003b, 151; see also 152)

This "reference to the future" is already implicit in the animal's comportment toward the virtual dimensions of its situation: its form and its meaning. It is neither contained within the present like a predetermined reality to be unpacked when the conditions are ripe, nor completely unrelated to the patterns or tendencies that emerge in the present. Rather, the future unfurls from the present, just like the creaturely melody whose open structure unfurls as behavior-in-a-situation: both from first note to last, and from last note to first.[13] It is the instability, indeterminacy, or imbalance of any given moment that keeps it open to both past and future possibilities:

> The future of the organism is not folded back in potential in the beginning of its organic life, as in a nutshell in its beginning. . . . Each present moment is supported by a future larger than any future. To consider the organism in a given minute, we observe that there is the future in every present, because its present is in a state of imbalance. (2003b, 155)

This approach to the temporality of behavior allows Merleau-Ponty to develop a more complex logic of *conditionality* as an alternative to both the behaviorist logic of causality and the antibehaviorist commitment to an unencumbered, decontextualized (and specifically human) free will. For Merleau-Ponty, even a flatworm has possibilities that are both structured and indeterminate:

> We must not figure that in each point of the flatworm there would be a hidden head that would pass through the nose with each incision; we must not

conceive these potentialities as acts, in a nutshell. It is probably thus that the organism is not what it actually is under the eyes of the observer. If the organism were reduced to its actual being, such a proliferation would be impossible. We must thus say that flatworms would manifest if . . . they thus have a conditional existence. (2003b, 182–83; see also 213, 238)

In sum, "The animal is not a machine" (2003b, 149; see also 158–66). The animal is not "programmed" or "hard-wired" to behave a certain way by virtue of its genetic constitution or its environment, nor does it remain indifferent to these aspects of its embodied, relational existence. Rather, the animal elaborates its own melodic line in conversation with the given situation, but it also offers itself in a more or less distinctive way to this situation. The crucial difference between a machine and a living being is that the latter has its own perspective on the world and therefore its own *relation* to the world as an Umwelt.[14] It is a subject of behavior, and not just an instance of it:

The machine functions, the animal lives—that is, it restructures its world and its body. The function of the machine has a meaning, but this meaning is transcendent; it is in the mind of the constructor, whereas in the apparatus there is only the trace of meaning. (162)

For Merleau-Ponty, the living subject of behavior is a being for whom the world exists and to whom it *matters*. This subject may or may not have a reflective awareness of this perspective on the world; there are different levels of awareness and meta-awareness. But the living being's power to elaborate, improvise, operate, and even "invent" itself is rooted in this capacity to express, through its own simple or complex behavior, its orientation toward something meaningful. Merleau-Ponty quotes von Uexküll:

Each subject weaves its relations like the threads of a spider web weave relations concerning things of the exterior world, and constructs with all its threads a solid network that carries existence. (Quoted in 2003b, 176)

From Merleau-Ponty's critical phenomenological perspective, behavior is not the mechanistic correlation of inputs and outputs, stimulus and reflex, but, rather, a dynamic interweaving and unfurling in which the organism both makes itself and is carried along by impersonal processes, patterns, and relations of which it is not the origin or starting point. This approach to behavior not only shifts the framework of analysis from "parts" to the whole but also transforms the theoretical vocabulary of classical behaviorism. We can still speak of nerves and their stimuli, but these concepts have a different meaning and play a different role in the analysis of behavior. For example, nerves are not the means by which the brain manipulates the rest of the body, nor are they "a container in which the instruments of such and such reactions were deposited, but [rather] the theater where a qualitatively variable process unfolds" (Merleau-Ponty 2008, 69). The body is not merely an input–output mechanism but rather a site of perception and expression, an "open totality" or gestalt: "an intersensorial system of equivalences that functions as a whole" (2003b, 218, 217). A chiasmatic relation emerges between behavior, as the comportment of the body toward a meaningful material context, and the body, as "a system of motor powers which crisscross in order to produce a behavior" (148). We could say, in the style of Gilles Deleuze, that behavior is the becoming-temporal of the body, while embodiment is the becoming-spatial of behavior. Or, in Merleau-Ponty's own words, "The body belongs to a dynamic of behavior. Behavior is sunk into corporeity" (183).

At the same time that the meaning of the organism and its behavior is transformed, so too is the meaning of the environment, now understood as an Umwelt toward which the animal comports itself. Stimuli are the "occasion rather than the cause" of behavior (2008, 31).[15] They "do not come to the sensory surface and . . . pull the strings which command the muscles. . . . There are no strings" (32). Rather, stimulation opens up a virtual range of indeterminate but nevertheless structured possibilities for response. These possibilities depend not only on the material configuration of the situation and the physiological structure of the organism but also on the way this particular organism comports itself toward this particular environment. For Merleau-Ponty,

> The stimulus often acts much less by its elementary properties than by its spatial arrangement, its rhythm, and the rhythm of its intensities. More generally, it happens very frequently that the effect of a complex stimulus is not foreseeable on the basis of the elements which compose it. (10)

In other words, patterns of behavior are not just formed through the constant conjunction of otherwise unrelated stimulus and response, or cause and effect; rather, what distinguishes the behavior of a living organism from the behavior of nonliving matter is the presence of a form or gestalt that structures behavior from the beginning: an open-ended pattern that shapes but does not determine how a certain kind of organism orients itself toward a certain situation.

Reinterpreting Behaviorist Research

How would this critical phenomenological account of behavior change the way we interpret the results of behaviorist experimentation? Recall the example of the monkey with which I began. What behaviorist accounts overlook is the role that the monkey herself plays in organizing the experimental situation in a meaningful way, in relation to a goal that motivates her and against the background of a whole network of intentional relations. In a phenomenological interpretation of behavior, the monkey is not just stimulated to act by the real presence of food; rather, she *perceives* the food as something desirable and as something that is not (yet) accessible. Part of what it means to perceive something in this way is to comport oneself toward a range of possibilities that exist not in the food itself or in the mechanism of cage and lever but in the situation as a whole, as it appears to a living being with its own perspective on the situation. This perspective is shaped both by the animal's own personal history and by the appetites, structures, and capacities that are typical for her species. But it also shapes the way this particular kind of animal, and even this particular monkey with her own experience, "offers" herself to stimulus. The food behind the barrier *matters* to the monkey; it matters enough to motivate her to find a solution to the problem of gaining access to the food. This relation of mattering opens a temporal arc through which the future of success or failure arises from within the structure of the present, in relation to habits and capacities that have developed over a personal and evolutionary past.

We need not attribute to the monkey an ineffable mental substance in order to support this claim; we need only observe and describe the monkey's behavior as a whole, without decomposing it into separate parts. When we consider the monkey as a subject of experience rather than an aggregate of reflex mechanisms, then we notice that, while all sorts of incidental gestures may accompany the first successful act of pressing the lever, these incidental gestures are not repeated in subsequent repetitions of the act. Rather, the monkey singles out the one *essential* gesture that will accomplish her goal. This suggests that her solution to the problem does not emerge through a random series of trial and error that is eventually narrowed down through repetition and conditioning. Rather, the monkey *learns* the relation between pressing the lever and gaining access to food; in the future, when she encounters different situations with the same basic form, she will know just what to do, not because she has been reprogrammed but because she has caught onto the meaning or "melody" of a solution.[16] Drawing on capacities that have developed in response to particular situations (for example, the lab rather than the rainforest), she improvises a solution to the problem. As long as the melody works, she will probably continue to sing it, but if it slips out of harmony with her situation, she may try changing her tune, or she may get stuck on the same old tune, to the point of developing pathological habits that are amplified rather than corrected by the frustrating experience of dissonance.

In any case, the monkey solves the problem, to the extent that she does, not just because she is a food-loving organism stimulated by the real presence of food but also because (*as* a food-loving organism, situated in *this* particular relation to something that is meaningfully apprehended as inaccessible food) she has been looking for a solution from the moment she perceived the problem as such. Our experimental subject is not like the fabled monkey whose random tapping on a typewriter accidentally produces the works of Shakespeare, without ever understanding its meaning. Rather, she has been guided from the beginning by the meaningful goal of gaining access to the food in this particular (and peculiar) situation.

For Merleau-Ponty, learning is different from training or conditioning; it is not simply the development of a consistent reaction in the organism to a certain stimulus from the environment; rather, it is an initiation into meaning. That meaning need not be formulated explicitly in order to be understood; we learn how to dance by dancing, for example, and the dancers "understand" the difference between a waltz and a foxtrot bodily, whether or not they can give a discursive account of the difference. To learn is to "build up aptitudes, that is, a general power of responding to situations of a certain type by means of varied reactions which have nothing in common but the meaning" (2008, 130). Once something has been learned, that meaning can be transposed into different but similar situations, like a melody that is played on different instruments, in different keys, and even with different rhythms without losing its melodic form.

In this sense, learning is "not a *real* operation"—it does not involve a change in the material components of a situation—but, rather, a *virtual* operation, a transformation of the *sense* of the world through the reorientation of living, learning subjects toward the relationships that structure their situation (Merleau-Ponty 2008, 99). Learning is a matter of "creating relations among possible 'solutions' and, on the other hand, among all of them and the 'problem,' by which their *value* is measured" (101). The monkey, no less than the human being, has access to this virtual dimension of value; it is precisely the value of gaining access to the food, and the problem of being separated from it, that has guided her prospective orientation toward finding a solution. This orientation is both toward the food itself, understood as a real entity with real, empirical properties, and also—precisely as something that is *understood* to be real—toward the *possibility* of gaining access to it (125). By limiting themselves to what is objectively observable, behaviorists miss the sense in which both the monkey and the observer are comporting themselves toward the situation in a certain way, with certain ends that structure their behavior in advance, but in an open-ended way, in light of particular problems to be solved by particular subjects oriented in particular ways toward overlapping situations.

Even in order to understand behavior as a set of objective correlations between stimuli and responses, observers must comport themselves toward the situation in a particular way, looking for certain kinds of patterns or clues, foregrounding some details and consigning others to the background—in short, organizing the "data" of sensation in relation to certain meaningful possibilities. This is not to say that the organism simply projects a meaning onto the situation, without regard for its material configuration. The subject of behavior is not a pure, disembodied consciousness with the power to decide the meaning of the world single-handedly; if it were such a subject, it would have no reason to *behave* in response to its situation. Rather, the behavior of an embodied, embedded subject involves "an inextricable intersecting of 'horizontal' and 'vertical' localizations—without the body being anywhere pure thing, *but also without it being anywhere pure idea*" (207).

Merleau-Ponty criticizes behaviorism for presupposing this complex web of intentional relations between the experimental subject and its Umwelt, while claiming to bracket out any references to subjectivity. He argues that the pretense of pure objectivity produces a conceptual incoherence for behaviorist theory:

> Behaviorism made its task easy by supposing, in our example, that the lever
> which regulates the door [of the cage that blocks access to food] can become
> the conditioned stimulus, not only of reflexes of prehension and mastication
> which take place in the presence of the goal, but also of the manipulations
> which have *preceded* the opening of the door. (2008, 95)

Behaviorism wants to study how the monkey is "conditioned" to press
the lever in order to get food. But to the extent that it restricts itself
to an objective report of each successive component of behavior as it
unfolds in linear time, from the perspective of the observer, it remains
unable to explain the shift from the monkey's blind fumbling toward
food, which appears to be stimulated by the real, physical presence
of food, to the conditioned reflex, which appears to be stimulated by
the real, physical presence of the lever. Before the accidental success
of pressing the lever for the first time, the lever would seem to play no
role in the linear chain of cause and effect that constitutes the monkey's
behavior. But at some point after this first success, and through the
continued positive reinforcement of repeated successful trials, the lever
becomes a relevant stimulus for the monkey—arguably, the *most* relevant stimulus, to the point where the mere presence of a lever, with or
without food, may cause the monkey to salivate. How can we account
for this change of stimulus if we remain at the level of the real? The
lever has no less real, physical presence before the monkey's conditioning than after. Why, then, does it function as a cause in the postsuccess
trials, but not in the presuccess trials? Exactly the same series of gestures may be produced by the stimulus of the food or the stimulus of the
lever. How can the observer tell whether it is the food or the lever that
is causing this behavior? As long as behaviorism excludes the perspective of the monkey from its analysis, along with the meaning that the
monkey's comportment brings to the total situation of the experiment,
it will be forced to treat the lever as both an "effect" of behavior caused
by the food and as "the cause of its cause" (96). But this is incoherent,
even in behaviorist terms:

> But if learning is really only a particular case of physical causality, it is dif-
> ficult to see how the order of temporal passage would reverse itself, how the
> effect could become the cause of its cause. For the "perception" of the lever or
> the goal to bring back the useful manipulations, it is not sufficient for them
> to have preceded it in objective time. . . . [What remains to be understood
> is] the relation which is established between the goal and the preparatory

actions, giving a meaning to the multiplicity of elementary movements which the latter combine and making of them an act in the proper sense of the word, a new creation after which the behavioral history is qualitatively modified. (96)

Behaviorism's claim to *objectivity* rests on a neutral observation of a linear series of stimuli and responses in an organism's behavior. But its claim to *predictive* power depends upon the identification of a pattern in this linear series and upon the interpretation of this pattern in terms of causal relations. If behaviorism is to have anything to offer prison wardens seeking new, experimental ways of "treating" prisoners, then it needs to find some way of converting its objective observation of *correlations* between stimulus and response into a causal narrative in which certain stimuli *produce* certain responses. But this is precisely where the incoherence lies. A tension emerges in behaviorism between the actual succession of events in time and the logical connection of causality.[17] The result is a theory that, in spite of its appeal to scientificity, lacks the means to explain its own results without importing unacknowledged assumptions to which it is not entitled by its own objective criteria.

By taking into account the prospective comportment of the monkey toward the virtual dimension opened up by her situation, or toward the possible futures immanent in her present Umwelt, we can explain much more clearly and coherently how an effect can become a cause, how a lever that was once irrelevant and perhaps even unnoticed can become a salient feature, and how the discovery of this lever may retrospectively shape the meaning of the monkey's past, present, and future behavior. Merleau-Ponty's focus on the animal as neither an input–output mechanism nor a pure consciousness but a living being that comports itself toward the surrounding world in a meaningful way allows for a more coherent—and ultimately, a more scientifically sound—account of behavior.

Behaviorism and the Production of Pathology

Not only are there inherent theoretical problems with classical behaviorism, but even where it is able to achieve consistent, repeatable results, the highly contrived nature of the laboratory situation imposes a strict limit on the explanatory capacity of behaviorism in complex situations outside the lab.[18] As a result, the behaviorist model may prove more useful for understanding—or even for *producing*—pathological behavior than for understanding the way behavior unfolds for the most part for most living organisms.

In his 1927 book *Conditioned Reflexes,* Ivan Pavlov describes an experiment, whose results he was unable to explain except by proposing a (counterintuitive) "freedom reflex." I quote this passage in full to convey Pavlov's own sense of both the problem and the apparent solution:

In the course of the researches which I shall presently explain, we were completely at a loss on one occasion to find any cause for the peculiar behavior of an animal. It was evidently a very tractable dog, which soon became very friendly with us. We started off with a very simple experiment. The dog was placed in a stand with loose loops round its legs, but so as to be quite comfortable and free to move a pace or two. Nothing more was done except to present the animal repeatedly with food at intervals of some minutes. It stood quietly enough at first, and ate quite readily, but as time went on it became excited and struggled to get out of the stand, scratching at the floor, gnawing the supports, and so on. This ceaseless muscular exertion was accompanied by breathlessness and continuous salivation, which persisted at every experiment during several weeks, the animal getting worse and worse until it was no longer fitted for our researches. For a long time we remained puzzled over the unusual behavior of this animal. We tried out experimentally numerous possible interpretations, but though we had had long experience with a great number of dogs in our laboratories we could not work out a satisfactory solution of this strange behavior, until it occurred to us at last that it might be the expression of a special *freedom reflex,* and that the dog simply could not remain quiet when it was constrained in the stand. This reflex was overcome by setting off another against it—the reflex for food. We began to give the dog the whole of its food in the stand. At first the animal ate but little, and lost considerably in weight, but gradually it got to eat more, until at last the whole ration was consumed. At the same time the animal grew quieter during the course of the experiments: the freedom reflex was being inhibited. It is clear that the freedom reflex is one of the most important reflexes, or, if we use a more general term, reactions, of living beings. This reflex has even yet to find its final recognition. In James's writings it is not even enumerated among the special human "instincts." But it is clear that if the animal were not provided with a reflex of protest against boundaries set to its freedom, the smallest obstacle in its path would interfere with the proper fulfillment of its natural functions. Some animals as we all know have this freedom reflex to such a degree that when placed

in captivity they refuse all food, sicken and die. (Pavlov 2003, 11–12; see also
Merleau-Ponty 2008, 123)

Pavlov explains the strange phenomenon of the "freedom reflex"
in terms of its apparent utility for survival: if an organism had not
evolved some sort of mechanism for "protest[ing] against boundaries
set to its freedom," it might curl up and die as soon as it found itself
backed into a corner or caught in a thicket. But this does not explain
why the same freedom reflex would cause some animals to protest
their captivity by struggling and seeking to escape, whereas others
protest by refusing food to the point of death. Nor does it explain why
the same friendly, tractable dog would first launch one form of protest,
then the other, and finally capitulate by accepting food and becoming
docile.

Rather than interpreting these responses as evidence of a freedom
reflex, Merleau-Ponty argues that "the word 'reflex' has no meaning
if it does not designate a specific reaction to certain determined exci-
tants: the reaction in question, however, is an indeterminate refusal to
respond to stimuli" (2008, 123). This indeterminate refusal to respond
suggests a different sense of freedom, not as a reflex hardwired into
the organism and counteracted by the reflex for food, but as a fragile
capacity to escape: to withdraw from stimulus, to tune out an intolerable situation, to sleep, or even to take flight into illness or neurosis.
An organism's capacity to escape or withdraw, even from a situation
where its basic needs are being met, is crucial for its ability to maintain
a meaningful relation to its situation.[19] We could explain this capacity
to withdraw as evidence of the organism's need to regulate the quanti-
tative balance of inputs and outputs; when the environmental stimulus
outweighs the opportunities for reacting to this stimulus, the organism
enters into a new sequence of behavior, seeking either to change its environment, to become insensible to it, or both. But to the extent that we
interpret this capacity in mechanistic terms, we miss both the *meaning*
of the animal's struggle against the constriction of its open, dynamic
relationship with the world, and also the *meaninglessness* with which
such constriction threatens the animal.

Merleau-Ponty acknowledges the possibility of a meaningless experience of the world—not as the default setting of a mechanistic organism, but as a pathological response to the disintegration or collapse of
a meaningful relation to the world:

> Our body does not always have meaning, and our thoughts, on the other
> hand—in timidity for example—do not always find in it the plenitude of
> their vital expression. In these cases of disintegration [such as illness], the
> soul and the body are apparently distinct; and this is the truth of dualism.
> But the soul, if it possesses no means of expression—one should say rather,
> no means of actualizing itself—soon ceases to be *anything whatsoever* and
> in particular ceases to be the soul, as the thought of the aphasic weakens
> and becomes dissolved; the body which loses its meaning soon ceases to be
> a living body and falls back into the state of a physico-chemical mass; it
> arrives at non-meaning only by dying. (2008, 209)

For Merleau-Ponty, life is not just a struggle to survive; it is a struggle
to maintain a meaningful, integrated, and open-ended relation to one's
environment as a whole, including the other living beings with whom
one shares a common Umwelt. The form of this environment can disintegrate; the melody of behavior can cease to unfurl in a way that
supports one's meaningful experience of the world. When this happens,
the body may appear as a mechanism subject to the laws of physics and
chemistry rather than a living perspective shaped by flexible norms
of behavior.[20] In this sense, there is a certain truth to behaviorist re-
ductionism, just as there is a certain truth to mind–body dualism. But
these are distorted truths, arising in pain, illness, and other pathological situations, rather than the norm of animal behavior.

Behaviorism has a knack for producing such pathological situations and observing how animals react to them, in an effort to build
an objective, scientific account of behavior as such.[21] But if Merleau-
Ponty's critical phenomenological account of behavior is right, then
classical behaviorists do not merely observe the objective behavior of
their experimental subjects; they *produce* the machinelike, *partes-
extra-partes* organisms that they seek to describe and explain. They
produce these organisms by narrowing an animal's Umwelt to a cage,
a maze, or a sensory deprivation chamber and then recording the effects of this constriction on its behavior. What is problematic about
these experiments, beyond their evident cruelty and lack of respect for
animals as subjects of experience, is the assumption that by isolating
one part of an animal's experience of the world, be it vision or touch
or emotional attachment—one can learn how this part works and how
it fits together with other parts to form the mechanism as a whole.
For Merleau-Ponty, "only a disintegrated consciousness can be paral-
leled with physiological processes, that is, with a *partial* functioning of

the organism" (2008, 204, emphasis added). The results of behaviorist research may be repeatable and consistent within a certain range of statistical error, but these results confuse the part with the whole; in the end, they are better suited to describing the behavior of an isolated, pathological subject than that of a healthy animal living and moving in the world. If we want to understand the behavior of living beings as such, then we must avoid chopping them into parts with the confidence that we will eventually find a way to put the parts together again. We must acknowledge both the animal's perspective on the world and our own perspective on the animal, without assuming that these can ever coincide.

This is why Merleau-Ponty's critique of behaviorism is so important for understanding the violence of solitary confinement and sensory deprivation in the context of U.S. prisons. Not only does it provide a theoretical framework from which to critically respond to the particular assumptions of Cold War experiments in thought reform and behavior control, but it also makes evident the complicity of behaviorism's core assumptions with the violence of its experiments and its applications.

Returning to Life

Ultimately, the problem with Cold War behaviorism and the behavior modification programs it inspired is that they fail to understand the difference that life makes. In seeking to understand living beings in terms of the causal mechanisms that occur within them, behaviorism overlooks the distinctive surplus of life over any of its constituent parts. Even worse, it exploits this surplus, even while failing to acknowledge its existence.

Recall the KUBARK manual's observation that prolonged solitary confinement and sensory deprivation tended to produce, among other things, "an intense love of any other living thing." What must life be like for this exploitation of living, loving relationality to be possible? What must behaviorism be like to provide the conditions for its exploitation? In order to make a definitive break with behaviorist assumptions and methodologies, without abandoning the insight that behavior is a privileged site for psychological and philosophical research, we need to rethink the meaning of life from a critical phenomenological perspective.

In *The Structure of Behavior,* Merleau-Ponty writes:

> The phenomenon of life appeared . . . at the moment when a piece of exten-
> sion, by the disposition of its movements and by the allusion that each move-
> ment makes to all the others, turned back on itself and began to express
> something, to manifest an interior being externally. (2008, 162)

Life is inherently expressive—which is not to say that it necessarily
involves symbolic language; rather, a living being, from the amoeba
to the poetic genius, articulates both a relation to itself and a relation
to something other than itself, something that sustains and supports
its own life. In other words, life implies a certain *bearing* in relation
to the other, a comportment toward a world shared with others. This
comportment has an open-ended form or gestalt: it signifies beyond the
sum of an animal's particular actions, thanks to the patterned relations
or "allusions" that each gesture makes to the others. This relationality
is constitutive of the living being as such; it is the intimate–extimate
source of the surplus that defines life.

In the Nature lectures, Merleau-Ponty theorizes these relations in
terms of pivots or hinges around which possibilities emerge and become
articulated: "Phenomena of life turn around certain hinges. Themes
are again dimensions, the establishment of a certain field of gravity.
There are not only events, but events of a more or less great import"
(2003b, 183; see 207, 220).[22] The structures of living comportment are
not static like a geometrical grid but, rather, flexible and hinged and
therefore capable of articulating the relation of one dimension to another: the virtual and the actual, the visible and the invisible, meaning
and materiality. This hinge structure defines life as

> a singular point where another dimensionality appears. . . . It surges forth
> by investment in life—by opening of a depth, that is, as not existing for the
> rest of life, as a being-other, a relative nonbeing—relative, the only nonbeing
> that there is to consider, natural negativity. (224)

> Life has both a fragility and an obstinacy: it will be, if nothing opposes it. Not
> a hard nucleus of being, but the softness of the flesh. Dissociate our idea of
> Being from that of the thing: life is not a separable thing, but an investment, a
> singular point, a hollow in Being, an invariant ontological relief, a transverse
> rather than longitudinal causality telescoping the other. . . . [It involves] the
> establishment of a level around which the divergences begin forming, a kind
> of being that functions like a vault . . . refusal of all or nothing. (238)[23]

Merleau-Ponty rejects an account of life that would reduce its meaning to an instinct for survival. Against Darwinists who seek to explain

every aspect of life in terms of its utility for the individual or the species, Merleau-Ponty argues:

> Life is not only an organization for survival; there is in life a prodigious flourishing of forms, the utility of which is only rarely attested to and that sometimes even constitutes a danger for the animal. (2003b, 186; see also 184)

The problem with Darwinian thinking is that it "gives the actual world the power to determine the only possible" (175). For Merleau-Ponty, by contrast, the surplus of relational life engenders possibilities that remain irreducible to any present actuality. As we have seen, the living being's comportment toward the virtual dimensions of its total situation, even in highly constrained contexts, engenders a meaningful reference to a future, a contingency and a range of possibilities that are not all mapped out in advance, but rather unfurl within a total ensemble of relations. The living perspective of the animal is the organizing principle of this comportment-in-an-Umwelt, but it is not the "origin" in the sense of single-handedly projecting the meaning of the world.

Human animals are no less relational than the nonhuman animals that have been our main focus in this chapter. In both *The Structure of Behavior* and the Nature lectures, Merleau-Ponty situates humans in a nonreductive continuity with other living beings. On the one hand, "humanity [is] nothing other than a species of animal" (2008, 162), but on the other hand, "the word 'life' does not have the same meaning in animality and humanity; and the conditions of life are defined by the proper essence of the species" (174).[24] Humans, along with some other social animals, have access to a symbolic level of form that is closed to many other animals; but *every* living being has some access to form, and each level of form is nested in the others (104–24).

Throughout the Nature lectures, Merleau-Ponty emphasizes the relations, not only within animals or between animals and their environment but also *among* animals. He speaks of an "inter-animality" (2003b, 173, 189), "intercorporeity" (76), or "interbeing" (208) in relation to which each animal emerges as the unsharable center of a shared nexus, with its own singular perspective on a common world. Each living body opens toward the bodies of others, for good or for ill; even consciousness must be understood "as we grasp it across the bodies of others" (167). No body is a complete, self-enclosed unit unto itself:

Things as what are missing from my body in order to close its circuit.

But this is also an opening of my body to other bodies: just as I touch my hand touching, I perceive others as perceiving. The articulation of their body on the world is lived by me in the articulation of my body on the world where I see them.

This is reciprocal: my body is also made up of their corporeality. My corporeal schema is a normal means of knowing other bodies and these know my body. Universal-lateral of the co-perception of the world. (218)

What happens when an intercorporeal living being such as this is confined for a prolonged period of time to a small, enclosed space, isolated from other living beings and from an open-ended relation to the world? What are the ethical, political, and even ontological implications of such confinement?

6 BEYOND DEHUMANIZATION

A Posthumanist Critique of Intensive Confinement

If they only touch you when you're at the end of a chain,
then they can't see you as anything but a dog. Now I can't
see my face in the mirror. I've lost my skin. I can't feel my
mind.

> —Arizona State Prisoner interviewed by Colin Dayan,
> in "Legal Slaves and Civil Bodies"

Malebranche would not have beaten a stone as he beat his
dog, saying that the dog didn't suffer.

> —Merleau-Ponty, *Nature: Course Notes*

IN 1971, the Attica Liberation Faction demanded an end to the dehumanization of prisoners in its "Manifesto of Demands and Anti-Depression Platform":

> We, the inmates of Attica Prison, have grown to recognize beyond the shadow of a doubt, that because of our posture as prisoners and branded characters as alleged criminals, the administration and prison employees no longer consider or respect us as human beings, but rather as domesticated animals selected to do their bidding in slave labor and furnished as a personal whipping dog for their sadistic, psychopathic hate. . . .
>
> We are firm in our resolve and we demand, as human beings, the dignity and justice that is due to us by right of our birth. We do not know how the present system of brutality and dehumanization and injustices has been allowed to be perpetuated in this day of enlightenment, but we are the living proof of its existence and we cannot allow it to continue. (In James 2005, 303, 308)

Almost forty years later, in December 2010, thousands of inmates in Georgia state prisons joined together across racial and ethnic lines to engage in a nonviolent strike action to protest their own dehumanization. In their press release, the prisoners called upon the Georgia Department of Corrections to "stop treating them like animals and slaves and institute programs that address their basic human rights" (Dixon 2010).[1] Their demands were strikingly similar to the demands made by prisoners at Attica: a living wage, access to educational opportunities and vocational training, better food and living conditions, better health care, greater access to families and loved ones, and an end to cruel and unusual punishment.

Much has changed in the U.S. prison system since 1971: behavior modification programs have declined in response to prisoner litigation, the prison industrial complex grew rapidly in the 1980s and '90s, supermax prisons and private prison corporations have emerged, and, more recently, cash-strapped state governments are trying to downsize a prison population that is increasingly expensive to maintain (Davis 2003; Alexander 2011; Archibold 2010).[2] Countless legal cases have challenged the constitutionality of prison conditions and practices in light of the Eighth Amendment, which forbids cruel and unusual punishment (Dayan 2005; Reiter 2012a).Why, then, has so little changed in U.S. prisoners' demands in the forty years since the 1970s? And what accounts for the persistent comparison between prisoners, animals, and slaves, which the protesters both claim and critique?

This chapter examines both the rationale behind prisoners' demands for specifically *human* rights in their refusal of treatment as animals and slaves and also the practical and theoretical limits of humanist discourse for addressing the prisoners' demands in a meaningful way. I argue that the hierarchical opposition of humans to animals that humanist discourse presupposes ultimately works against prisoners, who share vital interests in common with nonhuman animals held in prolonged, intensive confinement in factory farms, laboratories, zoos, and other sites. While the demand for human rights makes sense in a prison system that is still haunted by slavery and its (partial) abolition, it is not clear that humanist values always support the well-being of prisoners. As we have seen, the commitment to more "humane" forms of punishment in the early penitentiary movement did not prevent it from inventing insidious forms of violence such as solitary confinement and perpetual surveillance. And the rhetoric of humanism helped justify this violence in the name of rehabilitation, even when skyrocketing rates of mental and physical illness among prisoners suggested that the goal of rehabilitation was not being reached.

To the extent that advocates of prison reform, abolition, or both accept the terms of humanist discourse uncritically, we risk underestimating the violence of a tradition that was capable of declaring that "all men are created equal" even while condemning women, slaves, freed people of color, and prison inmates to various forms of civil and social death. This is not just a conceptual problem; the practical, political goals of effective prison reform, abolition, or both are at stake here: decent work for decent pay, healthy meals, supportive relations with others, and freedom from physical and emotional abuse. While some of these goals may be specifically human, they are not exclusively so. If Merleau-Ponty's account of animal ontology has merit, then all living beings share an intercorporeal, interanimal way of being to some degree. From this perspective, the dignity of the living being depends not on recognition of mental capacities above and beyond the physical substrate of the body but, rather, on respect for the particular forms of intercorporeality that support each animal's well-being. There may be specifically human ways of being relational, as Merleau-Ponty himself acknowledges (2008, 160–84; 2003b, 221–29, 274–84), but this human specificity presupposes and remains interwoven with a whole network of relations shared with nonhuman animals.

In this chapter, I develop a posthumanist critique of intensive confinement, not just as a violation of human rights but as a violation of (human and nonhuman) animal ontology. By intensive confinement, I mean a range of practices including solitary confinement, small-group confinement, sensory deprivation and sensory overload: any form of isolation that is structured in a way that diminishes or undermines an open-ended relation to the world and to other living beings. As Cold War experiments in behavior modification suggest, the second and third waves of solitary confinement in the United States go well beyond what is usually understood by the term "solitary confinement"; they deploy a range of techniques for social and sensory isolation, sometimes deliberately, as at experimental prisons such as Marion Penitentiary or the Lexington High Security Unit for women, and sometimes incidentally, as in the hypercrowded prisons of California.[3] While I prefer the term "intensive confinement" to name these practices, I will switch back and forth between this term and "solitary confinement" in the remainder of this book, since the latter is more widely known and identifiable as an issue of public concern.

Although I acknowledge the strategic value of demanding respect for the human rights of prisoners, especially given the extent to which humanist discourse has structured the U.S. legal system, I argue that a humanist framework is ultimately inadequate to address the vital concerns of prisoners as living, relational beings. This relationality can be exploited in innumerable ways, both under the guise of retribution and under the guise of humane reform. But as I hope to show, there is also something *more* generated by the resistance of human and nonhuman animals to the conditions of their confinement: a meaningful relation to others and to the world that exceeds the terms of one's own capture. Ultimately, we need a political and ethical phenomenology of constitutive relationality to address the needs and desires of prisoners as *human animals,* and not as humans *rather than* animals. The reason why it is degrading to be treated like an animal is because we routinely treat animals in a degrading way in order to dominate and control them. But, as I will argue, human and nonhuman animals share vital interests, perhaps more now than ever, given the increasingly pervasive biopolitical management of human and nonhuman populations.

The chapter begins with a discussion of the prisoners' rights movement from the 1960s to the 1980s and the emergence of the supermax prison as a repressive reaction to prisoners' political and legal resistance. I focus in particular on *Madrid v. Gomez* (1995), in which Justice Thelton Henderson sought to protect the "human dignity" of prisoners at California's Pelican Bay supermax penitentiary but ended up reinscribing the violence of prolonged solitary confinement within law.[4] My critique of humanist legal discourse leads to a wider discussion of dehumanization and racialization in U.S. prisons from the days of the convict lease system to the present. I argue that many practices of dehumanization are better understood as a form of *de-animalization,* given the relational ontology of animal life developed by Merleau-Ponty. The striking resonance between the effects of intensive confinement on human and nonhuman animals in both the prison industrial complex and the animal industrial complex lends support to the claim that in order to support the dignity of prisoners as living, relational (human) beings, we must go beyond the humanist legal discourse that has promised so much and delivered so little.

Cruel but Not Unusual: The Use and Abuse of Humanism
from the Penitentiary to the Supermax

In the 1890 case *In re Medley,* U.S. Supreme Court Justice Samuel
Freeman Miller found the solitary confinement of a Colorado prisoner
to be in violation of the U.S. Constitution.[5] He described the effects
of prolonged solitude on inmates in prisons such as the Walnut Street
penitentiary in stark terms:

> A considerable number of the prisoners fell, after even a short confine-
> ment, into a semi-fatuous condition, from which it was next to impossible
> to arouse them, and others became violently insane; others still, commit-
> ted suicide; although those who stood the ordeal better were not generally
> reformed, and in most cases did not recover sufficient mental activity to be
> of any subsequent service to the community. (*In re Medley,* 134 U.S. at 168)

Miller's decision, along with economic and other practical concerns,
greatly reduced the use of solitary confinement as a standard method
of confinement in U.S. prisons until the introduction of behavior modification programs under the guise of "treatment" in the 1960s and '70s.
But in spite of his recognition of its mental and physical harm, Miller
condemned solitary confinement not because it violated the Eighth
Amendment, which forbids "cruel and unusual punishments" but,
rather, because it violated Article I of the Constitution, which forbids
attainder or ex post facto law.[6] He found the imposition of solitary
confinement unconstitutional in this particular case because it imposed
a form of additional punishment after the sentence determined by the
courts, thus condemning the prisoner to a pain and infamy that ex-
ceeded the initial sentence (which was, incidentally, a death sentence).
As a remedy, Miller ordered Medley to be released not just from solitude but from prison altogether. But there was nothing in his decision
that condemned solitary confinement *as such* as an unconstitutional
form of punishment.

By the mid-twentieth century, solitary confinement and other forms
of intensive confinement had made a comeback in U.S. prisons. These
programs intensified the domination of inmates, especially for the politically active inmates of color, who were disproportionately targeted
for such programs. But they also intensified the resistance of prisoners
and prison activists, both within U.S. prisons and in the courts, where
a series of legal challenges exposed prison conditions to public scrutiny

and led to some concrete improvements in the treatment of prisoners. And yet, as Alan Eladio Gómez, Colin Dayan, Keramet Reiter, and others have shown, the legal and political resistance of prisoners in the 1960s and '70s was met with a counterresistance—amounting to a domestic counterinsurgency—through which the exception of punitive isolation increasingly became the rule, and tidied-up versions of "the hole" were normalized and extended to entire prison populations in new supermaximum-security prisons.

In his study of prisoners' resistance and institutional reaction at Marion Penitentiary in the 1970s and '80s, Gómez argues that the forerunner of the Control Unit, which is now a standard feature of supermax prisons, was first introduced in 1972 as a repressive re-sponse to a labor strike and protest by inmates at Marion Penitentiary (Gómez 2006, 60). Provoked by the beating of a Chicano inmate by a prison guard, a diverse group of prisoners including Chicanos, blacks, American Indians, and whites joined together across racial and ethnic lines "to confront the prison authority's deployment of living death as a strategy to control radical inmates" (58). Gómez comments:

> Prison was civil death, but through collective struggle, activist prisoners created a new form of civil life, a way to resist punishment and death by affirming life through the process of political transformation, collective ac-tivity, and alliances beyond the prison walls. (2006, 68)

In response to their protest, inmates were tear-gassed and left naked in their cells for three days. All prisoners were forced to participate in a behavior modification program called CARE (Control and Rehabilitation Effort), and 149 prisoners were kept in solitary confine-ment and sensory deprivation for eighteen months in steel boxcar cells (so called because they were nothing more than a concrete box with steel bars on one end). The inmates were finally released from solitary confinement following a successful appeal to the decision in *Adams v. Carlson* (1973),[7] in which the U.S. Court of Appeals for the Seventh Circuit found that the prisoners' Eighth Amendment rights had been violated (Gómez 2006, 77).

But this decision did not end solitary confinement at Marion Penitentiary; instead, it prompted the development of Control Units, whose constitutionality was challenged by prisoners in further law-suits, this time without success (Gómez 2006, 77). With each legal ex-change, the terms used for solitary confinement were altered in Marion

Penitentiary—from "segregation units" to "control units," from "punitive isolation" to "preventive detention"—but the practice of solitary
confinement remained and was even refined through the dialectics of
resistance and reaction. Marion Penitentiary became an incubator, not
only for radical prison politics but also for the development of current
supermax technologies. In 1983, the entire prison was locked down in
response to the murder of two prison guards by members of the Aryan
Brotherhood; the lockdown remained in place for twenty-three years,
turning Marion into the first de facto supermax prison (see Gómez
2006 for details).[8]

If we measured the value of the prisoners' resistance at Marion
solely in terms of objective institutional outcomes, we might conclude
that the movement was a dismal failure. There are more prisoners
held in solitary confinement now in the United States than ever before.
In fact, there are more prisoners in the United States now than ever
before: the United States has the highest rate of incarceration in the
world, as well as the highest total number of prisoners in any country
in the world (Bureau of Justice Statistics, Office of Justice Programs
2012). In 2008, the U.S. incarceration rate reached its peak: 1 in 100
adults behind bars. The rate goes up to 1 in 9 for black men between
the ages of twenty and thirty-four (Liptak 2008a).[9] The Control Units
designed to contain resistance at Marion Penitentiary have become
standard methods of preempting resistance and intensifying the control of prisoners in supermax prisons across the United States and in
more than fifteen other countries. No one knows exactly how many
supermax prisoners there are in the United States, nor even how many
supermax confinement units are currently in operation, but it is esti-
mated that there are between 25,000 and 80,000 prisoners in supermax
confinement across forty-four states.

These are sobering figures, and we ignore them at our peril. But if
we understand the prisoners' resistance movement in its own terms—
as *resistance,* and as a *movement* that continues to create solidarity
among relational beings in even the most nonrelational or antirelational situations, cutting across the racial, ethnic, class, gender, and
religious lines that otherwise separate them and block solidarity—then
we gain a different appreciation for this resistance. We risk missing its
significance if we fail to consider the prisoners' perspective on their
own situation, and the meaning that resistance generates for relational
beings in excess of what may be objectively achieved.

Keramet Reiter's account of prisoners' rights litigation in the United States from the 1960s to the 1980s supports the connection made by Gómez between prisoners' efforts to defend their rights through legal action and prison authorities' development of supermax technologies in reaction to prisoner litigation. By failing to condemn solitary confinement outright as a form of cruel and unusual punishment and by delineating exactly what the law would permit—sometimes down to the specific dimensions of an isolation cell—many district and federal courts have ended up inscribing a "just measure of deprivation" within the law, even in cases where they have explicitly affirmed prisoners' human rights (Reiter 2012a, 100). Thus, prisoners' rights litigation not only established *minimum thresholds* for prison conditions such as cell size, nutrition, sanitation, and so forth, but it also inadvertently provided a *basic template* for the design of supermax prisons in the 1990s and beyond. For example, in *Gates v. Collier* (1974),[10] a federal district court considered the constitutionality of punitive isolation in the Mississippi State Penitentiary or Parchman Farm:

> The inmates are placed in the dark hole, naked, without any hygienic material, without any bedding, and often without adequate food. It is customary to cut the hair of an inmate confined in the dark hole by means of heavy-duty clippers. Inmates have frequently remained in the dark hole for forty-eight hours and may be confined there for up to seventy-two hours. While an inmate occupies the dark hole, the cell is not cleaned, nor is the inmate permitted to wash himself. (*Gates,* 501 F.2d at 1305; quoted in Reiter 2012a, 95–96)

Although both the district court and the U.S. Court of Appeals for the Fifth Circuit acknowledged that such conditions violated prisoners' constitutional rights, they did not condemn punitive isolation as such, nor even the use of "the dark hole." Rather, they limited its use to one twenty-four-hour period and ordered that "adequate food, clothing, hygiene items, and temperature control" be provided (Reiter 2012a, 96). Strikingly similar decisions were made in *Pugh v. Locke* (1976), *Hutto v. Finney* (1978), and *Rhodes v. Chapman* (1981).[11] In each case, egregious violations of prisoners' rights were acknowledged and linked to punitive isolation, but rather than condemning such punishment itself, judges ordered specific changes to ensure that the conditions of punitive isolation met certain basic standards.

These standards were determined by a certain conception of what is necessary for human life, where life and necessity are understood in terms of mere survival rather than relational well-being. By focusing on the provision of basic needs such as food, water, and shelter, judges in these cases were able to evade the questions of whether "needs" are sufficient to define (human) life and whether intensive confinement itself might be a form of torture.[12] But as Reiter (2012a, 107) has shown, the courts' efforts to set minimum standards for the protection of prisoners' basic needs or rights has tended rather to reproduce and legitimate that minimum as a new *normal* standard for confinement—and even to help render this new standard litigation-proof.[13]

Court-ordered requirements for adequate lighting have given rise to supermax units that are illuminated twenty-four hours a day; demands for adequate sanitation and hygiene have produced sterile, hypertechnologized supermax "pods" in which prisoners are given access to showers three times a week through remotely operated doors, which they pass through without ever coming into contact with another person; the demand for adequate physical exercise has given rise to the same routine for access to empty yards where they can run around, again without contact with others; and so forth (see Reiter 2012a, 103–6).

Reiter's argument that prisoners' rights litigation has concretely shaped the development of supermax prisons is supported by Sharon Shalev's interview with an architect who worked on the design of Pelican Bay supermax, which opened in 1989 as one of the first purpose-built supermax prisons. The architect describes his design objective as follows:

> First to isolate . . . particular inmates from the rest of the population, to try to cut off as much as possible the communication that they have with that population or with the outside world, and to put them in an environment where it's both safe for staff and the other inmates that are around them to live . . . an environment that allows you to manage them without taking away their rights that they have. (Quoted in Shalev 2009, 102; see also Reiter 2012a, 106–8)[14]

Later, he adds:

> To be honest, given our past with litigation particularly here in California, we wanted to make sure that we were building something that would stand court scrutiny. (106–7)

This way of "respecting" the basic rights of prisoners—not as a minimum guarantee but as a norm to be targeted—suggests that unless judges are willing to condemn certain practices outright, humanist legal discourse remains inadequate to achieve its own explicit goal: the protection of (human) dignity. It suggests that there are no meaningful rights without privileges, if by "privilege" we mean anything in excess of the absolute minimum requirements for survival.

Case Study: *Madrid v. Gomez* (1995)

This tension between the right to human dignity and the humanist legal discourse meant to secure this right is especially evident in the 1995 Eighth Amendment case *Madrid v. Gomez.* Throughout the case, the treatment of prisoners at California's Pelican Bay supermax prison is compared to the treatment of animals. Some inmates were "hog-tied" with their hands and feet bound together, then left chained to a toilet or bunk for up to twenty-four hours (*Madrid,* 889 F. Supp. at 1168). Other inmates were confined to outdoor cages the size of a telephone booth and left naked or partially dressed, exposed to inclement weather and to the view of other inmates (at 1171). One inmate who was caged recalled feeling like "just an animal or something" (at 1171). The presiding judge in this case, Chief Judge Thelton Henderson, concluded, "Leaving inmates in outdoor cages for any significant period—as if animals in a zoo—offends even the most elementary notions of common decency and dignity" (at 1172). And yet, like the judges in *Pugh, Hutto,* and *Rhodes,* he stopped short of condemning punitive isolation, for all but the most vulnerable prisoners, as cruel and unusual punishment.[15] What is this "common decency and dignity" so often invoked to protect prisoners from abuse, and why does it tend to produce such negligible effects on their material well-being?

In *Madrid v. Gomez,* Judge Henderson affirms the opinion in *Spain v. Procunier* (1979)[16] that the "Eighth Amendment is based on the 'fundamental premise that prisoners are not to be treated as less than human beings'" (*Madrid,* 889 F. Supp. at 1245). Even if prisoners have forfeited their claim to certain civil rights by violating the law, they have not lost their right to "human dignity" (at 1244). The content of this right to human dignity is grounded in the satisfaction of "basic human needs," which are listed as "food, clothing, shelter, medical care, and reasonable safety" (at 1245).[17] Note the degree to which these basic human needs overlap with the needs of any animal; there is nothing on this list, except for clothing and perhaps medical care, that a horse or a bear would not also need in order to thrive. But precisely because "humans are composed of more than flesh and blood"—presumably, because they are not merely animals, but *human* animals or rational animals—Henderson argues that "mental health is a need as essential to a meaningful human existence as other basic physical demands our bodies may make for shelter, warmth or sanitation" (at 1261).

How does Henderson seek to protect this fundamental, apparently human need for mental health? And what *is* "mental health" anyhow? Henderson condemns the use of excessive force and the deliberate humiliation of prisoners, acknowledging that some of the techniques used at Pelican Bay violated "evolving standards of decency that mark the process of a maturing society" (*Madrid,* 889 F. Supp. at 1245, citing *Patchette v. Nix,* 952 F.2d 158 at 163 [8th Cir. 1991]). He acknowledges the evidence of expert witnesses such as Stuart Grassian, who found that 80 percent of the inmates held in prolonged solitary confinement in the SHU at Pelican Bay had either "massively exacerbated a previous psychiatric illness or precipitated psychiatric symptoms associated with RES [Reduced Environmental Stimulation] conditions" (at 1232).[18] He notes the typical effects of RES, or what Grassian later calls SHU syndrome, as "perceptual distortions, hallucinations, hyperresponsivity to external stimuli, aggressive fantasies, overt paranoia, inability to concentrate, and problems with impulse control" (at 1230). In passing, Henderson even acknowledges the court's observation during its own tour of the SHU that "some inmates spend the time simply pacing around the edges of the pen; the image created is hauntingly similar to that of caged felines pacing at a zoo" (at 1229). But Henderson stops short of condemning SHU conditions as a violation of prisoners' Eighth Amendment rights, concluding,

> Conditions in the SHU may well hover on the edge of what is humanly tolerable for those with normal resilience, particularly when endured for extended periods of time. They do not, however, violate exacting Eighth Amendment standards, except for the specific population subgroups identified in this opinion. (At 1280)[19]

The "specific population subgroups" for whom prolonged solitary confinement does count as "cruel and unusual punishment" are (1) prisoners who are already mentally ill, and (2) prisoners who are at "unreasonably high risk" of becoming mentally ill if held in SHU conditions (at 1267). Note the frankly biopolitical resonance of the term "population," which refers to prisoners as a statistical entity with no specifically human qualities, even in a ruling that celebrates and seeks to protect this population's (apparently) human need for mental "health."[20] How are concepts such as "humanity" and "mental illness" (understood as an affliction faced by human beings who are "more than flesh and blood") working together here to expose prisoners to almost intolerable violence, even while claiming to protect them from it?

Colin Dayan (2005, 2007) argues persuasively that the "exacting standards" of Eighth Amendment cases have done less to protect prisoners from cruel and unusual punishment, and more to expand the scope and intensity of the violence to which prisoners are exposed *within* legal limits. Henderson's decision in *Madrid v. Gomez* is no exception to this rule. On the one hand, he acknowledges that "contemporary notions of humanity and decency . . . will not tolerate conditions that are likely to make inmates seriously mentally ill" (at 1261). But on the other hand, by limiting Eighth Amendment protection to just those "population subgroups" who are already suffering from mental illness or are recognizably on the verge of it, he creates a loophole into which virtually every prisoner could fall. Prisoners who are already mentally ill or "unreasonably" close to mental illness (whatever that means, and however it is measured) are protected from conditions that would exacerbate their condition. They are recognized as human beings, with an intrinsic dignity that no civilized nation would dare to violate. But those who are not (yet) mentally ill—who display "normal resilience" to barely tolerable conditions—may be confined in a situation that, according to Grassian's research, produces mental illness in about 90 percent of the population. To put this more succinctly: unless prisoners can obtain a diagnosis of mental illness, they may be subject to conditions that typically produce mental illness.[21] In the legal discourse of *Madrid v. Gomez,* and of Eighth Amendment cases more generally, mental illness becomes both the benchmark for distinguishing torture from legitimate punishment and also the condition that one would need to satisfy in order to be exempt from torture; it becomes both a sign of human dignity and an alibi for dehumanizing treatment.

The most outlandishly brutal violence described in *Madrid v. Gomez* was directed against a mentally ill African American inmate named Vaughn Dortch, who was punished for biting an officer and smearing himself with feces by being immersed in scalding hot bathwater to the point where his skin peeled off in large clumps. A nurse testified hearing one officer remark, "[It] looks like we're going to have a white boy before this is through, that his skin is so dirty and so rotten, it's all fallen off" (*Madrid,* 889 F. Supp. at 1167). Dortch was caught in a nexus of multiple forms of physical, mental, racist, symbolic, and institutional violence. It would be a gross understatement to say that his human rights were violated—even if there is also some truth to this statement. It would also be a disservice to all prisoners, including Dortch, to focus on incidents of exceptional violence at the expense of the everyday forms of structural violence that support these exceptions and make them possible.

Colin Dayan notes the disappearance of the prisoner as a *person* and as a *subject,* even in legal decisions that have sought to guarantee their basic rights and needs:

> The intact person imprisoned in the SHU—who is not stripped naked, driven out of his mind, caged, mutilated, scalded, or beaten—disappears from these pages. Only the visible signs of stigma are recognized. If the slave could only legally become a person—possessing will and more than mere matter—when committing a crime, here the prisoner is legally recognized only insofar as he becomes a senseless icon of the human, either mentally impaired or physically damaged. . . .
>
> The Court's logic thus strips the victim of the right to experience suffering, to know fear and anguish. Legally, the plaintiff has become a nonreactive body, a defenseless object. Subjectivity is the privilege of those in control. In other words, the "objective component"—serious deprivations of even the most basic human needs—do[es] not matter once all the eggs of mental activity are in the basket of the perpetrator. (2001, 25, 26–27)

Given the complicity of human rights discourse with the perpetuation of prisoner abuse and with the broader history of racism in the United States, we need a different language to describe the harm of intensive confinement and domination in sites such as Pelican Bay penitentiary. How might we account for this violence without appealing to human dignity or human rights at the expense of nonhuman animals, and ultimately at the expense of human prisoners as well? What are the possible connections and forms of solidarity that we overlook when, instead of understanding both human and nonhuman animals as relational beings, we oppose one to the other through an appeal to something "more than flesh and blood"?

Racialization, Dehumanization, and De-animalization in U.S. Control Prisons

Since the emergence of supermax prisons in the mid-1980s, prison policy in the United States has focused less on the rehabilitation of the criminal subject than on the management and control of security risks posed by the prison population as a whole (Shalev 2009, 23–25). We have entered the era of the control prison, where the immobilization of inmates has become an end in itself rather than a way of breaking through to the inwardness of the criminal soul or even the outwardness of the criminal's antisocial behavior. By "control prison" I mean a prison whose main focus is the management of security risks posed by prisoners; this is what characterizes the third wave of "solitary" or intensive confinement in the United States. The prisoner has become a risk to be managed, a resistance to be eliminated, and an organism to be fed, maintained, and prevented from taking its own life. A supermax prison, in which inmates are held under constant surveillance in small solitary confinement units for twenty-three hours a day, is the paradigmatic example of a control prison, but lower-security prisons also function as control prisons to the extent that they focus more on risk management than on rehabilitation. Also, many lower-security prisons have a separate pod of supermax-level Control Units—a prison within the prison—and so it becomes difficult to distinguish between supermax and max, or even between supermax and a county jail.[22]

Many prisoners in U.S. control prisons have compared their experience of incarceration to the treatment of animals. One Washington State prisoner told anthropologist Lorna Rhodes, "I'm walking around here like a caged animal—it makes you feel so inadequate, so inferior, so *less than*. The thing that keeps me sane is knowing I'm strong-minded" (quoted in Rhodes 2004, 35). Another, upon being "received" into prison, said, "It's very humiliating. I feel like a lab rat" (quoted in Rhodes 2004, 100). This feeling of being reduced to an animal is often reinforced by gendered and racialized practices of dehumanization in U.S. prisons. Cassandra Shaylor notes in her 1998 study of California's Valley State Prison for Women (VSPW):

> Guards speak to and about the women as though they are subhuman. A pamphlet, produced by the Warden's office, is given to women when they enter the SHU and lists times for daily "feedings." Guards constantly use racial epithets, many of which are gendered, to refer to the women. They

call the prisoners "dogs," "niggers," "bitches," "whores" and "black bitches"; women refer to their cells as "cages." When women are denied privileges, they are put on what guards refer to as "dog status." (1998, 395–96)

Of the fifty-two women held in SHU at VSPW in 1998, 40 percent were identified as black, 21 percent as Hispanic/Mexican, and 5.9 percent as "Other" (Shaylor 1998, 394). These numbers reflect a more pervasive overrepresentation of African Americans and Latinos/as in state and federal prisons across the United States. They also reflect a complex history of slavery, abolition, reconstruction, Jim Crow, and the convict lease system, in which African Americans were both freed from slavery and hypercriminalized in ways that replicated and even intensified the dynamics of slavery.

In her 2002 paper "From the Convict Lease System to the Super-Max Prison," Angela Davis argues that the format for current penal policies, based on control rather than rehabilitation, is not the lofty humanitarianism of the early penitentiary system but the control of black bodies under slavery: the domination of disposable nonpersons or quasi persons (Davis 2002). As I argued in chapter 3, slaves occupied a curious position in U.S. law: they were considered property with respect to civil rights, but persons with respect to criminal responsibility. During slavery, slaves were already treated as domestic animals; they were bought, sold, inspected, and put to work according to the demands of the slave owner and overseer. After the abolition of slavery, the link between African American personhood and criminality was not dissolved but, rather, intensified by the convict lease system, which targeted freed slaves with disproportionately harsh sentences for the petty theft of food and farm animals. For example, in 1876, Mississippi passed what was known as the Pig Law, which granted sentences of up to five years in a state prison for the theft of a farm animal or any other property worth ten dollars or more (Oshinsky 1996, 40–41). The convict lease system perpetuated and exacerbated this simultaneous dehumanization and racialization, treating prisoners not just as animals but as *less than animals*. A 1909 legislative committee in Texas reported that "the life of a [Texas] convict is not as valuable in the eyes of the sergeants and guards and contractors as that of a dog" (quoted in Oshinsky 1996, 61). A 1934 critique of the convict lease system compared the iron cages in which convicts were transported to "those used for circus animals," except that these cages "did not have the privacy which would be given to a respectable lion, tiger or bear" (quoted in Oshinsky 1996, 59). Even the bodily wastes—and the wasted bodies—of prisoners were appropriated and sold for profit under the convict lease system:

> In 1871, state convicts were laying track and mining coal from Memphis to Knoxville. Each morning their urine was collected and sold to local tanneries by the barrel. When they died, their unclaimed bodies were purchased by the Medical School at Nashville for the students to practice on. (Oshinsky 1996, 58)

I argue that under conditions like these, prisoners are not only dehumanized, they are *de-animalized*. Not only their human dignity but also their dignity as living beings is violated and exploited. They are treated not only as laborers with productive capacities to be exploited but also as *natural resources* with material bodies to be exploited for their own sake, once their productive capacities have been exhausted.

While the last convict lease system was abolished in 1928, the exploitation of prison labor continues today. In U.S. federal prisons and in most state prisons, all able-bodied prisoners are required to work. They are paid between $0.17 and $1.15 per hour to produce goods such as furniture, clothing, and license plates and to run such day-to-day operations of the prison as food services, laundry, and even bookkeeping. State prisoners in Georgia and Texas do not have the right to be paid anything for their work (E. Brown 2010). In many states, private corporations such as Victoria's Secret, Starbucks, Nintendo, Microsoft, and Eddie Bauer contract prison labor to perform light industrial work, paying inmates between $1 and $3 an hour (Prison Policy Initiative 2003; Schwartzapfel 2009). But labor is not the only resource exploited by the current prison industrial complex; the sheer *existence* of prisoners constitutes a source of profit for private prison corporations that receive government contracts to manage and maintain prisoners. In her discussion of the connections between the convict lease system and the current prison industrial complex, Angela Davis quotes Steven Donzinger's 1996 report *The Real War on Crime*:

> In the criminal justice field, *the raw material is prisoners,* and industry will do what is necessary to guarantee a steady supply. For the supply of prisoners to grow, criminal justice policies must ensure a sufficient number of incarcerated Americans regardless of whether crime is rising or the incarceration is necessary. (Quoted in Davis 2002, 68)

Davis argues that to the extent that "black male bodies are considered dispensable," they are targeted for exploitation as raw material for the prison industrial complex (2002, 69).[23]

A Washington State prison officer interviewed by Lorna Rhodes confirms this pattern when he compares the intake of new prisoners to the task of receiving merchandise in a warehouse: "We are just like the guys who work loading docks—we're trying to *move* stuff" (quoted in Rhodes 2004, 101). Mark Medley, a maximum-security inmate at the Maryland Penitentiary, argues that prisoners are moved into different cells as part of a managerial plan rather than for the sake of rehabilitation or even security: "It's just that they have to liquidate their inventory as a matter of storage space" (Baxter et al. 2005, 215). And Laura Whitehorn, a political prisoner who spent fourteen years behind bars for her alleged involvement in the Resistance Conspiracy case, agrees: "The overcrowding means that people are treated like problems and like baggage" (Buck and Whitehorn 2005, 261).[24]

It is against this background of simultaneous dehumanization and de-animalization that the inmates of Attica and Georgia both invoke and refuse their treatment as animals and as slaves. Not only are prisoners treated as less than human in the current prison industrial complex, but they are also treated as *less than animal*; they are reduced to raw material for incarceration, physical mechanisms to be fed, worked, and controlled for profit. As I will demonstrate in the next section, this is a condition that human prisoners share with nonhuman animals in the current animal industrial complex. Even *animals* are treated as less than animals in laboratories and factory farms. They are treated as meat to be harvested and flesh to be experimented upon; they are confined to warehouse-like conditions where they cannot move freely or perform the most minimal gestures proper to their species; they are stocked and exchanged for profit, then dumped when global economic conditions make it no longer lucrative to maintain them.

The de-animalization of animal life is a condition that nonhuman animals share with many human animals caught in the prison industrial complex—particularly with those who have been racialized as black or brown and as more closely associated with nonhuman animality in the context of U.S. white supremacy. Allen Hornblum has reconstructed the details of medical experimentation on prisoners, most of whom were African American, at Philadelphia's Holmesburg Prison from the 1940s to 1974. The skin on their backs was marked off with a grid for the testing of everything from skin creams, perfumes, and detergents to radioactive isotopes, dioxin, and chemical warfare agents. While participants were paid a minimal amount for their services, they were not informed of the health risks or the pain they might undergo. Participants experienced what many nonhuman animals experience in similar experimental situations: blisters, rashes, skin-peeling, permanent scarring, chronic illness, and premature death. And they were perceived, as nonhuman animals are often perceived, as de-animalized flesh by the chief experimenter, Dr. Albert M. Klingman, who recalled his first visit to the prison in this way: "All I saw before me was acres of skin. It was like a farmer seeing a fertile field for the first time" (quoted in Hornblum 1998, xx).

What is it like to be the target not only of dehumanization but of a de-animalizing treatment that reduces one's corporeal existence to "acres of skin" or a mechanism to be reprogrammed? Denise Jones, an African American inmate at Valley State Prison for Women, analyzes her own situation in this way in a 1997 interview with Cassandra Shaylor: "They treat us like animals. No, you wouldn't treat an animal the way they do us here. I am sure they don't treat their dogs the way they treat us" (quoted in Shaylor 1998, 396; see also Dayan 2005, 72). By simultaneously rejecting her abusive treatment by the guards and distinguishing this treatment from that accorded to a dog or other animals, Jones both acknowledges the guards' logic of dehumanization and suggests that something else is going on here, something that is not quite captured by the phrase "treated like an animal." On the one hand, (black) prisoners are reduced to animals and so dehumanized; but on the other hand, precisely *as* dehumanized animals in a context that reduces most nonhuman animals to resources for human consumption and profit, while promoting others to the status of pets or honorary humans, (black) prisoners are further de-animalized, treated worse than (only the most privileged, anthropomorphized) animals.[25]

In his 1991 prison memoir *In the Belly of the Beast,* Chinese-Irish prisoner Jack Henry Abbott compares his own experience of intensive confinement to a radical dehumanization and reification, to the point of ontological violence:

> It is only a matter of time, if you love life too much or fear violence too much, before you become a thing, no longer a man. You can end up scurrying about like a rodent, lending yourself to every conceivable low, evil, degrading act

anyone tells you to do—either pigs or prisoners. There is a boundary in each man. . . . But when a man goes beyond the last essential boundary, it alters his ontology, so to speak. (67)

For Abbott, the prison system is not just degrading or dehumanizing; it is a violence against the ontological structure of life itself. Abbott expresses this violence in an extraordinary statement: "Solitary confinement in prison can alter the ontological makeup of a stone" (45). Solitary confinement does not simply dehumanize prisoners, cutting them off from the social relations that sustain them as social animals, and it does not only alter their very existence as living beings, pushing them beyond the boundary between humans and animals toward the nonliving status of a stone; solitary confinement is a violence so radical that it could even alter the ontology *of a stone*.

What does it mean for one's *ontology* to be altered by the experience of intensive incarceration? In what sense might one be both reduced to the status of an animal and reduced to something less than an animal, a piece of meat or even a stone, an inanimate token to be exchanged for profit? How are even prison guards and wardens reduced to the status of "pigs" in relation to the prisoners they keep under conditions of dehumanization and de-animalization? What is an animal, such that it could be de-animalized by intensive confinement, and in what sense does the animality of human beings expose those who are already structurally dehumanized by racism to a further de-animalization? And to what extent can the discourse of specifically *human* rights help us address the complicity between dehumanization and de-animalization in the context of the U.S. prison system?

In order to understand how inmates are both dehumanized and de-animalized through intensive confinement in today's control prisons, we need to compare the dynamics of the prison industrial complex and the animal industrial complex, reflecting on the ontology of animal life that this abusive treatment implies, even while reducing the animal to what it is not.

De-animalizing Prisoners

In the third wave of intensive confinement in the United States, the current era of the control prison, inmates face two extreme forms of intensive confinement: solitary confinement in a Control Unit, where they are deprived of any contact with others beyond the minimal touch of prison staff who fasten or unfasten their restraints through a slot in the cell door, and extremely overcrowded conditions in which two or three inmates may be housed in a unit designed for one person or in spaces that were never intended as living quarters, such as gymnasiums, common rooms, holding cells, and even hallways (Shalev 2009, 63). In this section, I will address the effects of both forms of intensive confinement on the well-being of prisoners as human animals.

Recall Dickens's description of a prisoner who has just been released from solitary confinement. The prisoner trembles, staggers, and appears to have suffered "a complete derangement of the nervous system." While the terminology has changed in the nearly two centuries since the penitentiary system was established in the United States, the symptoms of solitary confinement have remained strikingly consistent, both historically and geographically, and they continue to affect a large proportion of inmates held under such conditions.[26]

In 1982, Stuart Grassian interviewed fourteen of the fifteen prisoners held in solitary confinement in Block 10 of Walpole Prison in Massachusetts. The cells in Block 10 were 1.8 meters by 2.7 meters (or six feet by nine feet) in size. The prisoners had been isolated there for a median time of two months, ranging from eleven days to ten months. Since 1979, each unit had been sealed with a solid steel door blocking natural light, airflow, and a view to the outside; at the same time, all radios, televisions, and reading materials apart from the Bible had been confiscated. Grassian was brought into Block 10 as an expert witness in a class-action lawsuit on behalf of the inmates, who claimed that their conditions amounted to cruel and unusual punishment.[27] Many of the inmates were reluctant to speak at first, claiming, "Some of the guys can't take it—not me" (Grassian 1983, 1451). But a pattern of cognitive impairment, perceptual distortions, and affective strain soon emerged. Here are some excerpts from the prisoners' testimonies:

> I went to a standstill psychologically once—lapse of memory. I didn't talk for 15 days. I couldn't hear clearly. You can't see—you're blind—block everything out—disoriented, awareness is very bad. Did someone say he's coming out of it? I think what I'm saying is true—not sure. I think I was drooling—a complete standstill. (1453)

> They come by [for breakfast] with four trays; the first has big pancakes—I think I'm going to get them. Then someone comes up and gives me tiny

ones—they get real small, like silver dollars. I seem to see movements—real fast motions in front of me. Then seems like they're doing things behind your back—can't quite see them. Did someone just hit me? I dwell on it for hours. (1452)

Melting, everything in the cell starts moving; everything gets darker, you feel you are losing your vision. (1452)

I can't concentrate, can't read. . . . Your mind's narcotized. . . . Sometimes can't grasp words in my mind that I know. Get stuck, have to think of another word. Memory is going. You feel you are losing something you might not get back. (1453)

Deprived of everyday encounters with other people and confined to a space with radically diminished sensory stimulus, many inmates come unhinged from reality. Their senses seem to betray them; objects begin to move, melt, or shrink of their own accord. Even the effort to reflect on their experience becomes a form of pathology, leading one prisoner to "dwell on it for hours," and another goes into "a complete standstill." They cannot think straight, cannot remember things, cannot focus properly, and cannot even see clearly. What is the prisoner in solitary confinement at risk of losing, to the point of "not get[ting it] back"? And what is it about the supermax unit that precipitates this loss?[28]

Grassian has coined the term "SHU syndrome" to name the cluster of systems produced by long term confinement in a Secure Housing Unit or other supermax-level prison cell. He identifies six basic components of SHU syndrome: (1) hyperresponsivity to external stimuli; (2) perceptual distortions, illusions, and hallucinations; (3) panic attacks; (4) difficulties with thinking, concentration, and memory; (5) intrusive obsessional thoughts; and (6) overt paranoia (2006, 335–36). He notes that this particular configuration of symptoms is "strikingly unique" and that the perceptual disturbances in particular are "virtually found nowhere else" (337).

Prisoners in a Control Unit may have adequate food and drink, and the conditions of their confinement may meet or exceed court-tested thresholds for humane treatment. But there is something about the exclusion of other living beings from the space we inhabit and the absence of even the *possibility* of touching or being touched by another that threatens to unhinge us. We tend to view ourselves as individuals with our own separate, inherent capacity to think and perceive. At the same time, we acknowledge that humans are social animals and that we need other people in order to live a full and happy life. But the testimony of prisoners in solitary confinement suggests that we are much more deeply connected with and dependent upon other living beings than we tend to assume. We rely on a network of others, not just to survive or to keep ourselves entertained but also to support our capacity to make sense of the world, to distinguish between reality and illusion, to follow a train of thought or a causal sequence, and even to tell where our own bodily existence begins and ends.

Every time I hear a sound and see another person look toward the origin of that sound, I receive an implicit confirmation that what I heard was something real, that it was not just my imagination playing tricks on me. Every time someone walks around the table rather than through it, I receive an unspoken, usually unremarkable, confirmation that the table exists and that my own way of relating to tables is shared by others. When I do not receive these implicit confirmations, I can usually ask someone—but for the most part, we do not need to ask because our experience is already interwoven with the experience of many other living, thinking, perceiving beings who relate to the same world from their own unique perspectives. This multiplicity of perspectives is like an invisible net that supports the coherence of my own experience, even (or especially) when others challenge my interpretation of "the facts." These facts are up for discussion in the first place because we inhabit a world shared with others who agree, at the very least, that there is something to disagree about.

Prolonged isolation cuts prisoners off from this network of social, cognitive, perceptual, affective, and even ontological support, turning prisoners' capacity for meaning, and for meaningful relationships, against itself to the point of incapacitation. Without the support of other embodied subjects in a shared space, many prisoners find it difficult to sustain capacities that would otherwise seem inherent in the individual: the capacity to think clearly; to perceive objects in a reliable, trustworthy way; and to maintain emotional stability. But even when prisoners are not held in solitary confinement, the mere presence of other inmates does not guarantee any meaningful sense of social relation. In many lower-security prisons, and even in some supermax prisons, overcrowding forces inmates into spaces designed for half their current capacity (Archibold 2010; Shalev 2009, 63–64). While these inmates do experience social interaction, the constant exposure and forced contact with others tends to exacerbate feelings of anxiety and alienation rather than provide a sense of relief from isolation.

In this sense, the "solitary" of "solitary confinement" is a misnomer. It refers less to the empirical absence of other people than to the highly mediated, socially produced *isolation* of inmates. After all, even solitary SHU inmates are monitored twenty-four hours a day by guards, upon whom they are forced to depend for everything from food to toilet paper, and by whom they can be forcibly extracted from their cells, strip-searched, cavity-searched, pepper-sprayed, and spread-eagled on the floor in four-point restraints.

Today's control prisons do not merely leave inmates to their own solitary devices; they force prisoners to interact with guards in specific ways, punishing them with physical force or with further levels of deprivation when they fail or refuse to comply with the rules. The SHU is a highly mediated, intensely "social" space insofar as it leaves inmates no room to withdraw from the forced relationality of constant surveillance and control; and yet this forced relationality only compounds the social isolation of prisoners, structurally undermining the possibility of an open, reciprocal relationship with others. Here, as in the animal industrial complex that I will explore in the next section, the basic structure of intensive confinement emerges as a forced isolation that excludes the possibility of genuine solitude, and as a forced relationality that excludes the possibility of genuine relationships.

Judge Henderson acknowledges the complexity of social isolation in his decision in *Madrid v. Gomez*:

> Roughly two-thirds of the inmates are double celled; however, this does not compensate for the otherwise severe level of social isolation in the SHU. The combination of being in extremely close proximity with one other person, while other avenues for normal social interaction are virtually precluded, often makes any long-term, normal relationship with the cellmate impossible. Instead, two persons housed together in this type of forced, constant intimacy have an "enormously high risk of becoming paranoid, hostile, and potentially violent towards each other" (Grassian Tr. 12-1857; Haney Tr. 6-988-89). The existence of a cellmate is thus unlikely to provide an opportunity for sustained positive or normal social contact. (*Madrid,* 889 F. Supp. at 1230)

First person accounts of intensive (nonsolitary) confinement confirm this point. In his prison memoir, Abbott explores the depths of violence and mutual degradation that inmates become capable of when forced together within the violent structure of the prison industrial complex. Rape, murder, threats, humiliation, and constant noise produce in the prisoner a sense of anxiety that he may be violated or provoked to violate others at any moment:

> You can't stand the sight of each other and yet you are doomed to stand and face one another every moment of every day for years without end. You must bathe together, defecate together and urinate together, eat and sleep together, talk together, work together. (1991, 86)

> The closest you come to adjusting is this: you *will* yourself to sleep all day through most of the disturbances. After each meal you curl up, pull the blankets over you, put your pillow over your ears and sleep. It's a drugged sleep. (66)

Referring to his experience both in solitary confinement and in overcrowded group cells, Abbott concludes, "I have been denied the society of *others*: It is as simple as that" (106). The mere presence of others does not constitute the *society* of others; in fact, if there is no possibility of withdrawing from constant exposure to others, then contact may be as antisocial as solitary confinement.

Inmate John Woodland Jr. describes his own experience of the need for both social interaction and withdrawal in a philosophy seminar with Drew Leder at the Maryland Penitentiary in 1993:

> There's a degree of privacy, I think, that everybody needs and must have. In prison the degree of privacy you have also determines the degree of safety you feel that you have. If I'm in a single cell, I can lock the door and lay down and I'm cool. The only time I feel threatened is if the door's open. Then I know that I have to be on my toes. (Baxter et al. 2005, 209)[29]

Donald Thompson, another inmate in the same seminar, says:

> You may just want to socialize with one or two at a time, but you'll always find yourself in a situation where—even though it may be people you like and would want to talk to later—you're literally forced to say "Hi!" all day long. . . . Just sitting here, right now, I'm around the people I want to be around all the time, talking about things I want to talk about. I can really feel a sense of power. As soon as I walk out into that yard, that power is gone. (209)

What does this brief account of social isolation in prison teach us about de-animalization and the ontology of animal life? While we cannot answer this question in full before comparing the experience of human animals with nonhuman animals, it is important to note that both first-person and third-person accounts of the debilitating effects of intensive confinement mark the limits of a dualistic ontology opposing mind to body and human to animal. Why would social isolation produce physical symptoms such as headaches, heart palpitations, back and neck pain, digestive problems, dizziness, and loss of appetite in inmates—unless there were an essential relation between inmates' sense of embodied existence and their social relations with other embodied beings (P. Smith 2006, 488–90)? Likewise, why would physical isolation or forced proximity to others produce psychological and affective symptoms such as anxiety, paranoia, panic, obsession, poor impulse control, aggression, and self-mutilation—unless human beings relied on the physical presence of others, as well as the chance to withdraw from that presence, for their emotional stability and mental health (P. Smith 2006, 492)? And why would prolonged isolation produce perceptual distortions, hallucinations, and cognitive impairments (P. Smith 2006, 490–91)—unless there were not only a corporeal dimension but also an *intercorporeal* or social dimension to the basic mental processes that we usually take to be intrinsic to the isolated individual?

The basic physical needs of prisoners, such as food, water, and shelter, may be adequately provided in most U.S. prisons, but the experience of inmates in intensive confinement suggests that human beings need something more than just the fulfillment of basic physical needs in order to flourish, or even to sustain their own physical, emotional, and mental health. The question is whether this "something more" is unique to humans, or whether it is shared with other social animals who display similar forms of strain and dis-ease under similar conditions of intensive confinement.[30] In the next section, I survey the effects of intensive confinement on nonhuman animals in factory farms and laboratories, with a view not only to the points of intersection between human and nonhuman animality, but also to the philosophical implications of this intersection for a postanthropocentric animal ontology.

De-animalizing Animals

Animals in factory farms or laboratories face many of the same challenges as prison inmates, and suffer many similar effects on their physical, mental, and emotional health. They are often held in conditions of both extreme isolation and extreme proximity: in tiny cages where they can barely move or interact with other animals, yet often in such close confinement with other animals that they cannot help but be in constant contact with them.

As in the prison industrial complex, economic pressures have favored the intensive confinement of farm animals such as pigs and chickens for the sake of saving space and maximizing profit. This form of confinement tends to generate pathological effects in animals, posing challenges for industrial agriculture even while increasing profit margins. When animals are not able to turn around in their cages or pens, when they do not have the space or the conditions to perform certain behaviors, such as grooming, foraging for food, or even walking—behaviors that are typical for their species—then many animals begin to engage in behavioral disorders known as stereotypies: "abnormal, repetitious, and apparently meaningless behaviors [such as] gnawing, bar biting, and tail biting" (Novek 2005, 234). Stereotypies such as "pacing back and forth, running in circles, somersaulting, rocking, self-biting, bar-biting, earpulling, hair-pulling, eye-poking, etc." have also been noted in lab monkeys and in zoos (Reinhardt 2004, 3).

What is the meaning of these "apparently meaningless" behaviors and syndromes? We cannot interview nonhuman animals to ask them to describe or explain their own experience; instead, we must rely on careful observation and reflection, both comparing the animals' behavior with our own and also remaining attentive to the differences between different ways of being in the world, resisting (to the extent that this is possible) the temptation to project our own motivations onto other species. Take, for example, D. G. M. Wood-Gush and K. Vestergaard's discussion of the effect of intensive confinement on battery chickens, who are no longer able to engage in the exploratory behavior that is normal for their species:

> One may ask how important it is for the animal to perform this type of exploratory behavior when food is constantly present or generously provided or when nests are provided. Consider the domestic fowl in a single bird battery cage; food is constantly before it. Examination of its behavior . . . shows that it spends a considerable amount of time raking over the food pellets. Not all the behavior directed toward the food is truly ingestive, and some could be classified as extrinsic exploration. (1989, 162)

Like human inmates in intensive confinement, chickens on factory farms have their basic needs met: food, water, and shelter. And yet closer observation suggests that there is something more involved in the chickens' relation to food than the mere ingestion of nutrients. The chickens no longer *need* to scratch for food in the battery cage, and yet they continue to scratch. One may interpret this behavior as evidence that chickens are a kind of mechanism that comes "hardwired" for scratching; even in the absence of any good reason to scratch, they continue to do so because that is how they have been programmed to behave by their genetic constitution. On this interpretation, chickens are not responsive enough to their environment to modify their behavior to suit the environment. But another interpretation is possible. The gestures of searching for food, exploring the environment, sifting through the inedible to find the edible—all of these gestures are ways of relating to the world through movements of the body. They are expressive of a comportment, a pattern of behavior that is shared with other animals of their kind and that overlaps with the behavior of other animals commonly found in their environment, such as insects, worms, foxes, and hawks. The field of possible experience for a chicken is structured in particular ways according to the kind of animal that it is, but it does not exclude interaction with a multiplicity of other animals and other inanimate things. If this is the case, then one may interpret the chicken's behavior as an expression of its constitutive relationality as an animal whose existence entails *essential,* rather than merely incidental, relationships to a field of possible experience and to a multiplicity of other animals who appear in this field. On this interpretation, the chicken's obsessive scratching, even in the absence of any reason to scratch, would not indicate an indifferent mechanism at work in an animal-automaton; rather, it would suggest that the whole network of relations that otherwise sustain this animal in its Umwelt have been undermined or pathologically deranged. Wood-Gush and Vestergaard implicitly recognize this second way of interpreting the evidence when they argue that although the intensive confinement of farm animals "leads to apparently docile animals, it is an abnormal behavioral state and is contrary to the animals' welfare and natural dignity" (1989, 167).

The scratching behavior of battery chickens suggests an intrinsic, rather than extrinsic, relationship between chickens and their edible/inedible environment. But there are also other, more explicitly *social* forms of relationality that come under intense pressure in the factory farm. Jim Mason and Mary Finelli observe:

> The animals have no relief from crowding and monotony. In a less restric-
> tive environment they would relieve boredom by moving; confined animals
> cannot. When animals are crowded and agitated, they are more likely to
> fight. In the restricted space of confinement pens, less aggressive animals
> cannot get away to make the instinctive show of submission. (2006, 112)

Not only the foraging behavior of chickens but also complex social behaviors, such as displaying signs of submission in order to avoid a fight,
are undermined by conditions of intensive confinement. This suggests
that animals are not merely inconvenienced by intensive confinement;
they are blocked from behaving as the kind of animals they are, with
meaningful relationships to the world and to other animals, when they
are not given the space to perform the gestures and movements that are
intrinsic to their particular form of relational being. Mason and Finelli
argue that the extreme limitation of the space that an animal is allowed
to occupy not only affects that particular animal, understood as an
organism separable from its world, but also impacts the whole "social
structure," along with the conditions of relatively harmonious coexis-
tence and mutual flourishing that this social structure sustains. They
observe that, "prevented from forming stable social structures, birds
[on factory farms] may engage in abnormal and potentially injurious
pecking behavior" (2006, 112). This pecking can lead to the death of
weaker chickens, and even to a "cannibal" frenzy in which chickens not
only kill other chickens, but also eat them. In order to reduce this pecking behavior, and the economic damage that fighting among birds can
cause for the farming enterprise, their claws, the ends of their beaks, or
both are cut off, usually without anesthesia (N. Williams 2008, 375).[31]

Similar behavior has been observed in intensively confined turkeys
and pigs, and self-injurious behavior is so common among primates
in zoos and laboratories that an acronym (SIB) is used as short-
hand.[32] These nonhuman animal pathologies resonate with reports
of increased aggression, violence, and self-mutilation in intensively
confined human prisoners. Sharon Shalev argues that compulsive self-
harm is a desperate attempt to confirm one's existence in the absence
of intersubjective recognition—to feel *something* rather than nothing
(2009, 196).[33] As one prisoner explains, "You become so angry. It's an
outlet, but you have to vent it out. Even your own blood is something
real" (197). Another prisoner says, "I found myself curled up in a foetal
position rocking myself back and forth and banging my head against
the wall. In the absence of sensation, it's hard sometimes to convince

yourself that you're really there" (197). Stuart Grassian observed extreme forms of self-mutilation, to the point of autocannibalism, in his study of the Bedford Hills Correctional Facility for Women: "Many [inmates] became grossly disorganized and psychotic, smearing themselves with feces, mumbling and screaming incoherently all day and night, some even descending to the horror of eating parts of their own bodies" (2006, 351).[34]

In considering syndromes found in farm animals alongside SHU syndrome in human prison inmates, I do not wish to conflate the differences among the many animal species who experience pathological symptoms in conditions of intensive confinement; rather, I am suggesting that for each of these species, there is a network of relations with other living and nonliving beings that helps sustain a meaningful sense of Being-in-the-world. This sense is structurally undermined by conditions that do not allow for a mixture of contact and withdrawal in relation to other living beings in a shared but open-ended space.[35]

Like a Kitten

In closing, I wish to consider one of the countless experiments in sensory deprivation that were carried out on human and nonhuman animals such as cats, dogs, primates, rats, and mice in the 1950s–70s.[36] I look to this experiment in particular because I think it discloses, in a simple yet devastating way, the importance of intercorporeal relations for both human and nonhuman animals, even if these relations are structured in different ways that are specific to each species. In this experiment, behavioral scientist Austin Riesen confined newborn kittens whose eyes had just started to open in a dark room for twenty-three hours a day. For the remaining hour, he covered the kittens' heads with "fine percale" hoods that diffused the light but still allowed for normal breathing with "no signs of discomfort" in the kittens (1961, 22). Riesen wanted to test whether sensory deprivation from birth would affect the kittens' development of "visual placing" skills. At what point would a deprived kitten begin to relate actively to its environment by extending its paws toward a table onto which it was being lowered? As soon as one of the control animals from the same litter showed signs of visual placing, the experimental kitten-subjects were allowed one hour of unhooded light and were tested for their responses. At first, the experimental kittens showed no signs of visual placing, but within five hours of unhooded light, whether or not these hours were continuous, they began to anticipate the table with their paws.

Riesen makes a remarkable observation about the kittens' second hour of unhooded life. He notes that in this hour, "kittens typically spent considerable time sitting straight up and still, staring fixedly at the mother's face" (1961, 23). Riesen does not comment on the role that the mother cat's face might play in the kitten's ability to orient itself within a visual and spatial world. Instead, he moves on to discuss other experiments involving kittens and primates who were permitted an experience of light but were not permitted to move and so failed to develop "the protective eye blink" (23).[37] For Riesen, light, movement, and the experience of another animal's face are all separable "parts" in the development of basic motor skills; the point of the experiment is to disentangle these parts in order to discover which is most fundamental. The structure of his experiment places light, movement, and the face of the kitten's mother on the same ontological plane; they are all sources of "stimulus" to which the animal responds. In the end, the mother's face disappears from Riesen's analysis; he concludes, "In the absence of patterned visual input, autonomous rhythmic activity appears to gain the upper hand" (25). Stereotypies such as rocking, pacing, repetitive grooming, biting, and so forth emerge as if to compensate for the loss of complex, intercorporeal relations to another living being. But this compensation is itself a pathology, often leading to further isolation, alienation, aggression, or self-harm.

Riesen's experiment is one among many to highlight the affinities among human and nonhuman animals, even while committing violence against the latter for the sake of the former's curiosity. What would human prisoners have to be like in order to have their basic capacity to experience the world—to think, perceive, feel, and act in a coherent, stable way—undermined by the experience of intensive confinement? They would not have to be subjects invested with a unique set of human capacities, such as symbolic language or abstract reasoning, for it is precisely at the level of bodily perception, sensibility, and affectivity that prisoners find their relation to the world undermined. Rather, *they would have to be like a kitten,* whose primary orientation point in the world is not a simple preprogrammed instinct or a strictly individual capacity for "visual placing" but, rather, an intercorporeal relation with other animals, and especially with the mother who cares for it.

For the kitten who has been deprived of an open-ended field of visual experience from birth, the first orientation point in the world, the anchor for its own individuated experience of space, is the mother's face. For an hour or more, the kitten stares at this face, sitting straight and still, until it feels capable of loosening its gaze and expanding its visual experience of the world to include other objects and other dimensions of spatial depth and proximity. This orientation of the kitten's embodied perspective in space through the mediation of the mother's face dovetails with experimental evidence on human infants, in which the mother's face provides an anchor point and support for an infant's own developing sense of self as an individuated subject with a unique perspective on a shared world (Maclaren 2008; Merleau-Ponty 2008, 166–68). It also confirms the experience of adult human animals who find themselves thoroughly disoriented and even ontologically deranged by the prolonged deprivation of everyday interactions with other animals, both human and nonhuman.[38]

The disastrous effects of being deprived of a meaningful relation to other living beings in a heterogeneous world suggest that there is nothing exclusively human about the need for everyday intercorporeal experience. Even though there are significant differences between humans and other animals—as there are between bats and bears, monkeys and chipmunks—there is also a level of intercorporeal intentionality that human beings share with other social animals. What the opposition between humane and inhumane treatment fails to grasp is the degree to which it is not primarily as *human beings,* with a presumably inherent sense of dignity and freedom, that prisoners are affected by solitary confinement and sensory deprivation, but as *living beings,* sensible flesh with corporeal relations to other embodied beings and to an open field of overlapping experience in a shared world. It is as animals that prisoners are damaged or even destroyed by the supermax or SHU, just as their fellow animals are damaged or destroyed by confinement in cages at zoos, factory farms, and scientific laboratories.

Our overlapping, intercorporeal experience of other animate bodies, both human and nonhuman, sustains our own capacity to perceive the world as a meaningful context for our own lives. These interactions with other animals do not merely provide a source of pleasant diversion from what would otherwise be a monotonous life of solitude; as the experience of isolated prisoners suggests, these interactions are vital for sustaining our most basic sense of reality and living personhood and for differentiating the void of empty and meaningless space from an experience of the world as an open-ended context for meaning. Even though psychological terms like "SHU syndrome" are helpful for expressing the harm of prolonged solitary confinement and for listing its most common effects or symptoms, such terms fail to express the sense in which it is not just prisoners' "mental health" that is affected by prolonged solitary confinement, but their whole Being-in-the-world, their capacity to relate intentionally to objects within the world, to coconstitute with others a sense of shared reality, and to participate in a common situation that is accessible to a multiplicity of different but overlapping perspectives.

Every day, other living beings provide orientation points for our own perception of the world. The twitching of a dog's ears tells me that a car is coming before I actually hear it; a trail of ants coming into the house alerts me to the cookie crumbs I have inadvertently spilled on the floor; a quick exchange of glances lets me know that I wasn't the only one to hear that sexist comment. Intercorporeal relations with other living beings are necessary not only for preserving "mental health," although this is important (and it is also important to note that the psychological effects of prolonged solitude are shared by many nonhuman animals, to the point where mental health has become a basic zoo-management issue). But these intercorporeal relations are also vital for both human and nonhuman animals to orient ourselves spatially and affectively in a world shared with other living beings: to feel where we are and even who we are. The problem with intensive confinement in control prisons is not just that it treats human prisoners like animals, but that it *fails* to treat them like animals, where animals are understood as living beings whose corporeal and intercorporeal relations with other living beings in a shared, open-ended space sustain a meaningful sense of the form of life that is proper to their species.

The prisoners at Attica prison in the 1970s and in the Georgia state prison system in 2010 were right to protest their dehumanization and the treatment like animals or like slaves to which this dehumanization exposes them; in a system that is structured by oppositions between human and animal, black and white, domination and freedom, the recognition of someone as a human being with an intrinsic, inviolable human dignity may be all that stands between a minimal form of protection and radical form of exploitation.[39] But there is a further violence to which dehumanized prisoners are exposed, which is not quite captured in the humanist language of enlightenment that some prisoners have invoked and which may very well need to be invoked for strategic reasons. This is the violence of what I have called de-animalization: the reduction of a living, relational animal to a nonrelational thing to be stored, exchanged, or even destroyed without regard for its particular ways of being in the world. Perhaps human dignity is best protected when it is claimed not as the unique, exclusive property of the human but as a structure of open relationality shared with other living beings.

Intensive confinement, whether it is produced through forced solitude or forced contact with others, in the context of the prison industrial complex or the animal industrial complex, commits a form of structural violence against animal ontology. It threatens to break the hinges of an intercorporeality that human animals share with nonhuman animals—not only with the social animals whose forms of relationality most closely approximate our own, but with any animal that lives and grows by relying on the mutual support of other living, growing beings. Human and nonhuman animals alike are de-animalized through intensive confinement: reduced to input–output machines, mechanisms of stimulus and response, separable units of behavior that can be disorganized and reorganized according to the requirements of the animal industrial complex or the prison industrial complex. In order to find more fruitful ways of critiquing the abuse of both systems, in which human and nonhuman animals are confined to cages, pens, and cells across the world, we need to think beyond dehumanization, and beyond the anthropocentric worldview that supports it.

III
SUPERMAX PRISONS

7 SUPERMAX CONFINEMENT AND THE EXHAUSTION OF SPACE

> The world is not what I think, but what I live through. I am
> open to the world, I have no doubt that I am in communica-
> tion with it, but I do not possess it; it is inexhaustible.
>
> —Maurice Merleau-Ponty, *Phenomenology of Perception*

> I usedta live in the world / now i live in harlem & my
> universe is six blocks.
>
> —Ntozake Shange, *For Colored Girls Who Have
> Considered Suicide When the Rainbow Is Enuf*

THE THIRD WAVE of solitary confinement in the United States is
the era of the control prison. Its implicit, and often explicit, aim is to
control, contain, and incapacitate prisoners. Gone is the rhetoric of
rehabilitation or spiritual redemption. It has been replaced by a neoliberal rhetoric of risk management, security, efficiency, accountability,
and public–private partnerships. Even the official names of supermax-
level prison cells reflect the aim of control, along with a desire to
represent this aim as a legally acceptable administrative tool rather
than as an instrument of outright punishment. Among the most common names on this seemingly interminable list are Special Housing
Unit or Security Housing Unit (SHU), Control Unit (CU), Special
Control Unit (SCU), Administrative Segregation Unit (ASU or Ad-
Seg), Administrative Maximum Facility (ADX or Ad-Max), Intensive
Management Unit (IMU), and even Communication Management
Unit (CMU). A 2005 Bureau of Justice report found that 81,622 pris-
oners reside in some form of restricted housing (Solitary Watch 2012b).

If anything, these numbers have increased as isolation units continue to be built in prisons, jails, and juvenile detention centers across the country, although the recent financial crisis has led some policy makers to propose cheaper alternatives.

Critics compare supermax prisons to warehouses (Irwin 2005) or to "cold storage" for people (Human Rights Watch 1997).[1] And indeed, most of the prisons I have visited are located in light industrial areas. One drives—perforce, because there is hardly ever public transit to these places—past distribution centers, mini storage depots, trucking company headquarters, low-rent offices . . . and prisons. The visual distinction between these different sites is often negligible. The only thing that makes Charles Bass Correctional Complex in Nashville, Tennessee, stand out from the other businesses on Cockrill Bend Boulevard are the extra layers of razor wire beyond and between the standard chain link fences. A casual observer could mistake the grounds around Riverbend Maximum Security Institution, down the street from Charles Bass, for a suburban golf course. Wild turkeys and deer graze on the green hills by the river, red-tailed hawks and turkey vultures soar overhead, and fireflies light up along the stream in the evening. But the prisoners see almost nothing of this. If they are lucky, they will have permission to walk along neatly plotted sidewalks from one unit to the other, where they will be able to see the open sky above them. Most of the prisoners I work with in Unit 2 at Riverbend have not touched the grass or seen the stars in over twenty years. They are allowed an hour of recreation time a day in a cage they call the dog pen. Some choose to remain in their cells during rec time. "I feel safer there," said one prisoner.[2]

Advocates of supermax prisons portray inmates as "the worst of the worst": serial killers, rapists, and terrorists who pose an incontrovertible threat to society at large, and even to other inmates. But in practice, many inmates convicted of nonviolent crimes end up in Control Units because they have broken prison rules against fighting (which is sometimes unavoidable), refusing to work (for pennies an hour, or in some states for no wages at all), possession of contraband (which can include anything from weapons to spicy tortilla chips), or even self-mutilation or attempted suicide (Shalev 2009, 72).[3] Some inmates are placed directly into the SHU without having done anything to break the rules because they are presumed to be gang members or gang associates, or because they are vulnerable to attacks from other inmates.[4]

As a result, there is a disproportionate number of black, Latino, queer, and trans inmates held at the supermax level.[5] Control Units are also notorious as destinations for politically active prisoners or perceived "leaders" within the general prison population.[6] Once an inmate has landed in a supermax unit, it can be extremely difficult to get out; even minor infringements or perceived infringements of prison rules can set back one's date of release into the general prison population. Decisions about so-called administrative segregation are made internally within the prison, without the presence of judges or lawyers, and so the prisoner is at the mercy of prison officials who may or may not be sympathetic to her case.

What is it like to be confined in a supermax unit? A typical cell ranges in size from six feet by eight feet to eight feet by twelve feet; it is part of a "pod" of eight to ten cells arranged into two tiers. Cells are usually painted white or pale grey to reduce visual stimulus. Furnishings consist of a bed, a table and seat, a toilet, and a sink—all bolted in place. The door is constructed of perforated stainless steel resembling a dense wire mesh that obstructs the prisoner's view to the outside while allowing some natural light to filter through along with the sounds and smells of adjoining cells, or even the pepper spray used on prisoners during cell extractions.[7] There is a slot in the door, called a cuffport, tray port, meal port, or pie flap, through which food trays are exchanged and the prisoners' hands cuffed or uncuffed for removal from the cell. There are either no windows at all or just a small, high window that lets in light but does not afford any view of the outside. Fluorescent lights are kept on twenty-four hours a day, and surveillance cameras are continuously running.[8]

Prisoners are confined in solitude for 22 to 23.5 hours a day, with the remaining time spent—again, in solitude—in an outdoor exercise yard, surrounded by concrete or tightly woven security mesh walls that offer little or no view of the outside and only a small glimpse of sky.[9] These yards are often called "dog pens" or "dog runs" because of their resemblance to an outdoor kennel. Remotely operated doors allow prison staff to release prisoners from their cells for showers or exercise without coming into contact with them. In many supermax prisons, inmates communicate with guards through intercoms; some prisons even employ "tele-medicine" and "tele-psychiatry" sessions to minimize direct contact between inmates and staff (Haney 2003, 126). Depending on the prisoners' level of good behavior, they may be given access to books, radio, television, or video conference visits with loved ones. Often, the only television available in a supermax prison is a closed-circuit broadcast of training videos and religious programming. A prisoner in a Control Unit can go for years, even decades, without experiencing any form of touch beyond the chaining and unchaining of wrists through the cuffport in the door. Prisoners who refuse to present their hands to the cuffport for restraint are forcibly "extracted" from their cells and pepper-sprayed if they continue to resist; they may be put in four-point restraints (with both arms and both legs fastened to the ground) or in a restraint chair (in which arms, legs, and chest are strapped to the chair). Officers are entitled to perform strip searches or cavity searches of inmates whom they suspect of possessing contraband items. Often, these searches are conducted as a matter of routine.[10]

Anthony Graves, who was falsely accused of murder and spent over eighteen years on death row in Texas, presented the following testimony to a 2012 Senate Judiciary Subcommittee hearing on solitary confinement:

> I had no physical contact with another human being in at least 10 of the 18 years I was incarcerated. Today I have a hard time being around a group of people for long periods of time without feeling too crowded. . . . I will have to live with these vivid memories for the rest of my life. I would watch guys come into prison totally sane and in three years they don't live in the real world anymore. . . . Solitary confinement does one thing, it breaks a man's will to live and he ends up deteriorating. He's never the same person again. . . . I haven't had a good sleep since my release. My mind and body are having a hard time making the adjustment. I have mood swings that cause emotional breakdowns. Solitary confinement makes our criminal justice system the criminal. (2012b)[11]

What would it be like to have one's bodily contact with others reduced to the fastening and unfastening of restraints, punctuated with the most intimate probing of the surface and depths of one's body?[12] Not to be able to speak to anyone except through intercom or by yelling through a slot in the door? To be kept in solitude and yet exposed to constant surveillance and to the echoing noise of other prisoners?[13] What would it be like to be prevented from having a concrete experience of open, unrestricted space? Not to see the sky or the horizon for days, weeks, even years on end? Not to know if it's day or night apart from the schedule of one's feedings and allotted exercise times?[14]

It is impossible to imagine. And yet both the attempt to imagine solitary confinement and the impossibility of knowing what it is like without having undergone it—and perhaps even having undergone it—are crucial for resistance. The act of imagining opens up an *elsewhere* and an *otherwise* within our current situation; it allows us to transpose ourselves into another place and time, another social position, and another subjectivity. As such, it highlights both the incompleteness of the here and now—the sense in which even our current reality bears different possibilities within itself—and also the incompleteness of any single subject, given the degree to which our subjectivity is shaped by how we imagine others to be, and how we imagine they perceive us. Prisoners in solitary confinement are, by definition, excluded from the looping effects of social interaction; they are isolated in their cells, with no one to see or to look back at them, no one to touch or to receive their touch. And yet, precisely by virtue of their forced isolation, the prisoners' situation is mediated by countless others: the guards who keep them, feed them, and monitor their activities; the wardens who oversee the guards; the prison review board that continues their isolation in ninety-day intervals; the lawyers who prosecuted or defended them; the judge or jury who sentenced them; and us, the public who tolerates their ongoing isolation, even (or especially) if we are not even aware of it. Supermax prisoners are unperceived and unimaginable others, but they are *our* others, and a society that practices long-term, wide-scale solitary confinement cannot help but be shaped by our (non)relation to those who have been "disappeared" but who remain among us, and sometimes return to haunt us.

Many prisoners speak of their experience in supermax prison as a form of living death. On the one hand, their bodies still live and breathe, eat and defecate, wake and sleep (often with difficulty). On the other hand, a meaningful sense of living embodiment has for the most part drained out of their lives; they've become unhinged from the world, confined to a space in which all they can do is turn around or pace back and forth, blocked from an open-ended perception of the world as a space of mutual belonging and interaction with others. José Rubio, an inmate at Marion Penitentiary during the 1972 protests, described his experience of the Control Unit as "death on the installment plan" (quoted in Gómez 2006, 68). Eddie Griffin, another former inmate at Marion, called it "a Death Row for the living" (1993, 7). In his essay "Resisting Living Death at Marion Penitentiary, 1972," Alan Eladio Gómez argues that the Control Unit introduced at Marion

Penitentiary but now common across the United States "collapsed the legal and physical space between life and politics—and between punishment and death. . . . Designed as a breathing coffin, the CU was/is a space of permanent living death" (2006, 60–61). The Control Unit gives a concrete, material shape to the civil and social death of inmates, produced and reinforced by law; it forms "a state of exception from the rule of prison law within an already existing state of exception from the rule of civil law" (59–60).[15]

Other prisoners describe their confinement in the SHU or CU in terms of sensory deprivation or even ontological derangement. Luc Levasseur, who was held in solitary confinement for thirteen years with the exception of eleven hours a week, describes the purpose of a boxcar cell—a cement cube perforated on one side by steel bars, which look out onto another cement wall with a solid steel door—as follows: "to gouge the prisoners' senses by suppressing human sound, putting blinders about our eyes and forbidding touch" (Levasseur 2005, 47). Jack Henry Abbott, who estimates that he spent fourteen to fifteen years in solitary confinement in maximum-security prisons in the 1960s and '70s, writes:

> Something happens down there in the hole, something like an event, but this event can only occur over a span of years. It cannot take place in time and space the way we ordinarily know them. (1991, 45)

> My body communicates with the cell. We exchange temperatures and air currents, smells and leavings on the floor and walls. I try to keep it clean, to wash away my evidence, for the first year or so, then let it go at that. (46)

> If you are in that cell for weeks that add up to months [Abbott is referring to a strip-cell consisting of nothing but an open toilet in the center, sprayed around with urine and feces], you do not ignore all this and live "with it"; you *enter* it and become a part of it. (29)

Eddie Griffin describes the Control Unit at Marion Penitentiary:

> The cell itself contains a flat steel slab jutting from the wall. Overlaying the slab is a one-inch piece of foam wrapped in coarse plastic. This is supposed to be a bed. Yet it cuts so deeply into the body when one lays on it, that the body literally reeks with pain. After a few days, you are totally numb. Feelings become indistinct, emotions unpredictable. The monotony makes thoughts hard to separate and capsulate. The eyes grow weary of the scene, and shadows appear around the periphery, causing sudden reflexive action. Essentially, the content of a man's mind is the only means to defend his sanity. (1993, 7)

Why does prolonged solitary confinement bring about such dramatic perceptual, psychological, cognitive, and even ontological effects, not just in one or two prisoners but in 70 to 90 percent of all prisoners (Grassian 1983, 2006; Haney 2003)? In what follows, I draw on Merleau-Ponty's account of embodied perception and his account of spatial depth in order to develop a phenomenological account of the fundamental importance of corporeal, spatial, and social depth and of the devastating effects of blocking someone's access to these depths.

Touch and Corporeal Depth

For Merleau-Ponty, the body has a depth that is accessible, in different ways, to both touch and vision. The back of my head, my profile, the slump of my posture—these can be seen through the mediation of mirrors or photographs, but they are immediately accessible to touch and to the touchy-feely sense of proprioception in a way that unfolds differently from vision and yields a different range of possible meanings. The sense of the body's spatiality is different from the "objective space" of geometry:

> Experience discloses beneath objective space, in which the body eventually finds its place, a primitive spatiality of which experience is merely the outer covering and which merges with the body's very being. To be a body is to be tied to a certain world, as we have seen; our body is not primarily *in* space: it is of it. (2002, 171)

As an embodied consciousness (or conscious embodiment), I find myself "in" space and implicated in a nexus of causal relations: bound by the laws of nature, shaped by the evolutionary history of my species, constrained by my own physiology, and so forth. But I also experience myself as a spatial being with my own perspective on the world and my own felt sense of situated embodiment.[16] On the one hand, the body is a physical thing; it can be plotted on a grid, prodded by a doctor or scientist, located with a GPS receiver. But on the other hand, the body is the site of lived experience; I feel things, not just *in* my body but *as* a body. In this sense, I do not just occupy space, I *inhabit* it. My body is not merely inserted into objective grid space; rather, it is the perspective from which my experience of space, and even of my own body as a spatial being, unfolds. I perceive my situation neither as a god hovering above the world nor as a robot passively recording raw data about the world, but as a corporeal Being-in-the-world who is both constituted by that world and constitutive of its sense, understood in the twofold signification of meaning and direction. As embodied Being-in-the-world, I do not indiscriminately take everything in at the same level or to the same degree. Rather, I am drawn to certain things rather than others, picking out some objects in the foreground and relegating others to the background. These relations shift according to what concerns me most at this or that moment, and I am not always the one who determines my own concerns; the relation between body and world unfolds as a conversation, in a dynamic tension between passive givenness and active constitution.

My body is the primordial "here" from which I encounter every "there."[17] It is the root of my intentional consciousness and of my existence as a living being whose physiological and existential structures intermesh with the bodies of other living beings. The "here" of my own bodily perspective is both utterly inescapable and utterly mobile; it is a root and a vehicle for my open-ended exploration of the world. Movement is a vital component of this experience for Merleau-Ponty:

> My body is geared onto a world when my perception presents me with a spectacle as varied and clearly articulated as possible, and when my motor intentions, as they unfold, receive the responses they expect from the world. (2002, 292)

This "gearing of the subject onto his world . . . is the origin of space" (2002, 293). As I move through the world, interacting with objects and other subjects, a constantly changing but consistently patterned series of profiles or glimpses of the world unfolds from the perspective of my embodied consciousness. Each of these profiles is partial, revealing some aspects of the world while concealing others; I can never see the front and the back of an object simultaneously, but as I move around, my body "gears into" the heterogeneous texture of the world, and I gain a sense of the object as a whole that exceeds what I can experience in any given moment, but that nevertheless has a coherence or wholeness of its own. Precisely because perception is partial and perspectival, it is also inexhaustible; I can never complete my perception of even a simple object like a cup or a table, since it is only accessible to me through a temporally unfolding blend of presence and absence.

Part of what it means to exist as a subject *of* space and not merely *in* space, is the experience of touch. In *Ideas II* and *Cartesian Meditations*, Husserl already expresses the importance of touch for constituting a sense of one's body as one's own. My left hand touches my right hand, sensing its coolness and smoothness as an object in space; but my right hand also *feels* this touch as gentle or harsh, palpating or scratching, and if I shift the emphasis of my attention, I can just as easily feel like my right hand is actively touching my left as the reverse. Both hands belong to the same touching-touched Body, or *Leib,* which is not merely in space but of it, and which experiences its own physical being as an utterly singular localization of sense. My own hand "is more than a material thing, and the way in which it is mine entails that I, the 'subject of the Body,' can say that what belongs to the material thing is its, not mine" (Husserl 2002, 157). The singular localization of sensation in my own body allows me to experience the features of other things as belonging to them, and not to me; it supports the distinction between myself and not-myself, and ultimately between self and other. Husserl goes so far as to say that a *"subject whose only sense was the sense of vision could not at all have an appearing Body. . . .* Obviously, the Body is also to be seen just like any other thing, but it becomes a *Body* only by incorporating tactile sensations, pain sensations, etc.—in short, by the localization of the sensations as sensations" (2002, 158).

In *The Visible and the Invisible,* Merleau-Ponty elaborates Husserl's insight beyond its epistemological framework into an ontology of the flesh, or the chiasmatic structure of being. What fascinates Merleau-Ponty the most in Husserl's account of tactility is the crossing-over of touching and being touched, which verges on simultaneity but refuses to be synchronized into a single moment of experience. Touching encroaches on the touched, and vice versa, without collapsing the difference between them; the chiasm of touching and touched is the site of differentiation through mutual overlapping and divergence.[18] For Merleau-Ponty, this chiasmatic structure is not confined to the sense of touch; rather, it expresses the general structure of being, as discernible in the relation of vision and the visible, the visible and the tangible, and even in the relation of self and other. For Merleau-Ponty, it is impossible to see without also being exposed to the possibility of being seen:

> As soon as I see, it is necessary that the vision (as is so well indicated by the double meaning of the word) be doubled with a complementary vision or with another vision: myself seen from without, such as another would see me, installed in the midst of the visible, occupied in considering it from a certain spot. (1968, 134)

The vision of another vision, complementary to mine and yet irreducibly different, reveals the visible world as "the surface of an inexhaustible depth" (143).

> As soon as we see other seers, we no longer have before us only the look without a pupil, the plate glass of things with that feeble reflection, that phantom of ourselves they evoke by designating a place among themselves whence we see them: henceforth, through other eyes we are for ourselves visible; the lacuna where our eyes, our back, lie is filled, filled still by the visible, of which we are not the titulars. (143)

It is as one among others, and not as a solitary subject of experience, that *I see myself as visible* and the world as animated with meaning, beyond what I might personally project upon it. The apparent lack by which I am unable to see my own eyes or the back of my own head becomes a sheltering hollow for the fullness of the visible world to which I belong and from which I draw reserves of sense. I owe the richness of the world to this reversibility of self and other by which I am granted access to a "wild meaning" that holds open an inexhaustible experience of "carnal being, as a being of depths" (155, 136).

Merleau-Ponty's account of reversibility raises ontological as well as ethical and political questions about the structure of surveillance in a control prison.[19] If I am constantly monitored in my prison cell, without having a chance to return the other's gaze—or if I spend eight hours a day in the surveillance booth, watching prisoners who cannot see me watching them—what effect does this have on my experience of chiasmatic being? On the one hand, the positions of guard and prisoner are tightly bound to one another as subjects and objects of vision; on the other hand, the irreversibility of these positions disconnects them from each other, such that they do not interweave as "two halves of an orange" or "two segments of one sole circular course" (Merleau-Ponty 1968, 133, 138). It is not even clear that they belong to "one sole world" whose "landscapes interweave" such that "the little private world of each is not juxtaposed to the world of all the others, but surrounded by it, levied off from it" (142). And yet the prisoner and the guard are stuck in the same dreary landscape of segmented hallways, razor-wire perimeters, and booming concrete interiors. They are positioned differently within this landscape, to be sure, but it is not at all clear that the guards have greater access to the chiasmatic structure of being than do the prisoners, as long as they are bound to watch over them. What happens to the "inexhaustible depth" of the visible/tangible world when the embodied relations of self and other are so rigidly defined and enforced?

Spatial Depth and the Pure Depth of Night

Merleau-Ponty's most extended discussion of depth unfolds in the chapter on space in *Phenomenology of Perception*. Here, Merleau-Ponty proposes a concept of "primitive" or "primary spatiality" that unfolds from the bodily perspective of one who is touching and touched, seeing and seen. In every mundane perception, there is not only the encounter with an object but also the opening of a dimension of depth that marks my distance from and proximity to things. While length and width can be perceived as belonging solely to objects located in grid space, depth unfolds in phenomenological space, as part of the lived experience of subjects who are embedded in the very world that they perceive. From a Cartesian perspective, where space is understood as extension, depth is not meaningfully different from width; what appears as depth to me (and is therefore invisible, since it merely passes through a segment of empty space), is clearly visible and measurable from a third-person perspective perpendicular to the line between myself and the object. In other words: the experience of depth at point A on the grid is (more clearly expressed as) the experience of width at point B. Merleau-Ponty rejects such a "solution" to the problem of depth, first because the conversion of depth-for-me into width-for-the-other does not explain anything about our experience of depth as such, and second because the primary experience of space is not open to measurement but, rather, unfolds through the qualitative, and even affective, opening of a *dimension*.

For Merleau-Ponty, the "lived distance" of depth perception "binds me to things which count and exist for me, and links them to each other. This distance measures the 'scope' of my life at every moment" (2002, 333). In this sense, the experience of depth is not merely perceptual in a cognitive sense, but also affective or emotional. I am *moved* by things, and not everything moves me in the same way. Affective depth marks the emergence and unfolding of meaningful space, space that matters to what Heidegger would call my Being-in-the-world. To care about things—to be structured *as* care—is to be open to the way some aspects of the world leap out at me and seize me, while others recede into the background or even escape my notice.

In his discussion of depth, Merleau-Ponty raises the possibility of an experience of "pure depth": depth without a determinate object, "a spatiality without things" (2002, 330). He calls this experience of pure depth "night":

> Night is not an object before me; it enwraps me and infiltrates through all my senses, stifling my recollections and almost destroying my personal identity. I am no longer withdrawn into my perceptual look-out from which I watch the outlines of objects moving by at a distance. Night has no outlines; it is itself in contact with me; it enwraps me and its unity is the mystical unity of the *mana*. Even shouts or a distant light people it only vaguely, and then it comes to life in its entirety; it is pure depth without foreground or background, without surfaces and without any distance separating it from me. (330)

Night is the name for an experience of space unhinged from determinate objects and from the limits or outlines that distinguish self from nonself.[20] Recall the experience of prisoners in prolonged solitary confinement: the strange feeling of death in life, in which one's body begins to "communicate" with the cell, the outlines around things seem to melt, and the cell walls themselves begin to waver. Could the experience of endless day, as in the twenty-four-hour illumination of the supermax cell, be tantamount to an experience of night? Is supermax confinement an experience of pure depth, or is it an experience of space deprived of depth? And how exactly would we be able to determine the difference?

For Merleau-Ponty, the experience of night is fecund and generative; it exposes us to the prepersonal matrix from which our bodies individuate and to which they remain attached by a mystical umbilical cord. But even here, the experience of night is highly ambivalent; it stifles my reflections and threatens to destroy my personal identity just as much as it connects me to the *mana* of pure depth:

> Sometimes between myself and the events . . . the lived distance is both too small and too great: the majority of the events cease to count for me, while the nearest ones obsess me. They enshroud me like night and rob me of my individuality and freedom. I can literally no longer breathe; I am possessed. (2002, 333)

The experience of pure depth can be suffocating as well as liberating; affective depth, the site of mattering, can invert into a radical loss of meaning where nothing counts anymore. Supermax daylight, no less than the experience of night, threatens to destroy a prisoner's sense of personal identity—not because it is free from limits, but because it is confined to such strict limits that the open-ended field of experience that defines the world, and defines both self and other as coinhabitants of a shared world, begins to disintegrate.

What anchors and stabilizes the experience of pure depth is the correlation of an individuated, embodied perspective, a "here," with a world of stable, determinate objects, a "there." Merleau-Ponty calls this "clear space": "that impartial space in which all objects are equally important and enjoy the same right to existence" (2002, 287). Clear space is not opposed to night; it remains connected to pure depth, "thoroughly permeated by another spatiality thrown into relief by morbid deviations from the normal" (287). Nor is it drained of affective significance, as Shiloh Whitney observes:

> Our perceptual distance from the things that populate our world is not guaranteed. It depends on our ability to care, to become acquainted with affective entities that polarize space in their own right. This in turn lets us achieve "lived distance": a margin of respectful affective distance from things and others. (2010, 14)

Clear space is the sane, rational space of a world shared with others, a world in which things matter but in which their precise meaning is subject to constant mediation and negotiation. It is a sense of space maintained by both an engagement with the world and a capacity to sleep or withdraw from the world. Merleau-Ponty writes, "During sleep . . . I hold the world present to me only in order to keep it at a distance, and I revert to the subjective sources of my existence" (2002, 331). Sleep is the escape that both reconnects me to the experience of primary spatiality—to the night—and also allows me to retain and even recover my sense of personal identity, my distinction from the night, the root of my own subjective existence. The temporal rhythm of alternating night and day, sleep and waking, release and return, sustains the fabric of embodied subjectivity in a world that is experienced in depth, somewhere between the extremes of pure depth and objective space.[21]

In articulating his concept of pure depth, Merleau-Ponty cites schizophrenia as an example of those "morbid deviations from the normal" produced by an exposure to the night. He presents schizophrenia less as a mental illness than as a phenomenological disorder of

Being-in-the-world rooted in a pathological experience of space: "The schizophrenic no longer inhabits the common property world, but a private world, and no longer gets as far as geographical space. . . . The world can no longer be taken for granted" (2002, 335). For one reason or another—Merleau-Ponty does not speculate on the etiology of the disease—schizophrenia unhinges patients from a common world, afflicting them with an experience of the world not shared with other people. We could say that schizophrenia removes patients from "clear space":

> What protects the sane man against delirium or hallucination, is not his critical powers, but the structure of his space: objects remain before him, keeping their distances and, as Malebranche said speaking of Adam, touching him only with respect. What brings about both hallucinations and myths is a shrinkage in the space directly experienced, a rooting of things in our body [rather than in a shared world], the overwhelming proximity of the object, the oneness of man and the world, which is, not indeed abolished, but repressed by everyday perception or by objective thought, and which philosophical consciousness rediscovers. (339)

The schizophrenic is exposed to a prolonged experience of night: an experience that unravels the meaning of "experience" understood phenomenologically as the subjective basis for knowledge of the objective (that is, intersubjective or intercorporeal) world. Clear space, with its consistent correlations between self and other, body and world, keeps the night at bay; it carves "places" out of the pure depth of spatiality, and it institutes stable but flexible limits on the proximity and distance of things. In so doing, it preserves a hollow within the world for the reception of a body, and a hollow within the body for the reception of a world. Of course, clear space can also be reified into objective or grid space when the rationalist subject attempts to deny or overcome the lived experience of depth, in which case rationality also becomes a source of pathology. But there is a place (quite literally) for an experience of clear space somewhere between night and the grid of objective space.

In the final section of this chapter, I will overlap and diverge from Merleau-Ponty's analysis of schizophrenia in *Phenomenology of Perception* in order to develop my own account of SHU syndrome as a pathological experience of space, and so of embodied subjectivity. If schizophrenia is a pathology of space in which the world shrinks to the limits of my own private experience, and so destabilizes my sense of reality to the point where "the world can no longer be taken for granted," then prolonged solitary confinement amounts to a production of something like schizophrenia in the prisoner (Merleau-Ponty 2002, 335). I argue that supermax confinement is not a solution to the problem of finding a place to keep "the worst of the worst" from harming others. It is—among other things—a technology for producing what one could call mental illness, if "mental" were not too narrow a term to express the complex intertwining of body, mind, and world that I have just undertaken to describe.[22] Prolonged solitary confinement in a control prison threatens to exhaust the otherwise inexhaustible horizons of perceptual experience by blocking prisoners' concrete experience of depth in its spatial, affective, and social dimensions. It leaves prisoners feeling like their lives have been drained of meaning, like they are dead within life, no longer *of* space but merely *in* it. As we will see, prisoners held in solitary confinement have also developed a range of practices of resistance to the abolition of depth and the liquidation of meaningful space. But before I make the argument that intensive confinement threatens to "exhaust" prisoners' sense of space, I need to say a bit more about Merleau-Ponty's account of the inexhaustibility of thing and world.

The Inexhaustible Depth of the World

In *The Primacy of Perception,* Merleau-Ponty defines perceptual objects as "open, inexhaustible systems which we recognize through a certain style of development, although we are never able, in principle, to explore them entirely" (1964a, 6). But what if a person is confined for years on end in an eight-by-ten cell with no view to the outside, little room to move around, few if any new objects to encounter, no opportunity to rearrange the furniture, and strictly limited contact with other people? At what point might the "open, inexhaustible systems" of perception become exhausted?

First we must ask, What makes the object of perception inexhaustible? In *The Sense of Space,* David Morris addresses this question in relation to the experience of place. He argues that the difference between a hallucination and the perception of a real object is that "real things occupy place and they present, as Merleau-Ponty urges, an inexhaustible wealth of different aspects" (2004, 111). A hallucination exhausts itself in its momentary appearance to me, and only me. "The 'pink elephant' is a hallucination not merely because it is the wrong color, but because I cannot place it outside me, it just floats through the room with blatant disregard for place" (110). A place is a niche within space, a hollow for something to be encountered in depth. As we have seen, space becomes "clear"—it staves off the turbulence of night—by unfolding access to more or less stable and determinate places. For something to occupy a place, it must *be somewhere* in relation to my own body and in a context with other things around which this particular thing is to be found. A place is not merely a point or cluster of points in objective grid space; rather, it forms a system with my body, it is the site of a mutual interaction and correlation between self and nonself. In other words, a place is "there" in relation to my "here." As Morris puts it:

> Place is roughed up by movement. A ganzfeld [a homogeneous, unpatterned field of color that produces in the viewer an effect of sensory deprivation], on the contrary, manifests no difference; it is place ground down and smoothed out by the artist, homogenized by the bouncing of light; it is created by movement that obscures itself, and so presents no field or room in which things can appear for our moving body. (112)

A ganzfeld—like the smooth, homogeneous walls of the supermax prison cell—effaces the distinctions that would otherwise serve as anchors or signposts for the emergence of place. The ganzfeld is, in effect, a region of space that refuses to cohere into place, offering so little resistance to the gaze that a viewer exposed to a ganzfeld for an extended period of time without interruption typically experiences a temporary loss of vision or "fog." The ganzfeld *exhausts* the visual experience of space by *emptying* it of the distinctions that help pattern our experience in open-ended but consistent ways.[23] In a sense, it immobilizes an embodied perceiver by releasing the perceiver into a vacuum where nothing has any more affective pull than anything else, where the "respectful distance" of clear space has been exacerbated to the point of indifference.[24]

Morris argues for a "tight coupling between the inexhaustibility of things and the inexhaustibility of the places in which we move and explore things" (2004, 112). Something that is encountered in a particular place is never given absolutely, from all sides at once, but only in partial perspectives, each of which involves a blend of presence and absence. This incompleteness is crucial for the dynamic interrelation between body and world and for the inexhaustible perception of the latter. As Merleau-Ponty writes:

> *I have* the world as an incomplete individual, through the agency of my
> body as the potentiality of this world, and I have the positing of objects
> through that of my body, or conversely the positing of my body through that
> of objects, not in any kind of logical implication . . . but in a real implication,
> and because my body is a movement towards the world, and the world my
> body's point of support. (2002, 408)

I wish to supplement Morris's account of the relation between place
and inexhaustibility with one other crucial dimension: the experience
of other embodied subjects in a shared space of overlapping perspectives.[25] The perceptual object is inexhaustible not only because it is the
"other side" that completes the sense of embodied consciousness, and
not only because objects of perception are given to me from a partial
perspective in a determinate place outside of myself. What lends the
most radical sense of inexhaustibility to perception is the availability
of what I perceive to others with whom I share a partial perspective,
though our perspectives can never coincide. Things move me with
affective depth not only because of the anonymous indeterminacy of
night, and not only because things overflow my own private perception of them, but also because the world *matters to other subjects* in
ways that implicate me practically and emotionally and yet remain
ultimately inscrutable, thanks to the singularity of first-person consciousness. As Merleau-Ponty writes in his Nature lectures, "There is
a reference in me to space which is not mine" (2003b, 166; see also 167,
218). He makes a similar point in *Phenomenology of Perception*:

> Between my consciousness and my body as I experience it, between this
> phenomenal body of mine and that of another as I see it from the outside,
> there exists an internal relation which causes the other to appear as the
> completion of the system. (2002, 410)

My experience of a plurality of other embodied subjects in a shared
world holds open the incompleteness that, even at the individual level,
characterizes my perception of things and places. The perspectives of
self and other

> slip into each other and are brought together finally in the thing. In the same
> way we must learn to find the communication between one consciousness
> and another in one and the same world. In reality, the other is not shut up
> inside my perspective of the world, because this perspective itself has no
> definite limits, because it slips spontaneously into the other's, and because
> both are brought together in the one single world in which we all participate
> as anonymous subjects of perception. (411)

I propose to call this structure of overlapping perspectives the opening of *social depth* or, more precisely, *intercorporeal depth.* Intercorporeal depth is not merely added onto spatial depth; rather, it subtends it in ways that Merleau-Ponty may not make explicit but that are nonetheless latent or implicit in his texts. The overlapping of my own perspective with the perspectives of others literally fills out the dimensionality of my own perception. Confined to my own visual perspective, I can only see one side of a spatial object at a time; and yet the *sense* of a spatial object involves the potentiality to be seen from multiple perspectives. As a solitary individual, I have access to these other perspectives as they unfold for me successively in sequential time; I walk around the object, and I see the same thing from many different successive profiles. Every present profile implies a manifold of retained and protended profiles that are respectively slipping away and coming into view, such that what I *experience* is not only the particular slice of the object that is visible to me at any given moment but, rather, the object as a whole. But these multiple profiles that are accessible to me sequentially *in time* are also accessible simultaneously to a multiplicity of different viewers *in the space of a shared world.* The side of the cereal box that is hidden to me now is revealed to the person across the table, and the closer we are to one another, the more fully our perspectives overlap—*simultaneously,* spread out in space—without ever coinciding absolutely. This multiplicity of virtual and actual perspectives within my own experience of the world opens up the singularity of first-person consciousness to novelty and diversity in an open-ended way. Merleau-Ponty writes:

> No sooner has my gaze fallen upon a living body in process of acting than the objects surrounding it immediately take on a fresh layer of significance: they are no longer simply what I myself could make of them, they are what this other pattern of behavior is about to make of them. Round about the perceived body a vortex forms, towards which my world is drawn and, so to speak, sucked in: to this extent, it is no longer merely mine, and no longer merely present, it is present to x, to that other manifestation of behavior which begins to take shape in it. Already the other body has ceased to be a mere fragment of the world, and become the theatre of a certain process of elaboration, and, as it were, a certain "view" of the world. (2002, 411–12)

The overlapping of my own perspective as a moving, living body with the perspectives of other moving, living bodies does not only support my cognitive understanding of the world; it also shapes the emotional or affective landscape of a world that sucks me in and forms a "vortex" around my body. The body of the other is not merely a thing among things but an open-ended "pattern of behavior" defined by its habits of movement, activity, and response, in relation both to my own patterns of behavior and to the animate and inanimate things that we mutually encounter in places within a shared world. In this sense, body, thing, and other are not separate substances that exist first for themselves and only later enter into relation with each other; rather, they are mutually constitutive relata for whom the relation comes first; a separate identity emerges only through divergence. This process of mutual divergence leaves in its wake a zone of reversible relationality, or what Merleau-Ponty later calls "flesh" between myself and the other. In the context of *Phenomenology of Perception,* however, this zone is articulated in terms of an "anonymous existence" that belongs neither to myself nor to the other, but to both of us insofar as we participate in a mutually constitutive relationality:

> As the parts of my body together comprise a system, so my body and the other's are one whole, two sides of one and the same phenomenon, and the anonymous existence of which my body is the ever-renewed trace henceforth inhabits both bodies simultaneously. (2002, 412)

This social and perceptual depth is precisely what is blocked for the prisoner in supermax confinement: the spontaneous overlapping of perspectives with others, and the anonymity of belonging to a shared world in which one's own unique perceptual perspective is only one among many, where one is a participant in the plurality of a social world.[26]

What does it mean to be denied one's participation as an anonymous subject of perception? At first glance, it might seem counterintuitive to claim that the supermax prisoner is denied *anonymity.* Isn't anonymity precisely the problem for an inmate whose name has been replaced by a number, who wears a prison jumpsuit identical to every other prisoner's, and who is denied the sort of social interaction that could confirm, both in language and in bodily comportment, her existence as a person?[27] Yes and no. Without denying the pain of anonymity, I want to suggest that access to anonymity is part of what sustains a coherent sense of personhood. The capacity to withdraw and slip away into the night, disappearing from the gaze of others, releasing oneself from the confines of any particular place, is tantamount to the "sleep" that, according to Merleau-Ponty, allows me to "hold the world present to me only in order to keep it at a distance" and to "revert to the subjective sources of my existence" (2002, 331). Without this anonymity—without the possibility of becoming imperceptible, to borrow a phrase from Gilles Deleuze and Félix Guattari—I may no longer be able to sustain the complex dynamic of perception, which involves both engagement and withdrawal, both connection and distinction, both location in a place and relation to the "elsewhere" of a "larger place." The ambivalence of anonymity recalls the ambivalence of night, and the two concepts are not unconnected. On the one hand, night threatens the subject with self-loss and dispersal; but on the other hand, as pure depth, it reopens every reified space to the possibility of indetermination and becoming-otherwise. Night pulls one beyond oneself, into an open world of indeterminate and inexhaustible depth. Both night and sleep are necessary for sustaining the fabric of relations between self, other, thing, and world.

Prisoners who are shut up in their solitary cells and monitored from a distance by video camera twenty-four hours a day are both rendered anonymous, in that they are reduced to nameless, faceless existence in which they are constantly reminded that they do not matter to anyone. But they are also denied access to anonymity, in that they are unable to slip out of place, to withdraw from the fixity of any given place, from their eight-by-ten cells, and to withdraw from the meanings attached to those cells: "the worst of the worst," "beyond rehabilitation," "a hopeless case," and so on. To put this another way: Prisoners in solitary confinement are denied the *incompleteness* of perceptual Being-in-the-world, the double incompleteness of the body–thing system and the self–other system, both of which sustain the sense of a world with inexhaustible horizons. They are confined to their own side of the otherwise open circuit between their own perceiving bodies and the heterogeneous field of the world, understood as "the field of all fields" (Merleau-Ponty 2002, 408), the one world shared in common.

Cut off from an open-ended experience of space and a noncoercive experience of others, supermax prisoners risk losing the sense of themselves as persons who matter and to whom the world matters, on their own terms, as self-organizing and auto-affective Beings-in-the-world. They risk getting stuffed inside the theoretical position of the Cartesian cogito, the absolute individual that is shut up within itself, forced into a position that Merleau-Ponty argues does not exist except as a fiction devised by the intellectualist philosophers of cognition. As in the context of liberal individualism discussed in the introduction to this book, supermax prisoners are forced into an ideal(ist) position that nonincarcerated subjects never actually find themselves in, but that prisoners are forced to adopt through a coercive rearrangement of space: the position of solitary, solipsistic individuals made to bear the full weight of their own being, made "accountable" for everything they do, say, and are, and for the "choices" they make in a situation that is structured from top to bottom by domination and control.

What is it like to be forced into such a place, and what sort of strategies have prisoners developed to resist their situation? In the final section of this chapter, I turn to the first-person accounts of prisoners themselves in an effort to fill out the phenomenological dimensions of the analysis presented thus far and to (begin to) explore the social, political, and ethical implications of supermax confinement.

The Exhaustion of Space? Pathology and Resistance in the Supermax Prison

In her book *Total Confinement,* anthropologist Lorna Rhodes describes her first visit to a prison in Washington State. She observes an inmate, Jamal Nelson, in the solitary exercise yard. He is swinging his arms from side to side in widening circles until his knuckles start hitting the concrete walls. He continues to swing, splattering the concrete with blood, relentlessly marking the limits of the space allotted to him, as if oblivious to the pain and even to the walls themselves (2004, 3).

What would drive someone to do this? Again, we could invoke mental illness or SHU syndrome, and we could list the typical symptoms of such an illness or syndrome. But prisoners' first-person accounts of their experience in intensive confinement suggests that the genesis of such behavior rests in a disturbance or even derangement of the complex relations between self, other, and world in a confined space where, for the most part, experiences of spatial and intercorporeal depth are foreclosed. Recall the ontological "event" within prolonged solitary confinement described by Jack Henry Abbott, whereby the prisoner's body "communicates" with the cell, as if one had no choice but to "*enter* it and become a part of it." How does this indistinction between a place and its inhabitant come about in supermax prisons, and how do some prisoners manage to resist it?

In a philosophy seminar with Drew Leder at the Maryland Penitentiary in 1993, inmate John Woodland Jr. describes his maximum security cell: "It's just enough room to live in. No more. Nothing for relaxation. Nothing for feeling comfortable. Just enough room to live in" (Baxter et al. 2005, 208). He compares the space of the prison cell to the social space afforded to himself and other African Americans in an urban landscape carved up by racist oppression:

> One thing I noticed when I first came to the penitentiary is that the penitentiary design is similar to the high-rise projects in West Baltimore or East Baltimore or wherever. In prison it's the tiers; in the projects it's the floors. . . .
>
> Because wherever you go, east or west, you see African Americans and low-income people packed in on top of one another, with no real space. When you walk down the streets of most inner cities, you feel indifference to everything: "This isn't really part of me. I'm just existing here. This is not something I should care about or protect or build up. This is something I gotta deal with until I get out." I guess that's the same way we look at prison. (208–9)

What is it like to inhabit such a place (or nonplace)? Is "just enough room to live in" really enough room for life, or does it situate the prisoner in the twilight of a half-life or living death? How does one manage to care about a space (or care about oneself in a space) that is structured in a way that, for the most part, forecloses the intercorporeal experience of depth? In nonincarcerated space, walls tend to function as supports for embodied personhood: constitutive limits that carve places out of pure depth, both stabilizing and continuing the dynamics of embodied, relational consciousness. Walls offer protection and privacy; they mediate between inner and outer space. But what is the experience of walls like in a supermax unit, where the walls have no windows and the door does not open from the inside—where the white or gray ganzfeld gives the eyes almost nothing to "gear" into, just a smooth homogeneous surface or, in older prisons, a pockmarked surface carved with traces of other inmates, now absent?

We do not know what Jamal Nelson felt as he swung his arms into the walls of the exercise pen, bashing his own hands. But we do have reports from prisoners who have come back from the opacity of such an event or who have found different ways of negotiating their experience of intensive confinement. Jack Henry Abbott describes his twenty-three days in a blackout cell, where even his food was deposited through a revolving apparatus that did not let in a sliver of light:

> I heard someone screaming far away and it was me. I fell against the wall, and as if it were a catapult, was hurled across the cell to the opposite wall. Back and forth I reeled, from the door to the walls, screaming. Insane. (1991, 27)

There is perhaps no more literal experience of night than this: total darkness, the absence of perceptual limits, self-loss—and a violent reassertion of self, to the point of physical self-destruction and insanity. To bash one's hands or body against the walls of a cell is both to refuse and to confirm the enclosure of one's available space. Perhaps it is a way of emphatically marking the difference between body and cell in a situation where they have begun to merge, where the cell has become a kind of exoskeleton for the body. In chapter 1, I introduced Caleb Smith's concept of the "cellular soul" idealized by early penitentiary reformers (2009, 92). In its ideal form, the cellular soul would be redeemed through its separation from the world that had corrupted it; given time to reflect in solitude, the cellular soul would rectify itself, using the walls of the cell as a material and spiritual prosthesis for becoming an upstanding citizen, a self-contained and self-supporting individual. But in practice, the cellular soul became an inhabitant of its own tomb, not a resurrected citizen but a prisoner condemned to living death, "buried from the world" (quoted in C. Smith 2009, 39).

Building on Smith's work, and taking into account the structure of supermax spatiality and embodied subjectivity, I wish to argue that solitary confinement is equally a matter of "cellular embodiment." In theory, supermax prisoners learn how to "contain" themselves; they learn how to moderate their behavior in accordance with certain rules that give them access to more or less bodily comfort and more or less living space on the basis of a punishment–reward system. They learn to make rational choices as individuals within a stable, concrete structure.[28] But in practice, confinement in a supermax cell undermines prisoners' agency by blocking their experience of spatial and social depth, literally confining them to a Control Unit, where their only choices are already mapped out by a flowchart of automatic acts and consequences, punishments and rewards, that allow little or no room for negotiating the complexity of perceptual and social life within or beyond prison. Elliott Currie calls this "punitive individualism" (1998, 112; and quoted in Rhodes 2004, 84): individuals are made to bear the full weight of their existence, expected to be fully accountable for a situation over which they have little or no control and to take the blame for the damage that this structure does to their own embodied subjectivity. A person who bashes his or her own body against the cell walls is both refusing and confirming the logic of punitive individualism that structures cellular embodiment. The self-battering body makes a statement of sorts: these walls may confine me absolutely, but I absolutely refuse to be confined! There is a difference between my body and space, there is a "there" to which my "here" is correlated, and I will find it, even if I have to hurl myself against it, or even destroy myself in the process.

Other prisoners find different, less destructive ways of responding to their confinement in a tightly limited space. Robert King, a member of the Angola Three who spent twenty-nine years in solitary confinement in a dimly lit nine-foot-by-six-foot cell, writes:[29]

> Some days I would pace up and down and from left to right for hours, counting to myself. I learned to know every inch of the cell. Maybe I looked crazy walking back and forth like some trapped animal, but I had no choice—I needed to feel in control of my space. . . .
>
> At times I felt an anguish that is hard to put into words. . . .
>
> I talk about my 29 years in solitary as if it was the past, but the truth is it never leaves you. In some ways I am still there. (2010)

Like the act of bashing one's body into walls, the habit of pacing both resists and reinscribes the limits of place that block an experience of intercorporeal depth. But unlike bashing, pacing develops a more sustainable coping mechanism, a way of feeling "in control of [one's] space" even if one does not have the power to change places. Pacing is a bodily attempt to "take the measure" of the cell or cage, and in some way to take control over something that cannot be controlled.[30] The subject who paces is both refusing to sit still within the allotted space and refusing to destroy bodily integrity by bashing against the walls. It is a way of insisting that one is still a living, moving being, even though the world has been diminished to the point where one is no longer able to live and move freely and nonpathologically. It is also an expression of restlessness: I can't get comfortable in my own skin, but I can't get out of it, either. Pacing expresses not an acceptance of limits but, rather, a nervous retracing of them; it is a habit formed around the impossibility of habituating oneself to what is an intolerable situation. In this sense, it is a way of coping—but even this coping mechanism is still a pathology that can become its own compulsive trap. Habits of adaption to the narrow and solitary space of a supermax unit can become habits of maladaption to life outside of prison, or even on the main line in the general prison population. Many prisoners find that their time in confined space and solitude expands the amount of personal space they need after they get released. It is as if their sense of personhood had expanded to fit the narrow constraints permitted, and even though the cell walls were barriers to freedom and connection, they had adjusted to them, and maybe even identified with them in order to form a zone of comfort or safety (see Rhodes 2004, 34). As Robert King says, "In some ways I am still there."[31]

Supermax prisons are at least nominally meant to be structures of containment for the most brutal and violent prisoners—"the worst of the worst"—but they can also be furnaces for the superrefinement of criminal insanity. Lorna Rhodes's interview with Pete Owen, a long-term inmate of the Control Unit in a Washington State prison, confirms the possibility that, while intensive confinement is a suffocating, claustrophobic barrier to a full sense of personhood, it can also refine or distill a new form of personhood: CU superhumanity, hyperviolent but also calm and hyperrational. Owen says:

> You get a real bizarre second wind, it gets to be a different thing that is *made*—not broken—by the control unit. . . . A strong person with a strong will, it's gonna make them into something with a lot of violent potential. For months, years on end, you're in that little box—it comes down to no recognition of your being. And your human dignity becomes immense. (Quoted in Rhodes 2004, 174)

In this extraordinary statement, Owen reconfigures the meaning of "human dignity," removing it from the context of liberal individualism and its abstract respect for human rationality and transposing it into the supermax context of an extreme, even violent, hyperrationality, a sharp focusing of the will into a determination to resist absolutely the control of others. Rhodes notes that both prisoners and guards "use the term 'monster' to describe the prisoner who becomes increasingly hardened even as the building he lives in is likewise hardened to keep up with him" (2004, 175).[32] Both inmates who harden in response to the inflexible walls of their confinement and inmates who crumble in that space, maladapting through compulsive habits of self-harm, tend to find themselves trapped in the very situation that has produced them, since the more pathological they become as a result of intensive confinement, the less chance that they will ever be released from it until their full sentence has been served. At that point, they are often released directly into the public with no transition or counseling.

What can we make of these first-person accounts from prisoners in light of our previous discussion of Merleau-Ponty's account of inter-corporeal depth? Deprived of a regular, concrete experience of other embodied subjects in mutual interaction, and blocked from a regu-lar, concrete experience of spatial distance or variable depth, the pris-oner in supermax confinement risks coming unhinged from the world and being thrown into a pathological experience of space not unlike Merleau-Ponty's account of schizophrenia. The solid, homogeneous walls of the supermax Control Unit create a "place" that is tantamount to the pure depth of night in the sense that it threatens the subject with the dissolution of all meaningful boundaries, but this "place" is signifi-cantly unlike pure depth, and it is equally unlike the places of mutual interaction between body and world, self and other that shape our ex-perience of clear space. If pure depth is the opening of an inexhaustible dimension of embodied perception, to the point of releasing the subject from confinement in any given determinate place, then supermax con-finement is not an experience of pure depth. Rather, it is confinement in a place that drains space of its intercorporeal depth, a place that ex-hausts space and blocks the emergence of dimensionality. But if place is a niche within space, a limitation that helps us mediate and incor-porate the giddiness of pure depth, then the supermax Control Unit is not a place, either. Rather, it is a space that—through its extreme and rigid limitation and its liquidation of intercorporeal depth—destroys the boundaries that constitute a meaningful sense of place.

The supermax unit is precisely that: a unit, a block of objective grid space that a living, moving, embodied Being-in-the-world is forced to occupy like a piece on a chessboard, an absolute individual separable from the society of others and from the "larger place" of the world. This unit is measurable in feet or in "paces"—six by nine, eight by twelve—and yet the subjective *experience* of this space could never be expressed in terms of length and width; it can only be conveyed as the blocked experience of foreclosed depth that their occupants are forced to undergo in solitude. The irony is that—tragically, absurdly—the supermax prisoner is one of the only living beings whose experience of space matches the account of objective grid space given by Cartesian rationalists (or liberal individualists, for that matter). Nonincarcerated subjects are free to invest in the fictions of objectivity, autonomy, self-sufficiency, and individuality, all the while relying on their embodied experience of affective and intercorporeal depth to sustain a meaningful sense of Being-in-the-world. Only incarcerated subjects are forced to actually *exist* in such fictions, or to be broken by them.

And yet, in a testament to their resilience as living beings, some prisoners do manage to carve out a place of sorts in the evacuated, exhausted space of supermax confinement. To say so is not in any way to deny the cruelty of carceral technologies that wittingly or unwittingly produce pathological subjects, nor is it to downplay the harm to both those who resist and those who do not manage to resist, nor is it even to imply a hierarchy between those who survive and those who are broken by the supermax. Rather, it is to acknowledge the complexity of even the most homogeneous place insofar as it forms part of the circuit of embodied experience for a living human being. Lorna Rhodes observes:

> The "box" of the prison presents a smooth surface to the outside world, which is of course how it works as a place of disappearance. But inside, it has distinct internal separations. (2004, 3)

These internal separations function to individualize and arrange prisoners for the sake of management and control, but they also open cracks and fissures within the otherwise homogeneous space of the supermax. Many Control Units have ventilation grates through which inmates are able to communicate with each other. Even the walls themselves can become a means of connecting with other prisoners by tapping and knocking.[33] The cuffport in particular becomes a heightened site of exchange between inside and outside, prisoner and guard, even prisoner and other prisoners. Just as cell walls can become a kind of exoskeleton for the inmate, as if the material boundaries of the cell had fused with the inmate's own body, so too can the cell walls and cuffport become expressive of an intimate carnality forced into the publicity of constant surveillance. The cuffport becomes both a mouth and an anus, a site of possible interchange for the prisoner whose full participation in intercorporeality has been blocked.

Rhodes explains that some prisoners throw their own feces through the cuffport as an act of resistance and aggression by those who feel that they have no other way to fight back against guards who have almost total control over every aspect of their lives:

> In a world where your food is thrown at you through a hole, where the head of your bed is next to your toilet, where toilet paper has to be requested, throwing shit *says* something. (2004, 45)

Prisoners who throw their own shit at officers are using one of the last means of resistance, their own bodily wastes and the slots in their "cellular embodiment," as weapons against their keepers, saying, in effect, "If I'm nothing but a piece of shit, then you can eat my shit—and you can clean it up, too."[34] Not only do they spray officers with their filth, posing both a symbolic and a biomedical threat of contamination by another person's bodily fluids, but they also *make something happen,* initiating a whole series of actions that will ultimately rebound against the prisoners themselves with the violence of retaliation and punishment but that nevertheless exert an ambivalent kind of agency.[35] Shit-throwing prisoners recruit the bodies of guards as unwilling proxies for their own bodies, which remain locked in cells and blocked from almost all significant action. For some prisoners, even the violent retribution for behavior like this is experienced as a kind of perverse triumph. One prisoner interviewed by Rhodes says, "I want to fight those people that hurt me. And the only way I can fight them is to . . . leave 'em no choice but to come in on me" (quoted in 2004, 173). Another prisoner echoes this logic:[36]

> If I'm being good and they don't give me nothing, I can't take that kind of rejection. . . . I just went off, spitting, urinating, tearing up my cell, the whole nine yards. . . . If they feel like I'm gonna be a badass, why not be one? . . . They think they can control me, but I'm gonna be the one in control. (Quoted in Rhodes 2004, 55)

This (twisted, but understandable) logic of "control" can take extreme forms, as in the case of the mentally ill prisoner who proclaims with pride, "I *made* 'em cut off my thumb" (quoted in Rhodes 2004, 68).

Not only the cuffport but also the body itself becomes an ambivalent site of violence and resistance within supermax prisons. As Allen Feldman writes, quoting a statement from the Provisional Irish Republican Army (PIRA) during the so-called dirty protest at Her

Majesty's Prison Maze (or Long Kesh) from 1978–83, in which prisoners refused to shower and smeared feces all over their cell walls:

> The H-Blocks changed the whole way you thought about your body. . . .
> From the moment we hit the H-block we had used our bodies as a protest
> weapon. It came from the understanding that the Brits were using our bod-
> ies to break us. (Quoted in Feldman 1991, 179)

A dialectic of force and resistance sweeps up the bodies of both prisoners and guards.[37] On the one hand, guards are separated from prisoners by highly mediated space where prisoners are sealed within solid walls and monitored from a distance through constantly running surveillance cameras, with doors as the only threshold between inside and outside and cuffports as the only gaps, the only permeable points in this threshold. On the other hand, guards come into the most intimate contact possible with prisoners, cuffing and uncuffing their hands through cuffports, restraining their hands and legs, doling out squares of toilet paper or menstrual pads, dispensing food, searching their anal cavities, and sometimes getting feces or urine thrown in their faces. The separation between prisoners and guards cannot be absolutely enforced, and yet the dialectic of force and resistance that springs up between them remains asymmetrically weighted toward the guards, who have the power of *legitimate* physical violence on their side.

The most extreme manifestation of this asymmetry is the strip search, which could be traumatic for anyone but is especially so for the many prisoners who are survivors of sexual and physical abuse.[38] Laura Whitehorn, a political prisoner who spent fourteen years in prison in connection with the Resistance Conspiracy case, says:

> The point is not to locate contraband; it's to reduce you to a completely pow-
> erless person. . . . It reduces you to an object, not worthy of being defended.
> The message is, "your body is meaningless, why don't you want this man to
> put his hands all over you?" Very, very deeply damaging. . . .
>
> You have to exert an enormous amount of psychic energy to remove
> yourself from the situation, where this guy's running his hands all over
> your body. You end up exhausted at the end of the day, and your nerves
> are shot. Your only life is resisting these situations. (Buck and Whitehorn
> 2005, 262–63)

Yvonne Smith, a twenty-one-year-old African American prisoner in the SHU at Valley State Prison for Women, confirms this feeling:

> They don't do this because of "safety and security of the institution," they do it for humiliation. Some of them really like it. There is nothing we can do between our cells and the shower, no way we can pick anything up. [Women at VSPW were subject to strip searches every time they were taken out of their cells to go have a shower.] They're with us, watching us the whole time. They are just tryin' to break us down. (Quoted in Shaylor 1998, 391)

Claudia Johnson, another prisoner at VSPW, states this succinctly: "It is about humiliation and total loss of dignity, and I don't care what they call it. I call it rape" (quoted in Shaylor 1998, 392).

In a strip search, one's body, the site of corporeal and intercorporeal "mattering," is literally put into the hands of another whose insistent message is that the body of the person being searched does *not* matter, that it does not even properly belong to that person, and that it can only bear the meaning that is imposed on it by the violence of others. Laura Doyle interprets the practice of strip-searching and cavity-searching from the perspective of Merleau-Ponty's late work on the "flesh" (1968, 130–55) as an occupation of the chiasmatic space of the prisoner's body:

> To shove a fist or instrument into the anus against the will of the prisoner: it is to come between the parts of the fleshly person, to display mastery over the body (as mass) of the prisoner: it is to come between the parts of the fleshly person, to display mastery over the space contained and occupied by the body. (Doyle 2006, 186)

But Doyle also suggests that the capacity of the body to be forcefully penetrated bears witness, if only negatively and painfully, to its capacity for internal spaces of self-relation and bodily resistance. Even when prisoners are forced back on their own bodies and blocked from *external* experience of spatial depth, they may be able to retain and recover a sense of *internal* depth—an "inscape" or "breathing space"—within their own bodies:

> Here, perhaps, is where resistance lives. For, short of death, and sometimes regardless of desire, there is always an internal space—a breathing space quite literally as well as analogically; and while dense matter can be dominated, can be forced into this or that position, penetrated with this or that weapon, the breathing space cannot be. (188)

We may wonder if this breathing space is really inviolable, given prisoners' accounts of violation through strip searches and cavity searches. Is it not possible to dominate and occupy even a person's inner bodily space and psychic space? Is the domination and restriction of outer space not already a kind of invasion that transforms the prisoner into a cellular body and a cellular soul? Perhaps. But Doyle's confidence in "the capacity of *inter*corporeal exchange to revive and protect the *intra*corporeal self-relation and so to set once more in motion the processes of active being" does not blind her to the fact that "the capacity for metamorphosis resides in an interior space that is also an opening to violation" (194, 186). The body is the hinge of our being, the place where we are open to the world, and for that very reason it can be exploited and turned against us; but for the same reason, it is also a place where we can return to ourselves and rearticulate our bodily intimacy, recovering to whatever extent possible the phenomenological and ontological conditions of intercorporeal depth. The condition for the possibility of exploitation is also the condition for the possibility of resistance, since only a hinged, corporeal being could be broken in this way.

I have mentioned, very briefly, the existence of psychic space.[39] Psychic space, like the opening of an inner corporeal depth and like the affective dimensions of spatial and social depth, remains connected to the web of relations between body, thing, and other that together constitute a meaningful sense of the world. Psychic space is not just a metaphor, in other words, but a continuation and intensification of our everyday corporeal and intercorporeal experience of spatiality. When blocked from a concrete experience of spatial depth in maximum or supermaximum confinement units, many prisoners turn to psychic space as a source of depth and dimensionality, an "elsewhere" beyond the rigid framework of the prison cell. Mark Medley, an inmate in Drew Leder's philosophy seminar at the Maryland Penitentiary, uses what he calls "autistic thinking"—a retreat from the current reality of the prison cell into a world of fantasy and open-ended creation— as a way of resting or "sleeping" and sustaining a sense of meaningful worldhood in the midst of a situation that blocks both space and meaning.[40] Both the activity and engagement involved in projects like these and the disengagement or rest involved in fantasy or "autistic thinking" allow prisoners to structure their experience of space and time with a meaningful rhythm, an orientation toward something that matters to them, and to grant themselves the slackening of attention that allows each one of us to sustain the intensity of our absorption in the world. Some prisoners achieve this by drawing or writing poetry;

others challenge themselves with cognitive exercises.[41] Robert King made pralines out of sugar and pecans he had saved from meal trays, melting the sugar in a tin can over a fire made with collected scraps of toilet paper and whatever other paper he could scrounge up (King 2010). For me, one of the most extraordinary projects of reimagining psycho-social space within prison is currently unfolding in the collaboration between Herman Wallace and artist Jackie Sumell.[42]

Herman Wallace, Robert King, and Albert Woodfox are known collectively as the Angola Three. In the 1960s, each man found himself imprisoned for petty crimes at Angola Prison, a former slave plantation and current maximum-security state prison in Louisiana. Once in prison, they became politically active, and together they organized the first ever prison chapter of the Black Panther Party in 1971. They began educating prisoners on their legal rights, organizing for better prison conditions, and working toward desegregation of the prison population, but in 1972 Wallace and Woodfox were accused and convicted of murdering a prison guard; King was associated with the murder but not charged. All three have denied involvement in the murder, and the case against them is riddled with inconsistencies. But while King was released in 2001 following a legal action concerning another accusation, Wallace and Woodfox have remained in solitary confinement since 1972.

In 2003, artist Jackie Sumell began corresponding with Wallace during his two-year confinement to the part of Angola Prison called "the Dungeon," where even prisoners who are already in solitary confinement are subject to further crushing restrictions on their access to spatial and social depth. Sumell asked Wallace, "What kind of a house does a man who has lived in a six-foot-by-nine-foot cell for over 30 years dream of?" Since then, Wallace and Sumell have been working together to imagine, draft, build models, and create computer-aided design simulations of his dream home; together with the Community Futures Collective, Sumell is raising money to buy land in Wallace's hometown of New Orleans and to construct his dream home in reality. Wallace's plans for the house are quite modest. The house has many windows, but also differentiated rooms or "places." It is built of natural materials like wood and stone, and it is surrounded by trees, grass with stone pathways, gardens, and even a rooftop greenhouse. In a letter, Wallace explains his priorities: a well-stocked pantry with easy access from the garage for unloading groceries; a bedroom with a fireplace,

African art, mirrored ceilings, soft blue light, and a fake-fur bearskin on the king-sized bed; a six-foot-by-nine-foot hot tub (the same size as his current cell); an underground bunker accessible through a trapdoor in the fireplace; and, finally, a swimming pool with a large black panther insignia on the bottom. What is perhaps most remarkable about this "dream home" is that it is not very remarkable at all: not particularly extravagant or large, not unusual or fantastical, just a pleasant and comfortable middle-class house with a large hot tub, a striking swimming pool, and a trapdoor to a bunker. Call the bunker a fall-out shelter or a panic room, and drain the black panther image of its political significance, and this could be any number of ordinary U.S. homes built since the 1980s. What is extraordinary about this project is the web of relationships that the project has restored and created: Wallace's relation to Sumell and to the wider public that follows his story; his relation to the psychic, social, affective, and aesthetic depths of space; and his relation to a future in which his legal action may be successful, he may be released, and he may be able to dwell in the place he has so meticulously planned and imagined. There is nothing guaranteed about this future, but the relation to even a contingent future may help sustain the depth of the world within prolonged solitary confinement.

I have argued that a concrete experience of depth and of a shared space with other embodied subjects is constitutive of one's own embodied subjectivity. Depth has many layers—spatial, affective, corporeal, intercorporeal, and even imaginative. In the words of Renaud Barbaras, "depth is what 'makes room' *[donne lieu]* for things, that by which they 'take place' *[ont lieu]*. For things, taking (a) place *[avoir (une) lieu]* cannot mean occupying room but only adventing" (2004, 213). As we have seen, the supermax unit threatens to become a space without depth and without place or taking-place, without advent, without emergence. It threatens to become a dead space rather than a space of birth; an exhausted space with no elsewhere, no beyond. But even in this dead space, some prisoners are able to sustain a sense of "elsewhere," of a place beyond the Control Unit, and of a future that could be otherwise. Other prisoners—or the same prisoners at different times—come unhinged; they develop habits of pacing, throwing themselves at walls, throwing their own bodily wastes, creating disturbances that draw out the violence of guards, and even taking pleasure in the ambivalent agency of *making* someone react in violence. But even if they manage to survive solitary confinement without reacting in physical violence, the profound boredom of isolation is itself a form of violence. The space of the supermax is structured in a way that tends to exhaust a meaningful sense of space; it pushes experience to the point of collapse. Stuck in the same routine, within the same rigid walls, one's own corporeal and intercorporeal Being-in-the-world risks being evacuated as a site of mattering and care. What the testimony of prisoners and the work of Merleau-Ponty helps us see is that SHU syndrome is more than a mental illness afflicting individual subjects; it is a social, phenomenological, and ontological pathology, which neither the language of the clinic nor the logic of liberal individualism is adequate to express.

8 DEAD TIME

Heidegger, Levinas, and the Temporality of
Supermax Confinement

Do the time, don't let the time do you.

—Common prison adage

Trying to explain it is like trying to explain what an endless toothache feels like. . . . I wish I could paint what it's
like . . . slow constant peeling of the skin, stripping of the
flesh, the nerve-wracking sound of water dripping from
a leaky faucet in the still of the night while you're trying
to sleep. Drip, drip, drip, the minutes, hours, days, weeks,
months, years, constantly drip away with no end or relief in
sight.

—Tommy Silverstein, a prisoner who has
spent more than thirty-two years in solitary
confinement, "The Most Restrictive Alternative"

WHAT DOES IT MEAN TO *SERVE TIME*? To be at risk of having
time *do* you, or even *do you in*? Every prisoner must face this question
on some level. But time is an especially pressing issue for the supermax
prisoner who is isolated from others and confined to a tiny cell for
weeks, months, or even years. Just as security doors chop up supermax
space, so too does the prison schedule chop up supermax time; the supermax inmate is subject to a rigid schedule of feedings, showers, and
short sessions in the "dog run." Rather than multiplying differences,
this segmentation of time tends to undermine prisoners' sense of meaningful temporal distinctions; the constant repetition of the same makes
each day blend into the next, such that time seems both to grind to a
halt and to slip away without incident or event.[1]

This urgent demand to do nothing—to hurry up and wait—characterizes most aspects of prison life. For example, supermax inmates being taken to see a doctor or dentist must be ready to leave their cell two hours before the appointment. This is to make time for cell removal, which includes a mandatory strip search, handcuffing, and the fastening of belly chains or leg irons. A former prisoner explains:

> You're going to see the dentist, you're gonna be placed in a holding cell that's about the size of a phone booth, and you will stand there for three to four hours. Now you better hope that you didn't drink coffee that day or drink a lot of water because eventually you're going to have to use the restroom and if you complain that you have to use [it], they'll end up taking you back to your cell and you'll be put back on the three months waiting list to see the doctor. (Quoted in Shalev 2009, 155)

Waiting to do nothing—or waiting to avoid the punishment of further waiting so that one's basic needs or desires can be addressed—is an overwhelming feature of prison temporality, even beyond the most obvious occasion for waiting: for eventual release from prison.[2]

This temporal structure of waiting has a political effect: it reinforces inmates' dependence on prison authorities to receive even the most basic rights and privileges. Waiting for the arrival of something important—whether it is a meal, a bit of toilet paper, or a book from the prison library—both devalues the present and extends it indefinitely. Structurally, this overvalues the prison official as a source of (temporary and limited) release from an otherwise interminable waiting. The prisoner may resist the power of the prison official to grant or withdraw this sense of release—and in the final section of this chapter, I will discuss some of the forms that resistance may take—but in any case, the prisoner is bound to negotiate with this asymmetrical structure, not only of power but of *power over time*. The implicit message of intensive confinement is: You are no longer in charge of your own time. In the rhetoric of prison officials, "tough on crime" politicians, and the popular media, inmates have "done the crime" and now they must "do the time." But the testimony of prisoners in prolonged solitary confinement suggests that their capacity to *do time*—to exist as a temporal subject rather than an object persisting through time—is undermined by the whole structure of solitary confinement.

Contemporary supermax prisoners' exposure to constant artificial light can intensify this sense of living death, eroding the distinction between night and day, unhinging prisoners' diurnal rhythms both from natural cycles and from the social habits of friends and family outside prison, or even of other prisoners.[3] Insomnia is a common symptom of SHU syndrome, along with headaches, nervousness, muscular pain, digestive disorders, and other manifestations of psychic and corporeal stress. But even prisoners who do not suffer from the most dramatic symptoms of SHU syndrome often suffer from a profound boredom that alters their sense of time. Sam Gutierrez, an inmate at Stateville Maximum Security Prison in Illinois, says:

> For me, and for many like me in prison, violence is not the major problem; the major problem is monotony. It is the dull sameness of prison life, its idleness and boredom, that grinds me down. Nothing matters; everything is inconsequential other than when you will be free and how to make time pass until then. But boredom, time-slowing boredom, interrupted by occasional bursts of fear and anger, is the governing reality of life in prison. (Quoted in Morris and Rothman 1998, 203)

Another Washington State inmate interviewed by Lorna Rhodes says:

> It's pretty much like not living. You're locked in a cell twenty-three hours a day. . . . That's it. . . . It's boredom, real intense boredom. No outside air . . . you can't see out the windows. They don't treat you bad, but it's just that everything is so impersonal. It's like dealing with automatons. (Quoted in Rhodes 2004, 29)

Pushed to an extreme, this institutionalized boredom can become a form of violence against the living intentionality of the human animal. Blocked from engaging with the world in a meaningful way, the living, sensing, thinking, speaking person can turn against itself, buckling the hinges of its relational being. On the one hand, boredom may seem like a small price to pay for violent crimes like murder and rape. But the extreme boredom produced and reinforced by social and sensory deprivation can amount to a living death sentence that compounds the violence of crime rather than demanding something more or something different from the offender.

Jack Henry Abbott offers this account of the temporality of isolation: "Time descends in your cell like the lid of a coffin in which you lie and watch it as it slowly closes over you. When you neither move nor think in your cell, you are awash in pure nothingness" (1991, 44–45). He connects this feeling of living death to an overstimulation that has left him both raw and numb:

> I have been made oversensitive—my very *flesh* has been made to suffer
> sensations and longings I never had before. I have been chopped to pieces
> by a life of deprivation of sensations; by beatings so frequent I am now a
> piece of meat and bone; by lies and by drugs that attack my nervous sys-
> tem. I have had my mind turned into steel by the endless smelter of *time* in
> confinement. (37)

> When a man is taken farther and farther away from experience, he is being
> taken to his death. (53)

Abbott explains this transformation as an "event" that alters the ontology of the living human being and could alter the ontology even of
a stone. The hallucinations that often emerge in solitary confinement
are not just signs of mental illness but also ontological derangements
of time and reality:

> You are far from insanity, you are only living through an experience, an
> event. The mirages are real reflections of how far you have journeyed into
> that pure terrain of time. They *are* real. They bring you the now out-of-
> place things back into the desert that was once the felicitous garden of your
> memory. (48)

In the hole, time comes unhinged from the memory of the prisoner; it is
no longer *the prisoner's* time but, rather, a "pure terrain" that dredges
up events that are real but have no intrinsic relation to the inmate's
temporal subjectivity. They pass by like objects in a desert, inverting
the relation between hallucination and the perception of reality:

> Real things: these are the mirages in the desert. The real world is out of
> place in the hole, but the hole is nonetheless really there. It is time that
> no longer moves forward in human experience. You can walk, placing one
> foot before the other, across eternity in time. All the space you need is six
> or seven feet. The hole furnishes only that provision: you are living a dem-
> onstration of the theory of the infinite within the finite; the dream within
> the reality. (49)

> You become silent, contemplative, because you have become inverted. Your
> sense perception, having taken in everything, including yourself, within the
> finite confines of the hole, passes through the monotony and now rises up
> from the *other side,* the infinite, to haunt you with reality. (49)

For Abbott, this is not insanity, but "supersanity" (50). Prisoners
who manage not to disintegrate under the pressure of intensive confinement may feel like they contain an infinite universe within themselves. But even this survival strategy can deepen the gulf between the

isolated prisoner and the rest of the world, making it difficult to return to an open, dynamic relation to the world as a world, and not as a "pure terrain" of finite infinity and dream reality.

In the general prison population, Abbott's strategy for survival is to withdraw from the dizzying suffocation of prison through sleep or drugs:

> The closest you come to adjusting is this: you *will* yourself to sleep all day through most of the disturbances. After each meal you curl up, pull the blankets over you, put your pillow over your ears and sleep. It's a drugged sleep. (66)

At night, when it is quiet and there is not the constant distraction of the din of yelling prisoners, Abbott says, "You are with yourself again" (66). But even this expression suggests a doubling or splitting of subjects who are never simply alone but always *with themselves*—stuck to themselves, even in the absence of all other meaningful relations. To be confined in solitude is not just to be left alone but to be forced into an inescapable relation *to oneself*—and to no one else.

What does it mean to be *alone with oneself*: a relational being cut off from meaningful relations to others and yet condemned to an inescapable relation to one's own existence? The early penitentiary system had confidence in the capacity of human beings to be redeemed by self-reflection. But as we have seen, the capacity to reflect becomes a source of pathology and suffering rather than moral and spiritual transformation when it is cut off from the network of worldly, intercorporeal relations that would otherwise support meaning by allowing subjects to be absorbed in something or someone other than themselves. At what point does the arguably legitimate right of communities to punish offenders and even to limit their control over time and space become a form of violence against the prisoners' ontological status as temporal, spatial, intercorporeal subjects? When do the conditions of intensive confinement structurally undermine prisoners' capacity to *do* time, to make time, to comport themselves as living, temporal subjects—"a melody that sings itself"—rather than as objects that merely persist over time? In order to respond to these questions, we need to think about what it means to be a temporal subject, and how this temporality is rearranged or even deranged through prolonged solitary confinement.

In what follows, I draw on Heidegger's account of temporality in *Being and Time* to develop a preliminary phenomenology of time in the supermax. I argue that, ultimately, Heidegger's failure to engage robustly with the ethical dimensions of existence and his focus on the challenge of individuation rather than the violence of isolation limit his capacity to shed light on the specific deprivation of solitary confinement. I turn to Levinas's early work for a phenomenological account of solitude as a form of individuation in which the subject is encumbered by its own unsharable relation to being and desires an escape that is ultimately ethical rather than ontological. Heidegger's work helps open up the question of prison temporality; Levinas's work allows me to address the complicated violence of solitary confinement, in which the subject's own capacities for meaning, for relation, and for self-relation become instruments of its own undoing when unhinged from a meaningful relation to others.

Toward a Phenomenology of Prison Time

Many prisoners find themselves stuck within a present that seems to go nowhere, with little to lose and little to look forward to, waiting for a future release that may never come or that, when it does, might not deliver the longed-for sense of freedom. They find themselves haunted by a past that cannot be undone and that may return obsessively to dominate the present and drain the future of hope. What might phenomenology have to teach us about the meaning, and the risk of meaninglessness, in prisoners' experience of time, especially in isolation?

For Husserl, consciousness is essentially a temporal flow of impressions that are constantly different but unfold according to consistent basic structures. Even the experience of a simple spatial object would be impossible without the interplay of protention and retention through which consciousness anticipates future profiles of the object and retains past profiles as they slip away. The perceptual object as a whole is never given all at once; rather, it appears as a dynamic totality of past, present, and future perspectives.

In his critical appropriation of Husserl, Heidegger interprets the temporality of consciousness in relation to the concrete existence of Dasein as a Being-in-the-world for whom its own being is an issue (Heidegger 1962, 32). The relation between past and future possibilities is not just an epistemological issue for Dasein but also an existential one: at stake is not just one's theoretical understanding of the world but the meaning of one's life and death. As an existent who is thrown into a world with determinate historical possibilities, Dasein also *throws itself* toward these possibilities, such that Dasein not only *has* possibilities but *is* its possibilities. Dasein ek-sists in the dynamic tension between thrownness and projection, anticipation and repetition: between a future that is always to come *(Zu-kunft)* and a past that always already has been *(Gewesen-heit)*. From this perspective, the past is never simply finished; rather, it forms a heritage of possibilities that Dasein takes up in different ways, depending on its relation to the future. Jack Henry Abbott makes a similar point in his prison memoir:

> What happens in the past is the future, and so the past is not static, fixed. Human reality is like that. The events and decisions in personal history slide in and out of perspective, take on new meanings, just as the person does. (1991, 72)

For Heidegger, the productive limit of this future, and the source from which a meaningful experience of time springs, is death. Death marks a future that will never arrive in the present: an impossible possibility that can be neither experienced nor evaded (1962, 307). My own death can never become actual for me in a present or representable moment, but for this very reason, it discloses the meaning of possibility as such, unhinged from its apparent fulfillment in actuality. The impossible possibility of death has important implications for Dasein's relations with others. As Being-in-the-world, Dasein is also Being-with-others; it is always already involved in a social world populated by others *with* whom it understands and interprets its own possibilities. For the most part, as a thrown and falling existent, Dasein takes over the common, average understanding of the world that is disclosed by its cultural inheritance. It perceives the world according to trends and patterns that are not specifically its own but, rather, the product of a generic, anonymous, impersonal sociality that Heidegger calls the "they."

Dasein is torn out of this complacent absorption in the "they" by its own anxious Being-toward-death. No one can die for me or accompany me in the utter solitude of death; this possibility alone belongs to me exclusively, as my "ownmost" (Heidegger 1962, 294; see also 284). Heidegger goes so far as to say that anxiety before death discloses Dasein as a solitary existent: "solus ipse" (233). Anxiety makes the world appear uncanny and unfamiliar; I feel disconnected, no longer at home in the world. This disconnection is productive; anxiety individualizes Dasein and begins to set it free for the appropriation of its own possibilities. But anxiety is not sufficient to accomplish Dasein's individuation *in relation to* the world and to others; anxiety wrests Dasein from the everyday, but it does not in itself create a renewed connection to the world or to the concrete possibilities into which Dasein is thrown. For this, we must listen and respond to the call of conscience.

The call of conscience "summons" Dasein to its ownmost "Being-guilty" (Heidegger 1962, 314). We must be careful not to interpret this guilt in moral or religious terms; it is a sign not of original sin or even of criminal transgression but, rather, of existential and historical concreteness, the facticity of being thrown into a world that one did not choose but with which one must come to terms in one's own singular way. In order to accomplish this, Dasein must "become free for the call" of conscience; it must "choose itself" by *"wanting to have a conscience"*—in other words, by wanting to be responsible for its own existence from the ground up, even while admitting that it never could have established that ground for itself (334).[4] In the resolute anticipation of death, "one becomes free for one's own death" (308): not free to evade death or overcome finitude but free to accept one's own limits as a site of meaningful possibility rather than a mere obstacle.[5] Thanks to this finite freedom, past, present, and future possibilities become meaningful as *my own inheritance*: as both singularly mine and also part of a common heritage shared with others.[6]

While Dasein, understood as ecstatic Being-in-the-world, is a relational being, the "nonrelational" possibility of death isolates Dasein from others (Heidegger 1962, 294). For Heidegger, this isolation is a condition for the possibility of authentic Being-with-others, where social life does not suppress the individuation of Dasein but, rather, supports it. But what if one's Being-in-the-world has been reduced to four concrete walls and a steel mesh door? What if one's relation to others has been stripped away, not by the resolute anticipation of death but by a social and sensory isolation that threatens to reduce one's life to a living death? Are there not certain situations of extreme domination that can rob one of a meaningful relation to one's own death?[7] What could freedom mean—even if it is the finite freedom of being "free for death"—in a supermax prison where one's choices are already mapped out in a table of punishments and rewards, in relation to which the words "choice" and "responsibility" begin to lose their meaning? Heidegger may not agree with Sartre's claim in *Being and Nothingness* that the prisoner is always free to "project his escape," even if he can't accomplish this escape concretely (Sartre 1956, 483–84).[8] But to what extent does Heidegger's analysis offer a different way of thinking about freedom, possibilities, and death in the concrete situation of solitary confinement?

For me, the most productive possibility in *Being and Time* for understanding the temporality of solitary confinement is not Heidegger's account of Being-toward-death but his account of work and its relational assignment structure. In his classic discussion of the ready-to-hand, Heidegger shows how the presence of the tool or the ready-to-hand recedes in the midst of productive work. I am so fully absorbed in hammering that the hammer disappears as such; I comport myself toward the goal or the "in-order-to" that the hammer enables me to accomplish. It is only when the hammer breaks or goes missing that the network of referential implications involved in work becomes visible to me.

It is in this context that Dasein's relation to others is first discussed in *Being and Time*. One aspect of the network of references disclosed in relation to the ready-to-hand is a social reference to the others for whom I am working but whose presence in my own work process remains largely implicit:

> In the work there is also an assignment to the person who is to use it or wear it. The work is cut to his figure; he "is" there along with it as the work emerges. Even when goods are produced by the dozen, this constitutive assignment is by no means lacking; it is merely indefinite, and points to the random, the average. Thus along with the work, we encounter not only entities ready-to-hand but also entities with Dasein's own kind of Being, entities for which, in their concern, the product becomes ready-to-hand; and together with these we encounter the world in which wearers and users live, which is at the same time ours. Any work with which one concerns oneself is ready-to-hand not only in the domestic world of the workshop but also in the public world. (Heidegger 1962, 100)

Even when I am absorbed in solitary work, Dasein sustains an implicit relation to others *for* whom and *from* whom its work gains meaning. Merleau-Ponty expresses this point well in *Phenomenology of Perception*:

> In the cultural object, I feel the close presence of others beneath a veil of anonymity. *Someone* uses the pipe for smoking, the spoon for eating, the bell for summoning, and it is through the perception of a human act and another person that the perception of a cultural world could be verified. (2002, 405)

He adds, "The first of all cultural objects, and the one by which all the rest exist, is the body of the other person as the vehicle of a form of behavior" (406).

I will return to the temporality of work in the final section of this chapter when I discuss prisoners' strategies for resistance to the debilitating isolation of solitary confinement. But first I want to contrast Heidegger's account of the temporality of existence, where the challenge is to individuate oneself from a generic, impersonal form of sociality in order to appropriate the meaning of Being as such, with Levinas's early account of temporality, where a meaningful sense of time emerges *in response to the other,* and in the escape from a generic, impersonal relation to Being as such. While Heidegger's account of temporality—especially the temporality of work—sheds light on some of the strategies that prisoners have developed to survive solitary confinement, Levinas's account of the *ethical* meaning of temporality helps us understand the pain of isolation in its own terms, as a form of violence against the ethical and ontological relationality of the subject.

Levinas and the Solitude of the Instant

Levinas is best known for his ethics of infinite responsibility. I can never fulfill my obligations to others because the more I seek to respond, the more my responsibility grows; this infinite obligation for the other who faces me is multiplied indefinitely by the countless others who do not appear face-to-face but who are no less deserving of a response. While some readers have objected to what appears to be an unreasonably heavy weight of obligation placed on the single individual, such a reading fails to recognize Levinas's sustained critique of the assumption that the basic unit of subjectivity is the single individual.[9] For Levinas, subjectivity is the other-in-the-same, the one-for-the-other; the individual is already the denial or diminishment of a more fundamental relationality. The central challenge for Levinas is not how to limit the otherwise insupportable weight of responsibility for others (as is arguably the case with liberal theories of moral responsibility) but, rather, how to escape the otherwise unbearable weight of solitude, or what Levinas calls "bourgeois" individualism.[10]

For Levinas, solitude is not a particular quality or attribute of the existent but, rather, its fundamental condition; to exist is in a fundamental sense to exist alone, in solitude. This solitude is not something that the subject must accomplish by wresting itself out of an inauthentic form of sociality; the challenge is rather to escape from the suffocating weight of an unshared, solitary relation to being. No one shares the very fact of my existence with me; and this fact, this weight of existence upon the solitary existent, is unbearable without some sort of escape, some chance of "getting out of being by a new path" (2003, 73). The face of the other opens up this path by commanding me to responsibility and so pulling me into a future that is not strictly my own but, rather, the infinite time of responsibility for the other. *There is no time without the other* for Levinas; the solitary existent remains stuck in the present instant to the extent that it fails to encounter something beyond itself, something that is not a "thing" or an intentional object but an other who resists the subject's powers and puts them in question.

This solitude of the subject is fundamental for Levinas, but it is not simple, nor is it final. Solitude is instead the initial condition of a subject whose emergence as a personal existent from the background of impersonal existence already complicates its subjectivity in ways that allow for both its self-entrapment and its escape vis-à-vis the other. Even the barest schema of the subject, which Levinas calls "hypostasis," is already complicated by a hingelike structure between substance and process, noun and verb, existent and existence. On this account, the solitary subject is not a point from which intentional rays radiate outward but, rather, a fold in being, a hinge between the event of coming-to-be and the substantive product of this event. Its individuation is only superficially like that of the atomistic, self-enclosed individuals who, on Thomas Hobbes's account, spring out of the ground "like mushrooms, come to full maturity, without all kind of engagement to each other" (quoted in Benhabib 1992, 156). Rather, for Levinas the hypostasis of the subject is the condensation of a being that remains rooted to the ground and related to itself in a way that makes the relation to others crucial to its own being. This schema of a hinged, irreducibly relational being provides the template for corporeal life and sensibility in Levinas's later work, but in *On Escape, Existence and Existents,* and *Time and the Other* we already find an account of the body as both related to itself, encumbered with its own materiality, and also open to others in a way that can be both redemptive and exploitative.

What is the originary solitude of the subject like, and in what sense is it already complicated by relationality? In *Existence and Existents*—a text written in large part when Levinas was held captive in a Nazi work camp from 1940–45—the solitude of the subject is described in terms of an irreducible duality:

> The solitude of a subject is more than the isolation of a being or the unity of an object. It is, as it were, a dual solitude: this other than me accompanies the ego like a shadow. (Levinas 1978, 88)

If solitude is dual rather than singular, then solitary confinement is not just a matter of leaving prisoners alone but of locking them up *with themselves,* locking them in with their own shadow. In fact, the early penitentiary movement presupposes a similar duality when it locked prisoners in with themselves in order to make them reflect on their crimes and their criminal selves, to contemplate themselves as in a mirror, with no distractions or outside influences. But in the penitentiary, the presupposed duality of the person has different ontological and religious roots, based on the duality of a corrupt or corruptible earthly body and a contemplative, redemptive divine soul. For Levinas, the duality of solitude is wholly secular, even godless. The double who arises in the ontological event of hypostasis, and perhaps also in the political situation of solitary confinement, is not a redemptive other or even a redeemable self but, rather, a "viscous, heavy, stupid double, but one the ego *[le moi]* is with precisely because it is me *[moi]*" (1987, 56). This double is like a weight that I can neither put down nor adequately carry, because it is the weight of my own existence, the inert and inexpressive burden of having to be myself, with no escape.[11] In the words of Italian criminologists Dario Melossi and Massimo Pavarini, "Alone in his cell, the inmate is handed over to himself" (quoted in Rhodes 2004, 43). As Lena Constante, a Romanian political prisoner, puts it, "In this dungeon of a cell I became aware of my duality. I was two. For I was here and I saw myself here. I was two" (quoted in Doyle 2006, 188).

In what sense does solitude already imply a relation to oneself as a double, while blocking the relation to an other who is truly other or outside oneself? This is where Levinas's departure from phenomenological method becomes clear. Classical phenomenology begins with the first-person singular, with a consciousness to whom objects appear within the inexhaustible horizons of a meaningful world. Levinas's own research reaches beyond this terrain of phenomenology, inquiring not into the conditions for the possibility of meaningful experience but, rather, into the conditions for the possibility of an existent, its *being* or substantiality. Levinas's question is not how the world can appear to consciousness but how consciousness (a subject, an existent) can appear in the world. This is a question Husserl cannot ask, given his starting point of intentional consciousness and his methodological bracketing of questions of existence.

For Levinas, "the essential ambiguity of the 'I'"—as both noun and verb, substance and process, being and event—is an amphibological subject that both breaks with the impersonality of faceless existence and remains bound to it (1978, 79). To be conscious on this account is not merely to be intentionally directed toward a meaningful world but, rather, to have access to a nonintentional dimension of *uncon-sciousness*: in short, to be able to fall asleep. The hallmark of consciousness for Levinas is not attention but the capacity to withdraw one's attention from the world, to curl up in a corner and retreat into privacy, slipping under the radar of one's own intentionality (45, 49). In "Judaism and Revolution," Levinas has this to say about sleep and food: "Sublime materialism! . . . Sublime materialism, concerned with dessert" (in Levinas 1994b, 97). Consciousness is not opposed to unconsciousness, then, but presupposes it, just as one side of a hinge presupposes the other. This is not just a logical relation but an ontological and even a practical one. Consciousness rests in the hollow of unconsciousness, "back to back" with its sleepy underside (Levinas 1978, 99). Only a being who can slip away from itself in sleep can also sustain the efforts of consciousness.[12] In the impersonality of sheer existence, there is nothing but an insomnia without a subject, an impersonal wakefulness, an impossibility of both falling asleep and waking up.[13]

The hinged structure of (un)consciousness finds its temporal articulation in the instant, which for Levinas is neither within time nor fully outside of time but, rather, an exception prior to the "scission of being into an inside and an outside" (1978, 100).[14] This priority of the instant to time is ontological; it marks "the accomplishment of existence" in the form of an existent, the turning point or hinge between the insubstantiality of impersonal existence and the emergence of a substantive, a personal existent (76). The instant is thus not a simple point; it is already a relation between existence and the existent who emerges from it (76).[15] As the pivot between personality and impersonality, consciousness and unconsciousness, waking and falling asleep, the instant is like "a wink, made up of looking and not looking" (68).[16] The principle of noncontradiction does not apply to the instant because, as hinge or fold, it articulates the very possibility of differentiation itself, prior to determinate identities (76). As such, the instant provides the bare schema of a solitude that is not single but double: both alone and encumbered with oneself, both an event of beginning and a posited substance. The ambiguity of this position is what Levinas calls hypostasis, or the emergence of a person from the ground of impersonality. But before we can consider the implications of hypostasis, we need to concretize this abstract schema of the instant with a thicker description of what it feels like in everyday life.

For Levinas, consciousness relies upon its ability to suspend itself, "to sink into unconsciousness and thus accord itself a reprieve" (1978, 51). A reprieve from what? From the irremissible weight of having to be, the finality of an existence that haunts the subject who is unable to either assume the sheer fact of being or to negate it. The weight of being is not like a piece of baggage I could put down or hand to a porter to carry for me; it is the weight of my own existence: a weight that both encumbers my existence with unchosen burdens and also allows me to mark out a position for myself in the world, to start from somewhere, to posit myself as a being.[17] This weight is both a burden and a gift; it creates the problem of self-encumbrance or suffocation in one's own being but it also establishes the conditions for shifting this weight into a Being-for-others that will open infinite dimensions of responsibility, in a relation to time that lifts the tragic finality or definitiveness of existence. The weight of material existence is the sort of baggage we need in order to have a place in the world from which to offer hospitality, to transform the materiality of possession into gifts that offer food and shelter to others.

For Levinas, the subject does not posit itself through a heroic act of the will or an authentic existential choice; acts and choices already presuppose an existent, and even thrownness presupposes a world into which one is thrown. Levinas's inquiry leads him beneath the level of the world, beneath the drama of choosing or not choosing, to the conditions for the emergence of an existent as such. Levinas finds these conditions in the passivity of lying down, slipping into unconsciousness, and falling asleep. "To lie down is precisely to limit existence to a place, to position" (1978, 69). In falling asleep, my existence is localized; I sink into a position that roots my existence in its unconscious, material ground. I posit myself—or find myself posited—as an existent: not yet as a conscious subject, but as the *basis* for a conscious subject.[18]

This account of the subject's position—in the double sense of being positioned in space and posited as a subject—"makes the body the very advent of consciousness" (Levinas 1978, 71; see also 30, 35).[19] Again, the body is not opposed to consciousness, separable from it, or reducible to it; rather, it forms the position of consciousness in space, its materiality as an existent, and the root of its resistance to impersonal being. The body "is not posited; it is a position" (71). Embodiment is the site of the subject's subjectivation, its ambiguous or "amphibological" emergence as both event and noun or substantive, as both sides of the hinge of hypostasis.[20]

Levinas describes the affective dimensions of this embodied positionality in terms of fatigue (and elsewhere, in terms of malaise, shame, and nausea [2003, 63–68]). Fatigue is not opposed to effort; it arises as a kind of inversion within effort, an internal limit or complication. We feel the weight of our own existence when the hand that exerts an effort to hold onto something reaches the limits of its powers, letting the object slip away even as it strains to hold on more tightly (1978, 30). Fatigue marks the hinge or turning point between the effort of consciousness and the effortlessness of sleep.[21] The complications of fatigue articulate a hesitation or delay within the existent, a slippage between me and myself.[22] I want to stay awake, but I can't quite keep up with myself; awareness slips away even as I try to focus and concentrate. In these moments, I fall out of synch—not merely with the world, but with myself.[23] This hesitation can only arise in a complicated subject whose solitude is not single but already doubled.[24]

Not only fatigue, but also other bodily affects such as hunger and thirst produce this delay whereby the subject falls behind itself, but thereby posits itself as an existent:

> Sincerity with respect to objects [the sincerity of thirst, hunger, and the need for warmth] is a hesitation with regard to existence, which appears as a task to be taken up. A subject, an existent to take it up, will arise from that hesitation. (Levinas 1978, 45)

The temporality of this analysis is doubly complicated. Not only does hunger produce a hesitation *within* the existent, but it also posits the subject *itself* as an existent who takes up the task of its own existence and so doubles up with itself. A hesitation or delay arises—which is not yet a *temporal* delay in the full intercorporeal sense that Levinas will ascribe to time—between the feeling of hunger and the subject who feels it, between the impersonal tug of bodily needs and the apprehension of these needs by a consciousness. It is as if the feeling of hunger and thirst preceded, and even called forth, a subject who could "have" these feelings, who could experience them as consciousness. Levinas is pointing to an affective dimension of a hungry, thirsty life that is not strictly personal, that precedes the formation of a person but remains in relation to that person, such that the impersonal *soi* and the personal *moi* never quite match up.

This syncopation or delay between me and myself is not something that happens once and for all in an instant before time; rather, it arises again and again within the existence of an affective, embodied subject. Every instant is an exception to time within time, a complication that affects the conscious subject even in everyday experience. A not-yet-personal affect demands the emergence of someone to feel it; the gnawing feeling of hunger provokes the cry, "I'm hungry!" To be hungry is to feel this complication of existence on an affective level. Hunger is not just a lack of food; it is a gnawing-away of one's entrails, a feeling of bodily self-betrayal, of being at odds with oneself or out of step with oneself.[25] When good food is readily available, this feeling of tension or complication can be pleasurable; it is possible to enjoy one's needs, as Levinas points out in *Totality and Infinity*. But the prolonged deprivation of basic bodily needs provokes both the aversiveness of bodily pain and an existential or even ontological aversiveness, to the point where one can no longer bear to *be oneself,* where the hinge between *moi* and *soi* does not sustain consciousness but breaks it down.

In a passage that is even more intensely moving because of the circumstances under which it was written—in a Nazi forced-labor camp—Levinas suggests the political implications of his analysis:

> When one has to eat, drink and warm oneself in order not to die, when nourishment becomes fuel, as in certain kinds of hard labor, the world also seems to be at an end, turned upside down and absurd, needing to be renewed. Time becomes unhinged. (1978, 45)

Time becomes unhinged and the world turns upside down in experiences of severe bodily deprivation—because time and the world, and even the subject of experience, are sustained by a more fundamental nonintentional, unconscious, affective dimension of corporeal life. *Le moi* rests "back to back" with *soi-même,* like two gymnasts who rise up by leaning into one another, supporting each others' weight. This duality of *moi* and *soi* is already intrinsic to the solitary existent; and yet, confined to its solitude, deprived of everyday bodily relations with others, the existent breaks apart, encountering itself as a mute, shadowy double, no longer supportive of its own conscious subjectivity but destructive of it, like an unbearable weight.

Dickens captures this feeling in his imaginative reconstruction of what happens to prisoners at Eastern State Penitentiary:

> The weary days pass on with solemn pace, like mourners at a funeral; and slowly he begins to feel that the white walls of the cell have something dreadful in them: that their colour is horrible: that their smooth surface chills his blood: that there is one hateful corner which torments him. Every morning when he wakes, he hides his head beneath the coverlet, and shudders to see the ghastly ceiling looking down upon him. The blessed light of day itself peeps in, an ugly phantom face, through the unchangeable crevice which is his prison window.
>
> By slow but sure degrees, the terrors of that hateful corner swell until they beset him at all times; invade his rest, made his dreams hideous, and his nights dreadful. . . . Now, it is every night the lurking-place of a ghost: a shadow:—a silent something, horrible to see, but whether bird, or beast, or muffled human shape, he cannot tell. (1957, 107)

There is *not enough* in the experience of sensory and social isolation to support the relational individuation of an existent; at the same time, there is *too much* in the dark corners of that cell to allow for an authentic experience of solitude. Time slows down to a funeral pace, and even the "blessed light of day" afflicts the prisoner with its "ugly phantom face." The prisoner's growing sense of anxiety may disclose the world as uncanny or un-home-like *(unheimlich)*, but in a way that blocks the possibility of authentic appropriation. Rather than disclosing its ownmost potentiality-for-Being as Being-toward-death, isolation threatens the prisoner with both depersonalization and doubling. The anonymity of impersonal existence assumes a mocking, shadowy "face" that confronts the prisoner not with the meaning of Being but with the meaningless of being alone with no escape.

The *il y a* is Levinas's name for the sheer impersonality of existence without an existent. He introduces the concept not as an origin story but as a postapocalyptic one:

> Let us imagine all things, beings and persons, returning to nothingness. What remains after this imaginary destruction is not something, but the fact that there is *[il y a]*. The absence of everything returns as a presence, as

the place where the bottom has dropped out of everything, an atmospheric density, a plenitude of the void, or the murmur of silence. There is, after this destruction of things and beings, the impersonal "field of forces" of existing. There is something that is neither subject nor substantive. The fact of existing imposes itself when there is no longer anything. And it is anonymous: there is neither anyone nor anything that takes this existence upon itself. It is impersonal like "it is raining" or "it is hot." Existing returns no matter with what negation one dismisses it. There is, as the irremissibility of pure existing. (1987, 46–47)

This account of the *il y a* resonates with many accounts of isolation, both in carceral and noncarceral contexts. Christopher Burney, an English spy held in solitary confinement for eighteen months by the Nazis in Occupied France during World War II, said:

I feel a sense of impotence, an inexorable subjection to a machine of nameless horror. . . . Variety—is the very stuff of life. We need the constant ebb and flow of wavelets of sensations, thought, perception, action and emotion—keeping even our isolation in the ocean of reality, so that we neither encroach nor are encroached upon. (Quoted in Solomon et al. 1957, 360)

In her memoir *A Woman in the Polar Night,* Christiane Ritter describes the effects of a seemingly endless arctic winter as a depersonalization to the point of dissolution: "It is as though we were dissolving in moonlight, as though it were eating us up. The light seemed to follow us everywhere. . . . Neither the walls of the hut nor the roof of snow can dispel my fancy that I am moonlight myself" (quoted in Solomon et al. 1957, 357). She observes:

The extroverts among those who spend the winter here will always intrinsically create for themselves a sphere of activity and hence a sphere of reality, which will save them when no impulse comes from without. Those who find their pleasures in meditation, will withdraw into themselves, into regions of astonishing brightness; but those who are accustomed to yield to their inclination to idleness run the great danger of losing themselves in nothingness, of surrendering their senses to all the insane fantasies of overstretched nerves. (358)

This is what Merleau-Ponty, following Eugène Minkowski, called Night: not an object against which I can oppose myself as a subject but, rather, an atmosphere that "enwraps me and infiltrates through all my senses, stifling my recollections and almost destroying my personal identity" (2002, 283). It is what Jack Henry Abbott tried to gain a distance from by curling up, pulling the blankets over his head, and *willing* himself to sleep (1991, 66).

The insomnia that Levinas relates to the impersonality of sheer being, or the *il y a*, is not just a metaphor. In the supermax prisons that impose twenty-four-hour artificial light on prisoners, and even in the early penitentiary cells with their tiny, viewless windows, insomnia is the more or less pervasive condition of solitary confinement. There is no night in the supermax unit; but this permanent exposure to light has the (only apparently paradoxical) effect of unleashing the endless Night of the *il y a*, undoing the distinction between night and day.

In order to maintain the identity of the same, the individuated or hypostasized subject must exist in relation to others. By forcing the subject into a withdrawal from the world, prolonged solitary confinement disrupts the affective rhythm of hypostasized existence and makes it difficult or impossible for the subject to restore this rhythm. This prolonged, forced withdrawal from social relations confines the subject to itself, blocking its own paths of ontological or ethical escape and threatening to smother its affective resistance. As such, prolonged solitary confinement inhibits the subject's capacity to suspend itself, to withdraw from the world on its own terms, and to reawaken according to its own affective, intercorporeal rhythms. Both Levinas's reflections on ontological solitude and the research on solitary confinement suggests that we need everyday corporeal relations with others in order to *be ourselves,* not just because we define our particular social and psychological identities in relation to one another but also because we have a constitutive desire for the bodily presence of others.

The solitary subject literally comes unhinged without this concrete experience of affective intercorporeality. Why? Because even our solitude is dual; it is not simple or complete on its own but already complicated at the moment of its own hypostasis. Consciousness needs to be able to lose itself—on its own terms, in response to its own singular affective disposition—in order to sustain itself. This is the hesitation or complication that consciousness presupposes. The instant is the pivot around which consciousness sustains itself, both positing itself and withdrawing, awakening and falling asleep. This interval between me and myself, or between *moi* and *soi*—this instant—is the crack or fissure that sustains consciousness by allowing it to slacken its own intentional threads. But the interval intrinsic to the self cannot be sustained by the self alone. I can only bear the weight of my own existence thanks to an opening or escape that the bodily presence of others opens up for me by drawing the instant of my solitude into relation with a future that is not my own, but a time of Being-for-others, or infinite responsibility. We find the meaning of our lives, but also the strength to bear the weight of our own ontological solitude, in affective, intercorporeal and ethical relations with others. That is how the light gets in.

Resisting Living Death: Problems and (Partial) Solutions

Social and sensory isolation exploits the complicated structure of embodied subjectivity; it puts pressure on the hinges that sustain us, exploiting the complications of the subject in a way that turns its ontological duplicity against itself. What sort of resistance is possible against this forced self-betrayal? Levinas describes subjectivity itself in terms of resistance:

> Our existence in the world . . . is but the amplification of that resistance against anonymous and fateful being by which existence becomes consciousness, that is, a relationship an existent maintains with existence, through the light which both fills up and maintains the interval [of the present instant]. (1978, 51)

Consciousness is the amplification of a more basic affective resistance of the existent against existence: a resistance that is felt at the level of effort and fatigue, hunger and thirst, but that also describes the hinged structure of subjectivity as both conscious and unconscious, intentional and nonintentional, dependent on the bodily rhythms of sleeping and waking to sustain the weight of its own being. This affective rhythm of subjectivity is itself a resistance to the rhythmless monotony of the *il y a,* or of sheer impersonal existence. In chapter 9, I will argue that it also forms a root of our ethical-political resistance. In what follows, I explore some of the many ways in which prisoners in contemporary control prisons have managed to survive and resist the conditions of their confinement.

Most prisoners will tell you that in order to "do the time" rather than allowing the time to "do you," one needs to establish a daily schedule. For example, in *Survival in Solitary: A Manual Written by and for People Living in Control Units,* SHU inmate LuQman Abdullah Hayes shares his schedule:

5:00 AM	Wake up and wash up
6:30	Breakfast
8:00	Yard/Exercise
9:00	Wash up/read
11:30	Lunch
12:00 PM	Wash clothes, cell, etc.
1:00	Read/study/write, etc.
2:00	Hold class on unit on politics, history, economics, or general discussion on legal endeavors
4:00	Dinner
4:30	Back to reading, writing, studying, etc. (In Kerness and Teter 2008, 23)

This schedule helps Hayes stay active and engaged as a temporal *subject* rather than an object passively undergoing the passage of time. The creation of a schedule carves up the day into meaningfully different phases, each with its own activity or focus. It allows Hayes to manage his own anxiety, or to "break the worry habit," by giving him something determinate to look forward to and to distract him from gnawing regrets about the past (23; see also 27, 31). This segmentation of time into manageable parts that one can expect or forget may not be the key to Heideggerian authenticity (contrast Heidegger 1962, 386–89, 391–92, 397–400 on inauthentic temporality). Rather, they are strategies for keeping the *il y a* at bay and for holding open cracks in "being" through which something other than the present instant might be able to shine through. Letters, books, and newspapers are especially important for sustaining a relationship with others who are not physically present but who still demand a response and even a responsibility. I will have more to say about the importance of responsibility in chapter 9.

There is a great risk for prisoners in prolonged solitary confinement to get stuck in a moment that goes nowhere, closed into a circular repetition of the same. The "worry habit" can become an obsession that undermines the inmate's ability to think and perceive clearly. As inmates at Walpole Prison explained to Stuart Grassian:

> I went to a standstill psychologically once—lapse of memory. I didn't talk for 15 days. I couldn't hear clearly. You can't see—you're blind—block everything out—disoriented, awareness is very bad. Did someone say he's coming out of it? I think what I'm saying is true—not sure. I think I was drooling—a complete standstill. (Quoted in Grassian 1983, 1453)

I seem to see movements—real fast motions in front of me. Then seems like they're doing things behind your back—can't quite see them. Did someone just hit me? I dwell on it for hours. (1452)

In her own contribution to the manual, political prisoner Laura Whitehorn recommends "having several different schedules, and alternating them, to avoid having the days all melt into sameness, and to keep track of what day and date it was" (in Kerness and Teter 2008, 27). She also uses

exterior signals, such as changes in light, shift changes, regular noises from outside my cell, to keep track of time. The first few weeks I'd note a sound or other objective occurrence, then yell for the cops to find out what time it was, etc. (27)

Like many other prisoners, Whitehorn recommends reading, writing letters, studying, remaining politically active, and engaging in some form of creative activity: "Reminding myself that my place in the universe was as a sentient, loving, creative human being, not a caged animal, was helpful" (27; see also 16, 19, 20, 25, 35, 42). Some prisoners challenge themselves with cognitive exercises to keep their minds focused. Others create art out of the materials around them: newspaper, toilet paper rolls, soap, bread, coffee mate, unraveled sweaters or socks—whatever is available.[26] The temporality of engaging in a project or other challenge in which the mind reaches toward a solution or toward the completion of a task offers a temporary escape from the oppressiveness of an unchanging present, a way of forgetting oneself and focusing on something that matters.

But sometimes prisoners in intensive confinement resort to other, more ambivalent forms of escape. Some rely on drugs or pruno (a prison wine made from fermented fruit) to kill time. Participants in Drew Leder's philosophy seminar explain the temporary sense of escape offered by drugs: "Once I start getting high, the two hours is gone. You defy all time . . . because when you're so caught up in the drugs you've got *no concept of time*. . . . You're in that false world, *never-never land*. . . . It puts you in a state of mind where *you just don't care*" (in Leder 2001, 91–92). Even if this false sense of power over time may have been part of what landed one in prison in the first place, the "never-never land" of escape remains tempting for prisoners whose temporal horizons have all but collapsed. Another common strategy is to engage in fantasy or daydreaming as a way of escaping the crushing immediacy of confinement. Recall that Maryland Penitentiary inmate Mark Medley used extended fantasy, or what he calls "autistic thinking": "It's like a resting period for the mind, almost like sleep, but it can be used in a sense to resist being conditioned" (Baxter et al. 2005, 214). Taken to an extreme, this coping mechanism can become a way of disengaging from the here and now so radically that one slips into a delusional depersonalization.

Fantasy, drugs, and other forms of escapism function as stopgap replacements for the sense of escape that Levinas describes as a "new path" "out of being" (2003, 73). Prisoners who manage to "do" their time even when deprived of an open-ended relation to space, time, and others often find creative ways of establishing and sustaining a virtual relation to others, to the "outside," and to a future of open possibilities. They cultivate a sense of hope within an otherwise hopeless isolation. But sometimes the most sustainable relation to time in prison is not hope—if by hope we mean expectation of something good that will arrive in the future—but rather an immersion in what Levinas would call enjoyment, or "bathing in the element" (1969, 132). For example, in Drew Leder's discussions with prisoners at the Maryland Penitentiary, twenty-six-year-old maximum-security inmate Tray Jones disagrees with some of the older prisoners who emphasize the importance of studying, planning, and maintaining hope for the future:

> You know this dude you describe as mature, the one who dedicates himself to studies and casework, expecting a break in the courtroom, hopeful they'll get out of prison soon—when things don't happen they usually the ones to go crazy. They become frustrated grouches. Whereas the dude he was describing as immature—like me—*I enjoy the moment*. My case went just as far. I'm having fun designing this future too. But my present is so enjoyable because I'm not expecting and hoping. (In Leder 2001, 88)

Jones was not being held in solitary confinement, and it is not clear that his approach to time in confinement can be transferred to the SHU, or even to other prisoners in maximum security. His claim to be "enjoy[ing] the moment" may be an overstatement generated within a context of competition with other inmates who seem, from his perspective, to take themselves as older and wiser men. But he makes an interesting point about the relation between present and future. In a situation where one has very little control over any aspect of life, it makes sense to comport oneself toward the possibility of a future that could be otherwise. But this lack of control in the present can extend itself indefinitely into the future for inmates serving multiple life sentences, subject to strict rules and the sometimes arbitrary judgments of prison authorities, in a world where even the release from prison does not guarantee a job, a home, meaningful relationships with others, or anything else that distinguishes freedom from the mere absence of constraint. If hope for the future is to be anything more than a fantasy or a cruel joke—if it is to be a source of empowerment rather than self-deception—then the future must have an effective, dynamic relation to the present.

Later, Jones comments on the cruelty of time in a way that suggests that in spite of his youth and his apparent immaturity, he understands the risk of expecting too much from a situation that is beyond one's own control:

> Whatever way you look at it, whether it's in the drug world or not, time is real cruel. It moves us all and never gives us enough. . . . Everybody spends more time in the ground than they do on earth. So I'm trying to dedicate myself to getting rid of time. Because when I think about the future, that traps me, and my past traps me. The only thing I can do good with is this moment *right now*. (In Leder 2001, 92)

In the same seminar, a prisoner named Q says, "I don't dwell on the sentence because it can overwhelm you—you can actually go insane. You get caught up in this *time zone*." Charles Baxter agrees: "You can get tripping, Doc." Gary Huffman adds, "It's where your mind jumps time" (in Leder 2001, 88). To "jump" time is also to be jumped by it, to feel the doom of a situation where the possibility of release is a source not of comfort or hope but of impatience, frustration, rage, or depression. Q explains, "To me, time is like a dragon I have to slay. If I can master the present, I will have used my time to redeem time" (86). This is an extraordinary statement. On the one hand, time is represented as the prisoner's enemy; it is what he has been condemned to *serve*. On the other hand, if the prisoner can master or control his time in prison, he can use the "problem" of time against itself, as a resource rather than a curse and as a chance for redemption. This redemption is not strictly personal, nor is it a general, impersonal triumph over time's finitude or contingency. Rather, Q explains the meaning of redemption in terms of renewed social relations: "Then I can go back and offer something to people who never had to be in that situation [of imprisonment]" (86).

For Q, the redemption of time does not involve the personal death and rebirth imagined by Benjamin Rush, but it does involve a transformation of the relation between prisoners who have served their time and the community that is now positioned not only to receive them (with or without "tears of joy" and a "universal shout") but also to *learn from them* (Rush 1806, 157). The future anterior in Q's phrase, "I will have used my time to redeem time," situates this redemption in a realm of possibility, displacing the promise of redemption from the actuality of the present. Perhaps this was the mistake of the early penitentiary system: in spite of its many good intentions, the insistence on a forced redemption and the location of this redemption in an actual time and place created an expectation that could never be fulfilled, given the logic of actuality, expectation, and fulfillment.

Why is it so important for prisoners to feel in control of their own time? What does "control" even mean in relation to time, whether one is incarcerated or not? Can anyone be in control of time? My sense is that doing time, using time, feeling in control of time, even "getting rid of time" as Jones puts it, is a matter of affirming oneself as a temporal subject rather than just an object persisting over time. If one's perceptual relation to space is narrowed down to the point of being confined to sixty square feet, with the same objects in the same fixed positions at all times, then even the interplay of retention and protention that constitutes the experience of perceptual objects is foreshortened. The freedom that Husserl describes as an intrinsic aspect of perceptual experience—the freedom to walk around an object, to consider it from many different spatial angles, to return to it at will—is sharply curtailed if the horizons of one's experience are rigidly limited to the same small space for weeks, months, or years. To be a temporal subject is to maintain a creative relation to one's own temporal Being-in-the-world, not just to be carried along by clock time or calendar time but to *use* clocks and calendars as tools for organizing one's own day. These tools do not just measure the objective flow of time; their function is not just to allow the prisoner to count off the days until release. They also have a social meaning, and as such they imply a reference to other human beings, to a community of shared or common time. Minutes, hours, days, weeks, months, years: these are not just objective phenomena but also social phenomena. To measure one's own time in relation to these social markers is to participate, however distantly or virtually, in a social experience of time.

The resistance of prisoners to the structural unhinging of time and subjectivity in prolonged isolation is extraordinary. But even as we may admire and celebrate the resistance of these prisoners, we must remember that the possibility of resistance does not make solitary confinement any less violent or oppressive. Laura Whitehorn emphasizes the importance of remembering that one *will* be hurt by solitary confinement and that it is nothing to be ashamed of:

> I do believe that every one who has spent time in prison, double for control units, suffers physical if not also mental damage. Having this recognized— say, by the international anti-torture forces—helps. I think it was Stuart Grassian who observed that the women in the LexHSU developed illnesses as a result of the unit. When I read that, it helped me understand the damage to my own health that resulted or was exacerbated by the control unit time. (In Kerness and Teter 2008, 32; see also 18–19)[27]

All of these strategies are partial solutions or coping mechanisms, and they are vitally important as such, but they do not in themselves diminish the violence of intensive confinement. Work, timetables, and creative projects are not a replacement for intercorporeal support—nor is this support necessarily guaranteed by the physical presence of other people, especially in conditions of double-celling or overcrowded dorms on the prison main line. Even those who, like Robert King, manage to survive solitary confinement and even to emerge with great strength and dignity are often haunted by their experience. To be "still there" in one's prison cell, years after release, is to have one's Being-in-the-world altered by the spatial and temporal dimensions of confinement.

If the U.S. penal system is to return to its earlier mission of rehabilitating prisoners, and even if it is to make good on its current mission to make communities safer through its policies, we must find ways of punishing offenders that do not structurally undermine their capacities to learn, to relate meaningfully to others, and to become responsible members of an intercorporeal community. We must make the rhetoric of prison reform live up to its promises and its avowed ideals, and we must work to keep these promises and ideals open to critical engagement. Or we must dare to take prison abolition seriously as an ethical and political response to a system that, from the beginning, has harmed prisoners in the name of helping them.

9 FROM ACCOUNTABILITY TO RESPONSIBILITY

A Levinasian Critique of Supermax Rhetoric

> But the other absolutely other—the Other—does not limit
> the freedom of the same; calling it to responsibility, it founds
> it and justifies it.
>
> —Emmanuel Levinas, *Totality and Infinity*

> Without responsibility, straddling Nothingness and Infinity,
> I began to weep.
>
> —Frantz Fanon, *Black Skin, White Masks*

SUPPORTERS OF SUPERMAX CONFINEMENT often justify policies of extreme isolation and control through an appeal to safety, efficiency, and accountability (Riveland 1999, 6; Mears and Watson 2006, 251–56). Inmates who disrupt prison life with violence or other forms of disobedience create an unsafe environment for other inmates and for prison staff. Such prisoners must be isolated and removed from the general prison population so that the facility can continue to operate in a secure and efficient manner. This is how most prisons hold inmates accountable for their actions: they make the rules known to inmates in advance, and they follow strict guidelines for the administration of both punishments and rewards; inmates learn that their choices have consequences and know exactly what those consequences will be. It's all up to the individual to decide how to behave.

This appeal to individual choice and accountability may sound reasonable enough as long as the prisoners' perspectives are excluded or ignored. But even the most casual reflection on the meaning of accountability in a control prison generates multiple contradictions: What does "choice" mean for someone who is deprived of freedom to the greatest extent possible? To what extent is "good behavior" subject to choice? If behavior is merely a reaction to stimuli from the environment, as in the reductionist behavioral psychology that still dominates most prison policy in the United States, then wouldn't bad behavior be the result of a bad environment rather than bad choices on the part of the prisoner? What meaning can accountability have in 23½-hour-a-day lockdown, when there is literally no one available to whom one may give an account of oneself (Butler 2005)?

In addition to these formal contradictions, countless practical complications are generated by the rhetoric of individual choice and accountability in a control prison. For example, in California, prisoners classified as gang members or associates are confined indefinitely in the SHU, regardless of their actions; they are punished for who they are (or are presumed to be) rather than for their actions and choices within prison.[1] Even at lower-security prisons and jails, power dynamics can force prisoners into situations where breaking a rule is the only way to protect themselves against physical or sexual violence. Mentally ill or cognitively impaired inmates may not understand when they are breaking rules, or they may be mentally, physically, or emotionally unable to follow the rules, even if they do understand. Since solitary confinement exacerbates and even produces mental illness and cognitive difficulties in many prisoners, the longer inmates spend in the SHU, the less likely it is that they will be able to make the sort of "choices" that will allow them to be reintegrated into general population. Under circumstances such as these, the appeal to accountability in a control prison both *demands* responsibility from prisoners and *undermines* their capacity to respond ethically to others. At the same time, it shifts the weight of responsibility away from the prison system and onto individual prisoners, who are likely to appear incorrigible and resistant to rehabilitation, whether or not they actively fight the system.

Consider, for example, the testimony of Charles Samuels, director of the Federal Bureau of Prisons, to a 2012 Senate subcommittee hearing on solitary confinement:

> Inmate safety and wellbeing is of the utmost importance to the bureau, as is the safety of our staff and the community at large. As such, we do all that we can to ensure that we provide outstanding care, treatment and programming to federal inmates, giving them the best opportunity for successful reentry into their communities. (Solitary Watch 2012b, 4–5)[2]

When asked how many on-site mental health professionals were employed to administer to the needs of 490 inmates on lockdown at Florence ADX, a federal supermax prison, Samuels replied (after repeated efforts to evade the question by quoting more general statistics) that there were only *two*.[3] When pressed by Senator Dick Durbin to comment on whether he thinks this is sufficient and on whether he "could live in a box like that 23 hours a day" without "any negative impact," Samuels said, "I don't believe it is the preferred option" (Solitary Watch 2012b, 10).

In this chapter, I critically analyze the rhetoric of accountability in supermax prisons by drawing on Levinas's account of responsibility as the investment of one's arbitrary subjective freedom in an ethical responsibility for the other and a political solidarity with a community of others.[4] Levinas is best known for his concept of the face of the other as a site of infinite obligation. While there are rich possibilities for developing a critique of solitary confinement based on the systematic foreclosure of face-to-face encounters, I will focus on a lesser-known aspect of Levinas's work: his account of *critique* as the ethical provocation of philosophy and his account of *rhetoric* as a deployment of words against discourse, where discourse is understood as a primary ethical orientation toward an other who commands me to respond. Levinas's critique of rhetoric offers a vital supplement, and even a corrective, to his account of the face, which is often interpreted by Levinasians and non-Levinasians alike in nonpolitical or antipolitical ways. While it is beyond the scope of this chapter to argue the point at length, I hope to demonstrate that Levinas's critical phenomenology has something to offer radical political theory and practice, especially when read in conversation with postcolonial, Marxist, and feminist thinkers.[5] I conclude this chapter by reflecting on how the U.S. criminal justice system might live up to its name by offering programs that facilitate rather than undermine a sense of responsibility and solidarity among prisoners.

The Rhetoric of the Supermax

In his testimony to the 2012 Senate subcommittee hearings on solitary confinement, Charles Samuels defends restrictive housing as "a critical management tool that helps us maintain safety, security, and effective reentry programming for all federal inmates" (Solitary Watch

2012b, 6). Moments later, he admits that the Federal Bureau of Prisons has not undertaken a single study to determine the mental-health effects of restricted housing but states that the bureau would "welcome any research or literature regarding concerns in that area" (8). He also claims, "We do not consider any inmate to be held in isolation, though we are aware that some might use this term to refer to all restricted housing placement, regardless of the extent of contact with other individuals" (5). Samuels's testimony is an example of the kettle logic that structures much of the official discourse on supermax prisons: prisoners are not damaged by isolation; and even if they were, we could not have known because we do not have the research (although we welcome it); and besides, we do not isolate prisoners, we only place them in restrictive housing for the safety and well-being of themselves and others.

But what if outcomes do not meet the expectations set by the Federal Bureau of Prisons' commitment to providing "outstanding care, treatment and programming" to federal inmates? How does the biopolitical effort to manage and optimize the life of a population justify the cut between those to "make live" and those to "let die" (Foucault 2003, 241)? For Foucault, the biopolitical cut is made by racism: the death of abnormal, degenerate threats to life promise to improve the health, purity, and prosperity of the population as a whole (255). In the age of official color blindness, this racism operates covertly, both isolating a disproportionate number of brown and black people in prisons and jails and also appealing to their individual responsibility for criminal acts as an alibi for the racist structure of the criminal justice system, especially in relation to the war on drugs (Alexander 2010).

According to sociologist Loïc Wacquant, the United States is not just a society with prisons but "the first genuine prison society of history" (Wacquant 2001, 121). In this prison society, the risk posed by a surplus population of chronically underemployed, impoverished black and brown people is managed through a tightly meshed system of welfare for the women and incarceration for the men. The purpose of this "carceral-assistential complex" is

> to surveil, train and neutralize the populations recalcitrant or superfluous to the new economic and racial regime according to a gendered division of labor, the men being handled by its penal wing while (their) women and children are managed by a revamped welfare-workfare system designed to buttress casual employment. (97)

Within the prison itself, this management of "unmanageable" subpopulations is both intensified and generalized; men, women, and children alike are subject to "care," management, and control in a prison system that punishes their individual transgressions while putting them to work for pennies an hour. Within this system, "restrictive housing" functions as a prison within the prison; individuals who are unable or unwilling to function productively within the general population are identified, removed, and isolated for the sake of the whole. A California supermax prison administrator interviewed by Sharon Shalev defines the purpose of supermax confinement as the isolation of "predators" and those who "cannot be controlled or do not want to be controlled" so that the rest of the prison can function smoothly (quoted in Shalev 2009, 56; see also 208). This makes sense from a wildlife-management perspective: if there are dangerous predators, a good manager will identify and remove them to protect the health and safety of the general population. Gone are the religious motivations of solitary confinement in the early penitentiary system, underwritten though they were by biopolitical fantasies of "republican machines"; they have been replaced with a new form of neoliberal biopower, where the management and optimization of populations takes precedence over the spectacular punishment of bodies or the surveillance and discipline of individual subjects.[6]

Today's prisons are under pressure to demonstrate a certain level of efficiency, effectiveness, and accountability, whether or not they are run for profit. Prison administrators are accountable to the state or corporate entity that funds their operations, to the state and federal legislators that tolerate or support their existence, to the general prison population that apparently benefits from the removal of "predators," and to the public that they claim to keep safe and secure. But it is not clear that they are accountable to prisoners in isolation. One supermax correctional officer reflects:

> Do we have an obligation to take care of them? Yes. But do I have an obligation to provide him touching, feeling, contact with another human being? I would say no. He has earned his way to this unit and he's earned just the opposite. He's earned the need for me to keep him from other people. (Quoted in Shalev 2009, 142)

Those who have "earned" their way into isolation must "earn" their way out by working their way up the security ladder, one segment of good behavior at a time. Those with a "personal intent to disobey or not to follow directions," a desire "not to be controlled," or a commitment to creating (or becoming) a "management problem" remain in isolation (Shalev 2009, 56). As a prison architect in California explains, supermax confinement is intended "to give the inmate a chance to *decide* whether they want to stay there or not, and I think that's key to the success of a [supermax] is that the inmates now *decide their destiny*" (quoted in Shalev 2009, 134; emphasis added). This idea is so catchy, it comes with a slogan: "You did the crime, you do the time" (Rhodes 2004, 66).

But what can this slogan mean in a supermax prison where inmates are explicitly situated in a way that reduces, as much as possible, their capacity to make meaningful choices and to exercise personal autonomy? Chase Riveland defines a supermax prison as

> a highly restrictive, high-custody *housing unit* within a secure facility, or an *entire secure facility*, that isolates inmates from the general prison population and from each other due to grievous crimes, repetitive assaultive or violent institutional behavior, the threat of escape or actual escape from high-custody facility(s), or inciting or threatening to incite disturbances in a correctional institution. (1999, 6)

The same inmates who are isolated in this way are also enjoined to exercise their freedom to choose in a way that demonstrates in advance their capacity for making the right choices. They are positioned both as objects of supermaximum control and as independent, rational subjects, with a free will, who make good or bad choices for which they can and must be held accountable. But as Rhodes points out, accountability means nothing without someone to whom one may give an account of oneself:

> Prisoners like these have received the ultimate call to account for themselves, to hold still as icons of bad behavior. But no matter how many times they are counted and accounted for, they cannot account for themselves because their words are not allowed to "grab" those who contain them. (2004, 188)

The representation of inmates as both willful subjects and inert objects—while incoherent in itself—also overlooks the complexity of a system that, more often than not, puts prisoners in a double-bind situation where they are forced to "choose" between two intolerable options.

Some inmates will deliberately break prison rules in order to get removed from the main line, where they expect violence from another inmate, or simply to prove they are worthy of respect. As one prisoner explains:

> I have a choice, and I don't have a choice. . . . OK, [another inmate] is bad-mouthing me. . . . Right then and there I have a choice to go in there and beat him up and go to the hole . . . or ignore him and suffer greater consequences than going to the hole. . . . [My cellmates] would [say], "He is weak. He has no heart. He doesn't stand up for himself." (Quoted in Rhodes 2004, 67)

This paradox of both having and not having a choice echoes Fanon's reflection in *Black Skin, White Masks*: "I had to choose. What do I mean? I had no choice" (1967, 126). It is the double bind of the colonial subject, but it may also be the double bind of the late-modern subject more generally, to the extent that sovereign subjects are constituted as individually responsible for the injuries they sustain and for the fixed identities constituted in and through those injuries (W. Brown 1995).

There are other situations where prisoners are already suffering from some form of mental illness or cognitive impairment and are not able to follow the rules as well as other prisoners. Terry Kupers tells of mentally ill inmates having been shot by prison authorities because their medication slowed them down so that they could not react quickly enough to commands to hit the ground when disturbances broke out in the prison yard (1999, 25).

Still other inmates are confined to the SHU not for having broken a prison rule but simply for who they are or are presumed to be. These are the inmates classified as gang members or gang associates, a dispropor-tionate number of whom are black or Latino—even though one of the deadliest prison gangs in the United States is the Aryan Brotherhood. Classification as a gang member is managed on a points system, ac-cording to criteria such as tattoos, incriminating photographs, asso-ciation, telephone conversations and other forms of communication, information from debriefing reports or informants, and "staff infor-mation" (Shalev 2009, 75). These criteria are broad enough to capture virtually any prisoner in their net, and the reliance on circumstantial evidence means that some inmates are named as gang members just to settle a score.[7] While rule violators are given determinate sentences in the SHU, alleged gang members and associates are held indefinitely in the SHU, until they either prove that they have been falsely classified or they choose to "debrief" by providing prison authorities with ac-curate information about gang membership or activities. Colloquially, this policy is known among prisoners as "snitch, parole or die" (Shalev 2009, 81; see also Reiter 2012b). But snitching and dying are by no means mutually exclusive possibilities; former gang members face retaliation and murder upon release or reintegration into the general prison population.[8]

At least one supermax administrator interviewed by Shalev recognizes that "choice" may not be the best way to describe gang classification, debriefing, or even membership:

> Most of these guys didn't just come to prison and decide, "Gee, I think I'm going to be a gang member" and they go out and join a gang. Most of them had been associated with gang activities, many of them, since pre-teen. For many of them it was a family lifestyle—their fathers, their mothers, their brothers, sisters, aunts, uncles—the whole family network was associated with gang activity. (Quoted in Shalev 2009, 84)[9]

A former inmate adds more nuance to this situation:

> Why betray friends, people who you, who you grow up with . . . but you do not spend time with, just for a chance of going to the mainline. I don't see no honour in that. I think it's dishonourable. (Quoted in Shalev 2009, 84)

Some prisoners have used the rhetoric of accountability against the system that both demands it and destroys the conditions under which accountability could be meaningful. For example, the five core demands of the 2011 California prisoners' hunger strike include the following:

> Eliminate group punishments. Instead, practice individual accountability. When an individual prisoner breaks a rule, the prison often punishes a whole group of prisoners of the same race. This policy has been applied to keep prisoners in the SHU indefinitely and to make conditions increasingly harsh.[10]

The rhetoric of accountability, like the rhetoric of dehumanization discussed in chapter 6, is an ambivalent but perhaps inevitable effect of prison logic on prisoner's resistance. What are the ethical and political implications of this rhetoric?

The logic of supermax confinement both *binds prisoners to their actions,* by tracking and recording every act, outburst, or example of (bad) "behavior," and also *unbinds prisoners from their actions,* such that it does not matter what prisoners already classified as a certain kind of security risk do or refrain from doing. In either case, prisoners are assumed to be independent, autonomous, and ultimately nonrelational subjects: in control of their actions but not completely determined by them, and always capable of willfully making a different choice. As Lorna Rhodes puts it: "This tension about the shape of accountability raises the question of what it means to allow the 'social man' to wither on the other side of the bars while, at the same time, attributing to him an almost superhuman ability to exercise his will" (2004, 60).[11] But the greater the control and the more intense the confinement, the more impossible it becomes for prisoners to behave like separate individuals with a free will to make choices and to bear the full weight of the consequences of those choices. Prisoners find themselves in a Catch-22 situation where they cannot follow the rules even if they want to, or where they are punished whether or not they break the rules, or where the only avenue left for exercising some form of autonomy or self-defense is to break the rules, even if this means exposing themselves to an even harsher imposition of rules.[12]

In short, supermax prisoners are set up to fail. They are told to conduct themselves as autonomous subjects while under near-total control. They are told to reflect on the consequences of their actions in a situation that typically produces cognitive impairment and mental illness. They are told to accomplish a social and ethical transformation in a situation that blocks social and ethical relationships to others. They are *told* this in a way that both uses language and abuses it: by demanding accountability while excluding in advance the possibility of an interlocutor to whom one may give an account of oneself. Rather, the "account" is in prisoners' behavior: their compliance or noncompliance with a set of rules that can be observed and judged from a third-person perspective without engaging with the inmate as a subject.[13] This "objectivity" is construed as one of the merits of the current penal system: behavior seems to offer an objective measure of what inmates are capable of and what they are statistically likely to do in any given situation. Rehabilitation is defined, today as much as it was fifty years ago, in terms of behavior modification. Good inmates are those whose behavior complies with prison rules and norms, whether or not this is likely to translate into effective coping skills on the outside, after release.[14] The prisoners' own sense of honor or integrity and their relationships with others are reduced to instrumental factors in the optimization of behavior.

But if this is the most we can expect from criminal offenders—that they align their behavior with existing norms and rules and refrain from breaking the law—then justice is nothing more than the management of injustice. Justice is biopolitical in the sense that Foucault describes in *Security, Territory, Population*: it is the determination of "how to keep a type of criminality . . . within socially and economically acceptable limits and around an average that will be considered as optimal for a given social functioning" (2009, 5).[15] The question here is not how to make a legal prohibition stick to the body of a criminal, nor is it even how to discipline the criminal and instill the norms of good behavior; rather, it is how to manage the risk posed by criminal behavior, to reduce its harm, and to maximize the overall productivity of the population. Anyone who demands more from the criminal justice system in the twenty-first century must be a naive romantic, hopelessly out of touch with the harsh realities of crime and punishment.

Critical Phenomenology: Levinas and Fanon

Levinas opens his book *Totality and Infinity* with these words: "Everyone will readily agree that it is of the highest importance to know whether we are not duped by morality" (1969, 21). Is it naive to think that justice could mean anything other than the advantage of the stronger? Or is there more to justice than this? Prison officials and criminal offenders may agree on very little, but one assumption they tend to share is that justice is a matter of power, and power a matter of domination and control. But if this is true, then the logic of justice is war, and politics is nothing more than the "art of foreseeing war and of winning it by every means" (21). Rhetoric is, in effect, language in the service of war; it is the use of words to secure and enhance one's power, rather than a way of encountering the other in conversation. Levinas connects the logic of war to the "harsh reality" or "harsh object-lesson" of a regime that crushes everything and everyone that gets in its way, but he also connects war to "the very patency, or the truth, of the real" for Western philosophical thought (21). To the extent that knowledge is a matter of grasping something, of penetrating the real and possessing it as an object of knowledge, then philosophy is an art of war. Its aim is to cut through the opaque resistance of the world, canceling its otherness and securing it within a defensible theory. The totalizing ambitions of Western philosophy yield to a totalitarian logic of being and of politics:

> War is produced as the pure experience of pure being. The ontological event that takes form in this black light is a casting into movement of beings hitherto anchored in their identity, a mobilization of absolutes, by an objective order from which there is no escape. (21)

War forces people to

> play roles in which they no longer recognize themselves, making them betray not only commitments but their own substance, making them carry out actions that will destroy every possibility for action. . . . It establishes an order from which no one can keep his distance; nothing henceforth is exterior. War does not manifest exteriority and the other as other; it destroys the identity of the same. (21)

The logic of war, like the logic of the supermax prison, undermines the identity of subjects and objects, even while attempting to secure that identity, by foreclosing a relation to the outside beyond the totality.

But does war exhaust the meaning of being? Is even the peaceful acknowledgment of philosophers, political scientists, psychiatrists, and others that "we need other people" still based on the logic of war? How else might we understand the meaning of the world, the relations between self and other, knower and known, subject and world? In *Totality and Infinity,* Levinas proposes an *ethical reduction* of the totalizing logic of war. Ethical reduction is the method by which Levinas traces the conditions of what he calls "*objectifying cognition*" (1969, 67) or "objectifying thought" back to the "forgotten experience from which it lives" (28): the experience of an absolute other who teaches me something that I could not have derived from my own cognitive powers, namely, the ethical significance of the world.[16] Husserl reduces natural experience to transcendental consciousness, and Heidegger reduces consciousness to the more primordial structure of Being-in-the-world. Levinas's ethical reduction radicalizes the phenomenological project further, tracing both consciousness and Being-in-the-world to the hinged structure of created being, or the *creature.*

The creature is a consciousness who discovers in itself a *conscience*; it is a separated being who finds itself in relation to an absolute other who puts in question its spontaneous freedom and commands it to justify itself. In this sense, the creature is both for-itself and for-the-other; it is the "unity of spontaneous freedom, working on straight ahead, and critique, where freedom is capable of being called in question and thus preceding itself" (Levinas 1969, 89). The creature is not a subject who *needs* the other in order to be itself but, rather, a subject whose *desire* for the other reorients its existence in a critical and ethical direction, thus opening the possibility of ethical reduction:[17]

> And if the tracing back from a condition to what precedes that condition describes the status of the creature, in which the uncertainty of freedom and its recourse to justification are bound up, if knowing is a creature activity, this unsettling of the condition and this justification come from the other. (86)

In other words, the creature is a subject for whom truth is social justice. Levinas begins his ethical reduction of war with a series of questions:

> Does objectivity, whose harshness and universal power is revealed in war, provide the unique and primordial form in which Being, when it is distinguished from image, dream, and subjective abstraction, *imposes itself* on consciousness? Is the apprehension of an object equivalent to the very movement in which the bonds with truth are woven? (1969, 24)

His answer to these questions is no. The basic concepts of Western philosophy—truth, reality, being, objectivity—must be critically interrogated and reduced or "led back" to their more primordial, or even anarchic, ethical condition: the figure of the one-for-the-other, the other-in-the-same, infinity in the finite, the transcendence of the other in a separated yet responsible self. These relations of separation and transcendence "form the fabric of being itself" (81). Levinas's ethical reduction reveals ethical desire to be the anarchic condition of what is commonly understood as a social, biological, or economic need for social relations. In order to see how this is the case, we must follow Levinas's ethical reduction of war and of the "politics" that continues war by other means back to a revelation of truth as social justice. This reduction unfolds through the practice of what Levinas calls critique.

Critique is a variant of the phenomenological reduction: it "leads back" from an occurrent experience to the conditions that make that experience possible and meaningful. But critique differs significantly from the phenomenological, transcendental, and eidetic reductions in Husserl's work, and even from the variants of reduction in Heidegger's work (the hammer breaking down, anxiety disclosing the world as *unheimlich*) and from the more skeptical interpretation of the reduction proposed by Merleau-Ponty in the preface to *Phenomenology of Perception* (2002, xii–xvi). If anything, it is most akin to the scene that Fanon describes in *Black Skin, White Masks* in which a child says,

"Look, a Negro!" and so provokes in the racialized subject a whole series of affective, intellectual, social, and political questions that lead back from a normalized experience of French colonial identity to a critical interrogation of the whole system of colonization. There is no adequate response to the child's words or to the adult's inadequate apology ("Take no notice, sir, he does not know that you are as civilized as we" [1967, 113]), in part because the racialized subject has not been *addressed as an other* by these words but, rather, has been *singled out as an object,* frozen into a space where he is both excluded and isolated. Without a revolution or a wholesale transformation of the colonial situation, the critical provocation of the colonized risks becoming a vaguely tolerated monologue or a self-undermining pathology of anxiety, paranoia, and rage rather than collective action and solidarity among the colonized. The provocation that Fanon describes is both a critical opening for the racialized subject and a declaration of war against him—by a child, no less!—as well as a foreclosure of meaningful conversation between whites and blacks, colonizers and colonized. Fanon concludes *Black Skin, White Masks* with a final prayer: "O my body, make of me always a man who questions!" (232). With these words, he affirms the possibility of critique beyond the dead end of colonialism. As a prayer addressed to the body—a terrestrial site of divinity, if ever there was one—these final words are also an opening and an invitation to others: "At the conclusion of this study, I want the world to recognize, with me, the open door of every consciousness" (232).

What Fanon and Levinas share as critical phenomenologists, and what I find missing in Husserl, Heidegger, and even Merleau-Ponty, is the insight that the provocation of critique is not just the philosopher's curiosity or confusion but an interruptive *encounter with the other.* It is not just that I have decided to reflect on the structure of experience, nor is it that the coherence of my practical world has been disrupted and, in its disruption, the structure of Being-in-the-world has been disclosed. Rather, the other has *put me in question* and challenged me to question myself. For Fanon, the questioning of the racialized subject is first and foremost a violent dislocation, an amputation, and even an imprisonment: it cannot be the last word of critique, and it is not even clear that it is the first. The *no* and the *is not* of racism and colonial violence must be traced back to the "*yes* that vibrates to cosmic harmonies" and to the possibility of a collective struggle in which both blacks and whites "turn their backs on the inhuman voices" that foreclose a meaningful conversation between them (1967, 8, 231). Fanon asks the reader, "Why not the quite simple attempt to touch the other, to feel the other, to explain the other to myself? Was my freedom not given to me then in order to build the world of the You?" (231–32). This, too, is a critical provocation to perform an ethical reduction of the colonial situation to a renewed sense of creaturely humanity.

For Levinas, critique begins with the provocation of the other who puts me in question and commands me to justify myself. This command is not an act of war, rhetorical or otherwise; rather, it makes a break with the logic of war by addressing the subject as one who is both free and responsible. It does not destroy "the identity of the same" by shattering its corporeal schema and replacing it with a racial epidermal schema.[18] Rather, it critically engages this identity, asking, in effect: Who do you think you are? What do you have to say for yourself? For Levinas, we question ourselves, and ultimately we question being, because we have been *put in question* by an other, because we have been called to justify ourselves to one whose vulnerability is exposed to the potential violence of our arbitrary freedom. Without this experience of being put in question by an other, there would be no motivation for critique, nothing to interrupt the spontaneity of the for-itself, no command to reflect on the conditions of one's own freedom. Critique begins in shame—if by shame we mean the experience of being turned back upon oneself by a feeling of ethical exposure to the face of an other whose presence commands me to justify myself. Philosophy, the vocation of perpetual questioning, does not antecede this experience of being put in question by an other, which marks the birth of the philosopher as an ethical subject *and therefore* also as a speculative theoretical subject. In this sense, conscience precedes consciousness, and ethics is first philosophy.[19] Philosophy may be born in wonder, but wonder is born in shame.

The critical provocation of shame both highlights our freedom and conceals it by subordinating freedom to responsibility. But shame does not destroy my freedom; it merely commands me to justify this freedom and to invest it in ethical responsibility.[20] A freedom invested is a freedom divested of its arbitrary spontaneity, and so made meaningful. Ultimately, for Levinas, freedom is invested only in "Discourse and Desire, where the Other presents himself as an interlocutor, as him over whom I *can*not have power, whom I cannot kill . . . where, qua I, I am not innocent spontaneity but usurper and murderer" (1969, 84). At the very moment I am commanded not to murder, I appear to myself as both a murderer and a responsible subject; I discover both the violence of my arbitrary freedom and the "difficult freedom" of responsibility (Levinas 1997).

In what follows, I draw on Levinas's critique of war and rhetoric, and his ethical reduction of philosophical knowledge to justice and responsibility, to develop a critical phenomenology of accountability and choice in supermax prisons. I argue that the insistence on prisoners' individual accountability for their choices in a context where they have almost no control over their situation makes a mockery of ethical responsibility and political justice. Rather than challenging criminal offenders to face others in responsibility and to join others in solidarity, the control prison declares war on prisoners, disrupting their identity as separated subjects and condemning them to "an objective order from which there is no escape" (Levinas 1969, 21). An ethical response to crime, motivated by a demand for social justice rather than by punishment, "correction," or behavior modification, can help us envision new possibilities for criminal justice, both within prisons and beyond them.

An Ethical Reduction of Rhetoric

In the section of *Totality and Infinity* entitled "Truth Presupposes Justice," Levinas challenges us to imagine a world in which others do not matter and in which we may not even be sure they exist. In this imaginary world, truth is unhinged from justice, and the spontaneous freedom of the I is left to its own devices, unencumbered by the ethical command of the other. Levinas situates his account of this imaginary world (if we can even call it a "world") in relation to two philosophical figures: Gyges from Plato's *Republic* and the cogito from Descartes's First and Second Meditations.

Gyges is a shepherd who finds a magical ring that allows him to become invisible; he uses this power to rape the queen and murder the king. Plato introduces the figure of Gyges into the narrative of the *Republic* to raise questions about responsibility and freedom: What if I could evade the gaze of others and was no longer accountable to others for my actions? Doesn't power reveal that we are duped by morality, that only the weak have an interest in being responsible to others? Gyges raises the specter of a world where others do not matter and where, because they do not matter, I have no reason to consider them when I act or to constrain my actions for moral reasons. The implication is that without the gaze of others, I would have no conscience; I would become a will radically unhinged from an ethical orientation toward justice.

Descartes's cogito raises a different set of questions in response to a different scenario, where it is not that others do not *matter* but that I cannot be sure they *exist*. If the only thing I can know for certain is that I doubt or I think, and that therefore I am, then I remain in a doubtful relation to the existence of my own body, the world, and other subjects unless I can secure another absolute point outside my own existence, a pivot point or hinge with which to (re)connect to the world. The First and Second Meditations raise the specter of a cogito radically unhinged from the truth of the world, cut off from the possibility of knowing anything for certain beyond the indubitable fact *that* it exists.[21]

I will address these figures separately, since they raise different issues, both of which are relevant for my ethical reduction of SHU syndrome: a "world" without justice, and a "world" without truth.

"World" without Justice

Gyges inhabits a "world" of pure spectacle. Endowed with the power to see without being seen, he feels released from the obligation to take others into account. There are no witnesses to his actions and therefore no need for alibis. Whether or not God is dead, the magic of invisibility grants that everything is permitted. Gyges's ability to escape the detection of others allows him to act without having to bear the consequences of his actions; it frees his consciousness from the judgment of others and relieves him of his ethical conscience.

Gyges can do whatever he wants. But is he therefore free? Has he resolved the problem of existence that Levinas analyzes in his early work as the problem of escape, or of "getting out of being by a new path" (2003, 73)? Has he secured access to the truth, since no one can contest his possession of the world or punish his transgressions? Or has his life become meaningless in the absence of anyone to witness his actions and to demand from him a reason or justification? Has the world become a spectacle in which everything is permitted only because nothing is real?

Gyges embodies the fantasy of a subject who would be free as long as he is alone and unencumbered by obligations to others.[22] The temptation of Gyges is built into the logic of war: What if I could have it all to myself? What if I could get away with murder? This temptation is arguably one of the motivations of crime. After all, what is Gyges if not a murderer and a rapist? But the same temptation also structures the high-tech panopticon of supermax prisons where wardens are able to monitor inmates twenty-four hours a day through surveillance cameras, seeing without being seen; where the lights are never turned off in order to facilitate this surveillance; and where, in some prisons, even medical and psychiatric consultations are conducted by video monitor in order to minimize direct contact with inmates (Haney 2003, 126). In effect, the control prison sends this message to the inmate: You thought you were Gyges, you thought you could get away with murder. But you were caught in the act, and your punishment is to be put in a position that reverses Gyges's power: exposed to the gaze of others, but without the chance to return that gaze except in the most cursory way. You must become accountable for your actions, without knowing to whom or for whose sake you should give an account of yourself. And finally, you must prove yourself worthy of freedom in a situation that limits, controls, and monitors your every movement.

Following Elliott Currie, Lorna Rhodes calls this policy of making supermax inmates "accountable" for their actions even in the absence of anyone *to whom* to give an account of themselves—in the absence of an intercorporeal context that could make accountability meaningful as a form of responsibility to others rather than adherence to rules and regulations—"punitive individualism" (Currie 1998, 112; quoted in Rhodes 2004, 84). Inmates are both commanded to be individuals—to stand on their own, to rely on no one but themselves, to be autonomous—and also punished for being individuals, to the extent that individual autonomy involves the freedom to depart from the rules as well as to follow them. They are also punished for *not* being individuals, for falling apart in the social and sensory isolation of the SHU.

What would it take to "ethically reduce" the control prison and its Gygean structure to the ethical relations that make it possible and that are distorted and represented in the control prison as "accountability"? We must follow the rhetoric of individual choice and accountability back to the investment of spontaneous subjective freedom in an ethical responsibility that justifies it and so makes freedom meaningful beyond mere spontaneity. But before we can perform this ethical reduction of supermax rhetoric, we must examine another aspect of war and the rhetoric that sustains it: the solitary cogito and its "world" without truth.

"World" without Truth

If Gyges inhabits a "world" without justice, then the cogito in Descartes's First and Second Meditations—the solitary cogito, prior to the discovery of an absolute point of reference outside of itself—inhabits a "world" without truth. The *Meditations on First Philosophy* begin with the philosopher's attempt, for once in his life, to rid himself of false opinions and to establish an indubitable foundation for true knowledge. In the First Meditation, Descartes proves that as long as I am thinking—even if my thought takes the form of radical doubt—I know for certain that I exist. But this cogito remains threatened by the possibility of global deception by an evil genius until it can secure another absolute point outside its own existence: a hinge with which to (re)connect to the world. Descartes discovers this other absolute in the Third Meditation where he proves the existence of an omniscient, omnipotent, and perfect God by locating the idea of infinity within his own finite subjectivity and tracing this idea back to its only possible origin or cause: the existence of God himself. For Descartes, the possibility of a cogito that is radically deceived about everything but its own existence is merely a speculative possibility that emerges in the course of securing an indubitable ground for true knowledge of the world as it really is. But what if the Meditations had stalled here? What if the radical skepticism of the cogito became interminable? What if it failed to discover within itself something greater and older than itself?

Levinas argues that, for such a cogito, "thought would strike nothing substantial. On first contact the *phenomenon* would degrade into *appearance* and in this sense would remain in equivocation, under suspicion of an evil genius" (1969, 90).[23] Levinas describes this relation to the world as a parody of knowledge:

> He to whom the real had just presented itself, with an appearance that shone forth as the very *skin* of being, is being made game of. For already the *primordial* or the ultimate abandons the very skin in which it shone in its nudity, as a covering that announces, dissimulates, imitates, or deforms it. (91)

Without a relation to an absolute beyond the cogito's own self-evident existence, nothing could be known with any confidence; perception would become equivocal, no longer a site of access to the world but, rather, a source of illusion. What would this experience—or this unraveling of experience—be like?

Recall the statements made by prisoners at Walpole Prison in 1982:

> Melting, everything in the cell starts moving; everything gets darker, you feel you are losing your vision. (Quoted in Grassian 1983, 1452)

> They come by [for breakfast] with four trays; the first has big pancakes—I think I'm going to get them. Then someone comes up and gives me tiny ones—they get real small, like silver dollars. I seem to see movements—real fast motions in front of me. Then seems like they're doing things behind your back—can't quite see them. Did someone just hit me? I dwell on it for hours. (1452)

Aren't these people living the nightmare that Levinas, through his reading of Descartes, is asking us to imagine—a nightmare in which the distinction between reality and illusion becomes blurred to the point of unhinging the subject from an objective world?

By posing this question, I do not mean to suggest that prisoners in solitary confinement actively doubt whether or not other people exist, nor do I mean to suggest that they have been reduced to pure cogito, absolutely deprived of any relation to other subjects. After all, every inmate has some sort of contact with guards and other prison staff, and some are even able to communicate with other prisoners by sending "kites" (written notes) or by yelling across the cell tier. Many prisoners *know* that the cell walls are not wavering, that the pancakes are not shrinking, that the world is not melting. But the more radically they are deprived of everyday, embodied relations to others in the flesh, face-to-face, the more likely it seems that the world will become equivocal for them, as if phenomena have dissolved into mere appearances, as if "the skin of being" has become a source of illusion rather than a true manifestation of what is, as if they were being deceived or "made game of."

This perceptual equivocation is compounded by cognitive and even ontological confusion. To *dwell on something for hours,* without clarifying one's experience, is to be caught in a situation where the sheer capacity for thought—however absolute and indubitable—has become less a foundation for true knowledge than a source of pain and despair, producing panic, anxiety, and obsessive repetition. This is a situation where time stands still even as it slips away, where there is no escape from the weight of one's own indubitable, but therefore irremissible, existence.

How would an ethical reduction of SHU syndrome unfold, and where might it begin? I take as my transcendental clue a brief remark in Levinas's analysis of the spectacle unhinged from the conditions of true knowledge: "Apparition is a congealed form from which someone has already withdrawn" (1969, 98). The phenomenon that has dissolved into mere appearance or apparition is not a pure experience of the world *without* others; rather, it is already an experience of the world *deprived* of others, a world from which others have *withdrawn*. The thinker who sits down by the fire to perform his solitary meditations is not yet the bare cogito whose existence he proves in the First Meditation; rather, the thinker must *go back* to the cogito by withdrawing from the social relations that already support his everyday experience of the world, even if they also distract him with "false opinions" (Descartes 1996, 1: 1). Descartes's meditations unfold as a conversation with himself.

At the beginning of the Third Meditation, he declares:

> I will now close my eyes, I will stop my ears, I will turn away my senses from their objects, I will even efface from my consciousness all the images of corporeal things; or at least, because this can hardly be accomplished, I will consider them as empty and false; and thus, holding converse only with myself, and closely examining my nature, I will endeavor to obtain by degrees a more intimate and familiar knowledge of myself. (3: 1)

And yet, precisely as a conversation, Descartes's solitary meditations presuppose the ethical structure of "veritable conversation," in which there is something *about which* to speak because there is someone *to whom* to speak, someone who provokes critical reflection by putting me in question. As Levinas puts it, "Attention is attention to something *because* it is attention to someone" (1969, 99; emphasis added).

Or as Merleau-Ponty explains in a strikingly Levinasian passage in the *Phenomenology of Perception*:

> The philosopher cannot fail to draw others with him into his reflective retreat, because in the uncertainty of the world, he has for ever learned to treat them as consorts, and because all his knowledge is built on this datum of opinion. Transcendental subjectivity is a revealed subjectivity, revealed to itself and to others, and is for that reason an intersubjectivity. (2002, 421)

This claim may seem far-fetched to readers who are more sympathetic to Descartes's epistemological reduction than to Levinas's ethical reduction. After all, do I not pay attention to things or ask questions about the world, whether or not there is someone there to provoke them? But Levinas is not claiming that the ethical relation to an absolute other is an *empirical* condition for truth; rather, he is reducing knowledge to its *ethical–transcendental* condition. And even Descartes recognizes the necessity of a relation to something outside the cogito—something older than itself, yet discovered within itself—in order to secure its own true knowledge of the world. How does Levinas explain the ethical significance of truth in a way that both draws on the formal structure of the cogito in Descartes's Third Meditation and radicalizes his insight? In the following sections, I will track Levinas's ethical reduction of the object to the other and of rhetoric to language in order to explain why both perception and cognition come unhinged for many prisoners in solitary confinement.

From the Object to the Other

From the perspective of war, truth is objectivity; to know is to grasp objects as what they are, to catch them in the web of cognition by attaching one's own percept to an adequate concept. But in the preface to *Totality and Infinity,* Levinas asks whether objectivity is the primary way in which Being is disclosed to consciousness (1969, 24). "Does not lucidity, the mind's openness upon the true, consist in catching sight of the permanent possibility of war?" (21).

But as Stuart Grassian's research demonstrates, this simple task of grasping an object can become complicated for prisoners in prolonged solitary confinement. The distinction between objective reality and "image, dream, and subjective abstraction" can become blurred to the point of unhinging the subject from an objective world. The "harsh object-lesson" of war, which "does not manifest exteriority and the other as other" also risks losing touch with the objective world and "destroy[ing] the identity of the same" (Levinas, 1969, 21). In order to understand why prisoners' experience of objects, and even of their own personal identity, comes unraveled in solitary confinement, we need to put in question the logic of war and to trace "objectifying thought" back to the "forgotten experience from which it lives" (28). For Levinas, this forgotten experience is the encounter with an other who is not an object,[24] an other who *teaches* me something I did not already know: the idea of infinity.[25] This revelation of the other as teacher "constitutes a veritable inversion of *objectifying cognition*" (67): an inversion of knowledge as an instrument of war into knowledge "in the absolute sense of the term"—namely, as truth.

For Levinas, this ethical reduction of objectifying cognition to truth reveals the other as "the principle of phenomena" (1969, 92).[26] This is an extraordinary statement, and it reverses one of the central claims of classical phenomenology. For Husserl, thinking in the wake of Descartes, the "principle" of phenomena is the correlation of noetic acts with noemata in a singular, solitary consciousness. The full sense of objectivity may presuppose a concrete experience of other embodied subjects in a shared world, but the *principle* of phenomena remains the flow of noetic acts in a transcendental ego. But if the other is the principle of phenomena, then consciousness alone is not sufficient to produce a coherent experience of phenomena; solitary consciousness may have access to *appearances,* but to the extent that these appearances remain disconnected from the ethical revelation of an absolute other as teacher, they remain mere apparitions rather than phenomena that give me access to the things themselves. Levinas's key insight is that these subjective apparitions are not the building blocks of objectifying cognition but, rather, "a congealed form from which someone has already withdrawn" (1969, 98). Levinas traces even the structure of intentionality, the outward radiation of consciousness toward its objects, to the revelation of the other who teaches me the idea of infinity.[27] In other words, he reduces consciousness to conscience, and reveals *ethics as first philosophy.*[28]

Even in war, which excludes the other as other, a trace of this excluded or withdrawn other remains. War does not reveal the harsh truth of objectivity; it obscures this truth, and it even threatens to unhinge the subject from the objective world by excluding the other and destroying "the identity of the same." From the perspective of Levinas's ethical reduction of the totalizing logic of war, the sense of objectivity presupposes language or discourse as a privileged site of ethical relation:

> The objects are not objects when they offer themselves to the hand that uses them, to the mouth and the nose, the eyes and the ears that enjoy them. Objectivity . . . is *posited* in a discourse, in a *con-versation [entretien]* which *proposes* the world. This *proposition* is held between two points which do not constitute a system, a cosmos, a totality. (1969, 96)

The formal structure of this conversation between "two points" is borrowed from Descartes's Third Meditation, in which the cogito discovers within itself an idea of which it is not the cause, and that must have been "taught" or revealed by an absolute other. And yet the *sense* of conversation is not contained within the formal structure described by Descartes. This sense—both its meaning and its direction or orientation—can only be discovered by proceeding back from the formal structure to the "forgotten experience from which it lives" (Levinas 1969, 28): the ethical experience of being put in question by an other and commanded to respond, to justify oneself.

This is what it means to do philosophy: it is to perform the transcendental reduction as an ethical reduction, to discover the ethical experience from which our concepts live but that these concepts obscure to the extent that they are totalized within the framework of war. War is not the truth of being; rather, it is "the locus of truth is society" (Levinas 1969, 101). How might this ethical reduction of philosophy help us understand the experience of prisoners in solitary confinement?

From Rhetoric to Language

Recall the prisoner who told Stuart Grassian:

> I can't concentrate, can't read. . . . Your mind's narcotized. . . . Sometimes can't grasp words in my mind that I know. Get stuck, have to think of another word. Memory is going. You feel you are losing something you might not get back. (Quoted in Grassian 1983, 1453)

Another prisoner reported:

> I overhear the guards talking. Did they say that? Yes? No? It gets confusing. I tried to check it out with [a prisoner in the adjoining cell]; sometimes he hears something and I don't. I know one of us is crazy, but which one? Am I losing my mind? (1452)

What has happened to these prisoners, such that words they know begin to evade them, and even when they have a chance to speak to another prisoner, they are not sure who is more insane? This is a situation where not only perception but also language and thought have become equivocal, where meaningful discourse has become indiscernible from what Levinas calls rhetoric.

For Levinas, rhetoric is not merely an interested use of language; rather, it is an unhinging of language from the ethical situation of "veritable conversation." Rhetoric *inverts* the ethical inversion of war into discourse. In this sense, rhetoric is "antilanguage" (1969, 92) or "the inverse of language: the interlocutor has given a sign, but has declined every interpretation" (91). Rhetoric broadcasts "a mocking intention," a lie that evades direct refutation because it is not a matter of some particular error or distortion but, rather, a global inversion, a key change, a rendering-equivocal of the very status of the word and of the world (91). Someone gestures toward me, throws signs my way, but without opening the way to meaning, without questioning or responding in a conversation. Just as the equivocal world of the bare cogito turns phenomena into mere apparitions, rhetoric turns language against itself, using discourse in a way that *refuses to participate* in discourse, refuses to "propose" the world or to put the world in common.[29] This equivocation of language reinforces the equivocation of phenomena we addressed earlier:

> The inverse of language is like a laughter that seeks to destroy language, a laughter infinitely reverberated where mystification interlocks in mystification without ever resting on a real speech, without ever commencing. The spectacle of the silent world of facts is bewitched: every phenomenon masks, mystifies ad infinitum, making actuality impossible. (92)

A world where language has become equivocal is a world without principle, without the second, "earlier" or anarchic starting point of an absolute other, discovered by Descartes's cogito in the Third Meditation and recovered through Levinas's method of ethical reduction. It is an unworlded world where the idea of infinity has slipped into the bad infinite of endless reverberation and mystification. This connection between the unraveling of language and the unraveling of phenomena suggests that discourse and perception are mutually interrelated, and that both presuppose the other as interlocutor.[30] How might this analysis of rhetoric help us understand the experience of prisoners in solitary confinement?

A Levinasian Critique of Supermax Rhetoric

On the surface, it seems quite reasonable to claim that those who break the law must be held accountable for their actions. But in a country where passing a bad check can lead to more prison time than perpetrating massive corporate fraud, where criminal penalties for the possession of crack cocaine are still eighteen times greater than those for the possession of powdered cocaine (reduced from one hundred times greater by the Fair Sentencing Act of 2010), where a homeless woman can be arrested for trying to send her child to a better school district (J. Miller 2011)—this rhetoric of accountability makes a mockery of justice.

Supermax rhetoric demands accountability while undermining prisoners' capacity to act and to account for their actions. It declares war on the rebellious will of the prisoner, seeking to control, reshape, and (to the extent that this is still the goal of our penal system) to reform this transgressive will into a docile, well-behaved peacekeeper. Often, even prisoners who do transform themselves and others, making significant contributions to a meaningful sense of peace and justice, are not spared from punishment, control, and even execution.[31] As such, the justice system (oxymoron par excellence) rivets prisoners to their past and to their solitary existence, refusing to engage with them as others and structurally undermining their integrity as separated but responsible subjects. It confines prisoners to what Levinas calls the *il y a*—the equivocal par excellence—"beyond affirmation and negation" (1969, 93). Alone without solitude, exposed to the gaze of others without the possibility of cultivating a meaningful relation to them, confined to themselves and yet doubled with themselves, they are condemned to bear the weight of their own being without escape. The isolated cogito may be able to affirm its own existence with apodictic certainty, even (or especially) in solitude, but it cannot affirm the *world,* or even the phenomenon as a true appearance, without the other. As Levinas puts it, "It is not I, it is the other that can say yes" (1969, 93). Even the most successfully individuated subject cannot evade this ethical, political, and even epistemological imperative for "veritable conversation" with the other.

But if this is the case, then the rhetoric of accountability in control prisons does not affect just the prisoners in the SHU or just the prisoners in general population; it affects the entire "prison society" (Wacquant 2001, 121). To the extent that we support or even tolerate a penal policy based on control and isolation as a legitimate part of our justice system, we risk undermining our own humanity, or better yet, our own creaturely existence, as well as that of prisoners. Not just the legitimacy of penal institutions and procedures but *the meaning of the world* is at stake in these issues. By suspending the ethical conditions under which the world is proposed to another, and so becomes meaningful as a shared world or even as the gift of the other, we condemn ourselves as well as others to more or less extreme forms of social and civil death.

For Levinas, "Justice coincides with the overcoming of rhetoric" (1969, 72). To what extent is this overcoming of rhetoric already underway in U.S. prisons, and how might we facilitate the ethical reduction of the justice system to the conditions that make justice meaningful beyond its systematization? In *Total Confinement,* Lorna Rhodes recounts one warden's insight that the policy of total control undermines the humanity of the *prison staff,* as well as of the prisoners, by putting them in a position of unsustainable, irresponsible power over others. John Larson, Control Unit administrator at a Washington State prison, says, "We do not get our full humanity until these people go out into a normal situation" (quoted in Rhodes 2004, 208). Larson's observation that even the guards risk losing their humanity when put in the structural position of Gyges resonates with Levinas's claim that "not only modern war but every war employs arms that turn against those who wield them" (1969, 21). This is no less true for the philosophical tradition that identifies knowledge with possession and the knower with a solitary consciousness that is free to the extent that it remains unencumbered. The myth of the solitary, self-sufficient individual is a weapon that, in the context of the U.S. penitentiary system, has turned against the very subjects that solitary confinement aimed to reform, redeem, or resurrect.[32] What sort of policy shift could help us disinvest in the situation of Gyges and create a space in which both prisoners and prison staff have a chance to encounter one another—and themselves—as creaturely human beings, where the meaning of humanity is revealed in the face of the other who commands us to respond?

John Larson made a simple but powerful change in the Control Unit that he supervises: he instituted a policy of regular tier walks by mental health staff and unit managers that allowed prisoners on lockdown to interact with administrative staff on a reliable basis, giving them a chance to speak and be listened to, to sort out problems before they escalate, and to feel acknowledged by an other as someone who matters rather than as inventory in cold storage. Rhodes observes that, to a great extent, this policy works to derail the "mutual investment in 'war' that both staff and inmates can develop" (2004, 207–8). The regularity of these mundane, even quotidian interactions helped "create a kind of middle distance, neither hierarchical removal nor the dangerous intimacy so feared. In this context, words, not feces, are the medium of exchange" (205). This middle distance restores a sense of prisoners' humanity, both to themselves and to the prison staff: "It is human to be available, to listen, not to walk away from a cell front when the person on the other side is in the middle of a sentence" (206). It is human, but it is also creaturely in Levinas's sense of the word "creature," to engage in the *entre-tien* of conversation rather than waging war against the prisoner while hiding behind the rhetoric of security and care. Larson's aim is to transform "behavior" (prison code for bad behavior) "into words, with their potential for connecting the inmate to a version of himself that others can live with" (119). This is a significant departure from policies that rivet prisoners to fixed identities as criminal offenders or numbered inmates; it creates and sustains a discursive space into which offenders are invited, and even ethically commanded, to emerge as creatures who critically interrogate the power of their spontaneous freedom and the possibility of investing this freedom in a responsibility and solidarity that breaks with the logic of war.

The institution of regular tier walks in a Control Unit is a simple reform; it does not even begin to tackle the larger task of abolishing solitary confinement and other forms of intensive confinement, let alone the wider problems of mass incarceration, the hyperincarceration of racialized subjects, and the prison industrial complex. Since the financial crisis hit the United States in 2007, states such as California, Texas, and Georgia have cut back from three meals a day to two meals a day or even one meal a day on weekends.[33] Some states have tried to decrease the number of offenders held in prison custody, especially in more expensive forms of restricted housing. While this consideration of the economic bottom line does not in itself require a reconsideration of the ethos of the control prison—far from it—some prisons have begun to make positive changes as a result of both the imperative to save money and the pressure from activists, advocacy groups, news media, legislators, and the courts. For example, in Mississippi, Corrections Commissioner Christopher B. Epps has reduced the number of prisoners in solitary confinement from over a thousand in 2007 to three hundred in 2012 (Goode 2012). These changes were made in response to a court order to address the violence in Unit 32, a Control Unit at Mississippi State Penitentiary (formerly Parchman Prison). Prison officials reassessed the security risk of every prisoner in restrictive housing, releasing some into general population and creating a transitional area with recreational facilities, a group dining area, and rehabilitation programs for others. While many were skeptical about responding to violence with more freedom and privileges for inmates rather than less, the change was transformative. By 2010, the prison was able to close Unit 32 altogether. When asked at the Senate subcommittee hearings on solitary confinement how Epps managed to "pull this off politically" in "the state of Mississippi, which many folks up North may not look to for leadership," Epps replied, "Well, actually we were—we were being sued. . . . And we—we—and what happened was, you know, we did what we felt was right" (Solitary Watch 2012b, 29–30).

In California, economic pressures have led to a series of penal reforms, some of which have opened up new possibilities for mutually supportive relationships among prisoners. A program at the California Men's Colony, a minimum- and medium-security prison, pairs inmates with dementia and volunteer inmates who work as their personal caregivers (Belluck 2012). As the prison population ages, and as the combination of stress, inadequate food and health care, and sometimes a lifetime of substance abuse intensifies the debilitating effects of aging for many prisoners, more and more require extra care to help them deal with everything from personal hygiene to exploitation by other inmates.[34] While some state prison systems have hired more health professionals to deal with their aging prison population, and some nonviolent prisoners have been transferred to public nursing homes, California has invested in training prisoners to become caregivers, or Gold Coats, so named for the yellow jackets they wear to distinguish them from other prisoners. Gold Coats help dementia patients with daily routines such as eating, showering, and changing adult diapers; they also conduct exercise classes, accompany their patients to doctors' appointments, and help them navigate the potentially treacherous terrain of the yard and the chow hall. In order to be trained as a Gold Coat, prisoners must have five to ten years of "clean" behavior in prison; their volunteer work is noted on their record and may help them make parole, but nothing is guaranteed. One Gold Coat says, "Tomorrow ain't promised to none of us" (quoted in Donaldson et al. 2012).

While the Gold Coat program was designed to cut costs and to solve a health-management problem, it has also had an ethically transformative effect on prisoner-caregivers. One Gold Coat, Ramon Cañas, says, "[Prior to my caregiving work], I didn't have any feelings about other people. I mean, in that way, I was a predator." Now, he says, "I'm a protector." Another Gold Coat, Phillip Burdick, says, "I'm a person who was broken." Now, he cares for dementia patients who often "don't even say thank you" but "just pat me like that and I know what that means." Gold Coat Samuel Baxter says, "A year ago . . . I couldn't have said, 'You know what man, I'm going to go help this grown man get in the shower,'" and "get in there and help these guys wash theirself off." But the daily practice of caring for another who is both vulnerable and demanding has altered the way he thinks of himself and of others. "It humbles you" he adds in a video interview (all quoted in Donaldson et al. 2012). Baxter describes the inmate that he cares for: "He real independent, so I gotta let him tell me when he want his bed made. And that's cool, you know, cuz it's about him, not me." He reflects on the emotional demands of his work, which is more than just a job:

> You gotta be friends with these guys, you know what I'm sayin'? It's impossible to just come down here and say, you know what? I got a job to do and I'm gonna do it. It don't work like that. You gotta bond with them cuz if they don't trust you, you know, it's not gonna work.

These caregivers were not always so supportive of others; Burdick is serving a life sentence for beating a man to death with a hammer, Baxter shot and killed a coworker after a heated argument, and Cañas killed a hitchhiker who had stolen his car. But their caregiving obligations have allowed them to engage with others as responsible subjects and to explore their own emotional and ethical vulnerability in relation to others. As one Gold Coat wrote in an evaluation of the program, "Thank you for allowing me to feel human."

The Gold Coat program is remarkable, but it is not unique, nor does it require a large financial investment to get off the ground. What it does require is a radical critique of prison rhetoric that values punishment over rehabilitation and reduces rehabilitation to behavior modification rather than demanding and supporting a meaningful transformation of relationships among prisoners, staff, and the public. Another program that has helped support rather than undermine ethical responsibility among prisoners is a hospice program at New York's Coxsackie Correctional Facility. Coxsaskie is one of about seventy-five prisons across the country that connects prisoner volunteers with prisoners who are in the final stages of illness and death (Leland 2009). John Henson is a prisoner serving a sentence of twenty-five years to life for beating his former employer to death with a baseball bat in the course of an attempted robbery:

> Before hospice, Mr. Henson said he had given little thought to the consequences of his crime. Then he found himself locked in a hospital room with

another inmate, holding the man's hand as his breathing slowed toward a stop. (Leland 2009)

When the inmate was pronounced dead, Henson began to weep:

I don't even know why I was crying. Partly because of him, partly because of things that died within me at the same time. . . .

I was just thinking about why I'm in here and the person's life that I took. . . . And sitting with this person for the first time and actually seeing death firsthand, being right there, my hand in his hand, watching him take his last breath, just caused me to say, "Wow, who the hell are you? Who were you to do this to somebody else?"

Another hospice volunteer, Benny Lee, who has served more than a decade for manslaughter, says:

Growing up and in prison, I put up walls. But I have to be more emotionally receptive to these guys. This is going against everything I've tried to do. But I realize it's a change I have to make. . . .

It's helping me mature. . . . My views of life and death are changing. I was unsympathetic when it comes to death. I've had friends die, and I was callous about it. Now I can't do that. I've come to identify with these guys, not because we're inmates, but because we're human beings. What they're going through, I'll go through.

When we give up on whole groups of people and put them in cold storage in a control prison, then we deprive these people of the chance for ethical transformation, and we also deprive ourselves of the chance to learn from each other about ethical responsibility and political solidarity. Whether prisoners are held in expensive solitary confinement or cheap, overcrowded prisons, the ethos of intensive confinement undermines both the agency of prisoners and their capacity for ethically meaningful lives. If critical reflection is crucial for the cultivation of a responsible life and a commitment to justice, then the justice system is structurally *unjust* to the extent that it forecloses the ethical provocation of critique and seeks instead to manage, control, and contain criminal offenders.

The point of prison, if it is to have a point beyond punishment, revenge, and—more recently—profit, should be to challenge offenders to justify themselves and to give them a chance to be taught, in Levinas's sense of the word: a chance to engage in critique and self-questioning and to be ethically commanded by an other to put the world in common in language, as the gift of the other. It should be a chance and a challenge to repair one's relations of responsibility to the near and the far, to strangers and kin. When we isolate prisoners in solitary confinement, we deprive them of both the support of others, which is crucial for a coherent experience of the world, and also the critical provocation through which others call our own interpretation of the world into question and command us to give an account of ourselves. This command is especially important for those who have broken the law and so violated the trust of others in the community. If we truly want to address the harm of crime and to challenge criminal offenders to transform their lives, then we must put them in a situation where they have a chance and an obligation to explain themselves to others, to repair damaged networks of mutual support, and to lend their own singular perspective to the meaning of the world.

We ask too little of prisoners when we lock them into Control Units where they are neither allowed nor obliged to create and sustain meaningful, supportive relations with others. For the sake of justice, not only for them but for ourselves, we must put an end to the use of solitary confinement in this country, and we must begin the difficult but mutually rewarding work of bringing the tens of thousands of currently isolated prisoners back into the world. If Levinas is right and "justice coincides with the overcoming of rhetoric," then a philosophical critique of supermax rhetoric is long overdue (1969, 72). In the end, even the phrase "solitary confinement" may function as a rhetorical device that obscures the relation of nonincarcerated subjects to the supermax inmate. After all, this "solitude" is managed and enforced by prison staff who conduct twenty-four-hour surveillance of inmates, perform cavity searches and forced cell extractions, dole out toilet paper and sanitary napkins, and interact on a daily basis with inmates in countless other ways (not all of which are sanctioned by law). It is structured by bureaucrats, policy advisers, and legislators who promise to "get tough on crime." It is promoted by private prison corporations that reap enormous profits from the warehousing of prisoners in high-tech fortresses, often in communities where there are no other jobs. And it is tolerated by the community at large, to the extent that we are tempted to ask, Why should I care about what happens to a convicted murderer? Am I my brother's keeper? What is Hecuba to me? The tens of thousands of prisoners held in intensive confinement right now, and the over two million prisoners in prisons and jails, demand an ethical reduction of the justice system to the social justice of which it makes a mockery.

CONCLUSION

Afterlives

Here we are, the dead of all time, dying once again, only now
with the object of living. You have to get out of your self to
save yourselves.

—Subcomandante Marcos, quoted by
Pennsylvania inmate Tiyo Attallah Salah-El
in "A Call for the Abolition of Prisons"

THE SOCIAL DEATH OF PRISONERS in solitary confinement does
not just affect the individual or the family or the local community;
it affects all of us who live in a society in which black, brown, and
poor people of all races are criminalized and isolated in prisons for the
sake of someone else's security and prosperity. Urban centers across the
United States have been "securitized" through policing strategies that
compound the violence of mass incarceration while rendering this violence invisible (Glazek 2012; Wacquant 2009a, 2009b). The U.S. prison
system works both to perpetuate the social death of racialized subjects and to isolate privileged subjects in an ever-diminishing sphere
of secure spaces, from gated communities to green zones.[1] How do we
resist this social death drive from a position outside the prison walls, in
solidarity with those who have been isolated and excluded in the name
of peace and justice?

What we need is not a return to the goal of *rehabilitation*, which
retains its grip on the individual subject as a site of pathology, but
rather a *revolution* that transforms the "backyard colonialism" of our
prison society through a collective disinvestment in both punishment
and privilege. Fanon has much to teach us here:

> For colonialism has not simply depersonalized the colonized. The very
> structure of society has been depersonalized on a collective level. A colo-
> nized people is thus reduced to a collection of individuals who owe their
> very existence to the presence of the colonizer. (1963, 219–20)

For Fanon, both the colonizer and the colonized will be destroyed
through revolution, but this destruction is also the birth of a new sense
of humanity and new structures for social and political life. To assist
at this birth, we need to listen and respond to the voices of those who
have been most affected by the prison system, and we need to develop
new ways of thinking, speaking, writing, and acting in ethical responsibility and political solidarity with those who have been condemned
to social death, both in prison and beyond.

What would it take to come back to life after centuries of social death
and its avatars? In her book *Lose Your Mother,* Saidiya Hartman engages with both the ghosts of slavery and the promise of a new (this-
worldly) afterlife:

> This is the afterlife of slavery—skewed life chances, limited access to health
> and education, premature death, incarceration, and impoverishment. I, too,
> am the afterlife of slavery. (2007, 6; see also 45)

> To believe, as I do, that the enslaved are our contemporaries is to under-
> stand that we share their aspirations and defeats, which isn't to say that we
> are owed what they were but rather to acknowledge that they accompany
> our every effort to fight against domination, to abolish the color line, and to
> imagine a free territory, a new commons. (169)

The prison system, the criminal justice system, the welfare system, the education system, the public transportation system (or lack
thereof): all of these interlocking systems function as afterlives of slavery and social death. But the *critique* of these systems—the resistance
with which people join together in solidarity to make sense of their
experience and to work together to transform the world—this, too, is
an afterlife of slavery in resistance to social death. This resistant sense
of afterlife "requires the reconstruction of society, which is the only way
to honor our debt to the dead" (170). Hartman concludes her reflections
with an appeal to *"what we might become together* or the *possibility of
solidarity"* (231). Solidarity is an afterlife in common, an affiliation of
political solidarity, a kinship of purpose, rather than the false kinship
promised by a nostalgic attachment to identity.

The promise of "what we might become together" suggests a different sense of rebirth from the solitary resurrection that was expected of prisoners in the early penitentiary system. It suggests a collective rebirth of creaturely life and of the refusal to profit from the social death of others, no matter who they are or what they have done. As Marilyn Buck writes from behind prison walls:

> So, *we are you.* Except that we have—and do—live in a world that is incomprehensible at the subjective level to anyone who has not experienced imprisonment and almost absolute loss of control over one's self. (Personal correspondence, quoted in Rodríguez 2006, 180)

We are you: you could be here with us, if things had worked out differently. But you cannot understand or claim to understand what it is like to be locked down in a control prison without having undergone it yourself.

Part of this insight is shared by phenomenology: No one can directly experience the world *as* an other, at the "subjective level" of his or her own experience—especially when the experience in question is an absolute loss of control over one's self. At the same time, no one can isolate his or her experience from the complex web of ontological and epistemological entanglements with other living and nonliving beings. *We are you*: our subjective, unsharable experience of the world supports your own subjective, unsharable experience of a world that we have in common, whether we feel like sharing or not. The social death of prisoners sticks to the social life of those who have never set foot in a prison and could not possibly know what it is like.

But phenomenology is not enough. Phenomenology must become critical; it must engage not only with the epistemological and ontological conditions for the possibility of meaningful experience, but also with the ethical, political, and intercorporeal conditions that motivate and provoke our desire for meaning. Fanon, Merleau-Ponty, and Levinas are critical phenomenologists in this sense, even (or especially) as they push phenomenological method beyond its classical limits. But even critical phenomenology is not enough. We must also build a social movement of resistance to social death—a movement that makes good on the insights of critical phenomenology with ethical responsibility and political solidarity. Angela Davis reminds us of the collective power of resistance:

> Those of us with a history of active struggle against political repression understood of course, that while one of the protagonists of this battle was

indeed the state, the other was not a single individual, but rather the collective power of the thousands and thousands of people opposed to racism and political repression. (Quoted in Rodríguez 2006, 124)

In her autobiography, Davis recalls her response to the social movement that emerged in response to her own incarceration:

Chants thundered on the outside. . . . While the chants of "Free Angela" filled me with excitement, I was concerned that an overabundance of such chants might set me apart from the rest of my sisters. I shouted one by one the names of all the sisters on the floor participating in the demonstration. "Free Vernell! Free Helen! Free Joan! Free Laura! Free Minnie!" I was hoarse for the next week. (Davis 1988, 65; quoted in Rodríguez 2006, 126)

We are you. There is no meaningful sense of freedom for Angela Davis without the freedom of others whose names we may not recognize but who nevertheless make an ethical and political claim on our own creaturely existence. Who might we become together if we joined in solidarity to create new afterlives in resistance to social death?

NOTES

Introduction

1. See P. Smith 2006 for a detailed review of international studies on solitary confinement.

2. According to Craig Haney's 2003 study of Pelican Bay State Prison, a supermax prison in California, 91 percent of prisoners in the Secure Housing Unit (SHU) reported anxiety and nervousness; over 84 percent suffered from headaches, chronic fatigue, and difficulty sleeping; and 70 percent felt "on the verge of an emotional breakdown" (Haney 2003, 133). Similarly, ten of the fourteen prisoners interviewed by Stuart Grassian in his study of Walpole State Prison showed signs of "massive free-floating anxiety" (Grassian 1983, 1452), and all showed signs of what Grassian would later call "SHU syndrome": hyperresponsivity to stimulus; perceptual distortions (including hallucinations); panic attacks; difficulties with thinking, concentration, and memory; obsessional thoughts; paranoia; and problems with impulse control (Grassian 2006, 333–38). I will discuss this research in detail in chapters 6–9.

3. Seventy-five years later, Stephen Tillich, a Washington state supermax inmate, echoed this statement exactly: "It's like being in a tomb" (quoted in Rhodes 2004, 113).

4. Shaylor comments, "The 'blackness' of the SHU is reflected in both its racialized nature and the darkness of the cells themselves; the degree of force within the SHU is experienced by the women through physical brutality and sexual violence; the space of the SHU is oppressively small; mental stability is warped; the experience of passage of time is transformed; and communication flowing both into and out of the SHU is severely restricted" (1998, 415).

5. On mass incarceration and hyperincarceration in the United States, see Alexander 2010 and Wacquant 2001, respectively.

6. *Wikipedia,* s.v. Incarceration in the United States, accessed June 23, 2012, http://en.wikipedia.org/wiki/Incarceration_in_the_United_States.

7. For example, in 1993, 98 percent of those held in the Maryland Correctional

Adjustment Center, a supermax prison in Baltimore, were African American (J. G. Miller 1997, 227).

8. See Guenther 2012c for an explanation of my claim that Agamben fails to account adequately for ethical-political resistance.

9. See Alexander 2010, 153–56, 187–88. Rates of felon disenfranchisement are much higher for people of color than for whites. In California in 2009, African Americans were ten times more likely to be disenfranchised than whites. Hispanics make up 19 percent of California's population, but 36.5 percent of its disenfranchised (Shalev 2009, 41).

10. Bryan v. Walton, 14 Georgia 185 (1853).

11. Dred Scott v. Sandford, 60 U.S. 393 (1857).

12. Ruffin v. Commonwealth, 62 Va. 790, 796 (1871).

13. Avery v. Everett, 110 N.Y. 317 (1888).

14. See Meillassoux 1991 for insightful reflections on natal alienation in the context of African slavery. See also Agamben 1998 on inclusive exclusion, 17–29.

15. See V. Brown 2009 for an elaboration of this point in resistance to Patterson's concept of social death.

16. "Because the slave has no socially recognized existence outside of his master, he became a social nonperson" (Patterson 1982, 5).

17. Consider, for example, Frederick Douglass's exposure to the torture of his Aunt Hester, Sethe's inability to save her children from slavery except through infanticide in Toni Morrison's *Beloved,* and Sojourner Truth's forced reliance on the help of unreliable and unsympathetic white women to retrieve her son from being illegally sold to a slaveholder in another state (Douglass 1987, 343–44; Morrison 1998; Harris 1996, 325–28).

18. Arendt writes, "It seems that a man who is nothing but a man has lost the very qualities which make it possible for other people to treat him as a fellow man. This is one of the reasons why it is far more difficult to destroy the legal personality of a criminal, that is of a man who has taken upon himself the responsibility for an act whose consequences now determine his fate, than of a man who has been disallowed all common human responsibilities" (Arendt 1973, 300). But I think that Arendt underestimates the degree to which the legal personality of criminals can be destroyed in a situation of mass incarceration, as well as the sense in which some prisoners are "state-raised," interpellated as criminals more because of their class and race than because of their actions or speech.

19. "I have never accepted that I did this to myself. . . . That is the only reason I have been in prison this long" (Abbott 1991, 15).

20. Madrid v. Gomez, 889 F. Supp. 1146 (N.D. Cal. 1995).

1. An Experiment in Living Death

1. This form of punishment has made a recent comeback in the South with the resurgence of chain gangs and humiliation punishments. See Gorman 1997; Turley 2005; and the documentary film *American Chain Gang* 1999.

2. Caleb Smith suggests that "perhaps, in an American society increasingly dependent on plantation slavery and the racialized distinction between captive black bodies and free white minds, spectacular violence looked more and more like a shocking offense against 'humanity'" (2009, 9).

3. Of course, it is not at all clear that shame and pain are mutually exclusive. Louis Masur gives a somewhat different account of the dialectics of shame in the early U.S. penal system, arguing that the central mechanism of public punishment was shame—which backfired both when the public shamelessly harassed the wheelbarrow men and also when the public felt a sympathetic shame for their humiliated state—whereas the central mechanism of solitary confinement was meant to be guilt: a penitent reflection on one's sins, and the first step toward the redemption of the soul (1991, 84).

4. Rush makes a similar point in his 1812 book *Medical Inquiries and Observations on the Diseases of the Mind*: "All the operations in the mind are the effects of motions previously excited in the brain, and every idea and thought appears to depend upon a motion peculiar to itself" (quoted in Dumm 1987, 92).

5. "By removing men out of the reach of this exciting cause [of profane society and conversation], they are often reformed, especially if they are confined long enough to produce a sufficient chasm in their habits of vice. Where the benefit of reflection, and instruction from books, can be added to solitude and confinement, their good effects are still more certain" (Rush 1947a, 198). Even "Nebuchadnezzar was cured of his pride, by means of solitude and a vegetable diet" (201).

6. Rush himself offered the following principles of child rearing: (1) "It is as necessary to reward them for good as it is to punish them for bad actions," and (2) "all corporal corrections for children above three or four years old are highly improper and . . . solitude is the most effective punishment that can be contrived for them" (quoted in Takaki 2000, 26). Silence was also useful in childhood education as "a mechanical means of promoting virtue" (quoted in ibid., 198), since (in the words of Dr. John Fothergill's "Letter to a Friend in the Country," which Rush quotes approvingly), "to have the active minds of children put under a kind of restraint—to be accustomed to turn their attention from external objects, and habituated to a degree of abstracted quiet, is a matter of great consequence, and lasting benefit to them" (quoted in Rush 1947a, 198–99).

7. Note the similarity in language to later behaviorist accounts of "disorganization." I will discuss this literature at length in chapter 4.

8. This axiom is replaced with the following, decidedly less gothic, axiom in a later version of the same essay published in Rush's 1806 collection *Essays, Literary, Moral, and Philosophical*: "Let a large house be erected in a convenient part of the state. Let it be divided into a number of apartments, reserving one large room for public worship. Let cells be provided for the solitary confinement of such persons as are of a refractory temper. Let the house be supplied with the materials, and instruments for carrying on such manufactures as can be conducted with least instruction, or previous knowledge. Let a garden adjoin this house, in which the culprits may occasionally work, and walk. This spot will have a beneficial effect

not only upon health, but morals, for it will lead them to a familiarity with those pure and natural objects which are calculated to renew the connection of fallen men with his creator. Let the name of this house convey an idea of its benevolent design, but let it by no means be called a prison, or by any other name that is associated with what is infamous in the opinion of mankind. Let the direction of this institution be committed to persons of established characters for probity, discretion and humanity, who shall be amenable at all times to the legislature, or courts of the state" (Rush 1806, 150–51).

9. Actually, this is true only for the first-story cell blocks; the second story had no outdoor yard but had larger cells in compensation. Compare these to the cells at the Walnut Street Jail, which were more or less the dimensions of a tomb: eight feet by six feet by nine feet (Masur 1991, 82). See also Dumm 1987 on the smaller cells at Auburn Prison as a cause of the deaths and illnesses that occurred there, and also as a motivation for the change to a shared workspace.

10. See also "Eastern State Penitentiary" 2012a, 2012b.

11. Dumm comments, "These isolated subjects could be joined together by the machinery of republican government. Once set in motion by the dynamics of attraction and repulsion, heat and cold, flux and calm, the moderated passions of the citizenry would be harnessed to the never-ending project of self-adjustment" (1987, 111).

12. Caleb Smith connects this cellular soul to social contract theory, in which natural or animal life is sacrificed for the sake of the more stable security of being a citizen-subject (2009, 13–14, 31–52).

13. Dickens is not opposed to punishment in general; he holds that "the subject of Prison Discipline is one of the highest importance to any community" (1957, 52) and that the Auburn system is a humane but firm method of punishment that encourages reform in the offender and preserves both the safety and the dignity of the community as a whole, present and future. Dickens makes this clear in his notes about a House of Correction in South Boston that is run on the Auburn model: "If I thought it would do any good to the rising generation, I would cheerfully give my consent to the disinterment of the bones of any genteel highwayman (the more genteel, the more cheerfully), and to their exposure, piecemeal, on any sign-post, gate, or gibbet, that might be deemed a good elevation for the purpose" (51–52).

14. "And though he lives to be in the same cell ten weary years, he has no means of knowing, down to the very last hour, in what part of the building it is situated; what kind of men there are about him; whether in the long winter night there are living people near, or he is in some lonely corner of the great jail, with walls, and passages, and iron doors between him and the nearest sharer in its solitary horrors" (Dickens 1957, 101).

15. See chapter 7 for more about the importance of an experience of space shared in common with other living beings.

16. Only the English thief and the African American burglar seem to have retained a sense of personal integrity, the latter bragging to Dickens about his exploits and the former looking as if he would have "gladly stabbed me with his

shoemaker's knife" given half the chance (103). Not everyone is destroyed by solitary confinement, but Dickens observes that it afflicts the most sensitive, and the most open to reform, the most destructively. "That it is a singularly unequal punishment, and affects the worst man least, there is no doubt" (110). He also claims that women prisoners become more beautiful and are even "humanized" through prolonged solitude (104, 109). As problematic as these claims may be, Dickens still maintains a firm position against solitary confinement for any human being whatsoever.

2. Person, World, and Other

1. "The Objective world, the world that exists for me, that always has and always will exist for me—this world, with all its Objects, I said, derives its whole sense and its existential status, which it has for me, from me myself, from me as the transcendental Ego, the Ego who comes to the fore only with the transcendental-phenomenological epoche" (Husserl 1991, 26).

2. See Young 1990 and Merleau-Ponty 2002, 112–70, for phenomenological accounts of the tension between "I can" and "I cannot" in feminine bodily experience and disabled experience, respectively.

3. Husserl adds that the body is experienced as *my* body "only by incorporating tactile sensations, pain sensations, etc.—in short, by the localization of the sensations as sensations" (2002, 159). I will reflect on this point at greater length in parts II and III when I address the deprivation of touch in sensory deprivation experiments and the strange de-localization of sensation reported by prisoners in contemporary supermax prisons. Perhaps in order to sustain a sense of my own body, I need not only to be able to touch *myself* but also to be touched by others.

4. See, for example, Doane et al. 1959. I will address this research at some length in chapter 4.

5. Husserl writes, "In order to establish a mutual relationship between myself and an other, in order to communicate something to him, a Bodily relation, a Bodily connection by means of physical occurrences must be instituted. I have to go over and speak to him. Thus space plays a major role here and so does time" (2002, 176). Of course, once the sense of an other ego has been constituted, I can have relationships with others whom I never meet in person, who are accessible to me only through words or images, but Husserl's point is that the basic sense of "alter ego," or another person, is constituted through bodily relations.

6. Husserl notes, "With good reason it is said that in infancy we had to learn to see physical things" (1991, 79). This lesson is not learned by the solitary ego alone; we cannot even imagine what it would mean to learn to see without learning to see *"according to others,"* as Merleau-Ponty would put it (2002, 179). Human infants require the care of others even to survive past the first few years of infancy, but what is more important is that this care is not incidental, that the "empirical" or concrete experience of others performs a transcendental function, that we literally *and transcendentally* cannot form a meaningful experience of the world and of

ourselves in the world without intercorporeal relations with those who care for us, guide and shape our initial perceptions of the world, and support our bodily and psychic life to the point where we are capable of coherent experiences of the world, of ourselves, and of others. There is no point in trying to isolate which of these triadic components came first; they all emerge together, such that my own transcendental ego (including any meaningful experience of myself as a concrete person) really does belong to me and me alone, and yet any meaningful experience founded in this transcendental ego really does necessarily imply concrete relations to embodied others and material things.

7. Husserl makes a similar argument in *Ideas II*. In a passage following his claim that the sense "man" is transferred (within my experience) from the other to myself, Husserl reconfirms the priority of subjective to intersubjective being: "The intersubjective . . . *belongs to* all subjective existences (unities of appearance) as what 'appears' there in a higher sense" (Husserl 2002, 180; emphasis added).

8. This is especially true in cases of severe sensory deprivation—as we will see in chapters 4 and 6—but all solitary confinement involves some degree of sensory deprivation.

9. For example, a prisoner interviewed by Sharon Shalev reports, "[At] the front of [the] cell I saw the mesh, and I was just standing there and looking out, and all of a sudden it just starts moving like going like waving. . . . I didn't think to ask anybody else if they were experiencing that because I thought well they'll think I'm crazy if I say something like that, then they just take it as a weakness, you know, and laugh at you. So I didn't say anything about that" (2009, 193). I will discuss these and other perceptual distortions in isolation in chapters 4 and 6.

10. See part II for a detailed argument in support of this claim.

11. This was the case for Malcolm X, who read voraciously in prison and writes in his autobiography, "I preferred reading in the total isolation of my room" (1999, 177). But Malcolm X makes it clear that he was confined in a prison with a "heavy emphasis on rehabilitation," where he was not locked down in his prison cell but, rather, had access to a shared library, to conversations with other prisoners, and to written correspondence with people outside of prison.

12. A similar derangement occurs when one is exposed to constant light, as in the strip cell to which Abbott was confined for months at a time: "The light is present even when you close your eyes. It penetrates the eyelids and enters your visual sensations in a grayish-white glow, so that you cannot rest your eyes. It *throbs* always in your mind" (1991, 28). This is the visual equivalent of insomnia, which I will discuss in chapter 8. Note that, currently, in supermax prisons and in detention camps such as Guantánamo Bay, cells are illuminated by fluorescent lights twenty-four hours a day.

3. The Racialization of Criminality and the Criminalization of Race

1. They were arguably also punished *with slavery,* simply for being black. As Ladelle McWhorter explains in *Racism and Sexual Oppression in Anglo-America,*

indentured servants transported from Africa were deliberately singled out, separated from their European and Native American counterparts, and affixed with a "perpetual brand" of inexorable slavery and social death (2009, 63–96). As Virginia governor William Gooch said in 1723, "Such was the insolence of the free negroes at that time, that the Assembly thought it necessary . . . to fix a perpetual brand upon free negroes and mulattos by excluding them from that great privilege of a freeman" (quoted in Evans 1963, 414; see also McWhorter 2009, 75–96).

2. "The very terminology of slavery was retained under the convict lease system. Employers used the slaveholders' classification of laborers, according to their ability to work, into first, second, third, fourth, and fifth class hands. . . . Able-bodied males were referred to as 'full hands'; women and children prisoners were known as 'half-hands.' Company employers were reluctant to rent 'dead hands'—prisoners too old or too sick to work" (Adamson 1983, 560).

3. This racial disparity was even starker for women prisoners. In 1830, black women constituted 3 percent of the population of Pennsylvania but 70 percent of the population of Walnut Street. White women were 97 percent of the population but only 30 percent of the inmate population at Walnut Street (Patrick-Stamp 1995, 112).

4. Eastern State Penitentiary, n.d.

5. Angela Davis writes, "The birth of the English and American penitentiaries, whose most ardent advocates were passionately opposed to harsh corporal punishment, had little impact on the punishment regimes to which slaves were subjected. Neither did they effectively alter the ways in which white women were punished. As such they were implicitly racialized and gendered as new and less cruel modes of white male punishment" (2002, 64).

6. For example, in 1876, J. S. Hamilton & Co. leased convicts from the Mississippi State Penitentiary for $1.10 per month per prisoner and then subleased these prisoners for $9 per month to build railroads across the south (Oshinsky 1996, 43–44). Convicts forced to build railroads were not given food but were left to forage in the surrounding woods like "wild beasts" (quoted in ibid., 56). Convicts working on plantations were punished with lashes for such offenses as "slow hoeing," "sorry planting," or "being light with cotton" (45).

7. The *People's Advocate,* a Negro journal of Atlanta, Georgia, has the following observation on the prison showing of that state for 1892: "It is an astounding fact that 90 per cent of the state's convicts are colored; 194 white males and 2 white females; 1,710 colored males and 44 colored females. Is it possible that Georgia is so color prejudiced that she won't convict her white law-breakers. Yes, it is just so, but we hope for a better day" (quoted in Douglass 1893).

8. Oshinsky notes, "Not a single leased convict ever lived long enough to serve a sentence ten years or more" (1996, 46). The mortality rate for inmates in the South was 41.3 per thousand convicts, compared to a rate of 14.9 in the North (Shelden 2005).

9. Douglass continues: "Sunday was my only leisure time. I spent this in a sort of beast-like stupor, between sleep and wake, under some large tree. At times I

would rise up, a flash of energetic freedom would dart through my soul, accompanied with a faint beam of hope, that flickered for a moment, then vanished. I sank down again, mourning over my wretched condition. I was sometimes prompted to take my life, but prevented by a combination of hope and fear" (1987, 388). I will discuss the relation between slaves, convicts, and animals (or "beasts" and "brutes") in chapter 6.

10. Bruce Jackson relates this account of "rocking along easy" by Texas prison farm workers in the mid-1960s: "When you're working the convicts get tired and they say, 'Come on, you all, let's rock a while,' and they get together, you know, and that's the way they fool the boss. They come down with their axe and then they work it like it's stuck, they be resting, see. Then they take it, carry it out, hang it, carry it over their head real high: they resting. And they drop. But they ain't hitting as hard as they would if they's working. . . . They rocking. That's called 'Rocking along easy'" (quoted in Jackson 1999, 19).

11. This sensibility also comes through in the lyrics of popular music. See, for example, Bo Diddley's "Who Do You Love?": "Tombstone hand / And a graveyard mine / Just 22 / And I don't mind dyin'." Or Tupac Shakur's remarkable statement: "My music is spiritual. It's like Negro spirituals, except for the fact that I'm not saying 'We Shall Overcome.' I'm saying that we are overcome" (quoted in Holland 2000, 180). Consider also this incredible reflection by dancer and choreographer Bill T. Jones: "I will never grow old. My hands will never be discolored with the spots of age. I will never have varicose veins. My balls will never become pendulous, hanging down as old men's balls do. My penis will never be shriveled. My legs will never be spindly. My belly, never big and heavy. My shoulders never stooped, rounded like my mother's shoulders are. I will never need a son to massage my arms, as my father did. . . . I am not protected, remember? Old is for people who are protected. The unprotected have to die young" (quoted in Holland 2000, 175). Patricia Holland's book *Raising the Dead* offers a fascinating discussion of these and other invocations of death in black art and culture.

12. Fanon writes, "After the struggle is over, there is not only the demise of colonialism, but also the demise of the colonized" (1963, 178), and, "When there are no longer slaves, there are no longer masters" (1967, 219).

13. Fanon makes several other explicit references to colonialism as a form of generalized imprisonment: "To make him [the black man] talk pidgin is to fasten him to the effigy of him, to snare him, to imprison him, the eternal victim of an essence, of an *appearance* for which he is not responsible" (1967, 35). And: "Imprisoned in himself, locked into his artificial reserve, the negative-aggressive feeds his feeling of irreparable loss with everything that he continues to lose or that his passivity makes him lack" (78, quoting Germaine Guex).

14. Fanon quotes Jean Veneuse: ". . . an extremely painful and obsessive feeling of exclusion, of having no place anywhere, of being superfluous everywhere in an affective sense. . . . 'I am The Other' is an expression that I have heard time and again in the language of the abandonment-neurotic. To be 'The Other' is to

feel that one is always in a shaky position, to be always on guard, ready to be rejected and . . . unconsciously doing everything needed to bring about exactly this catastrophe" (1967, 76). Compare this with the statement of a supermax inmate interviewed by anthropologist Lorna Rhodes: "If I'm being good and they don't give me nothing, I can't take that kind of rejection. . . . I just went off, spitting, urinating, tearing up my cell, the whole nine yards. . . . If they feel like I'm gonna be a badass, why not be one? . . . They think they can control me, but I'm gonna be the one in control" (2004, 55). To be in "control" in this situation means having the power to provoke guards to enter his cell in riot gear and subdue him.

15. See Guenther 2012b for a detailed discussion of racialization and being "riveted" to one's identity.

16. Fanon writes, "The wealth of the imperialist nations is our wealth. . . . Europe is literally the creation of the Third World" (1963, 58).

17. Compare Jack Henry Abbott: "There is a boundary in each man. . . . But when a man goes beyond the last essential boundary, it alters his ontology, so to speak" (1991, 67), and, "Solitary confinement can alter the ontological makeup of a stone" (45).

18. Later, Fanon adds, "I am not the slave of the Slavery that dehumanized my ancestors" (1967, 230).

19. Compare this with the observation of an inmate at the Maryland Penitentiary: "It's just enough room to live in. No more. Nothing for relaxation. Nothing for feeling comfortable. Just enough room to live in" (John Woodland Jr., in Baxter et al. 2005, 208). See chapter 7 for a further discussion of this and other observations about the social and physical spaces of the prison and the projects.

20. From the oral argument transcript of *Miller v. Alabama,* last accessed June 23, 2012, http://www.supremecourt.gov/oral_arguments/argument_tran scripts/10-9646.pdf.

21. To follow up this line of inquiry, see for example Wacquant 2001.

22. Contrast this sense of mothering as shared responsibility and care with Fanon's characterization of the colonizer as "a mother who constantly prevents her basically perverse child from committing suicide or giving free reign to its malevolent instincts. The colonial child is protecting the child from itself, from its ego, its physiology, its biology, and its ontological misfortune" (1963, 149).

23. See Alessandrini 2009 for an insightful account of ethics without a subject in Fanon and Foucault.

4. From Thought Reform to Behavior Modification

1. An entire chapter could be written on the use of drugs to control the behavior of prisoners in the mid-twentieth-century United States, and even in current prisons. Common drugs include tranquilizers; muscle relaxers such as succinyl-choline chloride (Anectine); antipsychotics such as chlorpromazine (Thorazine), sometimes described as a "chemical lobotomy"; or fluphenazine (Prolixin), which

was often administered in such high doses that subjects lost "all control of voluntary muscles" and experienced "sensations of suffocation and drowning" and "feelings of deep horror and terror, 'as though he were on the brink of death'" (Mitford 1973, 25, 26). These drugs are, in effect, chemical forms of solitary confinement or sensory deprivation.

2. Edward Opton critiques the blurred line between treatment and punishment with a series of questions and answers: "When is torture not torture? When it is aversion therapy. When is brutality legal? When it is behavior modification. . . . When is punishment by the State not regulated by law? When it is prescribed by a psychiatrist" (1974, 605–6).

3. Robin Kelley offers a different response to this (rhetorical) question in *Freedom Dreams* (2002, 60–109).

4. I will discuss the KUBARK manual in more detail below. The SERE program was devised to help U.S. soldiers resist interrogation and other forms of manipulation should they be captured by enemy forces. In their 2008 "Senate Armed Services Committee Inquiry into the Treatment of Detainees in U.S. Custody," John McCain and Carl Levin argue that, although SERE techniques were only ever intended to help U.S. soldiers resist their captors, they had been improperly inverted and used against detainees in U.S. custody during the War on Terror (McCain and Levin 2008). And yet it would be false to claim that the United States had never used such techniques against its own prisoners until the War on Terror; such techniques were already used in coercive interrogation by the CIA in the early 1960s. See Otterman 2007 for a more detailed discussion of SERE and its relation to KUBARK and the U.S. War on Terror.

5. For more on MKULTRA, see Klein 2007 and Otterman 2007.

6. Lifton's language borrows from both behaviorism and Christianity, not unlike the eclectic approach of Benjamin Rush. In addition to using the language of being "reborn," which runs throughout his analysis, Lifton also compares the initial stages of thought reform as "ritualistic" repetition, "as if reciting a catechism" until the moment of "conversion" (1957, 642).

7. I bracket the questions of whether the Chinese ever did use such techniques or whether they were particularly "Chinese" or even particularly "Communist." I am interested rather in U.S. representations of Chinese/Communist techniques during the Cold War and in the rhetorical gestures necessary to make such techniques palatable for application to U.S. prisoners.

8. We will encounter Biderman again in *The Manipulation of Human Behavior* and in the CIA's KUBARK manual. In 1957, when this paper was published, Biderman was a researcher in the Office for Social Science Programs at the U.S. Air Force Personnel and Training Research Center at Maxwell Air Force Base in Alabama. He presented this paper in 1956 at a combined meeting of the Section on Neurology and Psychiatry with the New York Neurological Society at the New York Academy of Medicine as part of a panel discussion titled "Communist Methods of Interrogation and Indoctrination"; Lifton's paper

"Chinese Communist 'Thought Reform'" and a condensed version of Hinkle and Wolff's report were also presented at the same panel discussion. Biderman later became a senior researcher at the Bureau of Social Science Research in Washington, D.C.

9. Hinkle and Wolff (1956, 155) discuss the use of what we now call "stress positions," including chaining the prisoner's hands behind the back with forearms together for days or weeks, sometimes "milking" the prisoner's fingers to increase the pressure. The need for sleep was exploited by exposing the prisoner to constant light in his cell and interrupting him just as he began to fall asleep (129). Extremely hot or cold cell temperatures were another technique for reducing the prisoner's tolerance of isolation and for generally breaking down his resistance (129–30). Edgar Schein (1956, 160) also refers to the control of access to what we now call "comfort items" in Chinese POW camps and to the systematic use of rewards and punishments to control behavior or "train" the prisoners (169). These and other techniques were used at U.S. detention camps such as Guantánamo Bay and Abu Ghraib, as well as in U.S. domestic prisons.

10. "With the passage of time, the prisoner usually develops the intense need to be relieved of the pressures put upon him and to have some human companionship. He may have a very strong urge to talk to any human and be utterly dependent on anyone who will help him or befriend him. At about this time he also becomes mentally dull and loses his capacity for discrimination. He becomes malleable and suggestible and in some instances he may confabulate" (Hinkle and Wolff, quoted in Solomon et al. 1957, 360).

11. Both forms of sensory deprivation research generated controversy and lawsuits from experimental subjects who experienced years or even decades of debilitating effects as a result, but only one of these suits was successful (Klein 2007, 29–58; McCoy 2007). Even after sensory deprivation experiments were discontinued with human subjects, they were performed and continue to be performed on animal subjects such as primates, cats, dogs, mice, and rats.

12. Lilly's research was funded by the NIMH from 1954 to 1968; before that, in 1953, he had a post studying neurophysiology with the U.S. Public Health Service Commissioned Officers Corps.

13. The original context for this phrase occurs in Lilly's discussion of reports by solo sailors Captain Joshua Slocum and Dr. Alain Bombard, both of whom found themselves so overcome with feelings of love for other creatures that they were unable to kill or eat animals for food. As I will explain in the next section of this chapter, the phrase "intense love of any living things," is quoted (and grammatically corrected) by the writers of the coercive interrogation section of the CIA's KUBARK manual.

14. Lennart Nilsson's 1965 photo essay for *Life* magazine, "A Child is Born," crystallizes the image of the human embryo as a kind of astronaut, set against the cosmic background of the mother's body. See my analysis of this image in Guenther 2007a, 155–61.

15. Lilly suggests that, ultimately, even this intimate relation to the safety man could be dissolved: "When the safety man and the subject both consider it is safe for the Subject to become a self-observer free of the safety man, i.e., to enter solitude, these matters must be considered with great intensity and care" (Lilly and Shurley 1961, 244).

16. While issues of race are not explicitly addressed in either the KUBARK manual or the *Human Resource Exploitation Training Manual,* the techniques outlined in both manuals were explicitly intended for (often racialized) "Communist" enemies. The School of the Americas trained many of the interrogators/torturers who were responsible for countless deaths and injuries across South and Central America. Meltzer makes one brief reference to race, in a claim that echoes some of the racial "observations" in the post–Korean War literature on Chinese brainwashing techniques and even echoes some of the assumptions of antebellum slavery: "Many Negro patients who are thought to be malingering tend to play the part of a slow, somewhat confused and defective person who understands little of what is going on around him. Like members of other oppressed minorities, some Negroes have adopted a mask of dullness and unawareness when interacting with the Caucasian majority" (1961, 282). Note also the slippage in this passage between prisoners and patients.

17. See Otterman 2007, 146, 153, 200–215. See Klein 2007 for an analysis of the relation between the use of torture to "shock" and disorient prisoners and neoliberal economic policies that capitalize on the shock and disorientation of whole populations.

18. This is repeated and reinforced in the *Human Resource Exploitation Training Manual.* In regression, "the interrogatee's mature defences crumble as he becomes more childlike" (L-3). The interrogator's "capacity for resistance should be destroyed and replaced with a cooperative attitude" (H-2).

19. See also Elaine Scarry (1985) on the use of ordinary domestic objects to break down prisoners' sense of a coherent world and to isolate them in a painful body, as if betrayed by their own source of power and agency.

20. KUBARK attributed this (slightly modified) passage to Lilly 1956, 26, but it occurs in fact at Lilly 1956, 3.

21. Lazreg (2008, 111–69) gives a complex analysis of the gendered and sexual dynamics of torture in Algeria. For example, one French intelligence officer described his technique as follows: "An interrogation is like making love. An essential rule is to take your time, know how to hold yourself long enough till you reach the crucial moment, keep up the pain till it reaches its climax. Most of all do not go beyond this threshold or your partner will die on you. If you can motivate him, he'll talk. Well, you know, orgasm. Otherwise, he'll pass out. If you love women, lieutenant, you should understand" (quoted in Lazreg 2008, 127).

22. Judith Butler (2006, 45–46) discusses the vulnerable infant who is unable *not* to love whoever takes care of it, however poorly or abusively, noting, "Doubtless it seems better at that point to be enthralled with what is impoverished

or abusive than not to be enthralled at all and so to lose the condition of one's being and becoming" (45).

23. Many of the U.S. social scientists commissioned to research Communist "brainwashing" emphasize that there is nothing really new about Communist incarceration or interrogation techniques; their novelty is just in the rigor and intensity of their application. For example, in his 1956 paper, Schein comments, "Taken singly, there is nothing new or terrifying about the specific techniques used by the Chinese. . . . The only novelty in the Chinese methods was the attempt to use a combination of all these techniques and to apply them all simultaneously in order to gain complete control over significant portions of the physical and social environment of a group of people" (172; see also Hinkle and Wolff 1956, 164–65; Lifton 1957, 642). Lifton also argues that the only significant innovation of Chinese incarceration was the extent of its "milieu control": "The Chinese Communist prison, is probably the most thoroughly controlled and manipulated group environment that has ever existed" (1957, 643). And yet he also expresses admiration for this innovation: "Perhaps in a peculiar sense the world is indebted to the creators of this bizarre process for the valuable knowledge which it conveys—on an ethical as well as a psychological level" (644).

24. In November 1973, Schein wrote a letter to *Harper's Magazine* arguing that he had not advocated the Chinese methods in his presentation "Man against Man: Brainwashing" but had merely "described" them. But his transcript clearly shows more enthusiasm than mere neutral description (Opton 1974).

25. Like Schein, Groder went on to have a career as a psychiatrist and business consultant, cowriting two books: *Business Games: How to Recognize the Players and Deal with Them* (1980) and *Winning at Love: The Alpha Male's Guide to Success* (2010). In his author's bio for the latter book, Groder claims that, as an "alpha himself, Marty gleaned what he has presented in this book from working with the prisoners (most of whom are the dark side of alpha), from his clientele of highly successful people, and from his first failed marriage" (Groder and Webster 2010).

26. The High Security Unit at the Federal Correctional Institution in Lexington, Kentucky, served a similar function for women prisoners: "According to the testimony of Susan Rosenberg (later affirmed in a judgment by U.S. district court judge Barrington D. Parker Sr.), Rosenberg and her cellmates were asked to renounce their political convictions, and informed that the length of their terms of isolation depended upon their renunciations" (Eisenman 2009, n.p.). See Rosenberg 2011 for a detailed account of the HSU and of her experience as a political prisoner.

27. See Rodríguez 1996 for an incisive critique of the biopolitical, colonialist logic underlying both U.S. domestic prisons and detention camps in the War on Terror.

28. Rangel concludes his paper with this guarded endorsement: "Until better remedies are found, behavior modification, used in the proper manner, with the proper objectives, and subject to sufficient controls, offers a unique method for preparing our prison population for their return to society" (1975, 9).

29. Clonce v. Richardson, 379 F. Supp. 338 (W.D. Mo. 1974).

30. Groder reported eight success stories and two failures. Among the successes were four African Americans and two Caucasians; both "failures" were African American. The success stories "made successful adjustment to middle-class cultural norms" (Aynes 1975, 455). This judgment recalls the goal of the penitentiary and its work-based programs, except here the goal is a frankly secular conversion to the middle class.

31. For example, some prisoners, such as presumed gang members, are placed directly into restrictive housing regardless of their actions. I will discuss this policy at greater length in chapter 9.

5. Living Relationality

1. I will discuss one such appeal to human dignity in my analysis in chapter 6 of Judge Thelton Henderson's verdict in the 1995 Eighth Amendment case *Madrid v. Gomez*.

2. Compare Heidegger's account of Dasein as Being-in-the-world, where the "in" has the sense of a constitutive relationality of existent and world rather than the nonrelational sense in which water is in a glass (1962, 78–90). For Heidegger, Dasein does not include nonhuman animals (and does not even refer specifically to human beings); nevertheless, his account of world is helpful for articulating the difference between the behaviorist account of environment and the sense of Umwelt, or "surrounding-world," that Merleau-Ponty develops in his work, where even insects are treated as a form of Being-in-the-world (Merleau-Ponty 2002, 90).

3. Of course, there are more and less complex versions of behaviorism, but what they share is what Husserl would call the natural attitude: an approach to consciousness that seeks "natural" or empirical explanations of what, from a phenomenological perspective, admits of only an intentional analysis of relationships between constituting acts and constituted meanings. For example, in "Man's Adaptive Processes," presented at the symposium "The Power to Change Behavior," David Landy proposes a "physics of cultural change: when change is suppressed too long, like expanding gas molecules in a sealed container, the problems that demand solution expand and at last explode through the limits set by the closed society into drastic social upheaval" (Landy 1961, 48).

4. "It is not the stimuli which constitute the reactions nor which determine the contents of perception. It is not the real world which constitutes the perceived world" (Merleau-Ponty 2008, 88).

5. See Merleau-Ponty's essay "Phenomenology and the Sciences of Man" (in 1964a, 43–95) for his account of why this collaboration between phenomenology and Gestalt psychology is both justified and necessary. See also his *Phenomenology of Perception* (2002) for a more detailed account of perception from his critical phenomenological perspective, and Husserl's *Ideas II* (2002, 181–316) for an ex-

tended treatment of the relation between the body as viewed from a "naturalistic" perspective and the body in its "spiritual" *(Geistliche)* being.

6. "There is form whenever the properties of a system are modified by every change brought about in a single one of its parts and, on the contrary, are conserved when they all change while maintaining the same relationship among themselves" (Merleau-Ponty 2008, 47).

7. In an experiment conducted by F. J. J. Buytendijk and described by Merleau-Ponty, the sunfish displays a capacity to distinguish between food and nonfood, to learn, "an aptitude for choosing," and a "method of selection" in response to a series of manipulations in which the human experimenter mixes white and black bread together with chalk and bits of rubber (2008, 97). Merleau-Ponty comments, "It is not to a certain material [black speck/white speck] that the animal has adapted but, to speak a human language, to a certain kind of deception" (97). I will return to this notion of deception at the end of the chapter, when I consider the highly artificial context of mid-twentieth-century behaviorist experiments and their (often pathological) effects on experimental subjects, but for now I wish only to note the importance of form, even for the behavior of relatively simple organisms.

8. Francisco Varela, Evan Thompson, and Eleanor Rosch cite this passage approvingly in their influential book *The Embodied Mind* (1991). Merleau-Ponty's approach to behavior has inspired new approaches to cognitive science, known collectively as 4E (embodied, embedded, enactive, and emergent) cognitive science. For example: "Minds awaken in a world. We did not design our world. We simply found ourselves with it; we awoke both to ourselves and to the world we inhabit. We come to reflect on that world as we grow and live. We reflect on a world that is not made, but found, and yet it is our structure that enables us to reflect on this world. Thus in reflection we find ourselves in a circle: we are in a world that seems to be there before reflection begins, but that world is not separate from us" (Varelà, Thompson, and Rosch 1991, 4).

9. Earlier, Merleau-Ponty suggests that the model of an automatic telephone might be more appropriate, since it is "an apparatus which itself elaborates the stimulus" (2008, 13). But this metaphor is also limited, "since it would be a station which receives its instructions from convoys which it is charged to direct and which improvises the pathways and the switches according to their indications" (32). Later, in his Nature lectures on nature at the Collège de France, he abandons the metaphor altogether: "The organism is not just a telephone switchboard. In order to understand it, we must include in it the inventor or operator of the telephone" (2003b, 145).

10. Merleau-Ponty says something similar about language: "The first words must already have the kind of rhythm and accent which is appropriate to the end of the sentence, which is nevertheless not yet determined, except as the last notes of a melody are performed in its global structure" (2008, 87). See also 2008, 132; 2003b, 238.

11. "Unfurling" is a key concept in Merleau-Ponty's ontology of nature/culture.

See also 2003a, 119 and 152 and this passage: "The unfurling of the animal is like a pure wake that is related to no boat" (2003a, 176).

12. In *The Structure of Behavior,* Merleau-Ponty cites this passage indirectly via Buytendijk as "Every organism . . . is a melody which sings itself" (2008, 159). In the Nature lectures, he cites it directly (and more accurately) as "The unfurling of an Umwelt [is] a melody that is singing itself" (2003b, 173).

13. For a more detailed account of this temporality of possibility, see Morris 2008 and Guenther 2011b.

14. Some very simple organisms come close to a mechanistic relation to the world, but even these creatures display a capacity to "invent" themselves that sets them apart from the mechanistic model of life implicit in behaviorism. Animals like the medusa, the marine worm, and the starfish are so open and passive in relation to the environment that they cannot even be said to have an Umwelt (Merleau-Ponty 2003b, 168–70). They don't take account of the world; they receive nothing from it (169). They are "incomplete organisms" without the ability to regulate themselves or manipulate their environment. And yet, even the amoeba is sophisticated enough to elaborate its own structure, or *Bauplan*. This is what distinguishes even the simplest living organism from a machine: "The amoeba is a continuous birth, pure production. . . . Its *Bauplan* is endlessly recreated" (170). It is as if "our houses were born of a sort of purée, and each room contained a reserve of this purée" (170).

Even larvae, who instinctively rebuild their casing if it is destroyed, and who cannot help but make an effort to do so, are not simply *programmed* in their behavior. They have at least six possible ways of rebuilding, and even though they have no "consciousness" comparable to that of human beings or other higher animals, they make a kind of "choice" to rebuild in this way rather than that way, under the circumstances. Merleau-Ponty writes, "Hence a process appears as blindly conditioned. But on the other hand, there is a process in which [multiple] responses are possible; hence the hesitant activity" (2003b, 180).

Arguably, some more recent forms of robotics, such as those designed by Rodney Brooks, resemble the gestalt of living beings more closely and are even able to "learn" certain forms of behavior in response to their environment. But these newer robots do not operate on a behaviorist model of input–output mechanisms; rather, they take the gestalt of living beings as their biomimetic model.

15. "For the excitation itself is already a response, not an effect imported from outside the organism; it is the first act of its proper functioning" (Merleau-Ponty 2008, 31).

16. In *The Structure of Behavior,* Merleau-Ponty describes a cat who, if "trained to obtain its food by pulling on a string, will pull it with its paw on the first successful trial but with its teeth on the second" (2008, 96). Having learned the essential melody, the cat is immediately able to play different variations to achieve the same result; she does not need to be trained or conditioned to add new parts to the whole.

17. "The conditioned reflex theory presents stimulations and responses which succeed each other in an organism like a series of events external to each other and between which no relations can be established other than those of immediate temporal contiguity" (Merleau-Ponty 2008, 95).

18. "The reflex as it is defined in the classical conception does not represent the normal activity of the animal, but the reaction obtained from an organism when it is subjected to working as it were by means of detached parts, to responding not to complex *situations* but to isolated *stimuli* . . . and to 'laboratory behavior' where the animal is placed in an anthropomorphic situation" (Merleau-Ponty, 2008, 43–44).

19. I will have more to say about the importance of escape in chapter 8 on Levinas's early work.

20. See Merleau-Ponty's discussion (2003b, 148–49) of Arnold Gesell on behavior as an ambiguous tendency toward a norm and the openness of contingency or surprise. Behavior is not governed by physical laws but by norms, which by definition imply the possibility of a deviation from the norm. "All behavior tends toward a certain optimum," but at the same time, "a certain surprise" accompanies the design or pattern of behavior (149).

21. I will explore some of these situations in chapter 6. Some of the most egregious behaviorist experiments on nonhuman animals were conducted by Harry Harlow, a behaviorist psychologist who isolated baby monkeys in a chamber he called the "pit of despair" to see how they would react. Many of the monkeys became deranged, or even died. Harlow, Dodsworth, and Harlow 1965, Harlow, Plubell, and Baysinger 1973; see also Mason and Sponholz 1963.

22. I will address the "hinged" structure of life at greater length in chapter 8 in relation to Levinas's concept of hypostasis.

23. I will have more to say about the opening of a sense of depth in chapter 7 on Merleau-Ponty and the space of the supermax prison.

24. Merleau-Ponty makes a similar claim in the Nature lectures: "Animals, Husserl says, are only variants of humanity. We think that which is most universal in us starting from the most singular" (2003b, 77; see also 307).

6. Beyond Dehumanization

1. See also the demands of prisoners on hunger strike at Pelican Bay supermax prison in California in 2011–12 (Prisoner Hunger Strike Solidarity 2011) and at Red Onion State Prison in Virginia in 2012 (Solidarity with Virginia Prison Hunger Strikers, n.d.). While these demands do not invoke comparisons to slavery or treatment like animals, the substance and details of the demands are strikingly similar to those of prisoners in Georgia and at Attica.

2. In 2007, there were 264 privately run correctional facilities in the United States, holding approximately 99,000 adult inmates. Corrections Corporation of America, one of the largest private prison companies, employs over 17,000

(nonincarcerated) workers and claimed assets of $2.9 billion and revenue of $1.669 billion in 2009. Meanwhile, in states like California, which spearheaded the growth of the prison industrial complex in the 1980s, prisons have started granting early parole for nonviolent and elderly prisoners in an effort to reduce state expenditure on the very prisoners that, for the past three decades, it found profitable to incarcerate.

3. Brown v. Plata, 131 S. Ct. 1910 (2011); see also Cohen 2011.

4. Madrid v. Gomez, 889 F. Supp. 1146 (N.D. Cal. 1995).

5. In re Medley, 134 U.S. 160 (1890).

6. See also Dayan 2001, 19–20, for a further discussion of *In re Medley.*

7. Adams v. Carlson, 488 F. 2d 619 (1973).

8. The first purpose-built state supermax was the Security Management Unit (SMU) that opened in 1986 at the Arizona State Prison Complex in Florence, Arizona (Reiter 2012a, 72). It was followed by California's Pelican Bay State Prison in 1989. The first federal supermax was Florence ADX, which opened in Florence, Colorado in 1994.

9. The U.S. Department of Justice reported in 2009, "Among inmates held in custody in prisons or jails, black males were incarcerated at 6.6 times the rate of white males. One in 21 black males was incarcerated at midyear 2008, compared to one in 138 white males. At midyear 2008, black males (846,000) outnumbered white males (712,500) and Hispanic males (427,000) among inmates in prisons and jails. About 37 percent of all male inmates at midyear 2008 were black, down 41 percent from midyear 2000" (Bureau of Justice Statistics, Office of Justice Programs 2009).

10. Gates v. Collier, 501 F.2d 1291 (5th Cir. 1974).

11. Pugh v. Locke, 406 F. Supp. 318 (1976); Hutto v. Finney, 437 U.S. 678 (1978); Rhodes v. Chapman, 452 U.S. 337 (1981). See Reiter 2012a for a detailed discussion of these and other cases.

12. Arguably, the same logic of causality that pervades behaviorist science also seeps into the legal reasoning in such cases: unless a direct causal link can be made between punitive isolation and mental illness, then there is insufficient justification for banning its use. Colin Dayan (2001, 18, 23) gives a brilliant discussion of the gap between "basic human needs" and "human dignity." Dayan suggests, "Let us take the language of the law as a struggle between ways of thinking about what is human, what remains human even in instances of radical depersonalization" (18).

13. As Sharon Shalev puts it, "Former tools of last resort [are turned] into tools of first resort, or into the standard in prison conditions, moving the entire prison system to a new extreme which will then become its own de facto justification" (2009, 225).

14. The same architect reiterates this point later: "You've got your rights, but you don't have your privileges. And so, it's up to the inmates to learn to change" (quoted in Shalev 2009, 120). This statement is remarkably consistent with statements made in Reiter's interview with an Arizona architect who helped design

Florence ADX (which provided a template for Pelican Bay). This architect also states that the purpose of his design was to "take all their privileges away, [but] give them all their rights. . . . They can have their natural light, shower, exercise, all with one guy in the room at a time. . . . There's no right to have twelve people in your room together" (quoted in Reiter 2012a, 107). Reiter comments, "In other words, this Arizona Architect, although he did not explicitly reference the role of the courts, had internalized the basic minimum rights courts had accorded to prisoners throughout the 1970s, and he worked to physically institutionalize these rights—at the barest minimum level delineated by courts—in the supermax design. . . . So prison designers instituted a form of compliant resistance—building institutions to comply with the precise minimum standards courts had articulated for punitive isolation conditions, but resisting the provision of any unnecessary, or non-required privileges" (107).

15. Reiter comments on Henderson's own history: "Henderson, incidentally, is one of the more liberal judges in the federal court system. He was the first African-American lawyer to work for the U.S. Department of Justice, where he investigated the 16th Street Baptist Church Bombing in Montgomery, Alabama, and he has presided over a number of controversial cases in his career, including a case upholding environmental protections for dolphins, a case overturning a murder conviction of an alleged Black Panther, and, most recently, a class-action prison conditions case in California in which he ordered the release of more than 30,000 state prisoners. If any judge was predisposed to find the conditions of confinement in a supermax like Pelican Bay unconstitutional, it was Henderson" (2012a, 113).

16. Spain v. Procunier, 600 F.2d 189 (1979).

17. Henderson also cites Toussaint v. McCarthy (Toussaint IV), 801 F.2d 1080 at 1107 (9th Cir. 1986): "Human needs that prison officials must satisfy include food, clothing, sanitation, medical care, and personal safety" (*Madrid,* 889 F. Supp. at 1245). Note that social relations with others is absent from this list.

18. Not every individual prisoner experiences the adverse effects of solitary confinement, nor is the penitentiary the only site where the deleterious effects of prolonged solitude are produced. Grassian's research shows that similar effects may be observed in noncarceral situations such as solo expeditions at sea or by air, or even in isolations in small groups, such as in polar explorations; but he argues that the most radical adverse effects are produced when subjects perceive their isolation as a punishment that is intentionally inflicted on them (Grassian 2006, 347; compare 356–65). He also notes that the effects of solitary confinement are not restricted to human beings, but have also been observed in rats, monkeys, and dogs (365–66).

19. Earlier, Henderson cites *Toussaint III,* 597 F. Supp. at 1413–14 to support this conclusion: "Segregated detention is not cruel and unusual punishment per se, as long as the conditions of confinement are not foul, inhuman or totally without penological justification" (quoted in *Madrid,* 889 F. Supp. at 1262).

20. See Foucault 1990, 2003.

21. Colin Dayan puts it this way: "If you happen to be a prisoner, without any status explicitly recognized in law, you possess rights only insofar as you have lost your skin or your mind" (2001, 27).

22. Stephen Slevin was awarded a $22 million settlement in 2012 for inhumane treatment while he was a prisoner in New Mexico's Doña Ana County Jail. Arrested for driving while intoxicated, he was held in solitary confinement for two years without his case ever coming to trial. His mental and physical health deteriorated drastically, to the point where he was forced to pull his own tooth (Chuck 2012). While Mississippi and West Virginia recently abolished solitary confinement for juvenile offenders, and Montana has limited its use, many states still continue this practice (Casella and Ridgeway 2012; Fettig 2012; St. Cyr 2012).

23. "Whether this human raw material is used for its labor or as the forced consumers of commodities provided by corporations directly implicated in the prison industrial complex, it is clear that black male bodies are considered dispensable within the 'free world.' They are also a major source of profit in the prison world. This relationship recapitulates in complicated new ways the era of convict leasing" (Davis 2002, 69).

24. See also Shalev's interview with a unit manager at Pelican Bay: "Staff, because they're dealing with these guys daily on such a sterile level—lock them up, keep them locked up, don't touch them, keep yourself safe, search, search, it's a very, very mechanical, non-human process—staff get used to dealing with the inmates that way. . . . We deal with him as a product" (quoted in Shalev 2009, 176).

25. George Jackson makes a similar point in a 1970 letter to Fay Stender, in which he compares the reduction of black male prisoners to animals and beyond animals to meat, but he also complicates the connection between prisoners and animals by calling the wardens "pigs": "No black leaves Max Row walking. Either he leaves on the meat wagon or he leaves crawling licking at the pig's feet" (G. Jackson 1970, 31).

26. Similar symptoms are reported in the United States, Canada, Denmark, Germany, and South Africa—wherever the psychological effects of solitary confinement have been studied (P. Smith 2006). Between 83 percent and 91 percent of the inmates at California's Pelican Bay supermax prison report symptoms of "anxiety, headaches, lethargy, irrational anger, confused thought processes, and social withdrawal" while in solitary confinement. Hallucinations and other perceptual distortions afflict 40 percent (Haney 2003, 133).

27. See Colin Dayan's (2007) critique of the way cases claiming "cruel and unusual punishment" have for the most part worked against the interests of prisoners rather than protecting them. If the context of Grassian's research raises any doubts about its scientific neutrality, these doubts should be allayed by the consistency of his research with nearly every study of the psychological effects of solitary confinement. See Kupers 1999; Haney and Lynch 1997; Haney 2003. A dissenting voice in this literature comes from James Bonta and Paul Gendreau (1990), Canadian researchers who argue that while there is clinical evidence for the detrimental effects

of long-term solitary confinement, there are few, if any, negative effects produced by solitary confinement of less than ten days; but Bonta and Gendreau's research has been criticized for relying on evidence from voluntary solitary confinement rather than coerced solitude in prison. I have chosen to focus on Grassian's research in particular because he offers the most extensive and detailed reports of prisoners' first-person testimony.

28. The effects of prolonged solitary confinement overlap to a great degree with the effects of sensory deprivation (see Heron, Doane, and Scott 1956). It seems significant that the intensity of SHU syndrome at Walpole Prison increased dramatically after the steel doors were shut and the minimal stimulation of light, air, and a view to the outside was eliminated. In this chapter, I focus on the importance of a bodily relation to others for constituting and sustaining a sense of objective reality, but a further phenomenological exploration of the connection between sensory deprivation and solitary confinement is clearly warranted.

29. Woodland explicitly connects his experience of the space of a maximum-security prison to the space of racialized social housing (Baxter et al. 2005, 208–9).

30. Recall the behavior of the dog who demonstrated what Pavlov called a "freedom reflex." This dog also had its basic needs met, but it resisted the conditions of its confinement by whimpering, struggling, refusing food, and eventually—after much prodding—submitting to the situation.

31. Williams reports an interview with a corporate chicken farmer: "Q: Why do you de-beak them? / A: The chickens will, in their pecking order, pick on the weakest chicken. . . . Once they draw blood, then they just keep on going. They're quite cannibalistic. / Q: But when they are in a barnyard that usually doesn't happen. / A: No, but then the one who's being picked on can get away" (quoted in N. Williams 2008, 380).

32. Indeed, syndromes and their acronyms abound in the animal-management literature. Factory chickens are prone to "acute death syndrome" or "flip-over syndrome" due to overly rapid growth; other pathologies include "caged layer fatigue syndrome," a condition in which chickens who are unable to move in ways that are normal for their species become exhausted to the point of being unable to stand. Breeding methods designed to produce lean meat and accelerate growth expose pigs to porcine stress syndrome (PSS), in which they "literally drop dead from stress when they are weaned, moved to a new pen, mixed with strange pigs, or shipped to market" (Mason and Finelli 2006, 113). A similar "sudden death syndrome" affects intensively farmed cows and broiler breeder chickens.

On the topic of cannibalism in factory-farmed pigs, Mason and Finelli quote a 1976 text on hog farm management: "Acute tail biting is often called cannibalism and frequently results in crippling, mutilation and death. . . . Many times the tail is bitten first and the attacking pig or pigs continue to eat further into the back. If the situation is not attended to, the pig will die and be eaten" (quoted in Mason and Finelli 2006, 112). The risk of cannibalism leads many factory farms to crop the tails of pigs rather than to increase their living space.

33. See also Colin Dayan on the self-harm of prisoners: "The inmates have re-enacted the law's process of decreation on their own bodies, making visible what the law masks. And as if in a drama of historical revision, these expressions of derangement recall the Quaker dream of spiritual rebirth through solitude, but instead the raw materials of legal authority, once turned on the prisoners' bodies, commemorate the death of the spirit. . . . In this severe rephysicalizing of civil death, inmates make the wounding of the body recall the tortures of the mind. They have returned to the drawing and quartering, disemboweling, and bloodletting of old in order to testify to their continuation in other forms" (2001, 28).

34. Luc Levasseur, a prisoner formerly at Marion Penitentiary, confirms this in a report of his own experience on the inside: "One prisoner subjected to four-point restraints (chains actually) as shock therapy had been chewing on his own flesh" (2005, 48). In four-point restraints, the prisoner is spread-eagled, with both arms and both legs fixed in place on the floor.

35. Frances Crook, chief executive of the Howard League, explicitly compares overcrowded prisons to factory farms: "Prison is quite a toxic environment—don't forget it most resembles battery chickens. . . . People are cooped-up; they have a restricted diet and no natural light. If you are kept like that for several years it shortens your life" (quoted in Rickman 2012).

36. See, for example, Melzack 1954; Riesen and Aarons 1959; Mason and Sponholz 1963. While the example I have addressed at length here is fifty years old, research involving the sensory deprivation of animals continues and is especially common in research on brain plasticity. Mice are reared in the dark (Jiang et al. 2010), hamsters have their eyes removed at birth (Desgent, Boire, and Ptito 2010), and whiskers are plucked from rats (Sheikhkanloui-Milan et al. 2010), all in order to study (the limits of) the brain's capacity to develop new neural pathways in response to the organism's experience in and of its environment.

37. In Riesen's experiments on two chimps deprived of visual stimulation from the ages of five to ten months and ten to eighteen months, respectively, the animals showed "loss of recognition for food or food containers" and required about eight days to regain their former capacities to distinguish edible from inedible objects. Both animals also found it difficult to estimate distance and direction when reaching for objects or blinking protectively, and both improved dramatically after three days of "normal" perception. Both chimps also showed signs of trembling, twitching, and squinting.

38. It is not clear that intercorporeal relations with nonhuman animals are always enough to sustain a prisoner's sense of personhood and Being-in-the-world. Recall, for example, Dickens's account of the prisoner who raised rabbits in his cell, and who seemed to acquire their nervous habits in a way that only increased his suffering (1957, 103). Nevertheless, many prisoners report forming deep affective bonds with nonhuman animals, such as insects or rodents, who happen to enter the cell. A prisoner interviewed by Gustave de Beaumont and Alexis de Tocqueville in 1831 said, "This summer, a cricket entered my yard; it looked to

me like a companion. If a butterfly, or any other animal enters my cell, I never do it any harm" (quoted in Dumm 1987, 110). Research on the presence of companion animals in prison suggests that regular contact with nonhuman animals can have a profound impact on prison conditions, the rehabilitation of prisoners, and recidivism rates after release (Walsh and Mertin 1994). Programs connecting prisoners with companion animals in U.S. prisons include the Wisconsin Correctional Liberty Dog Program, Prisoners Training Dogs for the Disabled, and the Prison Pet Partnership at Washington [State] Corrections Center for Women.

Even in noncarceral situations, when people are lost at sea or trapped on an expedition, they often report developing what John C. Lilly calls an "intense love of any living things" and a revulsion "at the thought of killing food-animals" (1956, 3–4).

39. Dylan Rodríguez writes, "It may well be in the realm of *displaced time,* through the intersection between agency and temporality, that radical political praxis—in this case, articulating through an insurrectionist (and homosocial) captive black/brown masculinity ('*We are men! We are not beasts*' [in the Attica Declaration])—can fracture the death logic of the prison regime. For the Attica rebels, led by black and Puerto Rican insurgents, the political memory of slavery, displacement, and colonization—and the histories of domination borne on their bodies as that which transmogrified them into captive 'beasts' of burden—logically enacted a public demand for recognition as 'men.' The demand, in and of itself, was the displacement of a historical nonaccess to actualized subjectivity. Whereas the condition of death suggests time's closure for the biological body, the struggle to *make time live (or to relive time)*—discovering and reinventing history, constructing myth as social truth, short-circuiting state domination in the process of breaking protocol in the prison standoff—suggests the subversion of the prison's condition of reproduction" (2006, 216). See also Fanon's critique of dehumanization and his call for a new (postcolonial) humanism in *The Wretched of the Earth.*

7. Supermax Confinement and the Exhaustion of Space

1. The expression "cold storage" here is a reference to Laaman v. Helgemoe, 437 F. Supp. 269 (D.N.H. 1977), in which the presiding judge condemned "the cold storage of human beings" (at 307) and "enforced idleness" as a "numbing violence against the spirit" (at 293) (quoted in Dayan 2001, 23).

2. See also Brett Hartmann's letter from death row in Ohio: "I have the option to be out of my cell all day and socialize with the other 25 guys on any range(?), to go to an indoor gym 3 times a week or to an outside rec yard with grass and such, but something broke in me after surviving my last date and I have not cared to go to a gym or go outside for going on a year now" (quoted in Nolan 2012).

3. One survey found that fully 40 percent of supermax inmates had been placed in a supermax for "rule violations" (Mears and Watson 2006, 251). Some of

the rule violations that can land a prisoner in the SHU at Pelican Bay penitentiary include "[D] Tattooing or possession of tattoo paraphernalia; [G] Possession of $5 or more without authorization; [H] Acts of disobedience or disrespect which by reason of their intensity or context create potential for violence or mass disruptive conduct; [J] Refusal to perform work or participate in a programme as ordered or assigned; . . . [P] Throwing any liquid or solid substance on a non-prisoner; [T] Participation in gambling; . . . [W] Self mutilation or attempted suicide for the purpose of manipulation; and [X] Involvement in a conspiracy or attempt to do any of the above" (quoted in Shalev 2009, 72).

In her ethnographic study of control prisons in Washington State, Lorna Rhodes explains how fights with other prisoners can sometimes be inevitable as a way of gaining respect and establishing one's place in the social order of the prison (Rhodes 2004, 21–98).

Also, many mentally ill prisoners can break prison rules without even realizing it. One former SHU prisoner told Sharon Shalev, "I have seen inmates lose their mind completely because of the sound of a light where they are yelling at the light, cursing at the light, believing that for some reason the [authorities] planted some kind of noise inside the light purposely . . . and so the inmates that ain't strong minded, don't have something to hang on to, the light, the sound of the door, can make them lose their mind. . . . I found it strange, you know, how can a grown man, a very big, grown man, break down to a light. But that's what [that place] can do. And once you lose your mind, you don't know right from wrong. You don't know that you're breaking a rule. You don't know what to do exactly" (2009, 192; see also Kupers 1999, especially 9–38).

4. On the Kafkaesque policies and practices concerning classification as a gang member, see Shalev 2009, 74–76, 83–88; Haney 2003, 127; Arrigo and Bullock 2008, 633. Gang members are given indeterminate SHU sentences, which means that they will serve their entire prison term in the SHU unless they either prove that they have been falsely classified as a gang member or associate, or they "debrief" by renouncing gang membership and providing accurate information on the gang. Both of these options prove impossible for many inmates, either for social or pragmatic reasons. Craig Haney writes, "In fact, many prisoners are placed in supermax not specifically for what they have done but rather on the basis of who someone in authority has judged them to be (e.g., 'dangerous,' 'a threat,' or a member of a 'disruptive' group). In many states, the majority of supermax prisoners have been given so-called indeterminate terms, usually on the basis of having been officially labeled by prison officials as gang members. An indeterminate supermax term often means that these prisoners will serve their entire prison term in isolation (unless they debrief by providing incriminating information about other alleged gang members)" (2003, 127). I will return to the issue of gang membership in chapter 9.

5. See Arrigo and Bullock 2008; Stanley and Smith 2011. At Pelican Bay penitentiary in California, SHU inmates are 17 percent white, 12 percent African American, and 68 percent Hispanic (Shalev 2009, 69).

6. A former warden of Marion Penitentiary, Ralph Arons, explicitly said, "The purpose of the Marion Control Unit is to control revolutionary attitudes in the prison system and in the society at large" (quoted in Shaylor 1998, 398). See James 2003, 2005; and Franklin 1998 for interviews and narratives from U.S. political prisoners such as George Jackson, Assata Shakur, Mumia Abu-Jamal, Leonard Pelletier, Susan Rosenberg, Marilyn Buck, Laura Whitehorn, and Alan Berkman, all of whom have been held in maximum- or supermax-level prisons.

7. A former supermax inmate interviewed by Sharon Shalev reports, "The pods are very small, so any cell that they spray into, you know, is going to affect everybody in the pod. . . . Our fresh air was our toilet, as we flushed the toilet we stuck our heads in it to get fresh air because the pepper spray makes it very hard to breathe as your eyes burn and your nose runs and you're choking and coughing" (quoted in Shalev 2009, 166; see also 121).

8. In an interview for *Survival in Solitary: A Manual Written by and for People Living in Control Units,* Stuart Grassian says, "Keeping the lights on 24 hours a day in and of itself is known to cause significant psychiatric disturbances. It is going to interfere massively with the sleep/wake up cycle. We're talking about the need to maintain an adequate sense of alertness in the face of perceptual deprivation. Now if you add to that disturbance in the sleep/wake up cycle, you're going to increase the problem. So one of the worst things you can do for people is to keep the lights on 24 hours a day" (in Kerness and Teter 2008, 48).

9. Former inmate: "Everywhere you go, nothing's outside, everything's inside so you. . . . You never see the sun" (quoted in Shalev 2009, 153).

10. See Davis 2005, 62–64; Rosenberg 2011, 68–70, on the brutality of strip searches and cavity searches in women's prisons.

11. See also Graves's interview for the video *Democracy Now* (Graves 2012b).

12. A prisoner interviewed by Lorna Rhodes says, "I've got some people out there I know from the streets and I know they're going to give me a hug. But I won't be able to because it's embedded in my mind that when people touch me it has a negative effect, you know, that every time somebody touches me it's a cop" (quoted in Rhodes 2004, 34).

Supermax inmate Ronald Epps tells a similar story in his contribution to a survival guide for SHU prisoners: "Upon seeing me for the first time in over a year, a fellow prisoner shook my hand and then proceeded to put both arms around me to embrace me and I became visibly shaken and cringed up as if I had been physically violated. I had not had any physical contact with another human being in so long that I wasn't used to being touched. I had become super-sensitive to one of the basic human senses—the sense of human touch" (in Kerness and Teter 2008, 6).

13. For many prisoners, confinement—even solitary confinement—is characterized not by silence but by meaningless noise. In an interview for *Survival in Solitary,* Grassian says, "There has been a fair amount of evidence that it isn't a lack of sensory stimulation but a lack of perceptually informative, meaningful kind of stimulation that is really of importance. In other words, if you put someone in an absolutely quiet sort of room, you are going to get some degree of psychiatric

disturbance. Now, if you change those conditions, and you put that same individual in a room and add 80 decibels of white noise, you are going to get those disturbances much more quickly" (in Kerness and Teter 2008, 48).

Anthropologist Lorna Rhodes says of her own experience visiting a Control Unit, "Echoing in their hard-edged interior, their shouts are a blur of rage-saturated sound" (2004, 22). A prisoner interviewed by Rhodes says, "They put you in an environment where you can't talk to anybody else, you can't have any contact . . . unless you yell or scream. . . . The only thing you hear is the keys jingling" (quoted on 31). Rhodes argues that this sort of environment "fosters distorted forms of sociality patched together from the little contact that is available" (34).

Even now that most prisons require the use of headphones for music or television, the rumbling noise of ventilation systems, plumbing, and other mechanical noises, as well as the yelling, singing, screaming, or even talking of other prisoners, makes it difficult to hear oneself think. In my own experience facilitating a discussion group on Tennessee's death row, background noise is our biggest obstacle to communication. I return from the prison with my ears buzzing and my jaws aching from the effort of listening and speaking loud enough to be heard.

The words of prisoner-students in Drew Leder's philosophy class at the Maryland Penitentiary resonate with my own experience of maximum security noise: "You don't even have a sense of control over your speech. Since I've been in here, my speech has been affected, because I always have to hurry up and say something. And I'm a person who like to think about things before he goes out and speaks" (H. B. Johnson Jr., in Baxter et al. 2005, 210).

"It makes you loud. You've got to holler because it seems like you've always gotta talk over somebody or talk to somebody at a distance or that there's something separating you from that person" (John Woodland Jr., in Baxter et al. 2005, 210).

Eddie Griffin, a prisoner at Marion Penitentiary, connects this experience of noise to the experience of segmented space: "But even for the sake of security, the prison is laced with too many doors. Every few feet a prisoner is confronted by one. So he must await permission to enter or exit at almost every stop. A man becomes peeved. But this is augmented by the constant clanging that bombards his brain so many times a day until his nervous system becomes knotted. The persistent reverberation tends to resurrect and reinforce the same sensation, the same bleak feeling that originally introduced the individual into the Marion environment" (1993, 2).

14. A prisoner interviewed by Rhodes says, "Your lights are on all day. . . . It really kind of dulls all your senses. . . . It makes you numb. You get easily mad. You feel that everything they do is just to make you mad" (quoted in Rhodes 2004, 30).

15. Gómez continues, "Introduced during a state of emergency (when inmates went on strike after the Chicano inmate was beaten by a guard), the CU emerged as a weapon, a 'deathworld,' a 'dead zone' marking a particular moment of political repression. Incarceration implies a form of civil death, the deprivation of freedom

as punishment. . . . The very existence of political activists behind prison walls challenged the logic of advanced capitalism in the United States; resistance was unacceptable, the internal colonial other was to be buried alive, permanently isolated from human contact, sentenced to the punishment of living death" (2006, 60).

16. See also Husserl 2002, 223–316.

17. This insight is already expressed by Husserl in *Ideas II* and *Cartesian Meditations,* but Merleau-Ponty arguably makes it the center of his own critical phenomenology. In *Ideas II,* Husserl calls the Body *[Leib]* "the zero point of orientation, the bearer of the here and now" (2002, 61). It is "a material thing which, as localization field for sensations and for stirrings of feelings, as complex of sense organs, and as phenomenal partner and counter-part of all perceptions of things . . . makes up a fundamental component of the real givenness of the soul and the Ego" (165). In *Cartesian Meditations,* Husserl correlates the "here" of my own embodied experience with the "there" of the other's body in a way that is essential for the constitution of the sense of another person as another ego, with a singular experience of a common world (1991, 116–17).

18. See Guenther 2011b for a more detailed account of the chiasm and the logic of mutual divergence.

19. I will follow up on the ethical implications of this asymmetry in chapter 9 in my reading of the figure of Gyges in Levinas's *Totality and Infinity.*

20. Merleau-Ponty's account of "night" was inspired by Minkowski 1970.

21. I will address the "escape" of sleep at greater length in chapter 8.

22. Given the scope of this chapter, I have bracketed a discussion of the "other things" that shape the existence of supermax prisons: namely, a political climate of getting "tough on crime" even as crime rates decline across the United States, economic incentives driving the private prison industry, centuries of (largely disavowed) racist and class oppression in the United States, and so forth. See chapter 3 for a discussion of some of these issues in relation to supermax prisons.

23. This applies to the spatiality of one's own body as much as to the spatiality of things: "A thing, an arm, that appears no-place loses its thingliness, as if its inexhaustibility is exhausted when put into a region that exhausts spread-out difference" (Morris 2004, 112).

24. The inexhaustibility of space relies upon the heterogeneity of places within which more or less determinate things may be located. But it also depends on what Morris calls "a *larger place* that holds body and thing together and yet separate so that it is possible to adopt a moving relation to things in places, so that it is possible not to have the thing be exhausted by the enveloping movement of the body" (2004, 112). Ultimately, this "larger place" is the inexhaustible field of the world itself; at its most extreme limit, it is held open by the pure depth of night. And yet the depth of the world is not the same as pure depth, even if it is sustained by the latter at its limit.

25. Morris addresses intersubjectivity briefly but helpfully in his discussion of depth, arguing that "the body schema is originally one system with two terms,

namely, one's own behavior and the behavior of others" (2004, 164). He gives a fuller discussion of the social dimensions of existence in chapter 6, "Growing Space" (159–74).

26. This is arguably also an issue in Fanon's analysis of colonization. Fanon writes that "the Negro, because of his body, impedes the closing of the postural schema of the white man—at the point, naturally, at which the black man makes his entry into the phenomenal world of the white man" (1967, 160). In a racist, colonial society, white bodies and black bodies do not "comprise a system"; they do not form "one whole, two sides of one and the same phenomenon" (Merleau-Ponty 2002, 410). Or if they do, then it is not the system of meaningful experience and anonymous existence that Merleau-Ponty describes but, rather, a system of colonial domination in which the black man is both the privileged and the excluded other for the white man. Fanon argues that "the real Other for the white man is and will continue to be the black man. And conversely. Only for the white man The Other is perceived on the level of the body image, absolutely as the non-self— that is, the unidentifiable, the unassimilable. For the black man, as we have seen, historical and economic realities come into the picture" (1967, 161). For Fanon, this system of colonial domination produces psycho-social pathologies, both for whites and for blacks. "Here it is the war, this colonial war which radically disrupts and shatters the world, which is in fact the triggering situation [for mental illness]" (1963, 184; see also 181–233; 1967, 83–108, 141–209).

27. One prisoner explains this sense of anonymity in terms of stripping away the material objects that support the prisoner's sense of identity and represent the world he is leaving behind: "First they write down all the details of you, then they take your personal possessions and seal them up in a packet, then they take your clothes off you and put them in a numbered box, and finally you end up standing there with just a towel around your waist. What they're doing is reducing your identity stage by stage, slowly wiping you out as a person until you're only one more piece of flesh with a name and a number" (quoted in Doyle 2006, 193). Compare this to Orlando Patterson's account of the ritual initiation of slaves (1982, 51–62).

28. See Rhodes's interview with inmate Pete Owen, who frames his own struggles in terms of redemptive individualism: "Look at me. I didn't read at all before, I have an eighth grade education. But in there I learned to discipline myself. I want to read. I want to be an individual" (quoted in Rhodes 2004, 82). Rhodes analyzes the uptake of neoliberal rhetorics of "choice," "individuality," and "accountability" by prisoners (61–95).

29. The most detailed reporting on the Angola Three has been done by James Ridgeway for *Mother Jones* (Ridgeway 2009, Ridgeway and Casella 2012). See also Angola Three 2008. I will return to the Angola Three later in the chapter.

30. See David Morris's discussion of pacing in *The Sense of Space*: "The lion does not first take the measure of its cage in objective units, and then, finding it small, pace its confines; its elliptical, perpetual stride already is the 'measure' of

its environment, the 'measure' of an environment in which there is no striking distance, no safe remove; correlatively, the caged lion's stride is the 'measure' of an animal warped by confinement" (2004, 20).

31. Sharon Shalev relates the story of a man who was held in solitary confinement for a relatively short period of time in the 1960s but experienced a panic attack thirty years later when he underwent an MRI scan (Shalev 2009, 201). Another former prisoner who was held in solitary for four years now finds that she has to lock herself in the bathroom from time to time (201). Yet another explains his discomfort in public spaces like movie theaters: "After the movie's over and they turn on the light, you know, it's like I've been in the dark and all of a sudden the light comes on and boom all these millions of people around me, I'm like, you know, looking around like, okay, okay, who's gonna hit me, what's gonna happen, you know. I mean, you feel real uncomfortable and then all of a sudden you start shaking, you know, you feel your heart beat and then you realise, wait a minute, I'm at a theatre, what am I tripping on?" (202). Yet another says, "Sometimes I felt like I was losing my mind, or that I have lost it already, you know. . . . Holding conversations with myself . . . I had conversations with people. I mean dialogues, long dialogues with people. Some of them I knew, and some of them I didn't know. There were times when the darkness wasn't dark. I could see faces. . . . I think that I found out that I may be hallucinating when I touched my eyes and my eyes were open so I kind of knew I wasn't dreaming. After a while I thought that maybe I will die there. I really thought I would" (191).

32. One of the inmates interviewed by Rhodes says of another prisoner who has caught his "second wind," "He reminds me more of a majestic creature, like a shark or a tiger, one of the more solitary cats than he does a human being" (2004, 274). An inmate interviewed by Grassian speaks of his own experience: "I try to sleep 16 hours a day, block out my thoughts—muscles tense—think of torturing and killing the guards—lasts a couple of hours. I can't stop it. Bothers me. Have to keep control. This makes me think I'm slipping my mind. Lay in bed too much—scare yourself with thoughts in bed. I get panicky—thoughts come back—picture throwing a guard in lime—eats away at his skin, his flesh—torture him. Try to block it out, but I can't" (1983, 1453).

33. In her superb analysis of Merleau-Ponty and the space of the prison, Laura Doyle writes that communication between prisoners becomes possible, even in a context of very strict isolation, "by working this intercorporeal doubleness of the walls' simultaneous construction of inside/outside and isolation/connection" (2006, 194). Doyle interprets this as the prisoners' "remak[ing] the cell in the image of the chiasm" (195). She quotes the prison memoir of Lena Constante, who writes that when she discovered this acoustic potential, "the walls of my cell no longer separated me from the world. On the contrary" (quoted on 195). Psychiatrist and expert witness Craig Haney also notes that "the physical layouts of most such units—adjoining cells connected by plumbing, heating vents, and ventilation ducts—typically allow for some minimal form of communication between

prisoners (however strained and denatured the 'interaction' may be and however inventive prisoners must be to bring it about)" (2003, 151n2).

34. Luc Levasseur, a political prisoner incarcerated for twenty years in Florence supermax prison, writes, "Let's not kid ourselves about the prevailing attitude among the political and corporate elite and much of the voting public: prisoners are human waste. The more forbidding the penitentiaries, the more like garbage they define us" (2005, 52).

35. See Rhodes 2004, 43–49, for a more detailed discussion of this agency, as well as 61–95 for a fascinating discussion of "choice" and "responsibility."

36. This logic makes sense not only to the prisoners but also to the guards. Rhodes relates one officer's interpretation of an inmate's refusal to return his meal tray as a "statement" and a plea for attention: "[He wanted] everyone to stop what they were doing, 'now focus on me, this is my statement.' . . . He went so far, and he can't back down now. . . . You've got to [do it]—everyone has their own code. His statement was made by us coming in here, by us entering his cell" (in Rhodes 2004, 43). Here, again, the prisoner uses the guards' relative mobility and freedom to act as a proxy for his own immobility and containment. If he cannot storm out of the cell, at least he can make *them* storm *into* his cell. He can "say" something, make his "statement," without speaking a word. With one simple action—the action of doing nothing, of withdrawing the required action, of refusing to return the meal tray—he can set into action a chain of events at the end of which he will be restrained even further, will lose some of his privileges, may even add more time to his sentence, and may be physically harmed. But at least he made something happen. He made *them* do something as retaliation for his own confinement.

37. This interrelation between the bodies of prisoners and those of guards is made strikingly evident in a scene in the film *Hunger,* in which a prison guard at Long Kesh painfully washes his sore and bloody hands in the sink after beating prisoners to a pulp.

38. See Davis 2003, 60–83, for an analysis of how gender and sexual violence structure the U.S. prison industrial complex.

39. See Kelly Oliver's book *The Colonization of Psychic Space* (2004) for a fuller treatment of this concept.

40. "I would say that in a total panopticon environment, where you're virtually under twenty-four-hour surveillance, like at the new prison they've built in Jessup, Maryland, one way a man can resist the reforming idea of this system—the sort of feedback where the panopticon simulates the person's consciousness—is with autistic thinking, or total absorption in fantasy for an extended period of time. A person can just absorb themselves in creating a fantasy, can say, 'I'm building an island, and this is what my island will look like, and this is what my water source will be, and these are the kinds of plants or fruits I'll have on my island.' It's like a resting period for the mind, almost like sleep, but it can be used in a sense to resist being conditioned" (Mark Medley, in Baxter et al. 2005, 214).

41. A prisoner interviewed by Stuart Grassian says, "Got to try to concentrate.

Remember list of the presidents. Memorize the states, capitals, five boroughs, seven continents, nine planets" (quoted in Grassian 1983, 1453).

42. The collaboration between Sumell and Wallace is documented in Sumell and Wallace 2006, in Sumell 2010, and in the film *Herman's House* (2012).

8. Dead Time

1. For some SHU prisoners, the endlessness of solitary confinement may be quite literal; inmates who have been designated as gang members or associates may be placed in the SHU for their entire sentence, which for some inmates is thirty years or more. I will address the problems raised by gang member classification at greater length in chapter 9.

2. Even nonprisoners are struck by the inescapable imperative to wait when they visit prisoners or conduct officially approved classes or interviews (see Leder 2001, 1–2). I have found this in my own work facilitating a weekly discussion group at a maximum-security prison in Nashville. We are never quite sure whether, when we arrive at the appointed time, we will be able to proceed through the checkpoint to the meeting room. The prison may be on lockdown, or there may be a shift change for the correctional officers, or one of us may be turned away for inappropriate footwear, or the guard at the checkpoint may be unable to locate the memo that gives us permission to enter. There is both a sense of urgency—an imperative to plan carefully and respond to obstacles with agility—and also a sense of helplessness when something goes wrong that no amount of careful planning could have avoided. This tension between urgency and futility affects the prison volunteer's life once a week, but for prisoners and their close family members, it is something to be grappled with more or less constantly.

3. "The cells are often illuminated by artificial light 24 hours per day, and prisoners have no means of controlling the brightness or dimness in their units. Under these conditions, convicts may have difficulty determining whether it is day or night" (Arrigo and Bullock 2008, 625). The corrosive effects of this constant illumination can be inadvertently acknowledged even by claims to the contrary. A teacher who delivers videotaped courses to inmates in the SHU told Sharon Shalev that she did not observe any adverse effects on inmates, but she added that "some of the folks are not on the same timeframe, they have their days and nights mixed up, even though the programme starts normally around 8:30 in the morning, they may not be on that, on that time" (quoted in Shalev 2009, 184–85).

4. "Understanding the call is choosing; but it is not a choosing of conscience, which as such cannot be chosen. What is chosen is having-a-conscience as Being-free for one's ownmost Being-guilty" (Heidegger 1962, 334).

5. "Anxiety makes manifest in Dasein its Being towards its ownmost potentiality-for-Being—that is, its Being-free for the freedom of choosing itself and taking hold of itself" (Heidegger 1962, 232).

6. "Being-towards-death, as anticipation of possibility, is what first makes

this possibility possible, and sets it free as possibility" (Heidegger 1962, 307). "In anticipating this possibility, Dasein *makes* this possibility *possible* for itself as its ownmost potentiality-for-Being" (309).

7. See, for example, Jay Bernstein's (2001, 423–25) account of Theodor Adorno's critique of Heidegger. For Bernstein, as for Adorno, "being-towards-death takes the dying out of death" (425).

8. The full passage reads: "We shall not say that a prisoner is always free to get out of prison, which would be absurd, nor that he is always free to long for release, which would be an irrelevant truism, but that he is always free to try to escape (or get himself liberated); that is, that whatever his condition may be, he can project his escape and learn the value of his project by undertaking some action" (Sartre 1956, 483–84).

9. See Jill Stauffer's insightful Levinasian critique of liberalism in "How Much Does That Weigh?" (2010).

10. In *On Escape,* Levinas writes, "This conception of the 'I' *[moi]* as self-sufficient is one of the essential marks of bourgeois spirit and its philosophy. As sufficiency for the petit bourgeois, this conception of the 'I' nonetheless nourishes the audacious dreams of a restless and enterprising capitalism. This conception presides over capitalism's work ethic, its cult of initiative and discovery, which aims less at reconciling man with himself than at securing for him the unknowns of time and things. The bourgeois admits no inner division and would be ashamed to lack confidence in himself, but he is concerned about reality and the future, for they threaten to break up the uncontested equilibrium of the present where he holds sway" (2003, 50). This passage resonates with Theodor Adorno and Max Horkheimer's critique of bourgeois individualism: "Absolute solitude, the violent turning inward on the self, whose whole being consists in the mastery of material and in the monotonous rhythm of work, is the spectre which outlines the existence of man in the modern world. Radical isolation and radical reduction to the same hopeless nothingness are identical. Man in prison is the virtual image of the bourgeois type which he still has to become in reality" (quoted in C. Smith 2009, 115).

11. Levinas defines solitude in terms of "the definitiveness of the bond with which the ego is chained to itself" (1978, 84); "solitude is accursed not of itself, but by reason of its ontological significance as something definitive" (85). As the base of an existent whose materiality may be delivered over to the other in responsibility, solitude is not merely tragic and definitive but also a basis for responsibility, for hospitality, and for dwelling.

12. "Sleep is like entering into contact with the protective forces of a place; to seek after sleep is to gropingly seek after that contact. When one wakes up one finds oneself shut up in one's immobility like an egg in its shell" (Levinas 1978, 70).

13. Levinas describes insomnia as "the extinction of the subject" (1978, 67).

14. The question of hypostasis is the question of how such a distinction arises in the instant of the present and is posited in the form of a subject (whose being doubles with a having). Hypostasis is the very emergence of a distinction between

inside and outside; it is the hinge between the insubstantiality of being and the substantiality of the being, between verb and noun. Hypostasis gives rise to the sort of subject who can be crushed by the weight of its own being and whose precarious distinction between inside and outside can be undone by the radical deprivation of the presence of others. But it also gives rise to the sort of subject who could encounter an other who is radically outside, whose schema of inside–outside distinctions can be ruptured by someone absolutely beyond oneself. See Guenther 2009a for a further discussion of hypostasis.

15. The instant is "a relationship, a conquest . . . a relationship with and initiation into Being" (Levinas 1978, 76). Levinas also puts it this way: "An instant is not one lump; it is articulated," and, "The present contains a knot which its fading out will not untie" (1978, 18, 78).

16. The full passage reads: "This retreat of consciousness toward unconsciousness and this emergence of consciousness out of the depth of the unconscious do not occur in two different moments. Mental reservations murmur in the very activity of thought, as in a wink, made up of looking and not looking" (Levinas 1978, 68).

17. The existent is burdened with its own existence: "Existence drags behind it a weight—if only itself—which complicates the trip it takes" (Levinas 1978, 28; see also 27).

18. "Consciousness 'has' a base; it 'has' a place. This is the only sort of having that is not encumbering, but is a condition: consciousness *is* here" (Levinas 1978, 70).

19. "To the notion of existence, where the emphasis is put on the first syllable, we are opposing the notion of a being whose very advent is a folding back upon itself, a being which, contrary to the ecstaticism of contemporary thought, is in a certain sense a substance" (Levinas 1978, 81).

20. "The localization of consciousness is not subjective; it is the subjectivization of the subject. The scintillation of consciousness, the recess it forms *in the plenum,* does not refer at all to objective space, but is the very phenomenon of localization and of sleep—which is the uneventful event, the inward event" (Levinas 1978, 69).

21. Fatigue "presents itself first as a stiffening, a numbness, a way of curling up into oneself" (Levinas 1978, 30). Later, in *Totality and Infinity,* Levinas will use similar language to describe enjoyment: "Enjoyment is the singularization of an ego in its coiling back upon itself" (1969, 73). Only a being who is capable of coiling or curling up in enjoyment or sleep is capable of uncoiling itself in hospitality and responsibility for others.

22. "Fatigue marks a delay with respect to oneself and with respect to the present" (Levinas 1978, 31).

23. In fatigue, the existent "is no longer in step with itself, is out of joint with itself, in a dislocation of the I from itself, a being that is not joining up with itself in the instant, in which it is nevertheless committed for good" (Levinas 1978, 35).

24. "There is duality in existence, an essential lack of simplicity. The ego has a self, in which it is not only reflected, but with which it is involved, like a companion

or a partner; this relationship is what is called inwardness. . . . Existence casts a shadow, which pursues it tirelessly" (Levinas 1978, 28). This double—which is not yet an other—is both a burden and a basis for its own unburdening, both a knot and the condition for untying the knot (in Being-for-the-other). Levinas recalls the Russian folktale of Little John, who tries to get rid of his shadow by throwing his sandwich at it; but the "shadow, like a last and inalienable possession, still clings to him" (28). "To be an ego is not only to be for oneself; it is also to be with oneself" (88). "The verb to be is a reflexive verb: it is not just that one is, one is oneself *[on s'est]*" (28).

25. In *Otherwise Than Being,* Levinas writes that only "a subject [that] is of flesh and blood, a man that is hungry and eats, entrails in a skin" is "capable of giving the bread out of his mouth, or giving his skin" (1998b, 77). See also Marguerite Duras's moving account of hunger and starvation in *La Douleur,* in which she recounts her experience waiting for Robert Antelme, who was then her husband, to return from Dachau: "His hunger wheels around in your head like a vulture. You can't give him anything. You can always hold out a piece of bread in the void. You don't even know if he still has need of bread. You buy honey, sugar, pasta. You say to yourself, if he's dead I'll burn the lot. Nothing can help the way his hunger burns you. People die of cancer, of car accidents, but no, they don't die of hunger, they're finished off first. What hunger has wrought is completed by a bullet in the heart. I'd like to give him my life. I can't even give him a bit of bread" (1986, 34).

26. See Kornfield 1997 for examples of the incredible resourcefulness of imprisoned artists.

27. See also Troy Thomas's "Things a SHU Prisoner Should Know": "Prisoners who survive the SHU program should be told first that s/he was, is, in a trap—a situation where s/he was psychologically disabled and couldn't get out. Second s/he should be shown s/he didn't originally choose to enter a trap. Third, it should be pointed out that other prisoners were in similar traps. Fourth, tell the prisoners that it is possible to get out of the trap through restoring their will power and sense of self. . . . The process whereby the victim is 'psychologically incarcerated' in the oppressive SHU system is a subtle, but powerful force over which the victim/prisoner has little or no control, and therefore the victims need not feel either guilt or shame because of abnormal experiences, thus resulting in abnormal behavior" (in Kerness and Teter 2008, 18–19).

9. From Accountability to Responsibility

1. This practice was under revision as of February 2013 in response to over a year of hunger strikes at Pelican Bay and other California supermax prisons. Updates on the situation are posted on the Prisoner Hunger Strike Solidarity Web site, http://prisonerhungerstrikesolidarity.wordpress.com/.

2. The testimony of Samuels, along with that of others cited below, is collected in Solitary Watch 2012b.

3. The situation at Florence ADX (which, as it happens, was constructed in response to the resistance at Marion Penitentiary in the early 1980s) is currently the subject of a federal lawsuit alleging that the Bureau of Prisons "turns a blind eye to the needs of the mentally ill at ADX and to deplorable conditions of confinement that are injurious, callous and inhumane to those prisoners" (Cohen 2012).

4. I interpret Levinas's references to "fraternity" as an appeal to solidarity; this interpretation brings a feminist critique that is not already present in his work. See Guenther 2011a for a more detailed discussion of my reading of solidarity in the work of Levinas.

5. See Guenther 2012b and Guenther 2011c for a further elaboration of this point.

6. For a discussion of neoliberalism, biopower, and prisons, see Wacquant 2001, 2009a, 2009b.

7. On the Kafkaesque policies and practices concerning classification as a gang member, see Shalev 2009, 74–76, 83–88.

8. Prison authorities at Pelican Bay recognized this danger and sought to address it by creating so-called Transitional Housing Units (THUs) for inmates who have debriefed. They also created a new classification, "inactive gang member," to create a way out for inmates who have been isolated for so long that they no longer have any relevant information to "debrief" about. But even those labeled "inactive" can still be held indefinitely in the SHU at the discretion of prison authorities (Shalev 2009, 86, 87).

9. For first-person accounts of this entanglement of "family" and "gangs," see S. Williams 2004 and Jones 2010.

10. For the prisoners' other core demands, see California Prison Focus 2012. See also the demands of prisoners on hunger strike in 2012 at Red Onion State Prison in Virginia (Prisoner Hunger Strike Solidarity 2012).

11. To put this in Nietzschean terms: prisoners are told both that they must become animals capable of making and keeping promises and also that their promises are worthless on account of who they are and what they have done. This is slave morality at its finest. See Nietzsche 1989.

12. A prisoner interviewed by Dylan Rodríguez recognizes the futility of resisting routine cavity searches, even though he experiences them as a form of anal rape: "Every time I did this [resisted the cavity search], I lost. Every time I did this, I was beaten" (quoted in Rodríguez 2006, 205).

13. I don't mean to suggest that prisoners are never spoken to in the SHU; in accordance with the law, they receive regular hearings and medical screenings in which they are theoretically able to account for themselves as speaking subjects. But as Lorna Rhodes shows, these hearings do not guarantee that an inmate is "heard" (2004, 188).

14. See Haney 2003 on the dangers of "prisonization."

15. See also *Society Must Be Defended*" (Foucault 2003, 239–63).

16. "What counts is the idea of the overflowing of objectifying thought by a

forgotten experience from which it lives" (Levinas 1969, 28). "Revelation constitutes a veritable inversion of objectifying cognition" (67).

17. The SHU is structured to reduce the prisoner from a subject of desire to a
subject of need. As Dario Melossi and Massimo Pavarini noted in 1981, "Uprooted
from his universe, the inmate in solitary confinement gradually becomes aware
of his weakness, of his fragility, of his absolute dependence upon the administration, that is, on the 'other'; thus he becomes aware of himself as a subject-of-need.
This is what can be described as the first stage of reformation: transformation of
the real subject (criminal) into an 'ideal subject' (prisoner)" (quoted in Haney and
Lynch 1997, 4).

18. See Guenther 2012b and Guenther 2011a for a more detailed discussion
of (what I take to be) the potential for a Levinasian critical race theory. See also
Bernasconi 2008 and Drabinski 2011.

19. "If philosophy consists in knowing critically, that is, in seeking a foundation for its freedom, in justifying it, it begins with conscience, to which the other
is presented as the Other, and where the movement of thematization is inverted"
(Levinas 1969, 86). The movement of shame is not from inside out, like intentionality, but from outside in, like sensibility, and like the questioning that provokes
critique.

20. "Existence is not in reality condemned to freedom, but is invested as freedom. Freedom is not bare" (Levinas 1969, 84). Levinas also calls this investment
of freedom the foundation of reason (88). And he contrasts this investment of a
freedom that, prior to investment, "appear[s] to itself as a shame" with Sartre's
account of "the fall of my freedom" (Levinas 1969, 302–4).

21. "But I do not yet know with sufficient clearness what I am, though assured
that I am" (Descartes 1996, 2: 4).

22. Levinas articulates this fantasy as a question: "Is not truth correlative with
a freedom that is this side of justice, since it is the freedom of a being that is
alone?" (1969, 90). His point is that the free and unencumbered individual may be
represented as having a privileged access to truth (as certainty, apodictic truth),
but insofar as truth is justice (as ethical truth), this individual could not be further
from the truth. See Jack Henry Abbott's brilliant critique of the assumption that
freedom is essentially freedom from obligation to others (1991, foreword, 114–15).

23. This reading finds support in Descartes's own reflections: "I will suppose,
then, not that Deity, who is sovereignly good and the fountain of truth, but that
some malignant demon, who is at once exceedingly potent and deceitful, has employed all his artifice to deceive me; I will suppose that the sky, the air, the earth,
colors, figures, sounds, and all external things, are nothing better than the illusions
of dreams, by means of which this being has laid snares for my credulity; I will
consider myself as without hands, eyes, flesh, blood, or any of the senses, and as
falsely believing that I am possessed of these; I will continue resolutely fixed in this
belief, and if indeed by this means it be not in my power to arrive at the knowledge
of truth, I shall at least do what is in my power, viz, [suspend my judgment], and

guard with settled purpose against giving my assent to what is false, and being imposed upon by this deceiver, whatever be his power and artifice" (1996, 1: 12).

24. Levinas writes, "The relation with the face is not an object-cognition" (1969, 75). And, "The sense of our whole effort lies in affirming not that the Other forever escapes knowing, but that there is no meaning in speaking here of knowledge or ignorance, for justice, the preeminent transcendence and the condition for knowing, is nowise, as one would like, a noesis correlative of a noema" (90).

25. "The objectification and theme upon which objective knowledge opens already rests upon teaching" (Levinas, 1969, 69).

26. For Levinas, the knowledge of objects already presupposes a relation to infinity: "All knowing qua intentionality already presupposes the idea of infinity, which is pre-eminently non-adequation" (1969, 27). And, "The calling into question of things in a dialectic is not a modifying of the perception of them; it coincides with their objectification. The object is presented when we have welcomed an interlocutor" (69).

27. Even the givenness of phenomena is rooted in ethical experience: "Speech first founds community by giving, by presenting the phenomenon as given; and it gives by thematizing. The given is the work of a sentence" (Levinas 1969, 99).

28. "Ethics as First Philosophy," in Levinas 1989, 75–87.

29. "Language is universal because it is the very passage from the individual to the general, because it offers things which are mine to the Other. To speak is to make the world common, to create commonplaces. Language does not refer to the generality of concepts, but lays the foundations for a possession in common" (Levinas 1969, 76). While discourse calls for a response and responsibility, rhetoric makes a mockery of the search for meaning, blurring the distinction between doubt and confusion, language and silence, truth and error, sense and nonsense: "It is as though in this silent and indecisive apparition a lie were perpetrated, as though the danger of error arose from an imposture, as though the silence were but a modality of an utterance" (91). Rhetoric puts pressure on the systole and diastole, inspiration and exhalation, sleep and waking, hypostasis and escape of a subject who turns on its hinges and sustains itself through rhythmic alternation. In the (defaced) face of rhetoric, the hinged subject is forced into the very equivocal space of the hinge itself, at the point where the distinctions between inside and outside, self and other, and the like ought to be articulated but not conflated. This is what Agamben (1998) would call a zone of indistinction, or a gray zone.

30. "A world absolutely silent . . . could not even present itself as a spectacle" (Levinas 1969, 94).

31. Witness, for example, the executions of Tookie Williams in 2005 and Troy Davis in 2011.

32. Suicide rates for correctional officers are much higher than the national average, and even higher than rates for police officers and those in other related occupations. See, for example, B. Finley 2007.

33. See Archibold 2010, Alexander 2011, Keyes 2011, and *Huffington Post* 2011.

34. For a more comprehensive discussion of issues related to aging in prison, see the Human Rights Watch report *Old behind Bars: The Aging Prison Population in the United States* (2012).

Conclusion

1. See Sarah Ross's (2012) reflections on the symmetry between carceral spaces and suburban developments.

BIBLIOGRAPHY

Abbott, Jack Henry. 1991. *In the Belly of the Beast: Letters from Prison.* Introduction by Norman Mailer. New York: Vintage Books.

Adamson, Christopher R. 1983. "Punishment after Slavery: Southern State Penal Systems, 1865–1890." *Social Problems* 30 (June): 555–69.

Agamben, Giorgio. 1998. *Homo Sacer: Sovereign Power and Bare Life.* Translated by Daniel Heller-Roazen. Stanford: Stanford University Press.

Alessandrini, Anthony C. 2009. "The Humanism Effect: Fanon, Foucault, and Ethics without Subjects." *Foucault Studies* 7 (September): 64–80.

Alexander, Michelle. 2010. *The New Jim Crow: Mass Incarceration in the Age of Colorblindness.* New York and London: New Press.

———. 2011. "In Prison Reform, Money Trumps Civil Rights." *New York Times,* May 14. Accessed May 15, 2011. http://www.nytimes.com/2011/05/15/opinion/15alexander.html?_r=1&src=rechp.

Alford, Fred C. 2004. "Levinas and Political Theory." *Political Theory* 32 (April): 146–71.

American Chain Gang. 1999. Directed by Xackery Irving. DVD, Canoga Park, Calif.: Chain Gang Pictures/Cinema Libre Studio.

Andersen, Hans Christian. 1852. *Pictures of Sweden.* London: R. Bentley.

Angola Three (Herman Wallace, Robert King, and Albert Woodfox). 2008. "The Case of the Angola 3." Accessed July 15, 2012. http://www.angola3.org/thecase.aspx.

Archibold, Randal C. 2010. "California, in Financial Crisis, Opens Prison Doors." *New York Times,* March 23. Accessed May 15, 2011. http://www.nytimes.com/2010/03/24/us/24calprisons.html.

Arendt, Hannah. 1973. *The Origins of Totalitarianism.* New York: Harcourt, Brace, Jovanovich.

Arrigo, Bruce A., and Jennifer Leslie Bullock. 2008. "The Psychological Effects of Solitary Confinement on Prisoners in Supermax Units: Reviewing What We Know and Recommending What Should Change." *International Journal of Offender Therapy and Comparative Criminology* 52 (December): 622–40.

Aynes, Richard L. 1975. "Behavior Modification: Winners in the Game of Life?"
    Cleveland State Law Review 24, no. 3: 422–62.

Balibar, Étienne. 2002. *Politics and the Other Scene.* New York: Verso.

Barbaras, Renaud. 2004. *The Being of the Phenomenon: Merleau-Ponty's
    Ontology.* Translated by Ted Toadvine and Len Lawlor. Bloomington and
    Indianapolis: Indiana University Press.

Bauman, Zygmunt. 2004. *Wasted Lives: Modernity and Its Outcasts.* New
    York: Polity Press.

Baxter, Charles, Wayne Brown, Tony Chatman-Bey, H. B. Johnson Jr., Mark
    Medley, Donald Thompson, Selvyn Tillett, and John Woodland Jr. 2005.
    "Live from the Panopticon: Architecture and Power Revisited." With Drew
    Leder. In *The New Abolitionists: (Neo) Slave Narratives and Contemporary
    Prison Writings,* edited by Joy James, 205–16. Albany: SUNY Press.

Bayertz, Kurt. 1996. "Human Dignity: Philosophical Origin and Scientific
    Erosion of an Idea." In *Sanctity of Life and Human Dignity,* edited by Kurt
    Bayertz, 73–90. Dordrecht: Kluwer Academic.

Belluck, Pam. 2012. "Life, with Dementia." *New York Times,* February 26.
    Accessed July 11, 2012. http://www.nytimes.com/2012/02/26/health/dealing
    -with-dementia-among-aging-criminals.html?_r=1&pagewanted=all.

Benhabib, Seyla. 1992. *Situating the Self: Gender, Community, and
    Postmodernism in Contemporary Ethics.* New York: Routledge.

Bernasconi, Robert. 2008. "Sartre and Levinas: Philosophers against
    Racism and Antisemitism." In *Race after Sartre: Antiracism, Africana
    Existentialism, Postcolonialism,* edited by Jonathan Judaken, 113–27.
    Albany: SUNY Press.

Bernstein, Jay. 2001. *Adorno: Disenchantment and Ethics.* Cambridge:
    Cambridge University Press.

Biderman, Albert D. 1957. "Communist Attempts to Elicit False Confessions
    from Air Force Prisoners of War." *Bulletin of the New York Academy of
    Medicine* 33 (September): 616–25.

Biderman, Albert, and Herbert Zimmer, eds. 1961. *The Manipulation of Human
    Behavior.* New York: John Wiley and Sons.

Bonta, James, and Paul Gendreau. 1990. "Reexamining the Cruel and Unusual
    Punishment of Prison Life." *Law and Human Behavior* 14, no. 4 (August):
    347–66.

Brown, Elaine. 2010. "Prisoner Advocate Elaine Brown on Georgia Prison
    Strike: 'Repression Breeds Resistance.'" *Democracy Now,* December 14.
    Accessed July 12, 2012. http://www.democracynow.org/2010/12/14
    /prisoner_advocate_elaine_brown_on_georgia.

Brown, Vincent. 2009. "Social Death and Political Life in the Study of Slavery."
    American Historical Review 114 (December): 1231–49.

Brown, Wendy. 1995. *States of Injury: Power and Freedom in Late Modernity.*
    Princeton: Princeton University Press.

Bruchac, Joseph, and William Witherup. 1971. *Words from the House of the*

Dead: Prison Writings from Soledad Prison. New York: Greenfield Review Press.

Buck, Marilyn, and Laura Whitehorn. 2005. "Cruel but Not Unusual—The Punishment of Women in US Prisons." With Susie Day. In *The New Abolitionists: (Neo) Slave Narratives and Contemporary Prison Writings,* edited by Joy James, 261–73. Albany: SUNY Press.

Bureau of Justice Statistics, Office of Justice Programs. 2009. "Growth in Prison and Jail Populations Slowing: 16 States Report Declines in the Number of Prisoners." March 31. Accessed July 12, 2012. http://www.ojp.usdoj.gov /newsroom/pressreleases/2009/BJS090331.htm.

———. 2012. "Total Correctional Population." July 12. Accessed July 12, 2012. http://bjs.ojp.usdoj.gov/index.cfm?ty=tp&tid=11.

Butler, Judith. 2005. *Giving an Account of Oneself.* Bronx, N.Y.: Fordham University Press.

———. 2006. *Precarious Life.* New York: Verso.

California Prison Focus. 2012. "One Year Anniversary of Historic Hunger Strike." July 1. Accessed July 16, 2012. http://www.prisons.org/hungerstrike .htm.

Carlson, Eric T., and Jeffrey L. Wollock. 1975. "Benjamin Rush and His Insane Son." *Bulletin of the New York Academy of Medicine* 51 (December): 1312–30.

Casella, Jean, and James Ridgeway. 2012. "New Ban on Solitary Confinement for Child Prisoners in Mississippi." *Solitary Watch,* February 29. Accessed July 12, 2012. http://solitarywatch.com/2012/02/29/new-ban-on-solitary -confinement-for-child-prisoners-in-mississippi/.

Central Intelligence Agency (CIA). 1963. *KUBARK Counterintelligence Interrogation Manual.* In American Torture: The Official Website of Author Michael Otterman. Accessed July 4, 2011. www.americantorture.com /documents.html.

———. 1983. *Human Resource Exploitation Training Manual.* In American Torture: The Official Website of Author Michael Otterman. Accessed July 4, 2011. www.americantorture.com/documents.html.

Chuck, Elizabeth. 2012. "Man Spends 2 Years in Solitary after DWI Arrest." *MSNBC,* January 25. Accessed July 12, 2012. http://usnews.msnbc.msn .com/_news/2012/01/25/10233835-man-spends-2-years-in-solitary-after-dwi -arrest?lite.

"Civil Death Statutes: Medieval Fiction in a Modern World." 1937. *Harvard Law Review* 50, no. 6 (April): 968–77.

Cohen, Andrew. 2011. "The Supreme Court Declares California's Prisons Overcrowded." *Atlantic,* May 23. Accessed July 15, 2012. http://www .theatlantic.com/national/archive/2011/05/the-supreme-court-declares -californias-prisons-overcrowded/239313/.

———. 2012. "An American Gulag: Descending into Madness at Supermax." *Atlantic,* June 18. Accessed July 9, 2012. http://www.theatlantic.com/national

/archive/2012/06/an-american-gulag-descending-into-madness-at-supermax/258323/.

Currie, Elliott. 1998. *Crime and Punishment in America*. New York: Macmillan.

Daskal, Jennifer. 2008. "Locked Up Alone: Detention Conditions and Mental Health at Guantanamo." With Stacy Sullivan. *Human Rights Watch Report*, June 10. Accessed March 5, 2011. http://www.hrw.org/en/reports/2008/06/09/locked-alone.

Davis, Angela Y. 1988. *Angela Davis: An Autobiography*. New York: International Publishers.

———. 2002. "From the Convict Lease System to the Super-Max Prison." In *States of Confinement: Policing, Detention, and Prisons*, edited by Joy James, 60–74. New York: Palgrave Macmillan.

———. 2003. *Are Prisons Obsolete?* New York: Seven Stories Press.

———. 2005. *Abolition Democracy: Beyond Empire, Prisons, and Torture*. New York: Seven Stories Press.

Dayan, Colin [a.k.a. Joan]. 1999. "Held in the Body of the State: Prisons and the Law." In *History, Memory, and the Law*, edited by Austin Sarat and Thomas Kearns, 183–247. Ann Arbor: University of Michigan Press.

———. 2001. "Legal Slaves and Civil Bodies." *Nepantla: Views from South* 2, no. 1: 3–39.

———. 2005. "Legal Terrors." *Representations* 92 (Fall): 42–80.

———. 2007. *The Story of Cruel and Unusual*. Cambridge: MIT Press.

———. 2011. *The Law Is a White Dog: How Legal Rituals Make and Unmake Persons*. Princeton and Oxford: Princeton University Press.

D'Elia, Donald J. 1969. "Dr. Benjamin Rush and the Negro." *Journal of the History of Ideas* 30 (July–September): 413–22.

Descartes, René. 1996. *Meditations on First Philosophy*. Translated by John Cottingham. Cambridge: Cambridge University Press.

Desgent, Sébastien, Denis Boire, and Maurice Ptito. 2010. "Altered Expression of Parvalbumin and Calbindin in Interneurons within the Primary Visual Cortex of Neonatal Enucleated Hamsters." *Neuroscience* 171, no. 4 (December 29): 1326–40.

Dickens, Charles. 1957. *American Notes and Pictures from Italy*. London: Oxford University Press.

Dixon, Bruce A. 2010. "GA Prison Inmates Stage 1-Day Peaceful Strike Today." *Black Agenda Report*, December 9. Accessed March 6, 2011. http://www.blackagendareport.com/?q=content/ga-prison-inmates-stage-1-day-peaceful-strike-today.

Doane, B. K., W. Mahatoo, W. Heron, T. H. Scott. 1959. "Changes in Perceptual Function after Isolation." *Canadian Journal of Psychology* 13, no. 3: 210–19.

Donaldson, Nancy, Todd Heisler, Soo-Jeong Kang, and Catherine Spangler. 2012. *Dementia behind Bars. New York Times*. Video, 7:48. February 21.

Accessed February 22, 2012. http://video.nytimes.com/video/2012/02/25
/health/100000001367225/dementia-behind-bars.html.

Douglass, Frederick. 1893. "The Convict Lease System." In *History Is a Weapon*.
Accessed June 23, 2012. http://www.historyisaweapon.com/defcon1
/fredouconlea.html.

————. 1987. "Narrative of the Life of Frederick Douglass, an American Slave."
In *The Classic Slave Narratives*, edited by Henry Louis Gates Jr., 323–436.
New York: Signet Classics.

Doyle, Laura. 2006. "Bodies Inside/Out: Violation and Resistance from the
Prison Cell to *The Bluest Eye*." In *Feminist Interpretations of Maurice
Merleau-Ponty*, edited by Dorothea Olkowski and Gail Weiss, 183–208.
University Park: Penn State University Press.

Drabinski, John E. 2011. *Levinas and the Postcolonial: Race, Nation, Other*.
Edinburgh: Edinburgh University Press.

Du Bois, W. E. B. 1935. *Black Reconstruction: An Essay toward a History of
the Part Which Black Folk Played in the Attempt to Reconstruct Democracy
in America, 1860–1880*. New York: S. A. Russell.

Dumm, Thomas L. 1987. *Democracy and Punishment: Disciplinary Origins of
the United States*. Madison: University of Wisconsin Press.

Duras, Marguerite. 1986. *La Douleur*. Translated by B. Bray. London: William
Collins.

"Eastern State Penitentiary." 2012a. *Living Places*. Accessed June 23, 2012.
http://www.livingplaces.com/PA/Philadelphia_County/Philadelphia_City
/Eastern_State_Penitentiary.html.

"Eastern State Penitentiary." 2012b. *Surreal New Jersey*. Accessed June 23, 2012.
http://www.surrealnewjersey.com/eastern_state_penitentiary.htm.

Eastern State Penitentiary. n.d. "Timeline." Accessed June 23, 2012. http://www
.easternstate.org/learn/timeline.

Eisenman, Stephen. 2009. "The Resistable Rise and Predictable Fall of the U.S.
Supermax." *Monthly Review*, November. Accessed June 24, 2012. http://
www.monthlyreview.org/091116eisenman.php#fn18b.

Emerson, Ralph Waldo. 1983. "Nature [1836]." In *Essays and Lectures*, edited by
Joel Porte, 5–43. New York: Viking Press.

Evans, Emory G. 1963. "A Question of Complexion: Documents concerning
the Negro and the Franchise in Eighteenth-Century Virginia." *Virginia
Magazine of History and Biography* 71 (October): 411–15.

Fanon, Frantz. 1963. *The Wretched of the Earth*. Translated by Richard Philcox.
New York: Grove Press.

————. 1967. *Black Skin, White Masks*. Translated by Charles Lam Markmann.
New York: Grove Press.

Feldman, Allen. 1991. *Formations of Violence: The Narrative of the Body
and Political Terror in Northern Ireland*. Chicago: University of Chicago
Press.

Fettig, Amy. 2012. "Teenagers Too Often End Up in Solitary." *New York Times,*
June 5. Accessed July 12, 2012. http://www.nytimes.com/roomfordebate
/2012/06/05/when-to-punish-a-young-offender-and-when-to-rehabilitate
/the-dangers-of-juveniles-in-solitary-confinement.

Finley, Bruce. 2007. "Prison Horrors Haunt Guards' Private Lives." *Denver
Post,* March 25. Accessed July 16, 2012. http://www.denverpost.com
/ci_5510659.

Finley, James B. 1851. *Memorials of Prison Life.* Cincinnati, Ohio:
L. Swormstedt and A. Poe.

Foucault, Michel. 1979. *Discipline and Punish: Birth of the Prison.* Translated
by Alan Sheridan. New York: Vintage Books.

———. 1990. *The History of Sexuality: An Introduction.* Vol. 1. Translated by
Robert Hurley. New York: Vintage Books.

———. 2003. *"Society Must Be Defended": Lectures at the Collège de France,
1975–1976.* Translated by David Macey. New York: Picador.

———. 2009. *Security, Territory, Population: Lectures at the Collège de
France, 1977–1978.* Translated by Graham Burchell. New York: Macmillan.

Franklin, H. Bruce, ed. 1998. *Prison Writing in 20th-Century America.* New
York: Penguin.

Freedman, Sanford J. 1961. "Perceptual Changes in Sensory Deprivation:
Suggestions for a Conative Theory." *Journal of Nervous Mental Disease* 132,
no. 1 (January): 17–21.

Frost, Natasha A., Judith Greene, and Kevin Pranis. 2006. "The Punitiveness
Report—HARD HIT: The Growth in Imprisonment of Women, 1977–2004."
Institute on Women and Criminal Justice. Accessed July 15, 2012. http://
www.wpaonline.org/institute/hardhit/index.htm.

Gawande, Atul. 2009. "Hellhole." *New Yorker,* March 30. Accessed December 14,
2009. www.newyorker.com/reporting/2009/03/30/090330fa_fact_gawande.

Gaylin, Willard, and Helen Blatte. 1975. "Behavior Modification in Prisons."
Criminal Law Review 13: 11–35.

Gilmore, Ruth. 2007. *Golden Gulag: Prisons, Surplus, Crisis, and Opposition in
Globalizing California.* Berkeley and Los Angeles: University of California
Press.

Glazek, Christopher. 2012. "Raise the Crime Rate." *n + 1,* January 26. Accessed
July 9, 2012. http://nplusonemag.com/raise-the-crime-rate.

Gómez, Alan Eladio. 2006. "Resisting Living Death at Marion Penitentiary,
1972." *Radical History Review* 96 (Fall): 58–86.

Goode, Erica. 2012. "Prisons Rethink Isolation, Saving Money, Lives, and
Sanity." *New York Times,* March 10. Accessed July 11, 2012. http://www
.nytimes.com/2012/03/11/us/rethinking-solitary-confinement.html
?pagewanted=all.

Gordon, Avery. 2008. *Ghostly Matters: Haunting and the Sociological
Imagination.* Minneapolis: University of Minnesota Press.

Gorman, Tessa M. 1997. "Back on the Chain Gang: Why the Eighth Amendment and the History of Slavery Proscribe the Resurgence of Chain Gangs." *California Law Review* 85 (March): 441–78.

Grassian, Stuart. 1983. "Psychopathological Effects of Solitary Confinement." *American Journal of Psychiatry* 140, no. 11 (November 1): 1450–54.

———. 2006. "Psychiatric Effects of Solitary Confinement." *Journal of Law and Policy* 22: 325–83.

Graves, Anthony. 2012a. *From Death Row to Exoneration: Fmr. Texas Prisoner Anthony Graves on Surviving Solitary Confinement.* Democracy Now. Video. June 22. Accessed July 15, 2012. http://www.democracynow .org/2012/6/22/from_death_row_to_exoneration_fmr.

———. 2012b. "Testimony by Anthony C. Graves, Presented to the Senate Judiciary Committee, Subcommittee on the Constitution, Civil Rights, and Human Rights: 'Reassessing Solitary Confinement: The Human Rights, Fiscal, and Public Safety Consequences.'" June 19. Accessed July 15, 2012. http://solitarywatch.files.wordpress.com/2012/06/anthony-graves-texas -death-row-exoneree.pdf.

Gray, Francis Calley. 1848. *Prison Discipline in America.* London: John Murray.

Greene, Susan. 2012. "The Gray Box: An Investigative Look at Solitary Confinement." *Dart Society Reports,* January 24. Accessed July 9, 2012. http://www.dartsocietyreports.org/cms/2012/01/the-gray-box-an-original -investigation/.

Griffin, Eddie. 1993. "Breaking Men's Minds: Behavior Control and Human Experimentation at the Federal Prison in Marion." *Journal of Prisoners on Prisons* 4, no. 2: 17–28.

Groder, Martin, and John Van Hartz. 1980. *Business Games: How to Recognize the Players and Deal with Them.* New York: Boardroom Classics.

Groder, Martin, and Pat Webster. 2010. "About the Authors." Accessed June 23, 2012. http://www.winningatlovebook.com/authors.htm. In *Winning at Love: The Alpha Male's Guide to Success.* Minneapolis, Minn.: Bascomb Hill Books.

Guenther, Lisa. 2007a. *The Gift of the Other: Levinas and the Politics of Reproduction.* Albany: SUNY Press.

———. 2007b. "Le Flair animal: Levinas and the Possibility of Friendship." *PhaenEx: Journal of Existential and Phenomenological Theory and Culture* 2 (Fall–Winter): 216–38.

———. 2009a. "'Nameless Singularity': Levinas on Individuation and Ethical Singularity." *Epoché* 14 (Fall): 167–87.

———. 2009b. "Who Follows Whom? Derrida, Animals, and Women." *Derrida Today* 2, no. 2 (November): 151–65.

———. 2011a. "The Ethics and Politics of Otherness: Negotiating Alterity and Racial Difference." *philoSOPHIA* 1, no. 2: 195–214.

———. 2011b. "Merleau-Ponty and the Sense of Sexual Difference." *Angelaki* 16, no. 2: 19–33.

———. 2011c. "Shame and the Temporality of Social Life." *Continental Philosophy Review* 44 (March): 23–29.

———. 2011d. "Subjects without a World? An Husserlian Analysis of Solitary Confinement." *Human Studies* 34, no. 3 (September): 257–76.

———. 2012a. "Beyond Dehumanization: A Post-Humanist Critique of Intensive Confinement." In "Prison and Animals," ed. Susan Thomas and Laura Shields. Special issue, *Journal for Critical Animal Studies* 10, no. 2: 69–100.

———. 2012b. "Fecundity and Natal Alienation: Rethinking Kinship with Emmanuel Levinas and Orlando Patterson." In "Levinas and Race," ed. John Drabinski. Special issue, *Levinas Studies* 7: 1–20.

———. 2012c. "Resisting Agamben: The Biopolitics of Shame and Humiliation." *Philosophy and Social Criticism* 38, no. 1 (January): 59–79.

Haney, Craig. 2003. "Mental Health Issues in Long-Term Solitary and 'Supermax' Confinement." *Crime Delinquency* 49, no. 1 (January): 124–56.

Haney, Craig, and Mona Lynch. 1997. "Regulating Prisons of the Future: A Psychological Analysis of Supermax and Solitary Confinement." *New York University School of Law Review of Law and Social Change* 23, no. 4: 477–570.

Harlow, Harry F., Robert O. Dodsworth, and Margaret K. Harlow. 1965. "Total Social Isolation in Monkeys." *Proceedings of the National Academy of Sciences of the United States of America* 54 (July): 90–97.

Harlow, Harry F., Philip E. Plubell, and Craig M. Baysinger. 1973. "Induction of Psychological Death in Rhesus Monkeys." *Journal of Autism and Childhood Schizophrenia* 3 (October–December): 299–307.

Harris, Cheryl I. 1993. "Whiteness as Property." *Harvard Law Review* 106, no. 8 (June): 1707–95.

———. 1996. "Finding Sojourner's Truth: Race, Gender, and the Institution of Property." *Cardozo Law Review* 18 (November): 309–409.

Hartman, Saidiya. 2002. "The Time of Slavery." *South Atlantic Quarterly* 101 (Fall): 757–77.

———. 2007. *Lose Your Mother: A Journey along the Atlantic Slave Route.* New York: Farrar, Straus and Giroux.

Hebb, Donald O. 1961. "Sensory Deprivation: Facts in Search of a Theory." *Journal of Nervous and Mental Disease* 132: 40–43.

Heidegger, Martin. 1962. *Being and Time.* Translated by John Macquarrie and Edward Robinson. New York: Harper and Row.

———. 1995. *Fundamental Concepts of Metaphysics.* Translated by William McNeill and Nicholas Walker. Bloomington: Indiana University Press.

Herman's House. 2012. Directed by Angad Bhalla. DVD, Toronto, Ontario: Storyline Entertainment/Time of Day Films, 2012.

Heron, W., B. K. Doane, T. H. Scott. 1956. "Visual Disturbances after Prolonged Perceptual Isolation." *Canadian Journal of Psychology* 10, no. 1 (March): 13–18.

Hinkle, Lawrence E. 1961. "The Physiological State of the Interrogation Subject As It Affects Brain Function." In *The Manipulation of Human Behaviour,* ed. Albert D. Biderman and Herbert Zimmer, 19–50. New York: John Wiley and Sons.

Hinkle, Lawrence E., and Harold G. Wolff. 1956. "Communist Interrogation and Indoctrination of Enemies of the State: Analysis of Methods Used by the Communist State Police (a Special Report)." *AMA Archives of Neurology and Psychiatry* 76 (August): 115–74.

Holland, Sharon Patricia. 2000. *Raising the Dead: Readings of Death and (Black) Subjectivity.* Durham, N.C., and London: Duke University Press.

Hornblum, Allen M. 1998. *Acres of Skin: Human Experiments at Holmesburg Prison.* New York: Routledge.

Huffington Post. 2011. "Texas Prison System Goes to Two Meals a Day on Weekends to Cut Costs." October 22. Accessed July 16, 2012. http://www.huffingtonpost.com/2011/10/21/texas-prison-system-goes-to-two-meals-to-cut-costs_n_1025893.html?view=print&comm_ref=false.

Human Rights Watch. 1997. "Cold Storage: Super-Maximum Security Confinement in Indiana." Human Rights Watch report, October. New York: Human Rights Watch. Accessed June 25, 2012. www.hrw.org/reports/1997/usind.

———. 2012. "Old behind Bars: The Aging Prison Population in the United States." Human Rights Watch report, January 28. New York: Human Rights Watch. Accessed June 27, 2012. http://www.hrw.org/reports/2012/01/27/old-behind-bars-0.

Husserl, Edmund. 1970. *The Crisis of European Sciences and Transcendental Phenomenology: An Introduction to Phenomenological Philosophy.* Translated by David Carr. Evanston, Ill.: Northwestern University Press.

———. 1973. *Zur Phänomenologie der Intersubjektivität: Texte aus dem Nachlass.* Vols. 13–15. The Hague: Martinus Nijhoff.

———. 1983. *Ideas Pertaining to a Pure Phenomenology and to a Phenomenological Philosophy: First Book. General Introduction to a Pure Phenomenology.* Translated by F. Kersten. Dordrecht: Kluwer Academic.

———. 1991. *Cartesian Meditations: An Introduction to Phenomenology.* Translated by Dorian Cairns. Dordrecht: Kluwer Academic.

———. 2002. *Ideas Pertaining to a Pure Phenomenology and to a Phenomenological Philosophy: Second Book. Studies in the Phenomenology of Constitution.* Translated by R. Rojcewicz and A. Schuwer. Dordrecht: Kluwer Academic.

Irwin, John. 2005. *The Warehouse Prison: Disposal of the New Dangerous Class.* Los Angeles: Roxbury.

Jackson, Bruce, ed. 1999. *Wake Up Dead Man: Hard Labor and Southern Blues.* Athens and London: University of Georgia Press.

Jackson, George. 1970. *Soledad Brother: The Prison Letters of George Jackson.* New York: Bantam Books.

———. 1990. *Blood in My Eye*. Baltimore: Black Classic Press.

James, Joy, ed. 2003. *Imprisoned Intellectuals: America's Political Prisoners Write on Life, Liberation, and Rebellion*. New York: Rowman and Littlefield.

———, ed. 2005. *The New Abolitionists: (Neo) Slave Narratives and Contemporary Prison Writings*. Albany: SUNY Press.

Jiang, Bin, Kazuhiro Sohya, Abdolrahman Sarihi, Yuchio Yanagawa, and Tadaharu Tsumoto. 2010. "Laminar-Specific Maturation of GABAergic Transmission and Susceptibility to Visual Deprivation Are Related to Endocannabinoid Sensitivity in Mouse Visual Cortex." *Journal of Neuroscience* 30, no. 42 (October 20): 14261–72.

Jones, Arlando "Tray." 2010. *Eager Street: A Life on the Corner and Behind Bars*. Baltimore: Apprentice House.

Kelley, Robin D. G. 2002. *Freedom Dreams: The Black Radical Imagination*. Boston: Beacon Press.

Kerness, Bonnie, and Holbrook Teter, eds. 2008. *Survival in Solitary: A Manual Written by and for People Living in Control Units*. Santa Cruz, Calif.: Quiver Press.

Keyes, Scott. 2011. "State Budget Cutbacks Lead to an Unexpected Silver Lining: Prison Reform." *Think Progress,* February 7. Accessed July 16, 2012. http://thinkprogress.org/politics/2011/02/07/138507/state-budget-prisons/?mobile=nc.

King, Robert. 2010. "Experience: I Spent 29 Years in Solitary Confinement." *Guardian,* August 28. Accessed June 24, 2012. http://www.guardian.co.uk/lifeandstyle/2010/aug/28/29-years-solitary-confinement-robert-king.

Klein, Naomi. 2007. *The Shock Doctrine: The Rise of Disaster Capitalism*. New York and London: Macmillan.

Knott, Sarah. 2009. *Sensibility and the American Revolution*. Chapel Hill: University of North Carolina Press. Kornfield, Phyllis. 1997. *Cellblock Visions: Prison Art in America*. Princeton: Princeton University Press.

Kramer, Bernard. 1961. "Man in His Social Environment: Social Structure and Behavioral Change." In *The Power to Change Behavior,* edited by U.S. Bureau of Prisons, 27–40. Washington, D.C.: Bureau of Prisons.

Kupers, Terry. 1999. *Prison Madness: The Mental Health Crisis behind Bars and What We Must Do about It*. San Francisco: Jossey-Bass.

Landy, David. 1961. "Man's Adaptive Processes: Cultural Influences on Behavioral Change." In *The Power to Change Behavior,* edited by U.S. Bureau of Prisons, 41–51. Washington, D.C.: Bureau of Prisons.

Lazreg, Marnia. 2008. *Torture and the Twilight of Empire*. Princeton: Princeton University Press.

Leder, Drew. 2001. *The Soul Knows No Bars: Inmates Reflect on Life, Death, and Hope*. With Charles Baxter et al. Foreword by Cornel West. Lanham, Md.: Rowman and Littlefield.

Leiderman, P. Herbert. 1961. "Man Alone: Sensory Deprivation and Behavioral

Change." In *The Power to Change Behavior,* edited by U.S. Bureau of Prisons, 5–26. Washington, D.C.: Bureau of Prisons.

Leland, John. 2009. "Fellow Inmates Ease Pain of Dying in Jail." *New York Times,* October 17. Accessed July 11, 2012. http://www.nytimes.com/2009/10/18/health/18hospice.html.

Levasseur, Luc. 2005. "Trouble Coming Every Day: ADX—The First Year." In *The New Abolitionists: (Neo) Slave Narratives and Contemporary Prison Writings,* ed. Joy James, 47–55. Albany: SUNY Press.

Levinas, Emmanuel. 1961. *Totalité et infini: Essai sur l'exteriorité.* The Hague: Martinus Nijhoff.

———. 1969. *Totality and Infinity: An Essay on Exteriority.* Translated by Alphonso Lingis. Pittsburgh: Duquesne University Press.

——— 1978. *Existence and Existents.* Translated by Alphonso Lingis. The Hague: Martinus Nijhoff.

———. 1985. *Ethics and Infinity: Conversations with Phillipe Nemo.* Translated by Richard A. Cohen. Pittsburgh: Duquesne University Press.

———. 1987. *Time and the Other.* Translated by Richard A. Cohen. Pittsburgh: Duquesne University Press.

———. 1989. *The Levinas Reader.* Edited by Seán Hand. Translated by Seán Hand and Michael Temple. Oxford: Blackwell.

———. 1990. "Reflections on the Philosophy of Hitlerism." Translated by Seán Hand. *Critical Inquiry* 17 (Fall): 62–71.

———. 1994a. *Beyond the Verse: Talmudic Readings and Lectures.* Translated by Gary D. Mole. New York and London: Continuum.

———. 1994b. "Judaism and Revolution." In *Nine Talmudic Readings,* translated by Annette Aronowicz. Bloomington: Indiana University Press.

———. 1996. *Emmanuel Levinas: Basic Philosophical Writings.* Edited by Adriaan T. Peperzak, Simon Critchley, and Robert Bernasconi. Bloomington and Indianapolis: Indiana University Press.

———. 1997. *Difficult Freedom: Essays on Judaism.* Translated by Seán Hand. Baltimore: Johns Hopkins University Press.

———. 1998a. *Entre Nous: Thinking-of-the-Other.* Translated by Michael B. Smith and Barbara Harshav. New York: Columbia University Press.

———. 1998b. *Otherwise Than Being; or, Beyond Essence.* Translated by Alphonso Lingis. Pittsburgh: Duquesne University Press.

———. 1998c. "The Trace of the Other." In *Continental Philosophy: An Anthology,* edited by William McNeill and Karen S. Feldman, 176–85. Oxford: Blackwell.

———. 1999. *Alterity and Transcendence.* Translated by Michael B. Smith. New York: Columbia University Press.

———. 2000. *God, Death, and Time.* Translated by Bettina Bergo. Stanford: Stanford University Press.

———. 2003. *On Escape.* Translated by Bettina Bergo. Introduction and annotation by Jacques Rolland. Stanford: Stanford University Press.

Libby v. Comm'r of Corr. 432 N.E. 2d 486 (Mass. 1982).

Lifton, Robert J. 1957. "Chinese Communist 'Thought Reform': Confession and Re-education of Western Civilians." *Bulletin of the New York Academy of Medicine* 33 (September): 626–44.

Lilly, John C. 1956. "Mental Effects of Reduction of Ordinary Levels of Physical Stimuli in Intact, Healthy Persons." *Psychiatric Research Report of the American Psychiatric Association* 5 (June): 1–28.

Lilly, John C., and Jay T. Shurley. 1961. "Experiments in Solitude in Maximum Achievable Physical Isolation with Water Suspension of Intact Healthy Persons." Paper read at symposium, USAF Aerospace Medical Center, San Antonio, Texas, 1960. In *Psychophysiological Aspects of Space Flight,* edited by Bernard E. Flaherty, 238–47. New York: Columbia University Press.

Liptak, Adam. 2008a. "1 in 100 U.S. Adults behind Bars, New Study Says." *New York Times,* February 28. Accessed July 12, 2012. http://www.nytimes .com/2008/02/28/us/28cnd-prison.html?_r=2.

———. 2008b. "U.S. Prison Population Dwarfs That of Other Nations." *New York Times,* April 23. Accessed June 23, 2012. http://www.nytimes.com /2008/04/23/world/americas/23iht-23prison.12253738.html?pagewanted=all.

Lovell, David, and Clark Johnson. 2004. "Felony and Violent Recidivism among Supermax Prison Inmates in Washington State: A Pilot Study." University of Washington. Accessed July 22, 2011. http://www.son.washington.edu/faculty /fac-page-files/Lovell-SupermaxRecidivism-4-19-04.pdf.

Maclaren, Kym. 2008. "Embodied Perceptions of Others as a Condition of Selfhood? Empirical and Phenomenological Considerations." *Journal of Consciousness Studies* 15, no. 8: 63–93.

Malcolm X. 1999. *The Autobiography of Malcolm X.* New York: Ballantine Books.

Mason, Jim, and Mary Finelli. 2006. "Brave New Farm?" In *In Defense of Animals: The Second Wave,* edited by Peter Singer, 104–22. New York and London: Wiley-Blackwell.

Mason, William A., and R. R. Sponholz. 1963. "Behavior of Rhesus Monkeys Raised in Isolation." *Journal of Psychiatric Research* 1 (December): 299–306.

Masur, Louis P. 1991. *Rites of Execution: Capital Punishment and the Transformation of American Culture, 1776–1865.* Oxford: Oxford University Press.

Mayeux, Sara. 2010. "Prison Labor and the Thirteenth Amendment." *Prison Law Blog.* December 16. Accessed July 16, 2012. http://prisonlaw.wordpress .com/2010/12/16/prison-labor-and-the-thirteenth-amendment/.

McCain, John, and Carl Levin. 2008. "Senate Armed Services Committee Inquiry into the Treatment of Detainees in U.S. Custody." November 11. Executive Summary submitted to Department of Defense. Accessed June 27, 2011. http://www.tjsl.edu/slomansonb/9.7_SenateArmedSrvcRpt.pdf.

McConnell, James V. 1970. "Criminals Can Be Brainwashed—Now." *Psychology Today,* April, 14–16.

McCoy, Alfred W. 2007. "Science in Dachau's Shadow: Hebb, Beecher, and the Development of CIA Psychological Torture and Modern Medical Ethics." *Journal of the History of the Behavioral Sciences* 43 (Fall): 401–17.

McWhorter, Ladelle. 2009. *Racism and Sexual Oppression in Anglo-America: A Genealogy.* Indianapolis: Indiana University Press.

Mears, Daniel P., and Jamie Watson. 2006. "Towards a Fair and Balanced Assessment of Supermax Prisons." *Justice Quarterly* 23, no. 2 (June): 232–70.

Meerloo, Joost. 1951. "The Crime of Menticide." *American Journal of Psychiatry* 107 (February): 594–98.

Meillassoux, Claude. 1991. *The Anthropology of Slavery: The Womb of Iron and Gold.* Translated by Alide Dasnois. Chicago: University of Chicago Press.

Mellon, James, ed. 1988. *Bullwhip Days: The Slaves Remember: An Oral History.* New York: Avon Books.

Meltzer, Malcolm L. 1961. "Countermanipulation through Malingering." In *The Manipulation of Human Behaviour,* ed. Albert D. Biderman and Herbert Zimmer, 277–304. New York: John Wiley and Sons.

Melzack, R. 1954. "The Genesis of Emotional Behavior: An Experimental Study of the Dog." *Journal of Comparative and Physiological Psychology* 47 (April): 166–68.

Merleau-Ponty, Maurice. 1964a. *The Primacy of Perception, and Other Essays on Phenomenological Psychology, the Philosophy of Art, History, and Politics.* Translated by William Cobb. Evanston, Ill.: Northwestern University Press.

———. 1964b. *Signs.* Translated by Richard C. McCleary. Evanston, Ill.: Northwestern University Press.

———. 1968. *The Visible and the Invisible.* Translated by Alphonso Lingis. Evanston, Ill.: Northwestern University Press.

———. 1973. "Dialogue and the Perception of the Other." In *The Prose of the World,* translated by John O'Neill, 131–46. Evanston, Ill.: Northwestern University Press.

———. 2002. *Phenomenology of Perception.* Translated by Colin Smith. London: Routledge Classics.

———. 2003a. *L'Institution, la passivité: Notes de cours au Collège de France (1954–1955).* Paris: Belin.

———. 2003b. *Nature: Course Notes from the Collège de France (1956–60).* Translated by Robert Vallier. Compiled and with notes by Dominique Séglard. Evanston, Ill.: Northwestern University Press.

———. 2008. *The Structure of Behavior.* Translated by Alden Fisher. Pittsburgh: Duquesne University Press.

———. 2010. *Institution and Passivity: Course Notes from the Collège de France (1954–1955).* Translated by Leonard Lawlor and Heath Massey. Evanston, Ill.: Northwestern University Press.

Miller, Jerome G. 1997. *Search and Destroy: African-American Males in the Criminal Justice System.* Cambridge: Cambridge University Press.

Miller, Joshua Rhett. 2011. "Arrest of Homeless Connecticut Woman for
     Enrolling Son in School Illegally Sparks Debate." Fox News, April 26.
     Accessed July 11, 2012. http://www.foxnews.com/us/2011/04/25/arrest
     -homeless-connecticut-woman-enrolling-son-school-illegally-sparks
     -debate/#ixzz20Mz3ucLX.

Miller v. Alabama. 2012. "Oral Arguments." Last accessed June 23, 2012. http://
     www.supremecourt.gov/oral_arguments/argument_transcripts/10-9646.pdf.

Minkowski, Eugene. 1970. *Lived Time: Phenomenological and
     Psychopathological Studies.* Translated by Nancy Metzel. Evanston, Ill.:
     Northwestern University Press.

Mitford, Jessica. 1973. "The Torture Cure: In Some American Prisons, It Is
     Already 1984." *Harper's Magazine,* August, 16–30.

Morris, David. 2004. *The Sense of Space.* Albany: SUNY Press.

———. 2008. "The Time and Place of the Organism: Merleau-Ponty's
     Philosophy in Embryo." *Alter: Revue de phenomenology* 16: 69–86.

Morris, Norval, and David J. Rothman. 1998. *The Oxford History of the Prison:
     The Practice of Punishment in Western Society.* Oxford: Oxford University
     Press.

Morrison, Toni. 1998. *Beloved.* New York: Plume Books.

Nietzsche, Friedrich. 1989. *Genealogy of Morals and Ecce Homo.* Translated by
     Walter Kaufman. New York: Vintage Books.

Nolan, Hamilton. 2012. "Letters from Death Row: Brett Hartmann, Ohio
     Inmate 357-869." *Gawker,* May 25. Accessed July 15, 2012. http://gawker
     .com/5913076/letters-from-death-row-brett-hartmann-ohio-inmate-357+869.

Novek, Joel. 2005. "Pigs and People: Sociological Perspectives on the Discipline
     of Nonhuman Animals in Intensive Confinement." *Society and Animals* 13,
     no. 3: 221–44.

Oliver, Kelly. 2004. *The Colonization of Psychic Space: A Psychoanalytic Social
     Theory of Oppression.* Minneapolis: University of Minnesota Press.

Opton, Edward M., Jr. 1974. "Psychiatric Violence against Prisoners: When
     Therapy Is Punishment." *Mississippi Law Journal* 45, no. 3: 605–44.

Oshinsky, David M. 1996. *"Worse Than Slavery": Parchman Farm and the
     Ordeal of Jim Crow Justice.* New York: Free Press.

Otterman, Michael. 2007. *American Torture: From the Cold War to Abu Ghraib
     and Beyond.* London and Ann Arbor, Mich.: Pluto Press.

Patchette v. Nix. 952 F. 2d 158 (8th Cir. 1991).

Patrick-Stamp, Leslie. 1995. "Numbers That Are Not New: African Americans
     in the Country's First Prison, 1790–1835." *Pennsylvania Magazine of History
     and Biography* 119 (January–April): 95–128.

Patterson, Orlando. 1982. *Slavery and Social Death: A Comparative Study.*
     Cambridge and London: Harvard University Press.

Pavlov, Ivan Petrovich. 2003. *Conditioned Reflexes.* Translated by G. V. Anrep.
     Mineola, N.Y.: Courier Dover.

Prisoner Hunger Strike Solidarity. 2011. "Prisoners' Demands." April 3. Accessed July 12, 2012. http://prisonerhungerstrikesolidarity.wordpress.com /the-prisoners-demands-2/.

———. 2012. "Urgent Call for Support: Red Onion State Prison Hunger Strikers in VA." May 21. Accessed July 16, 2012. http://prisonerhungerstrike solidarity.wordpress.com/2012/05/21/urgent-call-for-support-red-onion-state -prison-hunger-strikers-in-va/.

Prison Policy Initiative. 2003. "Prison Labor." Accessed July 12, 2012. http:// www.prisonpolicy.org/prisonindex/prisonlabor.html.

Public Safety Performance Project. 2008. "One in 100: Behind Bars in America 2008." Washington, D.C.: Pew Center on the States. Accessed June 23, 2012. www.pewcenteronthestates.org.

Rangel, Charles. 1975. "Introduction: Behavior Modification." *American Criminal Law Review* 1 (Summer): 3–9.

Reinhardt, Viktor. 2004. "Stereotypical Behavior: A LAREF Discussion." *Lab Primate Newsletter* 43 (October): 3–4.

Reiter, Keramet Ann. 2012a. "The Most Restrictive Alternative: A Litigation History of Solitary Confinement in U.S. Prisons, 1960–2006." In *Studies in Law, Politics, and Society,* vol. 57, edited by Austin Sarat, 71–124. Bingley, U.K.: Emerald Group.

———. 2012b. "Parole, Snitch, or Die: California's Supermax Prisons and Prisoners, 1997–2007." *Punishment and Society* 14, no. 5 (December): 530–63.

Rhodes, Lorna A. 2004. *Total Confinement: Madness and Reason in the Maximum Security Prison.* Berkeley, Los Angeles, and London: University of California Press.

Rickman, Dina. 2012. "Prison Deaths and Overcrowding: Are the Two Linked?" *Huffington Post,* March 5. Accessed June 24, 2012. http://www .huffingtonpost.co.uk/2012/03/05/prison-deaths-overcrowding-howard -league-poa_n_1321771.html.

Ridgeway, James. 2009. "36 Years of Solitude." *Mother Jones,* March 2. Accessed July 15, 2012. http://www.motherjones.com/politics/2009/03/36-years -solitude.

Ridgeway, James, and Jean Casella. 2012. "Torturous Milestone: 40 Years in Solitary." *Mother Jones,* April 17. Accessed July 15, 2012. http://www .motherjones.com/politics/2012/04/angola-prison-3-herman-wallace-albert -woodfox-40-years-solitary-confinement.

Riesen, Austin H. 1961. "Studying Perceptual Development Using the Technique of Sensory Development." *Journal of Nervous Mental Disease* 132, no. 1: 21–25.

Riesen, Austin H., and Louis Aarons. 1959. "Visual Movement and Intensity Discrimination in Cats after Early Deprivation of Pattern Vision." *Journal of Comparative and Physiological Psychology* 52 (April): 142–49.

Riveland, Chase. 1999. *Supermax Prisons: Overview and General*

Considerations. Washington, D.C.: U.S. Department of Justice, National
  Institute of Corrections. Accessed June 24, 2012. http://static.nicic.gov
  /Library/014937.pdf.

Rodríguez, Dylan. 2006. "(Non)Scenes of Captivity: The Common Sense of
  Punishment and Death." *Radical History Review* 96 (Fall): 9–32.

Rosenberg, Susan. 2011. *An American Radical: Political Prisoner in My Own
  Country.* New York: Citadel Press.

Ross, Sarah. 2012. "Territorial Imaginations." *Art + Research.* Accessed July 15,
  2012. http://insecurespaces.net/territorialimaginations.html.

Rush, Benjamin. 1787. "An Enquiry into the Effects of Public Punishments."
  In *The American Museum or Repository of Ancient and Modern Fugitive
  Pieces, &c,* 2: 142–53. Philadelphia: Mathew Carey.

———. 1799. "Observations Intended to Favour a Supposition That the
  Black Color (As It Is Called) of the Negroes Is Derived from the
  Leprosy." *Transactions of the American Philosophical Society* 4:
  289–297.

———. 1806. *Essays, Literary, Moral, and Philosophical.* Philadelphia:
  Thomas and William Bradford.

———. 1812. *Medical Inquiries and Observations, upon Diseases of the Mind.*
  Philadelphia: Kimber and Richardson.

———. 1947a. "The Influence of Physical Causes upon the Moral Faculty [1786]."
  In *The Selected Writings of Benjamin Rush,* edited by Dagobert D. Runes,
  181–212. New York: Philosophical Library.

———. 1947b. "Lectures on Animal Life [1799]." In *The Selected Writings
  of Benjamin Rush,* edited by Dagobert D. Runes, 133–80. New York:
  Philosophical Library.

Salah-El, Tiyo Attallah. 2005. "A Call for the Abolition of Prisons." In *The New
  Abolitionists: (Neo) Slave Narratives and Contemporary Prison Writings,*
  edited by Joy James, 69–74. Albany: SUNY Press.

Sartre, Jean-Paul. 1956. *Being and Nothingness: An Essay on Phenomenological
  Ontology.* New York: Taylor and Francis.

———. 1963. Preface to *The Wretched of the Earth,* by Frantz Fanon, translated
  by Richard Philcox, xliii–lxii. New York: Grove Press.

Scarry, Elaine. 1985. *The Body in Pain: The Making and Unmaking of the
  World.* New York and Oxford: Oxford University Press.

Schein, Edgar H. 1956. "The Chinese Indoctrination Program for Prisoners
  of War: A Study of Attempted Brainwashing." *Psychiatry* 19, no. 2 (May):
  149–72.

———. 1961. "Man against Man: Brainwashing." In *The Power to Change
  Behavior,* edited by U.S. Bureau of Prisons, 52–64. Washington, D.C.:
  Bureau of Prisons.

Schmalleger, Frank, and John Smykla. 2007. *Corrections in the 21st Century.*
  New York: McGraw-Hill.

Schwartzapfel, Beth. 2009. "Your Valentine, Made in Prison." *The Nation,*

February 12. Accessed July 12, 2012. http://www.thenation.com/article
/your-valentine-made-prison#.

Shakur, Assata. 2000. "Assata Shakur Speaks from Exile: Post-modern Maroon
in the Ultimate Palenque; An Interview by Christian Parenti." October 24.
Accessed March 11, 2006. www.assatashakur.org/maroon.htm.

Shalev, Sharon. 2009. *Supermax: Controlling Risk through Solitary
Confinement.* Portland, Ore.: Willan.

Shange, Ntozake. 1997. *For Colored Girls Who Have Considered Suicide When
the Rainbow Is Enuf.* New York: Scribner.

Shaylor, Cassandra. 1998. "It's Like Living in a Black Hole: Women of Color
and Solitary Confinement in the Prison Industrial Complex." *New England
Journal on Criminal and Civil Confinement* 24: 385–416.

Sheikhkanloui-Milan, H., V. Sheibani, M. Afarinesh, S. Esmaeili-Mahani, A.
Shamsizadeh, G. Sepehri. 2010. "Effects of Electrical Stimulation of Dorsal
Raphe Nucleus on Neuronal Response Properties of Barrel Cortex Layer IV
Neurons following Long-Term Sensory Deprivation." *Neuroscience Bulletin*
26, no. 5 (October): 388–94.

Shelden, Randall G. 2005. "Slavery in the Third Millennium. Part II: Prisons
and Convict Leasing Help Perpetuate Slavery." Accessed May 19, 2011. http://
blackcommentator.com/142/142_slavery_2.html.

Smith, Caleb. 2009. *The Prison and the American Imagination.* New Haven
and London: Yale University Press.

Smith, Peter Scharff. 2006. "The Effects of Solitary Confinement on Prison
Inmates: A Brief History and Review of the Literature." *Crime and Justice*
34: 441–528.

Solidarity with Virginia Prison Hunger Strikers. n.d. "Ten Demands of ROSP
Hunger Strikers." Accessed July 15, 2012. http://virginiaprisonstrike.blogspot
.com/p/ten-demands-of-rosp-hunger-strikers.html.

Solitary Watch. 2012a. "FAQ." Accessed June 23, 2012. http://solitarywatch.com
/faq/.

———. 2012b. "Testimony from the U.S. Senate Judiciary Subcommittee on the
Constitution, Human Rights, and Civil Rights for Hearing on 'Reassessing
Solitary Confinement: The Human Rights, Fiscal, and Public Safety
Consequences.'" June 19. Accessed July 11, 2012. http://solitarywatch.com
/resources/testimony/.

Solomon, Philip, P. Herbert Leiderman, Jack Mendelson, and Donald Wexler.
1957. "Sensory Deprivation: A Review." *American Journal of Psychiatry* 114
(October): 357–63.

St. Cyr, Peter. 2012. "Former Inmates Describe Abuse in Solitary Confinement."
KOB Eyewitness News, February 29. Accessed July 12, 2012. http://www.kob
.com/article/stories/S2518465.shtml.

Stanley, Eric A., and Nat Smith, eds. 2011. *Captive Genders: Trans Embodiment
and the Prison Industrial Complex.* Edinburgh; Oakland, Calif.; Baltimore:
AK Press.

Stauffer, Jill. 2010. "How Much Does That Weigh? Levinas and the Possibility of Human Rights." *MonoKL: Reflections on Levinas* 5: 493–506.

Sullivan, Robert R. 1998. "The Birth of the Prison: The Case of Benjamin Rush." *Eighteenth-Century Studies* 31 (Spring): 333–44.

Sumell, Jackie. 2010. *The House That Herman Built.* Accessed July 15, 2012. http://www.hermanshouse.org/index.html.

Sumell, Jackie, and Herman Wallace. 2006. *The House That Herman Built.* Stuttgart: Merz and Solitude.

Takaki, Ronald. 2000. *Iron Cages: Race and Culture in 19th-Century America.* Oxford: Oxford University Press.

Tapley, Lance. 2010. "The Worst of the Worst: Supermax Torture in America." *Boston Review*, November–December. Accessed December 28, 2010. http://www.bostonreview.net/BR35.6/tapley.php.

Thorp, Willard. 1946. *The Lives of Eighteen from Princeton.* New York: Ayer.

Turley, Jonathan. 2005. "Humiliating Punishments and the Abuse of Judicial Power." September 18. Accessed June 23, 2012. http://jonathanturley .org/2007/08/18/humiliating-punishments-and-the-abuse-of-judicial-power/.

U.S. Bureau of Prisons, ed. 1961. *The Power to Change Behavior.* Papers presented at a seminar conducted by the Bureau of Prisons at an Associate Warden Training Program in April 1961. Washington, D.C.: Bureau of Prisons.

Varela, Francisco, Evan Thompson, and Eleanor Rosch. 1991. *The Embodied Mind: Cognitive Science and Human Experience.* Cambridge: MIT Press.

Venter, J. J. 2004. "Human Dignity and the Objectification of the Human Being." In *Does the World Exist? Plurisignificant Ciphering of Reality,* edited by Anna-Teresa Tymieniecka, 537–602. Dordrecht: Kluwer Academic.

Wacquant, Loïc. 2001. "Deadly Symbiosis: When Ghetto and Prison Meet and Mesh." *Punishment and Society* 3 (January): 95–133.

———. 2009a. *Prisons of Poverty.* Minneapolis: University of Minnesota Press.

———. 2009b. *Punishing the Poor: The Neoliberal Government of Social Insecurity.* Durham, N.C., and London: Duke University Press.

Walsh, P. G., and P. Mertin. 1994. "The Training of Pets as Therapy Dogs in a Woman's Prison: A Pilot Study." *Anthrozoos* 7, no. 2: 124–28.

Whitney, Shiloh. 2010. "A New Conception of Intentionality: Pure Depth as Affective Orientation." Paper presented at the Merleau-Ponty Circle annual meeting, September 22–25.

Williams, Nancy M. 2008. "Affected Ignorance and Animal Suffering: Why Our Failure to Debate Factory Farming Puts Us at Moral Risk." *Journal of Agricultural and Environmental Ethics* 21: 371–84.

Williams, Stanley Tookie. 2004. *Black Rage, Blue Redemption: A Memoir.* New York: Touchstone.

Williams, Vergil L. 1996. *Dictionary of American Penology.* Westport, Conn.: Greenwood.

Wood-Gush, D. G. M., and K. Vestergaard. 1989. "Exploratory Behavior and the Welfare of Intensively Kept Animals." *Journal of Agricultural Ethics 2*, no. 6: 161–69.

Yanni, Carla. 2007. *The Architecture of Madness: Insane Asylums in the United States.* Minneapolis: University of Minnesota Press.

Young, Iris Marion. 1990. *Throwing Like a Girl, and Other Essays in Feminist Philosophy and Social Theory.* Bloomington: Indiana University Press.

INDEX

Abbott, Jack Henry, xi, xxiv–xxvii, 36–37, 142–43, 147–48, 166, 181–82, 197–201, 212, 262n12, 265n17, 292n22
abolition: of death penalty, 54; of prison, 54, 127, 253–56; of slavery, xiv, xvii, xxviii–xxix, 41, 46–48, 51, 54, 61, 66, 126, 139
accountability, xxx, 161, 221–51
activity, 6, 11, 26, 30, 74, 153, 168–69, 191. *See also* passivity
actuality, 92, 178, 219, 244
ADX Florence, xii, 161, 223, 274n8, 275n14, 291n3
affect, xxx, 55, 87, 154–56, 171–79, 187, 191–93, 233; in Fanon, 55, 233; in Levinas, 209–14; in Merleau-Ponty, 171–80
Agamben, Giorgio, xvii, 47
agency, 183, 188, 193, 250
alter ego: in Husserl, 31–33, 173, 261
Andersen, Hans Christian, 15
Angola Prison, 40, 50
Angola Three, 184, 192
animal industrial complex, 128, 141, 143, 147–48, 157
anonymity, 189–90
anxiety: Being-toward-death, 201–2, 262, 239, 287n5; forced proximity

to others, 148–49; induced by solitary confinement, xi, 11–12, 22, 66, 147–49, 211, 215, 257n2, 276n26; sensory deprivation, 75
Arendt, Hannah, xxiv
Asklepieion program. *See* behavior modification: Asklepieion program
Attica prison, 125–26, 141, 156
Auburn system, 14–18, 21, 51
autonomy, xxii, 78, 81, 187, 237

bare life, xvii
basic needs, 82, 97, 118, 133–34, 137, 145, 149–50, 196; in Levinas, 210, 214. *See also* survival
behaviorism, xxi, xxix, 66, 69, 84, 91, 98–120, 266, 270n2, 271n7, 274n12; mechanistic model of cognition, xxviii, 7, 16, 24, 80, 106, 110, 118, 272n14. *See also* body
behavior modification, xvi, xxix, 65–99, 120, 126–30, 229; Asklepieion program, xxix, 91–99; CARE (Control and Rehabilitation Effort), 130; Cold War, xxix, 99, 101–3, 120; MKULTRA, 68; START (Special Treatment and

LISA GUENTHER is associate professor of philosophy at Vanderbilt University. She is the author of *The Gift of the Other: Levinas and the Politics of Reproduction.*